Studies in Irish Politics

Michael Marsh, *Series Editor*

Politics in Northern Ireland,
edited by Paul Mitchell and Rick Wilford

Contesting Politics: Women in Ireland, North and South,
edited by Yvonne Galligan, Eilís Ward, and Rick Wilford

FORTHCOMING

How Ireland Voted, 1997, edited by
Michael Marsh and Paul Mitchell

Published in cooperation with

Political Studies Association of Ireland

Politics in Northern Ireland

Marie, 1999.

Politics in Northern Ireland

edited by

Paul Mitchell and Rick Wilford

The Queen's University of Belfast

Westview Press

A Member of the Perseus Books Group

Studies in Irish Politics

Published in 1999 in the United States of America by Westview Press, 5500 Central Avenue, Boulder, Colorado 80301-2877, and in the United Kingdom by Westview Press, 12 Hid's Copse Road, Cumnor Hill, Oxford OX2 9JJ

Library of Congress Cataloging-in-Publication Data
Politics in Northern Ireland / edited by Paul Mitchell and Rick Wilford
p. cm.
Includes bibliographical references and index.
ISBN 0-8133-3527-2 (hc) — ISBN 0-8133-3528-0 (pbk)
1. Northern Ireland—Politics and government. I. Mitchell, Paul. II. Wilford, Rick, 1947– .
JN1572.A58P65 1999
320.9416—dc21

98-27569
CIP

The paper used in this publication meets the requirements of the American National Standard for Permanence of Paper for Printed Library Materials Z39.48-1984.

10 9 8 7 6 5 4 3 2 1

Contents

Tables

List of Acronyms

AIA	Anglo-Irish Agreement
APNI	Alliance Party of Northern Ireland
ASUs	Active Service Units
AV	alternative vote
BIC	British-Irish Council
BSE	bovine spongiform encephalitis
CAP	Common Agricultural Policy
CLMC	Combined Loyalist Military Command
Cmnd.	Command
CSJ	Campaign for Social Justice
DANI	Department of Agriculture
DCA	Belfast District Council Area
DFA	Irish Department of Foreign Affairs
DFP	Department of Finance and Personnel
DH	d'hondt
DUP	Democratic Unionist Party
ECHR	European Convention on Human Rights
EEC	European Economic Community
EOCNI	Equal Opportunities Commission for Northern Ireland
EPA	Emergency Provisions Act
EU	European Union
FEA	Fair Employment Agency
HC Debs.	House of Commons Debates
HMSO	Her Majesty's Stationery Office
ICPC	Independent Commission for Police Complaints
IGC	Intergovernmental Conference
INLA	Irish National Liberation Army
INTERREG	A Community Initiative to Assist Border Areas
IPLO	Irish People's Liberation Organisation
IPP	Irish Parliamentary Party
IRA	Irish Republican Army

LEADER	Links Between Actions for the Development of the Rural Economy
LSq	disproportionality
LVF	Loyalist Volunteer Force
MAFF	Ministry for Agriculture, Fisheries, and Food
MBW	Making Belfast Work
MEP	Member of the European Parliament
MP	member of parliament
NDPBs	nondepartmental public bodies
NI	Northern Ireland
NIASC	Northern Ireland Affairs Select Committee
NICRA	Northern Ireland Civil Rights Association
NICS	Northern Ireland Civil Service
NIEC	Northern Ireland Economic Council
NIFS	Northern Ireland Fertility Survey
NILP	Northern Ireland Labour Party
NIO	Northern Ireland Office
NISA	Northern Ireland Social Attitudes
NIWC	Northern Ireland Women's Coalition
PAF	Protestant Action Force
PAFT	Policy Appraisal and Fair Treatment
PCB	Police Complaints Board
PCC	Policy Coordination Committee
PCLCs	Police-Community Liaison Committees
PD	People's Democracy
PIRA	Provisional Irish Republican Army
PPRU	Policy Planning and Research Unit
PR	proportional representation
PSAI	Political Studies Association of Ireland
PTA	Prevention of Terrorism Act
PUP	Progressive Unionist Party
QUB	The Queen's University of Belfast
RTE	Radio Telefís Eíreann
RUC	Royal Ulster Constabulary
SACNI	Shared Authority Council of Northern Ireland
SDLP	Social Democratic and Labour Party
SDP	Social Democratic Party
SF	Sinn Féin
STV	single transferable vote
TD	Teachta Dála (Dáil Deputy, or member of the Dáil)
TSN	Targeting Social Need
UDA	Ulster Defence Association
UDP	Ulster Democratic Party

UDR	Ulster Defence Regiment
UFF	Ulster Freedom Fighters
UKUP	United Kingdom Unionist Party
UPNI	Unionist Party of Northern Ireland
USC	Ulster Special Constabulary
UUC	Ulster Unionist Council
UUP	Ulster Unionist Party
UUUC	United Ulster Unionist Council
UVF	Ulster Volunteer Force
UWC	Ulster Workers' Council
UWUC	Ulster Women's Unionist Council
VUP	Vanguard Unionist Party
WAC	Women's Affairs Committee

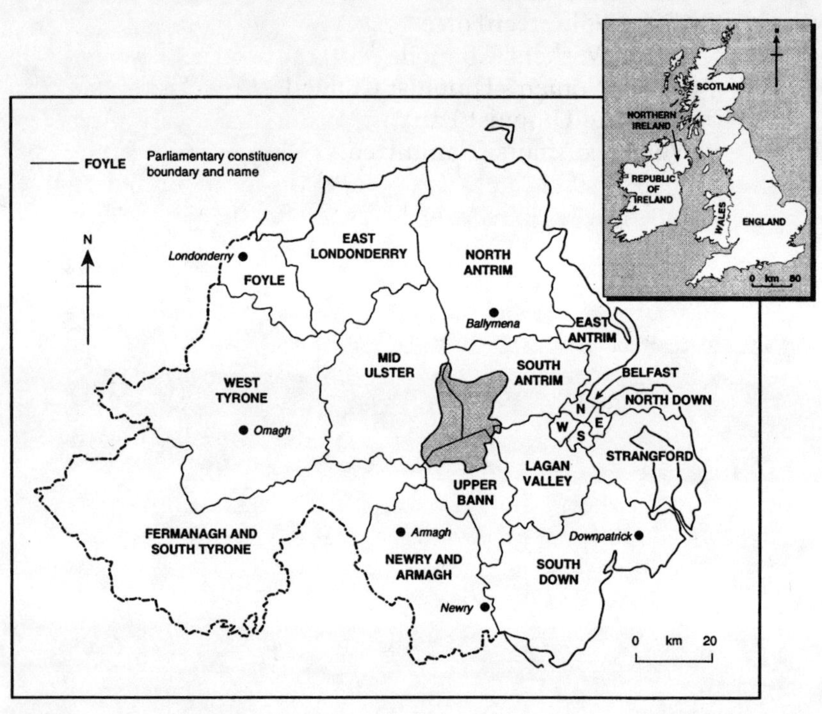

FOYLE
Parliamentary constituency boundary and name
N
Londonderry
FOYLE
EAST LONDONDERRY
NORTH ANTRIM
Ballymena
EAST ANTRIM
MID ULSTER
SOUTH ANTRIM
BELFAST
NORTH DOWN
WEST TYRONE
Omagh
N
E
W
S
STRANGFORD
UPPER BANN
LAGAN VALLEY
FERMANAGH AND SOUTH TYRONE
Armagh
NEWRY AND ARMAGH
Downpatrick
SOUTH DOWN
Newry
0 km 20
SCOTLAND
NORTHERN IRELAND
REPUBLIC OF IRELAND
WALES
ENGLAND
0 km 80

Preface

Given the sheer volume of books related to the Northern Ireland conflict, it is traditional and appropriate to offer some words of justification for producing yet another. The case is straightforward: Although there are some very good (and a lot of bad) books on Northern Ireland, none of them look much like a text for a course we would design on the politics and government of Northern Ireland. Perhaps understandably, most of the literature concentrates on only a few dimensions of "the conflict" and especially on constitutional policy and the ongoing search for a resolution of the antagonisms. While obviously not wanting to neglect these important topics (several chapters focus on conflict regulation and "solutions"), our feeling was that other important dimensions of politics tend to be relatively overlooked and undervalued. Therefore, in addition to the high drama of constitutional initiatives and negotiations, this book focuses on social structure, the paramilitaries, electoral and party systems, parliaments, policymaking, policing, and gender. We hope that the result is a well-rounded core text designed for university undergraduates, as well as for a wider public interested in politics in Northern Ireland.

Writing about contemporary politics does, of course, incur risks by threatening to create hostages to both ill and good fortune. However, though sensitive to the unfolding sequence of events, all of the contributors have been careful to embed their chapters within the rich body of scholarship that the study of Northern Ireland has generated. Although the book will appeal to a wider public audience, we have been motivated to cater primarily to the large and growing number of undergraduates attracted to the study of Northern Ireland's politics and for whom the sheer scale of literature is overwhelming. By combining genuine accessibility and considered scholarship, each of the authors helps to navigate students through the complexities of the politics of the region. Northern Ireland may be in the process of political transition. Accordingly, what the book provides, besides an analysis of alternative futures, is a set of guides that describe and explain both the opportunities and constraints that act on the prospects for change, whether they originate within its territory or beyond.

As this book is a collective enterprise, our primary thanks go to the eleven contributors who produced the chapters and responded in a timely fashion to the demands of interventionist editors. The inspiration for this book was the publication in 1992 of *Politics in the Republic of Ireland* (edited by John Coakley and Michael Gallagher), which, like the current book, was sponsored by the Political Studies Association of Ireland (PSAI). We would be more than gratified if, in due course, the current publication is deemed a worthy sister volume.

Politics in Northern Ireland would not have happened without the PSAI, and we thank its executive committee, publications committee, and members for their faith in this project. We are particularly indebted to the successive chairs of the publications committee: Brian Girvin, Michael Gallagher, and Michael Marsh. Michael Gallagher's close attention to detail on behalf of the PSAI during the early gestation of the project helped ensure its fruition. Our gratitude is also extended to Ruth Dilly, computer supremo in the School of Social Sciences at Queen's, for patiently solving all the technical traumas that befell us.

Although all conflicts are in a trivial sense unique, a central concern of the contributors was to reflect the internationalisation of the Northern Ireland conflict and to reap the benefits of analytical and comparative approaches to the politics of ethnic and national conflicts. Indeed, *Politics in Northern Ireland* is informed by a wider concern with the comparative politics of societies divided by ethnonational divisions.

Paul Mitchell and Rick Wilford
Belfast

1

The Past in the Present

FEARGAL COCHRANE

It was once wryly observed that Irish history was something Irishmen should never remember and Englishmen should never forget. In reality, the obverse has normally been the case, as Britain has sought to minimise the intrusion of Ireland into its domestic politics whereas the rival political groupings in Ireland have engaged in a selective recollection of their shared history. Unlike the Republic of Ireland or other countries that have emerged from violent beginnings (such as the United States of America), historical memory plays an important role in contemporary political behaviour within Northern Ireland—where questions over ethnicity, territoriality, power, and national identity, which determined the region's historical development, have not yet been resolved. Consequently, history (or, more precisely, historical myth) is invested with an importance that is not reflected in more stable societies. The central focus of this chapter, therefore, is to illustrate how the past structures the present—specifically, how the political development of Northern Ireland, leading in 1969 to the outbreak of the present civil conflict, is a product of that history.

Background to Partition

After the joint launching by the British and Irish governments of the Framework Documents in February 1995, Prime Minister John Major prepared to be interviewed by a local television journalist in Belfast. Just before transmission, Major asked, "Okay, Ken, where do you want me to start?" Feigning seriousness the reporter replied, "1690, Prime

Minister!" Deciding where to begin any account of Irish history is a matter of discretion and, to some degree, a political statement in itself. However, to understand the dynamics that led to the partition of Ireland, we must know something of the political forces that, by this time, had coalesced into the rival ideologies of unionism and nationalism.

Home Rule

The inability of Britain to successfully integrate Ireland politically or culturally into a viable model of common citizenship throughout the nineteenth century led eventually to calls for some degree of political autonomy. There were two views as to the extent this local autonomy should assume: complete independence, on the one hand, or some ambiguous form of devolution, on the other. There was also disagreement about the methods that should be used to achieve these ends. One group took the view that revolutionary nationalism was the only means available to attain the goal of independence. The lineage of this group can be traced through the Irish Republican Brotherhood and the emergence of Sinn Féin to the physical-force tradition of Irish republicanism that remains in Ireland today. The other strand within the emerging Irish nationalist movement was less ambitious in its goals and consequently more pragmatic in its political strategy. Once again, a line can be drawn from the reformist leadership of Charles Stewart Parnell and Isaac Butt to John Redmond and the "constitutional nationalism" practised today by the Social Democratic and Labour Party (SDLP) in Northern Ireland and by the main parties in the Republic of Ireland.

The most important point to note is that the home rule movement was neither revolutionary nor separatist. The initial principles of the Home Government Association were federalist, with separate legislatures being planned for England, Scotland, Wales, and Ireland, which would derive their authority from the United Kingdom parliament. The home rule movement became a political party in 1873; then, after the Westminster general election of January 1874 (when 59 out of the 100 Irish MPs were returned), it became the Irish Parliamentary Party (IPP) under the leadership of Butt and Parnell. The advocates of home rule were influenced by international events such as the northern victory in the American Civil War and the establishment in 1867 of Canada, where federalism had become *de rigueur* amongst political theorists.

This demand for limited self-government within the United Kingdom was opposed by British Conservatives who feared it could damage British authority in other parts of the empire. When Liberal leader William Gladstone announced his support for the cause of home rule,

the Conservatives accused him of treason, while Randolph Churchill would later declare, "Ulster will fight and Ulster will be right."

For many years the home rule issue was a hostage to Westminster arithmetic, as the influence of the Irish Parliamentary Party on the government depended upon the party's maintenance of the balance of power in the House of Commons. It was only in 1911, when the Liberal Party needed IPP support to reform the House of Lords, that the necessary legislation was pushed through. The Third Home Rule Bill was introduced by the Liberal government in 1912 (the previous two had failed in 1886 and 1893) and was opposed by the Conservatives and Unionists. In Ulster the unionist leader Sir Edward Carson, a Dublin-born lawyer, formed a private army called the Ulster Volunteer Force, and a "Solemn League and Covenant" was entered into by more than 400,000 unionists, many of whom signed their names in their own blood. This example of "public banding" is a key facet of Protestant political culture. The same phenomenon was seen more recently after the signing of the Anglo-Irish Agreement on 15 November 1985, albeit with less success. In this case, radical unionists formed "Ulster Clubs," as Edward Carson had done at the beginning of the century. As Alan Wright, the leader of this group, remarked in 1986: "It's a case of history repeating itself. In 1893 when the first home rule bill was presented to parliament, the unionists got together and formed a Unionist Club. So we decided that we needed a structure that everyone could come together under" (*Fortnight*, February 1986: 4).

In September 1914 the Government of Ireland Act became law, with two important qualifications: First, its operation would be suspended until after the ending of World War I and, secondly, a special opt-out would have to be provided for Ulster. Although the war had delayed the implementation of home rule, and perhaps forestalled the outbreak of civil war in Ulster, a mechanism still had to be found that would satisfy the unionists in the North of Ireland. In 1920, the British government introduced the Government of Ireland Act. This act became the basis for partition and established the region's political geography, which remains today. In particular, it proposed two subordinate legislatures in Ireland under the authority of Westminster: one for "Northern Ireland," incorporating six of Ulster's nine counties, and the other for Southern Ireland, with jurisdiction over the remaining twenty-six counties. Following the war of independence and subsequent negotiations between the British government and Sinn Féin, the Anglo-Irish Treaty was signed, enshrining the new territorial boundaries. Ironically, although six counties of Ulster were allowed to remain within the Union, their method of doing so was a form of home rule.

Political Cultures in the New State

The first prime minister of Northern Ireland was Sir James Craig, a man who claimed not to welcome the new state but who would go to his grave "ashamed if I did not go down with the ship too" (Buckland 1980: 50). Craig faced the unenviable task of creating a viable administration in the face of latent antagonism from the British government and open aggression from Southern nationalists and Catholics within the North, who felt that they had been corralled within an illegitimate regime and abandoned to the mercy of their unionist enemies. The political culture in the early years of the new state was therefore dominated by fear and uncertainty. This condition remains a feature of the unionist psyche today, and insecurity about their political surroundings is a central dynamic of contemporary unionists' political behaviour.

In 1920 unionists were aware that they had succeeded in obtaining a regional administration only by forming a paramilitary army, the Ulster Volunteer Force (UVF), and threatening to rebel against the British state. Fears about the tenuous nature of their position were heightened by the civil war that raged in the Free State from June 1922 until May 1923. The picture is clearer now, in retrospect; at the time, however, it was not obvious as to who would emerge victorious from this struggle: Had the anti-treaty republicans, led by Eamon de Valera, triumphed over the pro-treaty government, the future of Northern Ireland would have been seriously jeopardised. Unionist political culture during the early years of the Northern Ireland state was therefore one besieged by hostile forces. This situation translated into a desire for political domination and electoral cohesion, as it was feared that a loss of control to the nationalist community would have imperiled the very existence of the state itself. Many Protestants believed that if Northern Ireland were to disintegrate and they were subsumed politically into some sort of pan-nationalist Ireland, their cultural and religious freedom would also evaporate under the unyielding dogma of conservative Catholicism. Although such fears were debilitating, they also became an essential element of electoral cohesion. The unionist political leadership soon learned that the most successful electoral strategy lay in exacerbating these twin fears of "Rome rule" and "Catholic disloyalty," inasmuch as this could be relied upon to elicit the Pavlovian response among Protestants of voting for the Unionist Party (see Chapter 5).

The political culture among the nationalists was, conversely, one trapped in a state to which they held no allegiance, increasingly beset by the feeling that they were second-class citizens under the law. These feelings were heightened in 1925 after the report of the Boundary Commission, which had been a condition of the Anglo-Irish Treaty. In theory, this was given a remit to revise the border in line with local wishes. It was expected within nationalist circles that in border counties where nationalists formed a majority, such as parts of Fermanagh, Armagh, and Derry/Londonderry, they would be allowed a local opt-out from Northern Ireland into the Free State. The fear that this outcome might indeed ensue fueled the insecurity and uncertainty endemic within unionist politics. The Northern Ireland administration, mindful that the British government might take the opportunity to chip away at the geography of the state to the point that it became an untenable regime, made strenuous efforts to influence both the composition of the Boundary Commission and its eventual findings. The minister for home affairs, Dawson Bates, was the least subtle in this respect, drafting a memo that listed the military capability of the Northern Ireland government should a confrontation with the British state become necessary (Bardon 1992: 506). The commission's declaration that the boundaries should remain as they were confirmed the worst fears of the Northern nationalist community and strengthened its antipathy toward the Stormont regime.

Although "constitutional" (i.e., nonviolent) nationalists quickly established a dominance over Sinn Féin, they, too, adopted an ambivalent attitude toward the new regime, refusing to assume the role of official opposition, which would have conferred legitimacy upon the system. The degree of discrimination against nationalists between 1920 and 1972 is a matter of some debate. Abuses undoubtedly occurred (see Farrell 1980; Wilson 1989), but they were often haphazard and localised rather than systematic. Of course, the point could be made that electoral malpractice, together with partiality in housing and employment provision, occurred only when demographic circumstances demanded. Subsequently, however, nationalists have exaggerated the mistreatment in the same way that unionists have denied or downplayed it (see Whyte 1990: 61–64, for an outline of this debate). The effects on the political culture within Northern Ireland were certainly real enough. Many Protestants were living in conditions as bad as, if not worse than, those experienced by the Catholic community; influenced by the sectarian stereotypes provided by their leaders, they believed Catholics to be "enemies within" whose economic misfortunes were entirely self-inflicted.

Nationalists in Northern Ireland, meanwhile, were effectively leaderless, at least until the beginning of the civil rights movement in the late 1960s. Sinn Féin operated a policy of abstentionism and was of little practical use to the Catholic community, whereas the Nationalist Party, which did take its seats in the Stormont parliament, was excluded from power, becoming merely a decorative addendum to the political system. As a consequence of the party's disempowerment, "constitutional" nationalism became withdrawn and complacent, its conservative Catholic middle-class leadership "going through the motions" of opposition rather than taking up the political cudgels to fight for the grievances of those whom they purported to represent. For much of the period from 1920 to 1972, nationalist politics were in disarray, both philosophically and organisationally, functioning as little more than the political wing of the Catholic Church hierarchy: "Its basic unit of organisation was not the electoral ward but the parish. . . . Nationalist candidates were not selected, they were anointed" (Eamonn McCann, cited in Arthur 1984: 56). It was not unusual for seats to go uncontested due to the predictability of the electoral results, as demonstrated by the fact that between 1929 and 1969, 37.5 percent of all seats were unopposed and in a 52-seat lower chamber, unionists never held fewer than 32 seats (Arthur and Jeffrey 1988: 33).

Northern nationalism became alienated from the state, creating a constituency which believed that unconstitutional action and physical force was a legitimate means of political redress. Unionism, on the other hand, having originally been antipathetic to the notion of a devolved parliament for six counties of Ulster, soon became mesmerised by its potential. The preservation of the political regime (i.e., Unionist Party rule) became the *modus operandi* of successive administrations, whose political fixation lay neither with ideas nor ideologies but with the numbers game. A negative equation was quickly established—namely, that the loss of political control by the Unionist Party would lead to the immediate destruction of the state by "disloyal" nationalists; hence the necessity to do everything possible to reinforce unionist political hegemony and electoral cohesion. Eventually, owing in part to British government ambivalence and lack of interest, unionists made the fatal mistake of believing that Stormont was an autonomous entity, rather than simply a region of the United Kingdom that had been given a measure of self-government. Prime Minister Edward Heath was to disabuse unionists of this assumption in March 1972 by proroguing Stormont and introducing direct rule.

The Politics of Blood Sacrifice

The leader of the Irish Parliamentary Party, John Redmond, supported the British cause during World War I, confident that the long struggle for self-government was over. The unionists also cooperated, and although their leader, Edward Carson, did not personally care for British War Secretary Lord Kitchener, he offered the latter 35,000 men on condition that they would be retained in a single division. Although the unionists got their 36th (Ulster) Division, Irish nationalist support for the war quickly dimmed, due mainly to the continued postponement of home rule and the human costs of the conflict. Vast numbers of people disillusioned with the IPP's support for the war transferred their allegiance to Sinn Féin (formed by Arthur Griffith in 1906), which was overtly abstentionist and committed to political, economic, and cultural independence. On Easter Monday 1916, a small band of republicans staged an uprising in Dublin. The central figure behind the Easter Rising was Patrick Pearse, a cultural nationalist committed to the romantic ideal of a historic Gaelic race. Catholicism was tied into this philosophy, with blood sacrifice seen as a form of religious martyrdom—that is, as a reenactment of Christ's crucifixion that would ultimately lead to Ireland's resurrection. It was no accident, of course, that the episode took place at Easter. Shortly before the Rising, Pearse commented rather chillingly: "[W]e may make mistakes in the beginning and shoot the wrong people; but bloodshed is a cleansing and sanctifying thing" (Foster 1988: 477). Other nationalist leaders who took part in the Rising, such as James Connolly, were, until the very last moment, sceptical of this fatalistic vision. Mocking a Pearseian metaphor, he declared: "We do not think that the old heart of the earth needs to be warmed with the red wine of millions of lives. We think anyone who does is a blithering idiot" (Foster 1988: 478–479). Republicans seized government buildings at the centre of Dublin and engaged in a week of street fighting with the British army, at the end of which more than 450 people had been killed. The leaders signed a declaration of independence and proclaimed Ireland to be an independent Republic. Support for the Rising was minimal at the beginning and assumed such historical importance only because of the draconian British response: Fifteen rebel leaders were executed one by one over the period of a fortnight, martial law was imposed, and large numbers of innocent people were arbitrarily imprisoned.

A reorganised militant Sinn Féin took advantage of the public mood and routed the Irish Parliamentary Party in the 1918 Westminster election, winning 73 seats to the IPP's 6. By 1919 extreme republicans had formed the Irish Republican Army and had gone to war with Britain, a conflict that lasted until the 1921 truce and the eventual signing of the Anglo-Irish Treaty. Ironically, then, Pearse had his blood sacrifice; it became the driving force that eventually led to the birth of an independent Ireland. His comment at the funeral oration of republican leader O'Donovan Rossa in 1915 turned out to be correct, but only because a foolhardy British government played the part that he had written for it: "Life springs from death, and from the graves of patriotic men and women spring living nations." The caveat should be added that Britain was at war and fighting for its own survival in 1916 at a time when life was cheap. Therefore, although the executions should be judged in their historical context rather than with the benefit of hindsight, the political consequences cannot be denied. Once again we can see how the past informs the present, just as a modern parallel can be drawn between the blood sacrifice of 1916 and the republican hunger strike in the summer of 1981, when ten republican prisoners fasted to death in the H-Blocks of the Maze prison. Their immediate demands were based upon their being recognised as political prisoners, but they were conscious of the wider blood-sacrifice tradition in Irish history (O'Malley 1990: 119–120).

The Battle of the Somme in 1916 also inscribed the concept of blood sacrifice into the Ulster Protestant psyche, though in a fashion radically different from the effect of the Easter Rising on Irish nationalism. The event was given added piquancy by the fact that it began on 1 July, the same date as the Battle of the Boyne. (The latter is now celebrated on 12 July because of changes in the calendar.) Many of those who took part in the Somme were aware of the irony, adding their own vernacular—"No Surrender" and "Remember 1690"—as they went into battle. In the first two days of the Battle of the Somme, the 36th Division suffered more than 5,000 casualties. In the tightly knit community of Ulster, the death toll seemed all the greater. It should be remembered, of course, that Irish nationalists also lost their lives in France; among the most prominent was William Redmond, brother of John. Since July 1916 the Somme has been etched into the collective consciousness and political culture of Protestant Ulster. It added to the sense of solidarity and community, particularly against the backdrop of political insecurity that accompanied the aftermath of the Easter Rising. In acknowledgement of the importance of the battle, a Somme Heritage Centre exists in Northern Ireland today. Unlike the separatist effects of the Rising on Irish nationalism, the blood sacrifice at the Somme had a bonding impact on Ulster unionism. The memory of the human price paid in defence of British interests has been evoked on many subsequent occasions (especially during periods of heightened constitutional uncertainty) to remind the British government of the debt owed to the Ulster unionist community.

State Formation

In the aftermath of World War I, it became clear that the two conflicting sovereignty claims within Ireland could not be reconciled through constitutional compromise. Following the Anglo-Irish War and subsequent treaty negotiations, the British government decided that the most prudent course of action was to partition the island, creating two "states": one in "Northern Ireland" composed of six of Ulster's nine counties, and another for the remaining twenty-six counties of Ireland.

Northern Ireland: A New Political Landscape

The new political system that dominated Northern Ireland from 1921 to 1972 is best understood as a by-product of the power struggle between Britain and Ireland: "Neither a nation nor a full state, its creation in 1920 was the joint by-product of British and Irish state- and nation-building failures" (O'Leary and McGarry 1993: 107). Essentially it was an unwanted child (even among unionists), and the circumstances of its birth contain the seeds of its eventual demise. The political architecture of Northern Ireland was designed to ensure the existence of a stable unionist majority that enjoyed sufficient autonomy to carry out devolved local government responsibilities. Successive British administrations came to view Northern Ireland not as the acme of liberal-democratic state building but, rather, as an effective mechanism for removing a seemingly insoluble problem from its domestic political agenda.

This dubious "out of sight, out of mind" school of statecraft was one of the central reasons for the disintegration of the Stormont regime in 1972. Instead of assuming political responsibility for the region when it became obvious that necessary political reforms had not been introduced and that events were escalating out of control, successive British governments had neither the administrative structures nor the political will power to take remedial action until it was too late. Although the unionists had not welcomed the new state as the achievement of a political ideal (many, including Edward Carson, viewed it as a defeat and felt guilty that they had abandoned unionists in the other three counties of Ulster and in the rest of Ireland to the clutches of Irish nationalism), they soon embraced it as a protective buffer against both a duplicitous and untrustworthy British government and an antagonistic population in the rest of Ireland. Unionists became so enamoured of their new situation that they eventually developed a form of political *anorexia nervosa*, building a warped self-image such that when they looked in the mirror they saw a vibrant liberal-democratic polity reflected back. Those with clearer vision saw a one-party state with no rotation of government, a moribund (at times geriatric) political class within both unionism and nationalism, and a sectarian abuse of power by one section of the community.

This distorted self-image, coupled with the failure to understand the limits of their position, led to the eventual undoing of unionist power and the political regime in 1972. Due in part to British disinterest, many unionists had come to believe by the 1960s that Stormont was indeed an autonomous "state"—but it was not. Powers that were devolved from Westminster could just as easily be revoked, as they were in 1972. This tendency to inflate the significance of the new regime was epitomised by the Stormont building itself, a huge white edifice on a hill overlooking Belfast where part-time MPs gathered periodically to serve a population of barely one and a half million. The physical scale and imposing presence of the building were seen by unionists as symbolic of its importance and permanence.

Under the terms of the 1920 Government of Ireland Act, Stormont was empowered to pass what have been termed "internal" rather than "external" laws. Aside from the overarching sovereignty of Westminster, a number of reserved powers were not devolved to the new administration—notably in the area of foreign policy, where Stormont was denied the right either to sign international treaties or to conduct external trade. Westminster maintained exchequer controls such as the levying of income tax, customs and excise duties, and corporation tax. Northern Ireland was therefore placed in the paradoxical situation of being an autonomous self-governing and supposedly self-sufficient region whilst being denied any real powers to raise revenue or control its economy.

The Development of Unionist Politics

Some commentators have suggested that the progress of unionist politics from 1920 onward was driven not by behavioural factors but by structural ones. This argument asserts that the creation of a provincial parliament in 1920 locked the region into parochial and narrow forms of political expression. The system institutionalised sectarian politics and made a virtue out of the unionist *versus* nationalist division. The rationale of electoral politics became a person's religious affiliation, as a badge of ethnic identity, rather than what that person believed in beyond this sectarian baseline, and led ultimately to intercommunal breakdown and armed conflict. This structural argument is used today by those who could be described as civic unionists rather than ethnic unionists, to lobby for the political integration of Northern Ireland into the rest of the United Kingdom.

It seems clear enough that environmental factors such as religious balance and external antagonism decrease the "political space" within which the forces of moderation can operate. The actual terms of partition are a case in point. From the unionist perspective, the central rationale of the state was that its majoritarian nature would provide sufficient operational and ideological security to ensure its perpetuation. However, in retrospect it can be seen that far from copper-fastening what the region's first prime minister, Sir James Craig, would later refer to as "a Protestant Parliament and a Protestant state," its majoritarian nature created an illusory security as the Unionist Party came to rely on that majority. Elections, therefore, became a surrogate census rather than the democratic expression of competing philosophies or ideologies. To this extent, subsequent unionist failures can be blamed partly upon the flawed political structure that they inherited.

But how could a party that had organised itself in opposition to home rule have been able to monopolise political power for the duration of the devolution experiment? The most crucial factor in explaining the character of unionist politics in this period was the Unionist Party's concern to maintain communal solidarity and electoral cohesion. The success of the party from 1920 to 1969 was due largely to its capacity to achieve unity. Yet this unity was paradoxical, inasmuch as the unionist leaders were members of what has been described as an Ulster "squirearchy" (Arthur 1984: 62), guiding a movement that was predominantly working class in an age of abnormally high unemployment. How can this apparent anomaly be explained? The Unionist Party's success in obtaining cross-class support was partly due to the role of the Orange Order, which provided a bonding effect between classes and Protestant denominations. It perpetuated the notion of a common identity that must be defended in the face of both English and Irish antagonism and propagated the belief that such an identity could be achieved only through group solidarity. By emphasising the tradition of fraternal equality among its members, together with the existence of an external threat, the Orange Order tended to blur class distinctions and helped to reconcile the Protestant working class to the leadership of the landlords and wealthy businessmen.

The significance of Orangeism within the Unionist Party is illustrated by the fact that between 1921 and 1969 only three members of the cabinet were not in the Order. Once again, the modern parallels are obvious: The current leader of the Ulster Unionist Party, David Trimble, is a leading member of the Orange Order, and he rose to prominence in July 1995 with his role in the first Siege of Drumcree—a role that played a significant part in his elevation shortly afterward to the leadership of the party.[1] However, although the leaders of the Orange Order were members of the same "squirearchy" that dominated the Unionist Party, it was by no means an instrument of social control operated by the Protestant hierarchy. The support of the

Protestant working class for what was essentially a conservative government was not a collective act of deference but, rather, the rational belief that it suited the interests of working-class Protestants if upper-class Protestants maintained control. Their perception was that the alternative (i.e., disruption of group solidarity) would have jeopardised the general Protestant interest—namely, the distinctive religious and cultural values by which they defined themselves. This belief was perpetuated during the Stormont administration despite their experience, paradoxically, of relative poverty.

From the Protestant viewpoint, therefore, Catholic political mobilisation was a prelude to unity with the Irish Free State, which would ultimately worsen their already beleaguered economic situation and dilute or even extinguish the cultural and religious values at the centre of Protestant communal identity. Thus, an uneasy social contract was entered into whereby the working class gave tacit agreement to the rule of the Protestant upper class, so long as the latter prevented the spread of Catholic mobilisation and protected the former from absorption into the Irish Free State. This concept of a social contract leads us to consider the degree of "political space" available before the system collapsed around the ears of the Unionist Party leadership. But how do we reconcile the position of Sir James Craig in 1921, when he made some effort to secure a rapprochement with the nationalists and the Catholic hierarchy—"[W]e will be cautious in our legislation. We will be absolutely honest and fair in administering the law" (Buckland 1980: 51)—with his oft-quoted remark in 1934—"All I boast of is that we are a Protestant Parliament and a Protestant State" (Buckland 1980: 109)?

It was not long after power had been devolved from Westminster that divisions emerged among the Unionist Party leaders over the extent to which they should simply cultivate the support of the Protestant working class or make a serious attempt to establish a self-sufficient liberal-democratic political system. Paul Bew, Peter Gibbon, and Henry Patterson (1979) have identified the debate within unionism as a struggle between the "populists" and the "anti-populists." Centred around Sir James Craig, the populist grouping embarked upon a reckless programme of public expenditure in the hope that it would secure working-class support and thereby preserve unionist unity. The anti-populist group had its nucleus within the Ministry of Finance; its chief protagonists were Hugh Pollock, the minister for most of the period between 1921 and 1943, and his chief civil servant, Sir Wilfred Spender. The anti-populists insisted that Northern Ireland should live within its means and were concerned that Craig's flagrant public spending would alienate the British government who were paying the bills. Although the populists were aware of this possibility, they believed that they had little alternative but to placate the Protestant working class since to not do so would result in personal failure and a general disruption of the unionist political monolith.

This debate was not operating in a political vacuum, of course: Developments in Britain forced the populists to adopt policies that their opponents claimed the economy could ill afford. After World War II, the Stormont government found it increasingly difficult to maintain parity with Britain in social services spending. The election of a Labour government in 1945 witnessed a dramatic expansion in welfare provisions as well as expensive health and education reforms in line with the recommendations of the Beveridge Report. Despite its antipathy to socialism, the Unionist government felt obliged to implement similar measures, as it believed that failure to do so would have led to inevitable electoral defeat. The success of the Protestant ruling class in securing working-class disunity can be attributed to a combination of sectarian rhetoric and economic competition during a period of continuing unemployment. The outdoor relief riots of 1932[2] were taken as evidence, certainly by the populist wing of the Unionist Party, of the fragility of unionist unity and the leadership's dependence upon Protestant working-class support. Subsequently, the Unionist Party set out to show that, in contrast to transient and ephemeral class alliances, the Protestant working class had the same identity, the same cultural and religious values, and the same blood ties as Protestants higher up the social ladder. This message from the leadership that they were blood-brothers rather than just business partners was made more acceptable when continuing unemployment and competition for work brought both sections of the working class into direct economic competition. In 1938 the unionist leadership was challenged by liberal sections of the middle class, which called upon the government to assume a more interventionist role in the economy. Sir James Craig (later Lord Craigavon) found himself openly opposed by a section of his own party that was disillusioned with the government's handling of social and economic issues. Calling themselves Progressive Unionists, this group put forward twelve candidates at the 1938 Stormont election. The manifesto of this middle-class faction was aimed at a working-class electorate, focusing mainly on the problems of unemployment and inadequate housing for the low paid.

The failure of the Progressive Unionists to loosen the Unionist Party's grip on power was largely due to external circumstances—specifically, the more militant brand of Irish nationalism issuing from the Free State in the late 1930s. De Valera's more overt republicanism (or, more precisely, his republican rhetoric) enabled the Unionist government to articulate its well-worn sectarian *leitmotif* and to fight the election on the traditional border issue. The introduction of a new constitution in 1937 not only cemented the separatism between North and South but created new reasons for it. Articles 2 and 3 of the constitution defined the thirty-two counties of Ireland as the "national territory" and emphasised the Irish government's right to legislate for the whole of that national territory. And Article 44 recognised "the special position of the Holy Catholic Apostolic and Roman Church as the guardian of the Faith professed by the great majority of the citizens." However, the constitution also legitimised the existence of the other denominations within the state and guaranteed "freedom of conscience and the free profession and practise of religion" (Chubb 1982: 50). Though not containing any explicit threat to other religions, the constitution clearly offered little for Protestants or unionists to enthuse over; indeed, many viewed it as evidence of the Free State's aggressive intentions toward Northern Ireland. Given this context, it is not surprising that the Progressive Unionists failed to capitalise on the government's poor economic performance. The terms of political debate shifted accordingly, from economic issues to interminable wrangling over partition. Craigavon castigated the Progressive Unionists, other liberals, and socialists as "wreckers" and "compromisers," and led the Unionist Party to overwhelming victory, increasing its majority by 6 seats and removing the Progressive Unionists as a credible electoral threat.

As noted earlier, although political powers had been devolved to Stormont by the Government of Ireland Act, the region remained financially integrated within the U.K. *via* the Treasury (see Chapter 7). The importance of this anomaly became increasingly obvious after World War II as the interests of British and international capital came into conflict with the ethno-national rationale of the "state." The equilibrium that had been attained through the policy of allocating resources to party supporters was upset by the arrival of new companies and foreign investment, thus weakening the powers of patronage by which the elite retained power over the masses. A new middle class was created, one that did not owe allegiance to the old unionist oligarchy. The Stormont government was anxious to secure the huge subsidies available from the U.K. Treasury; yet as it did so, the autonomy of the Northern Ireland government diminished accordingly.

By stressing the benefits to Northern Ireland that the welfare state provided, and by contrasting this situation with the one in the Republic, the Unionist government effectively conceded the link between material prosperity and political allegiance. In 1943 the Northern Ireland Labour Party (NILP) began a campaign against the primitive nature of local health services: Northern Ireland had the highest infant mortality rate in the U.K. and the highest rate of death from tuberculosis. The winter of 1942 saw an outbreak of strikes at Short Brothers and other engineering plants, with further stoppages following in 1943. Between March and April 1944, the NILP coordinated a series of strikes among engineering workers in the shipyard and Shorts that resulted in the arrest of five shop stewards. In the 1944 election, the NILP set the political agenda; although it won only 2 seats (both in Belfast), it garnered a large percentage of the vote. Although the Unionist government attacked the socialists, it agreed to introduce whatever social reforms were passed in Britain, thereby acknowledging the demands of Protestant workers as articulated by the NILP.

Developments in Nationalist Politics

Two important points need to be mentioned in relation to the evolution of nationalist politics. The first is that, virtually overnight, nationalists within Northern Ireland were transformed from a majority into a minority community. For them, partition was obviously a much more important element of the Anglo-Irish Treaty than the oath of allegiance, which tended to dominate the Southern agenda. The legacy of partition for Northern nationalists was a sense of abandonment. As far as they were concerned, they had been cut off from their countrymen and left to the mercy of their unionist enemies. This feeling was exacerbated after 1925 when the Boundary Commission simply ratified the existing position.

The second major formative experience for Northern nationalists after 1920 was their treatment within the new state. Despite the inclusive rhetoric of Craig in the early 1920s, Catholics quickly became alienated from the regime. It soon became apparent that conventional political activity was unlikely to redress their grievances since they were consigned to permanent minority status within the new boundaries. Although there are numerous reasons as to why the Unionist Party clung to power with such determination—nationalists wishing to secede from the state, civil war in the South, de Valera's rise to power, and antagonism from the British government—the fact remains that nationalists were not well served by the Stormont system.

By the mid-1920s the Nationalist Party had eclipsed Sinn Féin, which was committed to a policy of abstentionism and increasingly regarded as irrelevant by a Catholic community that wanted representation on socioeconomic issues rather than nationalist dogma. This trend was reinforced as politics became more visible after 1920. Stormont and local government were seen to be taking real decisions affecting the everyday lives of the Catholic population. And with the onset of the economic depression in the late 1920s and early 1930s, these socioeconomic issues became all the more vital. The very fact, therefore, that the Nationalist Party was willing to participate in politics gave it an advantage over Sinn Féin. In the 1925 Stormont election, the Nationalists won 10 seats and Sinn Féin only 2. Although the Nationalists were able to outpoll Sinn Féin, they could not present a real political challenge to the Unionist Party. In nearly fifty years of trying, the only piece of legislation they succeeded in passing at Stormont was the Wild Birds Act of 1931, hardly a striking blow against unionist political hegemony. The high point for the Nationalist Party came during the 1929 Stormont election, when it won 11 seats. This event can be set in context if we consider that throughout the history of the Stormont regime from 1920 to 1972, not only was the Unionist Party never out of office, but its low point occurred in 1925 when it won 32 seats.

When unionists reacted to this dip in their political fortunes by abolishing proportional representation (PR) in 1929, nationalists became even more resigned to their minority status, but also more complacent. They abandoned any illusions about challenging the system and behaved instead like county councillors, highlighting the specific grievances of their constituents. At the time, nationalists saw the abolition of PR both as a direct attack on them and as an attempt to gerrymander the electoral system (see Chapter 4). In retrospect, however, the picture is more complex and remains a subject of some debate. If the abolition of PR to reduce the number of nationalist MPs at Stormont was indeed the intention, we should have seen a dramatic fall in the number of nationalist seats after 1929. However, no such drop occurred. It seems more likely that the change to the electoral system was an attempt to damage independent unionists and the Labour Party. This view is supported by Craig's statement: "What I want to get into this House . . . are men who are for the Union on the one hand and who are against it and want to go into a Dublin Parliament on the other" (Arthur 1984: 51). Craig was aware that in a straight fight between the two sides, unionists would win every time. Streamlining the political system by supplanting proportional representation consequently removed the smaller parties, strengthened the unionist vote, and weakened the nationalist position at Stormont.

Owing to its disempowerment, constitutional nationalism became moribund. As a party, the Nationalists never took to the task of opposing the government wholeheartedly and, from the outset, were ideologically opposed to the state. They refused to accept the title of "Official Opposition" for fear of conferring legitimacy and permanence upon the system. It was not until 1965 that they agreed to undertake this role in response to Terence O'Neill's reform programme (see below). It could be argued that had the Nationalists entered the fray with greater gusto, they may have achieved more and exerted a greater influence upon Northern Ireland politics, perhaps even forestalling or preventing the disintegration of the regime.

Constitutional nationalism became increasingly complacent, but the physical-force tradition fared little better. Effectively abandoned by the Free State and having witnessed the defeat of the anti-treaty faction in the civil war, the proponents of this tradition had to watch de Valera come to power and legitimise what they regarded as an unconstitutional regime. Their erstwhile leader, worried about IRA action drawing British aggression upon the Free State during World War II, implemented the Offences Against the State Act in 1939, thereby introducing internment without trial for his former comrades. Ideologically, there was nowhere for Irish republicanism to go. The republicans' abstentionist policy saw Sinn Féin wiped out in the 1929 election as Northern nationalist concerns turned to more practical issues such as poverty, unemployment, and slum housing. It was to be several decades before the IRA regrouped and made another attempt to effect political change through "armed struggle." Exasperated at the state of nationalist politics in the 1950s, the IRA launched its "border campaign," which lasted sporadically for the six years between 1956 and 1962. This campaign failed for three reasons. First, by this stage, the IRA had become extremely rusty as a fighting force. Its guerrilla activity resulted in the deaths of twice as many republicans as policemen, six of whom were killed during the six-year period. In fact, the IRA itself was never more than an irritation to the government, partly because its tactics were aimed at destroying property rather than at killing people. Secondly, the Border Campaign failed because it received very little support from the Catholic community within Northern Ireland. Some saw it as an embarrassment in their relations with the Protestant community and a potential threat to their economic and social position, whereas others opposed it because it never seemed coordinated or large-scale enough to be a serious threat to the status quo. Thirdly, there was a tough security response. Internment was introduced on both sides of the border, and the B-Specials were given a free hand to round up suspects. Indeed, because of their largely rural makeup, the B-Specials knew the border counties intimately and were familiar with many of the active republicans in the area.

The failure of both constitutional nationalism and physical-force republicanism to effect significant change within the state led to a groundswell of frustration within the Catholic community as well as to the emergence of new organisations and a new form of politics.

What we have come to know as "people power" became the outlet for Catholic frustration. New pressure groups were formed, people took to the streets, and the old political structures were swept away.

State Breakdown

The fall of the *ancien régime* was intrinsically linked to the growth of popular protest in the late 1960s. As a result of the civil rights movement and the reaction to that mobilisation by the Northern Ireland administration, the British government was sucked rapidly into the very maelstrom it had spent most of the century trying to circumnavigate.

Origins of the Civil Rights Movement

It is important to see the civil rights movement in Northern Ireland not as an isolated outbreak of popular mobilisation but as a product of a political environment that extended well beyond the boundaries of the state, with links to the civil rights struggle in the United States. One parallel between the political developments of the late 1960s and those of the early years of the decade was the emergence of Terence O'Neill as successor to the aging Lord Brookeborough. O'Neill's arrival introduced a new tone into the Unionist Party and, hence, to the Stormont government as well.

Brookeborough's rather stern unionist perspective—in particular, his refusal to admit that political reforms were required within the state—was replaced with a leadership that preached the gospel of inclusiveness and consensus. O'Neill made it clear from the beginning that the political status quo was unacceptable; Catholics were faring worse than Protestants within the state, and, accordingly, something would have to be done about it. A few days after becoming leader, he announced to the Ulster Unionist Council (UUC) that "our task will literally be to transform Ulster. To achieve it will demand bold and imaginative measures." And later, at the beginning of 1964, he declared that the central objectives of his government were to make Northern Ireland economically stronger and to "build bridges between the two traditions within our community." In short, the signals he was sending to the Catholic community were positive ones, implying that Catholics were no longer disloyal citizens to be given a wide berth but, rather, equal members of the state who should be encouraged to achieve their full (and as yet unrealised) potential.

To some degree, the depressed nature of Northern nationalism facilitated a more liberal articulation of Ulster unionism. Another key factor was, of course, the changing nature of the Southern state. De Valera had made way for Seán Lemass, and the Republic's enunciation of a policy of peaceful coexistence with the Northern regime increased the political space available to O'Neill and facilitated his more inclusive rhetoric. In material terms, many people, both unionist and nationalist, saw O'Neill as the sort of vibrant and dynamic leader who could meet the economic challenges of the future in a way that his predecessor could not. Indeed, both political and economic expectations were rising. Outside Northern Ireland, in both Europe and America, the early 1960s were a decade of hope; yet within only a few years the mood in Northern Ireland had shifted from toleration and conciliation to communal strife, political instability, and violence.

The key question is, Why did the civil rights movement emerge at the very time that the government was seeking to introduce reform? The general answer is that O'Neill's rhetoric failed to meet the level of expectation within the Catholic population; yet it had gone far enough to instill fear within some sections of the Protestant community that he had conceded too much and had jeopardised the Stormont regime. Gerry Fitt later remarked wryly that the only difference between O'Neill and his predecessors was that "while Craigavon and Brookeborough had walked over the Catholics with hob-nail boots, O'Neill walked over them with carpet slippers" (Gordon 1989: 5).

In retrospect, it is clear that, although O'Neill may have wanted to achieve reconciliation within the state, he did not think it was necessary to target nationalist grievances directly. In his view, unemployment differentials and housing anomalies did not require specific legislation. There was no systematic policy of discrimination on religious grounds, no flaw in the structure of the state that required attention. On the contrary, he held up the Stormont system as a paragon of virtue and specifically described it as superior to the unpleasant class warfare so apparent within the Westminster system. In O'Neill's opinion, the problems that would later become the main concern of the civil rights movement were not *structural* but *behavioural*. The issue as he perceived it was sectarianism itself rather than the more fundamental causes that underpinned it. And what was needed, therefore, was not a major programme of institutional reform but better community relations; hence his campaign of gesture politics such as visiting Catholic schools and his soothing public speeches. This analysis was fundamentally misconceived, however. O'Neill underestimated the grievances of the Catholic community together with the political temperature within the unionist population, and his reform programme was destined to be seen as inadequate. As Paul Arthur has concluded: "He could only have succeeded if Catholics had been prepared to anaesthetise their attitudes and aspirations for the duration of his premiership while he set about 'educating' the Protestant mind. However, his patronising efforts did not encourage acquiescence from either community" (Arthur 1984: 99).

The civil rights movement grew out of this unwillingness to remain passive. The main Catholic grievances concerned abnormally high levels of unemployment, the lack of an equitable system of housing allocation, and what they considered to be a system of electoral malpractice. Instead of tackling these problems head-on, O'Neill chose to pursue a macroeconomic policy that would, as a by-product, improve the living standards of the Catholic community. His policy of favouring the Seán Lemass dictum that "a rising tide lifts all boats" left him open to accusations that he was interested not so much in reconciliation as in preserving Unionist Party hegemony and the survival of the state. It could be observed that he did successfully play the Orange Card himself against the NILP at election time. However, if this was his primary goal he made a quite cataclysmic miscalculation, as the main consequence of his premiership was unionist political disintegration followed by the destruction of the Stormont system. Perhaps the truth is not that he didn't want to reform the state but, rather, that (1) he misunderstood the scale of what was required and (2) was unable to lead his government toward the sort of reform demanded by the Catholic community. When his words were not followed with deeds, many nationalists grew disillusioned with the O'Neill regime. Of course, when viewed from the perspective of the radical unionists, it was precisely what he was saying rather than doing that was important: They saw him as being hell-bent on introducing real reforms that would be detrimental to the Protestant community and the very fabric of Northern Ireland.

O'Neill's strategy of pursuing general economic growth, accompanied by conciliatory gestures toward nationalists, began to unravel after the publication of the Wilson Report in February 1965. This economic plan announced a number of ambitious proposals, including a new ring-road for Belfast, a new city in the middle of Northern Ireland, a second university, four new motorways, and a new housing policy. However, with the practical implementation of the report came a sharp decline in O'Neill's popularity among Catholics. Having been led to believe that their grievances would be listened to and tackled, they found their raised expectations dashed by decisions over both the name and location of the new town, Craigavon, and over the siting of Northern Ireland's second university in the mainly Protestant town of Coleraine rather than in the larger and predominantly Catholic city of Derry/Londonderry.

It would be fair to say that 1965 was the turning point for O'Neill's leadership, sowing the seeds of the later civil rights campaign. This was the year when modernising rhetoric was overtaken by more symbolic events. In particular, O'Neill's attempts to forge a more cooperative relationship with the Lemass-led government in the Republic fueled a sustained campaign by radical unionists, notably Ian Paisley, who insisted that O'Neill was a traitor both to Protestantism and to Ulster. Although O'Neill's meetings with Lemass were met by a good deal of popular support at the time, they acted as a form of Chinese water-torture on the government. O'Neill underestimated Paisley, seeing him as little more than a bigoted loudmouth who did not represent mainstream opinion. In retrospect, it is clear that although some of his views may have been too radical for all but a narrow constituency, Paisley was able to tap into the more general fear, frustration, and anger felt by those within the Protestant community who may not have shared all of his convictions. Indeed, these emotions were exacerbated as Catholics began to confront the state and its institutions. Although much of the civil rights agenda was concerned with practical grievances such as housing and employment, many Protestants increasingly came to see it as an attack on the Stormont system and as an attempt to overthrow the state.

The civil rights movement was not essentially concerned with the ideology of Irish nationalism. Rather, its key grievances focused on socioeconomic conditions, mainly in the areas of employment and housing, together with electoral malpractice. It is also important to note that the scale of nationalist grievance was not uniform: There was an overall sense of discontent amongst the Catholic population, but this fluctuated in intensity depending on the scale of abuse or maladministration in the particular locality. Accordingly, Derry/Londonderry became the focus for much of the civil rights campaign, as it was there that unemployment and gerrymandering were most extreme. In February 1967, for example, unemployment in the city of Derry/Londonderry stood at a massive 20 percent compared to the U.K. average of around 2.5 percent and the Northern Ireland average of 8 percent. The Cameron Commission would later find that the electoral system was weighted in the unionists' favour in Derry city, Armagh city, Omagh town, Co. Fermanagh, and Dungannon Urban and Rural District Council. The commission also found that housing policy was distorted for political ends in Derry, Omagh, and Dungannon. The demands made and the reforms called for concerned not an end to partition or the establishment of a thirty-two-county Irish republic but, rather, equality under the law.

The first stirrings of what later came to be officially known as the Civil Rights Movement occurred in 1959, when a pressure group called National Unity was formed in an effort to reform the Nationalist Party's rather moribund structure. Five years later, in 1964, the Dungannon-based Campaign for Social Justice (CSJ) was established. The primary aim of the CSJ was to publicise the discrimination against Catholics in Northern Ireland. It was led by the members of the "respectable" Catholic middle class and aimed most of its attacks at British politicians. Then, in 1967, the Derry Housing Action Committee was set up; an unreservedly socialist movement, it demanded an immediate house-building programme in the area. In tandem with the flowering of grassroots organisations, this campaign was broadened by the election victory of Gerry Fitt in West Belfast. Standing as a Republican Labour candidate in the 1966 Westminster general election, Fitt had a personable style that contrasted sharply with the rather dour and lifeless image of unionist MPs. The easy-going Fitt quickly gained allies within the British Labour Party who were concerned about the slow pace of reform in Northern Ireland.

NICRA: From Protest to Mass Movement

A new dynamism was brought to the movement with the formation of the Northern Ireland Civil Rights Association (NICRA) in February 1967. Although it shared the general aims of the earlier CSJ, NICRA advocated a policy of nonviolent direct action. It was also less esoteric and more practical than the CSJ, calling for immediate reform in the areas of housing and employment. However, NICRA was by no means a cohesive organisation. It was more of an umbrella group encompassing a number of other local organisations including the Derry Housing Action Committee. When the desired reforms failed to materialise, street politics escalated. In February 1968, NICRA held a press conference in London and announced that it was going to step up its campaign to expose Stormont's record on inadequate housing for the Catholic community. Subsequently, on 24 August 1968, the first civil rights march was staged. The six-mile procession in Co. Tyrone between Coalisland and Dungannon, along the model of the American civil rights demonstrations, was not attended by great numbers; but the crucial factor is that it received a great deal of local publicity and served as a template for future protests.

Predictably, it was in Derry that the civil rights campaign graduated from a loose collection of highly motivated and concerned activists to a mass movement that shook the government to its foundations and brought the glare of the world's media to Northern Ireland. NICRA planned to hold a march in Derry on 5 October 1968. Even by Irish standards this prospect resonated with symbolism. From the unionist perspective, Derry/Londonderry was akin to a holy city. Historically, it had withstood the siege of James II in 1689, protected the Protestant heritage (except among those who happened to be Presbyterian), and was thus infused with a sort of religio-cultural importance unparalleled in any of the other five counties. Unionists were thus unlikely to welcome the prospect of civil rights demonstrators parading through the city and breaching the walls that their forebears had so stoutly defended. A clash between the two groups was inevitable, and the government—specifically, the minister for home affairs, William Craig—banned part of the march's route. Ignoring the ban, the march went ahead as planned, and when the RUC intervened to block the route of the demonstrators, a riot ensued. Violence spread throughout the city, resulting in the injury of seventy-seven civilians and eleven RUC men. The Cameron Commission found that police handling of the march was "in certain material respects ill-co-ordinated and inept. There was use of unnecessary and ill-controlled force." But whatever the rights and wrongs of it, the political effects were clear. First, the marchers had won the propaganda battle. They were calling for civil rights and being hit over the head by a police force cast in the role of oppressive agents of the state. Secondly, Catholics' confidence in O'Neill's reformist credentials was mortally wounded; their confidence in the impartiality of the police, which was shaky at the best of times, evaporated, leaving the stage bare for the entry of more militant activists.

NICRA may well have remained a relatively insignificant pressure group had it not been for the reaction of the Stormont government and the RUC to the civil rights agitation. Television coverage of the police's heavy-handed response to a seemingly innocuous group of peaceful demonstrators was crucial in opening a Pandora's Box that led to a generation of sectarian conflict within Northern Ireland. In a decade well attuned to the concept of peaceful protest, the British government was embarrassed beyond endurance by the sight on the evening news of nonviolent British citizens being assaulted by the police. As a result of the publicity surrounding the civil rights agitation, O'Neill was summoned to London and forced to accept a package of reforms that, it was hoped, would defuse the situation. On 22 November 1968, after several heated cabinet meetings, O'Neill announced a five-point reform programme:

- Londonderry Corporation was to be abolished and replaced by a development commission appointed by the government.

- The most offensive sections of the Special Powers Act were to be repealed.
- Local government was to adopt a fair points system of housing allocation based on need.
- An ombudsman was to be appointed to investigate specific grievances.
- Universal suffrage in local government elections was to be considered.

This programme created a dilemma for members of the civil rights movement: Should they continue turning the screw on the government in the hope of winning further concessions, at the risk of more instability and greater confrontation with loyalist counterdemonstrators? Or should they wait for the government to deliver its promises? NICRA, the Nationalist Party, and the Derry Citizens' Action Committee called off further street protests until the government had been given a chance to introduce its reforms.

At this point it looked as if the crisis could be weathered. However, in Belfast, on the morning of New Year's Day 1969, approximately forty members of the radical student grouping People's Democracy (PD) gathered at Belfast City Hall to march the seventy five miles to Derry. What followed was a bizarre game of mass hide-and-seek between the marchers and roaming gangs of irate loyalist counterdemonstrators. When the students were ambushed at Burntollet bridge on the outskirts of Derry, it was clear that the stakes had risen dramatically, dispelling any lingering hopes that nationalists would remain in mute witness for O'Neill's reforms to be delivered. This march, together with its aftermath, polarised both sides. As Frank Wright (1987: 194) has observed, nationalists took the government's inability to protect the students as evidence that the reform programme was at best a token gesture and that the status quo remained intact. Conversely, many unionists interpreted the PD's breaking of the moratorium on marches as evidence that their activities were not primarily concerned with redressing socioeconomic grievances but, instead, represented a covert attack upon the state itself and the Protestant community within it. Mistrust concerning the motives and agenda of the "other" community produced a negative dynamic that easily spiraled into sectarian animosity.

Reclaiming Executive Authority

On 14 August 1969 the British army arrived in Northern Ireland to restore order and prevent the spread of sectarian violence. But the autonomy of the Northern Ireland government incurred a further dent, as the British were now able to exert an executive as well as financial influence upon the Stormont regime. Initially, the troops were perceived as serving a traditional peace-keeping role and were welcomed by the Catholic community as a protection against sectarian attack. There was relatively little fighting at this time between the army and the nationalist community. At the beginning of 1970, however, two factors changed the role of the army. First, as it was directed not by London but by the Stormont government, it was squeezed between the nationalist community and the government. The troops' attempts to impose control in working-class Catholic areas of Derry and Belfast led to the perception that they were acting as the military wing of the Unionist Party. House raids conducted insensitively by the army, and the Falls Road curfew in 1970, took a massive psychological toll on the Catholic population, and the infuriated community became a fertile breeding ground for the IRA. Secondly, the relationship between Catholics and the army changed because the troops were not, as advertised, protecting Catholics from Protestant attacks. The result was a rapid increase in IRA recruitment, which suddenly gained credibility as a defensive force. Ulster Defence Association (UDA) numbers also rose sharply as a consequence of Protestants being burned out of their homes and a widespread fear that the state was at the point of disintegration (see Chapter 2).

As the violence escalated, the conflicting pressures on the Stormont government became more intense. On the one hand, radical Protestants such as Ian Paisley demanded a tougher security response and blamed the breakdown of law and order on the weakness of the unionist leadership. However, when Brian Faulkner became prime minister in March 1971 and emphasised that a stronger security policy would be pursued, while Stormont's "autonomy" would be reasserted, concerns rose among audiences outside Northern Ireland. Although this message was welcomed by a majority of Protestants, it was not what British Prime Minister Edward Heath wanted to hear, as he was trying to convince parliament that the reform programme in Northern Ireland, introduced by Terence O'Neill, was continuing to progress. It became increasingly clear that the policies of Stormont and Westminster were diverging.

The climax of this conflict between policy approaches occurred on 9 August 1971 with the introduction of internment (detention without trial), an event that more than any other led to the total breakdown of the system in 1972. Unable to control violence, which rose dramatically after its introduction, internment also worsened both the relationship between the Stormont government and the Catholic community, on the one hand, and their standing with the British administration, on the other. Nationalist politicians withdrew from Stormont and announced their intention to set up an alternative assembly, while British troops were attacked to a greater degree by the IRA. The upsurge in violence further irritated the British government, which began to put more pressure on Faulkner's administration.

The final nail in the coffin of the Stormont regime was driven home in Derry/Londonderry on 30 January 1972 (later known as Bloody Sunday) when an illegal anti-internment march was fired upon by British paratroopers, resulting in the death of fourteen civilians. The international fallout from this event, together with everything that had gone before, left British Prime Minister Edward Heath with little option but to curb Stormont's responsibilities. The British government had decided to take all major powers—most notably, security, law, and order, as well as judicial powers—away from the devolved parliament and to administer these functions centrally through a Secretary of State. Unable to accept the reforms, the Unionist government resigned. Direct rule was introduced on 1 April 1972, and William Whitelaw became the first Secretary of State for Northern Ireland. A new phase in the political history of Northern Ireland was about to begin.

Conclusion

The political history of Northern Ireland from 1920 until the breakdown of the Stormont regime in 1972 is a story of missed opportunities and myopic political vision. However, although the circumstances of its birth may have been an accidental by-product of a larger British/Irish negotiation, Northern Ireland was not doomed to sectarian strife from the outset. The series of political actions and inactions that combined to produce an explosive cocktail in 1969 were a product of the negative interaction between the protagonists, the demonising of the "other" and that "other's" antagonistic motivations, and a constitutional apparatus incapable of producing a polity built upon consensus rather than division. As unionism and nationalism retreated further into their solid communal blocs, the political stability produced by unionist electoral success would mask a tumour at the heart of the body politic. The British government had been shaken out of its apathy by civil disorder; by the time it recognised that a fundamental problem existed, the opportunity for remedial action had passed. Considering the proclivity of both nationalists and unionists to invoke suitable historical examples as templates for their contemporary political behaviour, perhaps the last word on the period should be left to a European writer of a suitable vintage:

> Machiavelli, when writing *The Prince* in the year 1513, observed that political disorders might be compared to human disorders. "As the doctors say of a wasting disease," he wrote, "to start with it is easy to cure but difficult to diagnose. After a time unless it has been dealt with at the outset it becomes easy to diagnose but difficult to cure." He went on [to] say that "political disorders can be quickly healed if they are seen well in advance but when, for lack of diagnoses, they are allowed to grow in such a way that anyone can recognise them remedies are too late" (Boyd 1984: 12).

References and Further Reading

Arthur, Paul, 1984. *Government and Politics of Northern Ireland,* 2nd ed. London: Longman.

Arthur, Paul, and Keith Jeffrey, 1988. *Northern Ireland Since 1968.* Oxford: Basil Blackwell.

Bardon, Jonathan, 1992. *A History of Ulster.* Belfast: Blackstaff Press.

Bew, Paul, Peter Gibbon, and Henry Patterson, 1979. *The State in Northern Ireland, 1921–72: Political Forces and Social Classes.* Manchester: Manchester University Press.

Boyd, Andrew, 1984. *Northern Ireland: Who's to Blame?* Cork: Mercier Press.

Bloomfield, Ken, 1994. *Stormont in Crisis.* Belfast: Blackstaff Press.

Buckland, Patrick, 1980. *James Craig.* Dublin: Gill and Macmillan.

Catterall, Peter, and Sean McDougall (eds.), 1996. *The Northern Ireland Question in British Politics.* London: Macmillan.

Cochrane, Feargal, 1996. "'Meddling at the crossroads': The decline and fall of Terence O'Neill within the unionist community," pp. 148–168 in Richard English and Graham Walker (eds.), *Unionism in Modern Ireland.* London: Macmillan.

______, 1997. *Unionist Politics:The Politics of Unionism Since the Anglo-Irish Agreement.* Cork: Cork University Press.

Chubb, Basil, 1982. *The Government and Politics of Ireland,* 2nd ed. London: Longman.

Farrell, Michael, 1980. *Northern Ireland: The Orange State,* 2nd ed. London: Pluto Press.

Foster, R. F., 1988. *Modern Ireland 1600–1972.* London: Penguin.

Gordon, David. 1989. *The O'Neill Years: Unionist Politics 1963–1969.* Belfast: Athol Books.

Kennedy, Dennis, 1988. *The Widening Gulf: Northern Attitudes to the Independent Irish State 1919–1949.* Belfast: Blackstaff Press.

McCann, Eamonn, 1980. *War and an Irish Town,* 2nd ed. London: Pluto Press.

O'Dochartaigh, Niall, 1997. *From Civil Rights to Armalites: Derry and the Birth of the Irish Troubles.* Cork: Cork University Press.

O'Leary, Brendan, and John McGarry, 1993. *The Politics of Antagonism: Understanding Northern Ireland*. London: Athlone Press.

O'Malley, Padraig, 1990. *Biting at the Grave: The Irish Hunger Strikes and the Politics of Despair*. Belfast: Blackstaff Press.

Purdie, Bob, 1990. *Politics in the Streets: The Origins of the Civil Rights Movement in Northern Ireland*. Belfast: Blackstaff Press.

Walker, Graham, 1985. *The Politics of Frustration: Harry Midgley and the Failure of Labour in Northern Ireland*. Manchester: Manchester University Press.

Whyte, John, 1990. *Interpreting Northern Ireland*. Oxford: Oxford University Press.

Wilson, Tom, 1989. *Ulster: Conflict and Consent*. Oxford: Basil Blackwell.

Wright, Frank, 1987. *Northern Ireland: A Comparative Analysis*. Dublin: Gill and Macmillan.

2

Political Violence and the Paramilitaries

ADRIAN GUELKE

In the second half of 1994, twenty-five years after British troops were first deployed on the streets of Belfast and Derry/Londonderry in aid of the civil power, the main republican and loyalist paramilitary organisations declared ceasefires. Although the principal paramilitary organisations on both sides of the province's sectarian divide were formed after the start of Northern Ireland's troubles, which are usually dated from 5 October 1968 (see Chapter 1), a common belief was that the ceasefires marked the end of the troubles—at least in their current phase, if not for all time. That perception was encapsulated in the banner headline with which the announcement of the ceasefire by the Provisional Irish Republican Army (IRA) was greeted: "It's over" (*Belfast Telegraph*, 31 August 1994).

However, the hopes for a permanent end to the troubles were rudely shaken on 9 February 1996, when the Provisional IRA announced the end of its ceasefire shortly before its volunteers detonated a bomb at Canary Wharf in London. This incident was followed by further smaller-scale acts of violence in London. But, initially, the peace between the paramilitaries in Northern Ireland itself held. The renewal of the Provisional IRA's campaign reflected, among other factors, the organisation's frustration at the delay to the start of all-party talks as a result of an impasse over the issue of the decommissioning of paramilitary weapons. At a hurriedly arranged summit in London on 28 February 1996, the British and Irish governments attempted to relaunch the peace process by setting 10 June 1996 as a date for the start of all-party negotiations, following elections to a Northern Ireland Forum. Although the justification for these elections was that they would provide the negotiators with mandates from the electorate, the British government's endorsement of the elections had been a concession to the Ulster Unionist Party, made in the context of the Conservative Party's difficulties in sustaining a majority in the House of Commons.

Ironically, the results of the elections (held on 30 May 1996) were a setback for the Ulster Unionist Party, which lost support to the Democratic Unionist Party, particularly compared to the party's performance in the 1992 general election (see Chapter 5). Sinn Féin, the political wing of the Provisional IRA, substantially increased its share of the vote in comparison with elections in Northern Ireland in 1992, 1993, and 1994. This unexpected outcome put Sinn Féin in a strong position to press its claim to be included in negotiations, regardless of whether there was a renewal of the Provisional IRA's ceasefire. However, a new ceasefire remained a firm condition of the British and Irish governments for Sinn Féin's participation. At the same time, parties linked to the loyalist paramilitaries easily achieved sufficient votes to secure election to the Forum and, hence, places in the negotiations, subject to the loyalist paramilitaries' continued observance of a ceasefire.

The start of multiparty negotiations (without Sinn Féin) on 10 June 1996 was followed by the bombing of Manchester city centre by the Provisional IRA on 15 June 1996. A further escalation in the Provisional IRA's campaign occurred when a bomb attack was launched on the British army's main military base in Northern Ireland at Lisburn on 7 October 1996. Loyalist paramilitaries responded to the resumption of republican paramilitary violence in Northern Ireland with a renewal of their "tit for tat" campaign, although no claims of responsibility accompanied these attacks so as to avoid compromising the position of their political wings. In May 1997 the Chief Constable of the Royal Ulster Constabulary (RUC), Ronnie Flanagan, stated that breaches of the loyalist ceasefire had been committed by each of the constituent parts of the Combined Loyalist Military Command (CLMC). Throughout 1996 and the first half of 1997, the multiparty talks were deadlocked over how the issue of the decommissioning of paramilitary weapons should be addressed. The impasse was broken after the Labour Party won the British general election in May 1997 and, in government, made a determined effort to secure a new Provisional IRA ceasefire. Despite Sinn Féin's strong criticism of the new Secretary of State's handling of the issue of Orange Order parades, this new ceasefire was achieved, coming into effect on 20 July 1997. It was greeted by much greater scepticism than the original ceasefire of 31 August 1994.

After briefly reviewing the history of the principal paramilitaries since the start of the troubles, this chapter examines the steps that led up to the ceasefires. In this context it explores the decisions of the paramilitary organisations to halt their campaigns of violence. Next, it provides a discussion of why the Provisional IRA first ended and then restored its ceasefire and how these events have affected the prospects for a durable peace in Northern Ireland. It concludes with a speculation about what the future might be for paramilitary organisations within Northern Ireland politics in a variety of contexts, including that of an enduring truce between republicans and loyalists.

The Nature of Paramilitaries

Outside of Northern Ireland the term *paramilitary* is generally used to refer to state security forces that lie between the civilian police and the military. In Northern Ireland, unusually, it is used to refer to nongovernmental organisations that have used or threatened to use political violence. Admittedly, the term *terrorism* has also been quite widely used, especially by the mass media, to refer to political violence in Northern Ireland, and some scholars have drawn on the literature on terrorism in their analysis of the conflict (Bruce 1992: 268–290). However, fitting the Northern Ireland conflict into the framework for the analysis of terrorist groups has proved difficult for a number of reasons. First, within other Western liberal democracies, terrorist groups have been a fringe phenomenon involving a handful of activists operating at the extreme ends of the political spectrum, with very little public support and without the capacity through their violence to raise fears of civil war, as the actions of the paramilitaries have periodically done in Northern Ireland.

Secondly, terrorism within other Western liberal democracies has been almost exclusively associated with a relatively narrow range of forms of violence, such as hijackings, bombings, and assassinations, involving covert action by small groups. By contrast, paramilitary violence in Northern Ireland has encompassed a much wider range of actions. On the loyalist side in particular, parading in a show of force has been a common way in which the paramilitaries have sought to demonstrate their strength. And both republican and loyalist paramilitaries have exercised control of an area by administering so-called punishment beatings to petty criminals. Thirdly, engaging in covert violence has been the *raison d'être* of terrorist groups such as the Red Army Faction in Germany and the Red Brigades in Italy. When their covert violence has been ended, such groups have dissolved and disappeared. Though primarily associated with covert violence, the paramilitaries in Northern Ireland on both sides of the sectarian divide have also taken part in a range of activities, including their engagement through political wings in conventional party politics, that provide the basis of their continued existence in the absence of campaigns of covert violence.

At the same time, the term *militia,* referring to nonstate groups engaged in political violence during the Lebanese civil war or in the ongoing ethnic conflicts in the former Soviet Union, has not found favour in Northern Ireland. It is not difficult to explain why. First, Northern Ireland has been spared state breakdown on the pattern of Lebanon, parts of the former Soviet Union, or many states of sub-Saharan Africa. Violence reached a peak in terms of fatalities in Northern Ireland in 1972 (see Table 2.1). It was the point at which state security forces were at their weakest, not in terms of numbers but in terms of their capacity for maintaining law and order. The local security forces had been discredited as a result of the role that their partisanship had played in the onset of the troubles, and the British army was still in the process of getting to grips with its task (see Chapter 8). Secondly, the political conditions in Northern Ireland did not permit the overt violence associated with militias. It is possible that if the white supremacist militias in the United States, which achieved notoriety in the wake of the Oklahoma City bombing in 1995, had emerged into the limelight earlier, then the term *militia* might have seemed more appropriate in the Northern Ireland case. In particular, military-style exercises and shows of force in which the American militias have engaged have also been a characteristic of loyalist paramilitaries. Indeed, shows of force have been the primary form of activity with which short-lived loyalist organisations, such as the Third Force, Ulster Clubs, and Ulster Resistance, have been associated.

Shows of force, patrolling, and the self-proclaimed posture as defenders favoured by the loyalist paramilitaries have also led to the application of the term *vigilantes* to these organisations. Moreover, in the case of the republican paramilitaries, the term *guerrillas* has been quite commonly used in the mass media, particularly outside the British Isles. The different characterisations of loyalist and republican paramilitaries reflect not just the different types of activities with which they tend to be associated but also their opposing political outlooks. However, to represent them as being at opposite ends of a left-right political spectrum would be to oversimplify the situation. Such a characterisation is belied both by the social conservatism to be found in republican paramilitaries and by the influence of socialist ideas on loyalist paramilitaries. Nevertheless, there is no doubt that the republicans have seen themselves as revolutionaries, just as the loyalists have perceived their role as being to extinguish the fires of revolution.

TABLE 2.1 Number of Deaths Due to the Security Situation: 1969–1996

Year	*RUC*	*RUCR*	*ARMY*	*UDR/RIR*[a]	*Civilians*	*Totals*
1969	1	–	–	–	13	14
1970	2	–	–	–	23	25
1971	11	–	43	5	115	174
1972	14	3	105	26	322	470
1973	10	3	58	8	173	252
1974	12	3	30	7	168	220
1975	7	4	14	6	216	247
1976	13	10	14	15	245	297
1977	8	6	15	14	69	112
1978	4	6	14	7	50	81
1979	9	5	38	10	51	113
1980	3	6	8	9	50	76
1981	13	8	10	13	57	101
1982	8	4	21	7	57	97
1983	9	9	5	10	44	77
1984	7	2	9	10	36	64
1985	14	9	2	4	26	55
1986	10	2	4	8	37	61
1987	9	7	3	8	68	95
1988	4	2	21	12	55	94
1989	7	2	12	2	39	62
1990	7	5	7	8	49	76
1991	5	1	5	8	75	94
1992	2	1	4	2	76	85
1993	3	3	6	2	70	84
1994	3	–	1	2	56	62
1995	1	–	–	–	8	9
1996	–	–	1	–	14	15
Totals	196	101	450	203	2262	3212

[a]Figures include data on the Royal Irish Regiment (Home Service Battalions).
Source: The Chief Constable's Annual Report 1996 (1997), p. 85.

For republicans as self-defined revolutionaries, the organs and agents of the state constitute the most obvious legitimate targets for violence, whereas for loyalists the targets are the sources of revolution. However, both sides have interpreted the concept of legitimate target very broadly. Thus, republican paramilitaries have justified attacks not merely on off-duty members of the security forces but also on those who have retired or resigned from the security forces. Politicians have been targets, too; so have judges. Even contractors supplying routine services of a nonmilitary nature to the security forces have come under attack from republican paramilitaries. Loyalist notions of what constitutes a republican have at times been elastic enough to encompass virtually any politically active nationalist. Further, under the supposition that the communities from which the republicans draw their sustenance can be coerced into repudiating "their" men of violence, loyalists have at various junctures justified indiscriminate attacks on Catholics, most chillingly under the slogan "Any Catholic will do."

Yet neither the aim of revolution nor that of the suppression of revolution fully accounts for the violence used by the respective paramilitaries. Both have attacked prison officers in the process of waging campaigns over the treatment of their imprisoned members. And both have inflicted violent punishments on petty criminals to underline their control of a particular neighbourhood and to emphasise their role as protector of these communities. Such a role fits in readily with the defensive remit of loyalist paramilitaries. However, it is not confined to them. Republican paramilitaries have also been keen to project themselves as community defenders, against criminals within the community, against loyalist paramilitaries, and against the security forces. In addition, both republican and loyalist paramilitaries have been at the forefront of expressions of community anger, including rioting that has occurred in reaction to controversial decisions or actions by the authorities. The fund raising of the paramilitaries has involved them in other forms of violence as well, bank robberies being particularly associated with republican paramilitaries and protection rackets with loyalist ones (Maguire 1993: 273–292). At various times during the troubles, these secondary activities have loomed sufficiently large that it has been possible to argue that for at least some members of the paramilitaries they have assumed greater importance than their organisations' ostensible political objectives. This dimension of their activities has prompted comparison of the paramilitaries with gangsters and mafias. A concern following the ceasefires in 1994 was the continuation of some of these forms of violence, such as the killing of drug dealers, punishment beatings of those deemed by the paramilitaries to be antisocial elements, and the orchestration of rioting, as occurred in nationalist areas in July 1995 following the early release of Private Lee Clegg (a soldier who had been convicted of murdering a joyrider).

The victims of paramilitary violence extend beyond even the broad categories described above. Inadequate or bungled warnings of bomb attacks were quite a common cause of fatalities in the first decade of the troubles, and mistakes as well as misidentifications have added to the toll of deaths throughout the conflict. Even more important has been a general readiness of the paramilitaries to put the lives of bystanders at risk in their pursuit of those they deemed legitimate targets. For example, in the bombing of the Droppin' Well disco in Ballykelly in December 1982, the Irish National Liberation Army (INLA) killed six civilians as well as eleven soldiers, their primary target. In December 1987 the Provisional IRA killed Lord Justice Maurice Gibson and his wife in a car bomb attack close to the border with the Irish Republic as they were returning from holiday. And a Protestant was one of the seven fatalities in an attack by the Ulster Freedom Fighters (UFF) on the Rising Sun bar in Greysteel in County Derry in October 1993. Internecine warfare between paramilitaries on the same side of the sectarian divide and power struggles within individual paramilitary organisations provide another category of victims.

Brendan O'Leary and John McGarry have analysed the Irish Information Partnership's figures for fatalities in the twenty-year period from July 1969 to June 1989. They show that republican paramilitaries were responsible for 57.7 percent of total deaths as a result of the troubles; loyalist paramilitaries, for 25.3 percent of deaths; and the security forces, for 11.8 percent of deaths (O'Leary and McGarry 1993: 36). Analysis of these figures has revealed four main categories of death:

- paramilitary killings of civilians (44.2 percent of all deaths);
- war between nationalist paramilitaries and the security forces (34.8 percent of all deaths);
- internecine conflict and self-killings within paramilitary organisations (6.7 percent of all deaths); and
- killings of Catholic civilians by the security forces (5.3 percent of all deaths). (O'Leary and McGarry 1993: 28)

These data probably slightly understate the level of loyalist paramilitary violence in Northern Ireland during the troubles as a whole since they exclude 1990–1994, a period when killings by loyalist paramilitaries surpassed those by republican paramilitaries (see O'Duffy 1995). Note that, in Table 2.1, the official figures provide a breakdown of the victims into a number of categories, but not a breakdown of the agencies of violence.

Malcolm Sutton (1994) has listed every fatality of the Northern Ireland conflict, including those killed in Great Britain, the Republic of Ireland, and continental Europe from 14 July 1969 to 30 December 1993—a total of 3,285 deaths. Of these, republican paramilitaries were responsible for 1,926 deaths (58.6 percent); loyalist groups, for 911 deaths (27.7 percent); the British forces, for 357 deaths (10.9 percent); and the Irish Republic's forces, for 3 deaths. In the case of 88 other deaths, it was either not possible or not appropriate to identify the perpetrators (Sutton 1994: 195).

The relative importance of the various forms of violence varies among the different paramilitaries, thus seeming to demand an analysis of the violence committed by every paramilitary group. Since names can be put to approximately fifty different groups that have threatened, engaged in, or claimed responsibility for acts of political violence in Northern Ireland, such a task would be dauntingly complicated. In practice, however, Northern Ireland paramilitary politics is less complex than it appears to be, based on the number of groups or names of groups it has generated. First, it is possible to classify every such group as either republican or loyalist. Secondly, throughout the course of the troubles as a whole, a single organisation has dominated the paramilitary scene on each side of the sectarian divide: the Provisional IRA on the nationalist side and the Ulster Defence Association (UDA) on the unionist side. Other significant republican paramilitaries have been the Official IRA, the Irish National Liberation Army (INLA), the Irish People's Liberation Organisation (IPLO), and the Continuity Army Council, whereas significant loyalist paramilitaries include the Ulster Volunteer Force (UVF), the Red Hand Commandos, Tara, and the Loyalist Volunteer Force (LVF).

One factor that has appeared to multiply the number of loyalist paramilitaries has been their use of *noms de guerre*—most notably, the UFF for the UDA and the Protestant Action Force (PAF) for the UVF. The PAF provided the UVF with a vehicle for the continuation of violence in the midst of a "ceasefire," whereas through the device of claiming responsibility for assassinations in the name of the UFF, the UDA was able to escape proscription until 1992. The use of *noms de guerre* has been less common among republican paramilitaries, but by no means unknown. In particular, the massacre of ten Protestant workers in January 1976 at Kingsmills in south Armagh was claimed in the name of the Republican Action Force, which, in fact, was a cover name for members of a local unit of the Provisional IRA. Seven years later, in November 1983, an attack on a Pentecostal church at Darkley in county Armagh was claimed in the name of the Catholic Reaction Force, a cover name for members of an INLA unit. In these two cases, the use of *noms de guerre* reflected the reluctance of republican paramilitaries to admit responsibility for sectarian attacks where there was no semblance of a legitimate target relative to even the loosest republican notions of that concept.

Most of the significant loyalist paramilitary organisations emerged in the early years of the troubles. Although power struggles were common inside the loyalist paramilitaries from the outset, the scope for local initiative was such that groups could be formed independently of one another and did not follow the republican pattern of being the product of a split from an older organisation. The exception is the LVF, the product of a split in the UVF in 1996 and a vehicle for opponents of the peace process. The IRA divided in December 1969 into the Provisional IRA and the Official IRA. INLA represented a further split from the Official IRA in December 1974. However, claims of responsibility in the name of INLA were not made until January 1976, by which time the organisation was believed to be responsible for at least twelve deaths (Holland and McDonald 1994: 358). The IPLO emerged in 1986 as a result of a power struggle within the INLA, and the Continuity Army Council appeared in late 1995 as a result of disaffection with the peace process in the ranks of the Provisional IRA. However, the Continuity Army Council also had roots in an earlier split within Sinn Féin over the issue of whether the party should take up any seats it won in elections to the Dáil. The dropping of abstentionism had led to the formation of Republican Sinn Féin in 1986. Until the emergence of the Continuity Army Council, Republican Sinn Féin had lacked a military wing. Two aspects of the republican splits deserve highlighting. First, with the exception of the emergence of the IPLO, these splits have resulted from dissidents' assertions that continuing the "armed struggle" against British rule in Ireland should be accorded priority over the pursuit of republican objectives by nonviolent political means. Secondly, the splits have been characterized by a high propensity for bloodletting between the contending factions.

In recognition of the dominant role played by the Provisional IRA and the UDA, the next two sections of this chapter will focus on the evolution of the strategies of these two principal paramilitary organisations. Subsequently, the discussion will turn to the question of the relationship of paramilitaries in general to the politics of the wider society.

The Provisional Irish Republican Army

The Provisional IRA was formed in December 1969 as a result of a split within the existing IRA. This split was followed in January 1970 by a similar division in Sinn Féin, the political wing of the republican movement. The Provisionals represented a revival of the physical-force tradition within republicanism that had seemingly been discredited by the failure of the IRA's border campaign between 1956 and 1962. The abandonment of this campaign because of lack of support from the Catholic community had led to a reaction against militarism within the republican movement. A new leftist-oriented strategy of political mobilisation on social and economic issues took the place of the previously single-minded commitment to end partition by force. In the context of Northern Ireland, the hope was that the strategy's emphasis on social and economic issues would help to forge a class-based alliance capable of transcending the province's sectarian divide. The onset of the troubles largely destroyed that hope, with the consequence that the strand of the republican movement that attempted to sustain the left-leaning strategy was unable to secure mass support. As the Workers Party, however, it later achieved a measure of political success in the Republic of Ireland.

During the first decade of the troubles, the Provisional Republican movement operated in the belief that the key to its goal of a united Ireland lay in bringing about a British withdrawal from Northern Ireland. Specifically, in the early 1970s the largely Southern leadership of the movement made the crude calculation that just as Britain had been forced to withdraw from Aden because the number of British soldiers being killed in that conflict became politically unacceptable, so too it could be forced to withdraw from Northern Ireland (Maguire 1973: 69–70). The Provisional IRA conducted its campaign of violence against the security forces on the basis that victory lay just around the corner. The Provisionals welcomed the failure of successive political initiatives of the British government during this period on the assumption that it added to the disillusionment of opinion on the U.K. mainland with Northern Ireland—a disillusionment that sooner or later was bound to result in British withdrawal.

The Provisional IRA's expectation was disappointed when the British government opted for a policy of direct rule on a long-term basis in 1976. The Provisionals were forced to recognise that they had to adjust their strategy to take account of the strength of the British commitment to remain in Northern Ireland. This shift in thinking broadly coincided with changes in the leadership of the movement whereby Southerners were gradually displaced by a new generation of Northern radicals. Yet the goal of a united Ireland remained the same. Indeed, in one respect it was strengthened. The Northern radicals had no time for notions of a federal Ireland through which the Southern leaders had attempted to woo loyalists. The big change was the commitment by the Northern radicals to sustain a long war to achieve the goal of a united Ireland. This commitment brought other changes in its wake. Among these was a partial reorganisation of the Provisional IRA on a cell basis so as to improve the security of its Active Service Units (ASUs), which carried out bombings and shootings. Securing the resources to sustain the campaign of violence took precedence over the number of operations mounted by the ASUs at any one time. The

result was a fall in the number of operations carried out by the Provisional IRA.

This lower level of violence confronted the leadership of the Provisional republican movement with a problem: How could it sustain the political credibility of the "armed struggle" in these circumstances? A solution soon presented itself. The British commitment to direct rule—offering the two communities a form of government that was the least unacceptable—was accompanied by a policy of criminalising political violence by treating paramilitary offenders in the same way as ordinary criminals. This policy produced a crisis in Northern Ireland's prisons. Although the leaders of the Provisional Republican movement were accused of manipulating the prisoners for their own political ends, in fact the initiative for the prison protests came largely from the prisoners themselves (O'Malley 1990; Beresford 1987). In 1980 and again in 1981, republican prisoners went on hunger strikes in support of their demands to be treated differently from ordinary criminals. In 1981 ten prisoners died before the hunger strike was called off.

Within the Catholic community the hunger strikes generated mass support for the prisoners. Many who disagreed with the strategy of political violence nevertheless identified with the aspiration for a united Ireland that provided the motivation of those who took up arms; hence they tended to be sympathetic to the prisoners' demands. Bobby Sands's stunning victory in the Fermanagh and South Tyrone parliamentary by-election in April 1981 underlined the strength of support for the prisoners. It also demonstrated to the Provisional leadership that there was a possibility of securing mass support through the ballot box for Sinn Féin, the political wing of the movement. An electoral strategy had two obvious attractions to the movement, overcoming anxieties that such a strategy would blunt the movement's commitment to revolution: (1) It gave political meaning to a sustained campaign of violence at a lower level, and (2) it provided an avenue for employing the political energies of the multitude of sympathisers who were drawn into campaigns on behalf of the prisoners but could not be absorbed into the Provisional IRA, particularly in the context of the strategy of the long war. At the same time, the fact that the Provisional IRA's campaign of violence continued through the course of the prisoners' protests reassured the leadership that involvement in elections would not necessitate the abandoning of the "armed struggle."

The thinking behind the addition of an electoral dimension to the strategy of the long war was encapsulated in a speech by Danny Morrison at Sinn Féin's 1981 *ard fheis* (annual conference), in which he declared: "Who here really believes that we can win the war through the

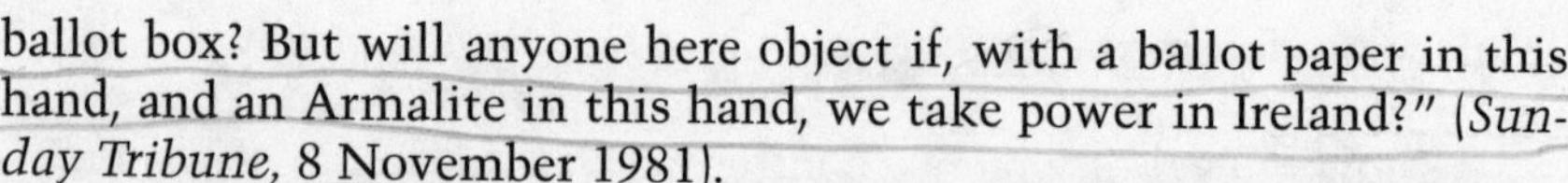

ballot box? But will anyone here object if, with a ballot paper in this hand, and an Armalite in this hand, we take power in Ireland?" (*Sunday Tribune*, 8 November 1981).

The strategy of the "ballot bomb" (*Iris* 1982: 3) was initially very successful, deriving much of its impact from the assumption on the U.K. mainland that there would be negligible support for Sinn Féin, given its characterisation in the media as the political wing of a terrorist organisation. Consequently, the vote for Sinn Féin in the elections for the Northern Ireland Assembly in 1982 exceeded all expectations. That Sinn Féin was able to secure more than 10 percent of the vote among the electorate in Northern Ireland was in itself shocking to British opinion. Little comfort was drawn from the fact that Sinn Féin had attracted the support of a minority of the Catholic minority. Further, when Sinn Féin followed up its success in the Assembly elections by increasing its share of the vote in the 1983 Westminster general election to more than 13 percent, while also securing the election of its president, Gerry Adams, as the MP for West Belfast, it even seemed possible that Sinn Féin might overtake its nationalist rival, the Social Democratic and Labour Party (SDLP).

One of the main aims of the Anglo-Irish Agreement of November 1985 was to give a boost to the electoral fortunes of the SDLP. In this it was successful (see Chapter 5). The SDLP made gains, though only partly at the expense of Sinn Féin. The culmination of this process occurred when Gerry Adams was defeated in the West Belfast constituency by Joe Hendron of the SDLP in the Westminster general election of 1992. The apparent waning of its challenge to the SDLP put pressure on the republican movement to reevaluate its strategy. Another factor added to that pressure: An important assumption behind the strategy of the long war was that polarisation between unionists and nationalists ruled out any possibility of political agreement across the sectarian divide. However, following the unionists' reconsideration of their position after they failed to bring down the Anglo-Irish Agreement through protests on the streets, that assumption no longer appeared to be entirely safe. A limited measure of convergence in the position of the political parties was evident. It encouraged the Secretary of State, Peter Brooke, to launch a political initiative in January 1990. Its aim was to establish the basis for comprehensive negotiations on Northern Ireland's future among the province's constitutional parties.

The initiative raised expectations of a political settlement involving the constitutional parties among the general public. But this was an alarming development for the republican movement, since it seemed likely that Sinn Féin would become marginalised in the context of such a settlement and it was questionable whether the credibility of

the long war could be sustained in these circumstances. As it was, doubts were growing within the republican movement about the political effectiveness of the Provisional IRA's campaign of violence. Once direct rule had been made more palatable to constitutional nationalists through the Anglo-Irish Agreement, the existence of a stalemate was no longer of such benefit to the republican movement. Thus, in an interview in 1990 a spokesperson for the General Headquarters Staff of the Provisional IRA characterised British strategy as one seeking to undermine the will of republicans by emphasising that the IRA could not hope to win—a proposition the spokesperson acknowledged to be more credible than claims British ministers had made in the past that the IRA could be defeated (*An Phoblacht/Republican News,* 1990).

At the political level the response of the republican movement to these pressures was to issue statements through Sinn Féin that sought to underline the reasonableness of republican demands by invoking international norms, particularly the principle of self-determination, and also by indicating Sinn Féin's readiness to enter into negotiations with the other political parties about the future of Ireland. In 1987 Sinn Féin published a document entitled "A Scenario for Peace" (*An Phoblacht/Republican News,* 1987). That was followed by *Towards a Lasting Peace in Ireland in 1992* (Sinn Féin 1992). At the time of their publication, these documents attracted relatively little attention. It was only in retrospect, with the development of the peace process, that they came to be seen as important steps in the evolution of the strategy of the republican movement and, through their use of the language of peace, as paving the way to the 1994 ceasefire. The 1987 document advocated elections to an all-Ireland constitutional conference in the context of a declaration of intent by Britain to withdraw. Outwardly, the approach of the 1992 document was not markedly different. It sought a declaration by the British and Irish governments "outlining the steps they intend taking to bring about a peaceful and orderly British political and military withdrawal from Ireland within a specified period" (Sinn Féin 1992: 12). This "specified period" would begin after the two governments had agreed on a set of principles including the necessity for there to be a transfer of sovereignty to an all-Ireland government. However, the 1992 document contained hints of changes in republican thinking.

Although convincing the British government to adopt a policy of withdrawal remained a central aim of the republican movement, the 1992 document raised the possibility of a change in strategy to achieve this end—specifically, by posing the alternative of "an effective unarmed constitutional strategy" to that of "continuing armed resistance" (Sinn Féin 1992: 16). In a section on "Armed Conflict in Ireland," the document also discussed the possibility of an alternative to the "armed struggle," concluding that "the development of such an alternative would be welcomed by Sinn Féin" (Sinn Féin 1992: 10). However, this statement was counterbalanced by others envisaging a continuation of the Provisional IRA's campaign for the foreseeable future. Ronnie Munck argues that the 1992 document nevertheless represented a new departure in republican thinking, and he contrasts its realism with the theology of the 1987 document (Munck 1995: 165–168).

By the time of the 1992 document, a high-level channel of communication had been opened up between the British government and the republican movement. It dated back to a meeting between Martin McGuinness and a leading government official in October 1990 (Coogan 1995: 338). One of the purposes of these contacts was to attempt to persuade the republican movement of British neutrality on the constitutional issue, a message emphasised in a speech by Secretary of State Brooke in November 1990, when he declared that Britain had no strategic or economic interest in Northern Ireland (Bew and Gillespie 1993: 240). The same line of argument regarding British neutrality as a result of the Anglo-Irish Agreement had been put to Sinn Féin by the SDLP in talks between the parties in 1988 (Sinn Féin 1989: 23). The two parties' motives for talking were different: The SDLP was seeking an end to the Provisional IRA's campaign of violence, whereas the aim of Sinn Féin was cooperation among nationalists on common objectives or, as it was to be put at a later date, the creation of a pan-nationalist front. Initially, Sinn Féin's desire to cooperate with the SDLP was explicable simply as a tactical response to the threat of the party's marginalisation in the event of a political settlement across the sectarian divide. Its development into a central plank of an alternative unarmed strategy was linked to a further change in republican thinking involving an acknowledgement that the Provisional IRA's campaign of violence was an obstacle to securing Protestant assent to a united Ireland; indeed, this was the theme of a speech given in June 1992 by Jim Gibney, a leading figure in Sinn Féin (Coogan 1995: 339).

The possibility that the republican movement might be drawn into a peace process attracted greater interest from the British government and the SDLP following the failure of the second round of talks among the constitutional parties in the autumn of 1992. Then, early in 1993, there were further exchanges of messages between the British government and the republican movement, and in April of that year the leader of the SDLP, John Hume, entered into talks with the Sinn Féin President Gerry Adams. When news of these talks quickly leaked out, they were greeted with a large measure of cynicism by political commentators. They tended to be seen as a ploy by the SDLP to counter criticism of its stance during the second round of the negotiations among the constitutional parties in 1992. That there was rather more to the talks became apparent in September 1993, when Hume and Adams announced that they had reached agreement on a set of proposals to put to the British and Irish governments.

The reaction of nationalist opinion to the possibility of an end to the violence overcame the initial caution of the two governments. However, the unacceptability to unionists of any initiative originating from Sinn Féin prompted the governments to bypass the unpublished Hume-Adams proposal. They issued their own set of proposals in the form of the *Joint Declaration for Peace* (often known as the Downing Street Declaration) on 15 December 1993 (HMSO, 1993). But this outcome clearly fell short of what the republican movement was seeking as the basis for an end to the campaign of violence against British rule. Sinn Féin asked for clarification of the terms of the Declaration, which it received in May 1994. That was followed by rejection of the terms of the Declaration by a special conference of Sinn Féin in July 1994. In fact, despite this apparent setback to the peace process, the leadership of the republican movement had by now become persuaded that this was a propitious moment to adopt an unarmed strategy, especially in light of the support for such a step from influential elements of the Irish-American lobby. On 31 August 1994, the leadership of the Provisional IRA issued a statement to the effect that, starting at midnight, there would be "a complete cessation of military operations" (*Belfast Telegraph*, 31 August 1994).

In justifying the ceasefire, Sinn Féin leaders emphasised the strength of nationalist forces. They also made much of the comparison between the peace process in Northern Ireland and South Africa's transition. These were important considerations in the thinking of the leadership, not mere attempts to rationalise the failure of the strategy of the long war. This point was well stated by journalist David McKittrick:

> What is clear is that this is not an IRA surrender. The organisation has the guns, the expertise and the recruits to go on killing; it has not been militarily defeated. Rather, it has allowed itself to be persuaded that in the circumstances of today it stands a better chance of furthering its aims through politics than through violence. (*The Independent*, 1 September 1994)

An example of the Provisional IRA's capacity was the huge damage done by two bombs in the City of London in 1992 and 1993. A source of unionist anxiety about the whole peace process since its inception in 1993 was that it had been brought about through tacit concessions by the British government to the republican movement, which the government had made because of the threat that the mainland campaign of the Provisional IRA posed to the British economy. Although many unionists were reassured by the terms of the Downing Street Declaration, the strength of the Irish dimension in the Framework Documents issued by the two governments in February 1995 (HMSO 1995) rekindled unionist suspicion.

The British government responded to the unionists' fears by seeking progress on the dismantling of paramilitary arsenals as a prior condition for all-party talks. Specifically, in March 1995 the British government insisted that some actual decommissioning would have to take place in advance of negotiations on the future of Northern Ireland, a position from which the Irish government retreated when it appreciated the implications of such a stance for progress in the peace process. The result was an impasse between the British government and the republican movement, since the Provisional IRA was unwilling to surrender any arms without prior progress toward a political settlement. The stalemate appeared to have been broken in November 1995, on the eve of President Clinton's visit to Northern Ireland, by the face-saving device of the appointment of an international commission under former U.S. Senator George Mitchell. In January 1996 the Mitchell Commission issued a report recommending that decommissioning should take place in parallel to all-party talks, but also that the parties should be required to sign up to a set of principles that committed them to pursue their political objectives by exclusively peaceful means.

However, by this time there was considerable dissent within the ranks of the Provisional IRA over the ceasefire, due to the lack of political movement since the publication of the Framework Documents in 1995. Such dissent raised the spectre of a split within the organisation. There was also disquiet over the prospect that the Mitchell Commission might impose conditions on Sinn Féin's participation in negotiations. This unease was compounded by the response of the British government to the Mitchell Commission report in which it insisted on the further condition of elections ahead of negotiations. Two events followed: the abandonment of the ceasefire (after a vote on the issue by the Army Council of the Provisional IRA) and the bombing of Canary Wharf (in London). Throughout the ceasefire, units of the Provisional IRA had been kept in a state of readiness to resume the campaign. A dummy run of the Canary Wharf bombing had actually preceded the British government's response to the Mitchell Commission's report. However, Sinn Féin leaders insisted that the British

prime minister's statement in the House of Commons on the Mitchell Commission report had been the final straw. They also contended that the end of the ceasefire did not mean that the party had abandoned its commitment to a peace strategy.

Despite the Provisional IRA's repudiation of the ceasefire on 9 February 1996, it did not resume operations on the same scale as that before 31 August 1994. The Provisional IRA's relative restraint during 1996 and the first half of 1997 can be attributed to a variety of factors. The security forces were successful in thwarting a number of major operations in both England and Northern Ireland. Divisions within its ranks over policy may have been a factor in limiting the effectiveness of the organisation. The electoral ambitions of Sinn Féin provided a further reason as to why their leadership should have pressed the case for restraint on the military wing. Sinn Féin did particularly well at the ballot box throughout 1996 and 1997. In the Forum elections of May 1996, Sinn Féin won 15.5 per cent of the vote. And in the British general election of May 1997, Sinn Féin won 16.1 percent of the vote and 2 seats, whereas in the local elections later that month the party won 16.9 percent of the vote and secured the election of 74 councillors. Sinn Féin's success came about only partly at the expense of its main nationalist rival, the SDLP. A notable feature of the elections in Northern Ireland in 1996 and 1997 was the increase in the overall size of the nationalist vote, reflecting change in the composition of the electorate. Sinn Féin also increased its vote substantially from a very low base in the general election in the Republic of Ireland in June 1997. In addition, a Sinn Féin TD was elected for the first time since the party had dropped its policy of abstentionism in relation to the Dáil in 1986.

However, the most important reason for which there was not a full-scale resumption of the Provisional IRA's campaign of violence was that the Sinn Féin leadership wished to keep the door open to participation in negotiations on the future of Northern Ireland. This preference was evident in its exploration of the possibility of a resumption of the ceasefire in late 1996, a process brought to an end on 28 November by a statement by the prime minister, John Major, rejecting the proposals put to the government by John Hume. The election of the new Labour government in Britain quickly led to negotiations through officials with Sinn Féin over the terms for a resumption of the Provisional IRA's ceasefire. These included assurances that (1) Sinn Féin would be allowed into the multiparty negotiations within a short period of the resumption of the ceasefire; (2) that the two governments would act to prevent the issue of the decommissioning of paramilitary weapons from delaying negotiations on the substantive constitutional issues; and (3) that a target of May 1998 would be set for the completion of negotiations. The willingness of the British government to meet these terms resulted in the "unequivocal" restoration of its 1994 ceasefire by the Provisional IRA on 20 July 1997.

The Ulster Defence Association

The violent reaction of the Catholic community to the introduction of internment in August 1971 prompted the formation of the UDA. It brought together a number of locally based vigilante organisations that had sprung up in working-class loyalist estates with the onset of the troubles in the late 1960s. The UDA responded to what it saw as a broadly based Catholic rebellion with shows of strength on the streets and a campaign of random assassinations of Catholics. This campaign intensified after the British government imposed direct rule in March 1972, which loyalists perceived as a betrayal. Like other loyalists, members of the UDA believed that the power-sharing Executive that the British government succeeded in establishing in 1974 was intended to be a stepping stone to a united Ireland because of the provision in the settlement for a Council of Ireland. The UDA played a key role in the general strike of Protestant workers in May 1974 that brought down the power-sharing Executive. At the time, the UDA had approximately 25,000 dues-paying members (Nelson 1984: 104).

The political influence of the UDA and other loyalist paramilitaries declined after the Ulster Workers Council strike, despite their pivotal role in its success. But their violence continued unabated. According to Michael McKeown's (1989) calculations, between 13 July 1973 and 12 July 1977 loyalist paramilitaries were responsible for 40 percent of the fatalities from political violence in Northern Ireland. However, in the following quadrennium, from 13 July 1977 to 12 July 1981, their share of killings fell to 12 percent of the total (McKeown 1989: 41–43). Two developments in 1976 had contributed to significant changes in the UDA leadership's perceptions of the conflict—changes that altered the pattern of UDA violence in particular: (1) The advent of the Peace People convinced UDA leaders that Catholics in general did not support the Provisional IRA's campaign of violence, and (2) the acceptance by the British government of direct rule as a long-term option dampened fears of betrayal by Britain.

Under the leadership of Andy Tyrie and John McMichael, the UDA began to seek a politically constructive way forward. In 1979 the New Ulster Political Research Group, set up under the aegis of the UDA leadership, published a document entitled *Beyond the Religious Di-*

vide (New Ulster Political Research Group 1979). It advocated an independent Northern Ireland as offering a context in which the sectarian divide could be transcended through the removal of the constitutional issue sustaining the divide. But the idea had little appeal to ordinary members of the UDA, and the attempts of the leadership to secure electoral support for its new departure were a failure. Nevertheless, despite the crisis in the prisons in 1980 and 1981, as well as the Anglo-Irish Agreement of 1985, the leadership was largely able to restrain its members from carrying out random attacks on Catholics. Accordingly, throughout the 1980s UDA violence remained at a relatively low level, although the leadership had no compunction about justifying the killings of republicans—a category that it was willing to define quite broadly. The leadership also exercised political restraint. In January 1987, the Ulster Political Research Group published a document entitled *Common Sense,* advocating power sharing in Northern Ireland as a way out of the impasse resulting from the Anglo-Irish Agreement (Ulster Political Research Group 1987).

In December 1987 John McMichael was murdered by the Provisional IRA. His death was followed by the resignation of Andy Tyrie as supreme commander in March 1988. The repercussions of an inquiry into security-force leaks to the loyalist paramilitaries, including the uncovering of an army intelligence agent within the UDA in January 1990, brought about further changes to the leadership of the UDA. The new leadership saw the restraint that the UDA had exercised during the 1980s as a product of the corruption of the old guard and was determined to demonstrate its effectiveness by matching the violence of the Provisional IRA blow for blow. The result was a sharp increase in assassinations by the UFF, the *nom de guerre* used by the UDA for covert operations. During the first round of negotiations among the constitutional parties between 30 April and 4 July 1991, the UDA joined other loyalist paramilitaries in an umbrella organisation, the Combined Loyalist Military Command (CLMC), which maintained a ceasefire inside Northern Ireland for the duration of the talks. After the failure of the talks, the loyalist paramilitaries intensified their campaign of violence. The British government eventually responded to the new militancy of the UDA by proscribing the organisation in August 1992.

Initially, the loyalist paramilitaries were suspicious of the peace process that the two governments launched in December 1993. For example, in March 1994 the monthly linked to the UDA, *Ulster Defender,* welcomed unionist claims of the demise of the Downing Street Declaration in an editorial entitled "An All Ireland Diversion" (*Ulster Defender* 1994a). However, when the Provisional IRA declared its ceasefire on 31 August 1994, the CLMC followed suit on 13 October 1994. Whereas the loyalist ceasefire was made explicitly conditional on "the continued cessation of all nationalist/republican violence" (*Ulster Defender* 1994b), the CLMC statement went much further than had any statement from a member of the republican movement in expressing remorse over the deaths of the innocent victims of the troubles. The emphasis being placed on politics in the new situation by the loyalist paramilitaries was reflected in the prominence that they now gave to their political wings, the Ulster Democratic Party (UDP) in the case of the UDA and the Progressive Unionist Party (PUP) in the case of the UVF. The fringe loyalist parties, as they were dubbed, quickly established a reputation for political moderation, advocating compromise and political accommodation. For example, they adopted a cautious stance on the Framework Documents issued by the two governments in February 1995, as illustrated by the commentary on the documents by the leader of the Ulster Democratic Party, Gary McMichael (*Ulster Defender* 1995). However, the fringe loyalist parties remain committed to the unionist camp and have followed the lead of the Ulster Unionist Party on issues such as participation in talks including Sinn Féin. Furthermore, their moderation might be interpreted as partly motivated by the desire to win respectability on the grounds of their purportedly greater willingness to compromise than other unionists.

One interpretation of the loyalist ceasefire is that it demonstrates the wholly reactive character of the loyalist paramilitaries. The weakness of this argument, however, is that loyalist violence through the course of the troubles has by no means followed the pattern set by republican paramilitaries. Indeed, it is evident that relatively little interplay has occurred in the evolution of the strategies of the Provisional IRA and the UDA. The positive loyalist response to the Provisional IRA's ceasefire owed more to the paramilitaries' recognition that they faced isolation within the Protestant community if they continued their violence in these circumstances than it did to any appreciation of the reasons for the Provisional IRA's decision. In particular, the leaders of the loyalist paramilitaries were astute enough to recognise that interpreting the Provisional IRA ceasefire as a surrender, and acting accordingly, was a more sensible course of action than allowing themselves to be put in a position where they would be held solely responsible for the continuance of the Northern Ireland conflict.

The resumption of the Provisional IRA's campaign of violence in February 1996 placed a considerable strain on the loyalist ceasefire. However, thanks to the efforts of the leaders of the political wings of the paramilitaries, and given that the breach of the Provisional IRA ceasefire was initially limited to a relatively small number of incidents in London, it held for several months, with one minor exception. Specifically, the Mid-Ulster UVF was responsible for a bomb scare at Dublin airport in early May 1996. As tensions rose in Northern Ireland over the issue of Orange Order marches during the summer of 1996, there were further and more serious incidents of loyalist paramilitary violence. Some of the violence was attributable to opponents of the peace process within the loyalist paramilitaries. Attempts by the leadership to discipline the dissidents failed, culminating in the standing down of the Mid-Ulster UVF and the formation of a new grouping, the Loyalist Volunteer Force (LVF), outside the control of the CLMC.

The leadership of the PUP and the UDP gained widespread media coverage during 1996 for their pleas to loyalist militants not to respond to provocation by republicans. Both the Progressive Unionist Party (with 3.5 percent of the vote) and the Ulster Democratic Party (with 2.2 percent of the vote) gained representation in the Northern Ireland Forum elected at the end of May 1996. The positive image acquired by the two parties continued and was reflected in electoral successes in 1997. Indeed, the PUP's most prominent spokesman, David Ervine, won 14.4 percent of the vote in Belfast South in the British general election of May 1997, and later that month the PUP won 6 seats on local councils across Northern Ireland compared to the 4 seats won by the UDP.

Conclusion

The truce between the paramilitaries during the 1994–1996 period did not lead to a complete cessation of paramilitary violence in Northern Ireland—partly because of the inability of the paramilitaries' leaders to exercise total control over their members, and partly because of the existence of fringe groups not committed to the ceasefires. But the most important reason was that the main paramilitaries never intended the ceasefires to apply to their use of violence for secondary purposes. Consequently, although many fewer people have been killed by the paramilitaries since 1994 than in the years before (again, see Table 2.1), violence and the threat of violence remain significant factors in the politics of Northern Ireland despite the Provisional IRA's restoration of its ceasefire in July 1997. The continuing controversy over the decommissioning of paramilitary arsenals has underlined that threat; but even if progress on this issue is made in the multiparty talks, a comprehensive political settlement would almost certainly be required to banish violence from the politics of Northern Ireland. However, the obstacles to a settlement with both broad support in the two communities and the capacity for permanency are formidable. Indeed, even a transitory arrangement will be difficult to achieve, given the current positions of the major political parties.

In the absence of a political settlement, the major paramilitaries seem likely to survive, even if their current truce holds. A reason for predicting that the paramilitaries will endure whatever happens is the range of functions they perform. However, the same reason might also provide the basis for their evolution into organisations that no longer merit the description *paramilitary*. At best, they might develop into exclusively constitutional political parties, although it seems unlikely that such a development would precede a comprehensive political settlement. Another possibility is their evolution into mafias. And, of course, it is possible that there will be a return to war between the paramilitaries. Republicans and loyalists have radically conflicting views of the balance of political forces in Northern Ireland, which may lead one side or the other to launch a violent challenge if it feels betrayed by the outcome of negotiations or by the actions of the British and Irish governments. In this respect, moreover, the perceptions of the paramilitaries do not differ radically from those to be found in the principal constitutional parties on either side of the sectarian divide.

One result of nearly thirty years of violence has been the polarisation of politics between the two communities such that the constitutional parties have acquired a better understanding of the perspective of the paramilitaries in their own communities than of the perspective of constitutional parties from the other community. The fact that it has proved easier to secure an end to the main campaigns of political violence than to get agreement across the sectarian divide is evidence of the strength of political polarisation between the communities. The question remains: Can the truce between the paramilitaries survive without a lasting political settlement between unionists and nationalists?

References and Further Reading

An Phoblacht/Republican News, 1987. Dublin: Sinn Féin. 7 May.

______, 1990. Dublin: Sinn Féin. 28 June.

Beresford, David, 1987. *Ten Men Dead: The Story of the 1981 Irish Hunger Strike*. London: Grafton Books.

Bew, Paul, and Gordon Gillespie, 1993. *Northern Ireland: A Chronology of the Troubles 1968–1993*. Dublin: Gill and Macmillan.

Bruce, Steve, 1992. *The Red Hand: Protestant Paramilitaries in Northern Ireland*. Oxford: Oxford University Press.

The Chief Constable's Annual Report 1996. Belfast: Royal Ulster Constabulary.

Coogan, Tim Pat, 1995. *The Troubles: Ireland's Ordeal 1966–1995 and the Search for Peace*. London: Hutchinson.

HMSO, 1993. *Joint Declaration: Downing Street, 15 December 1993*. Belfast. December.

———, 1995. *A New Framework for Agreement: A Shared Understanding Between the British and Irish Governments to Assist Discussion and Negotiation Involving the Northern Ireland Parties*. Belfast. February.

Holland, Jack, and Henry McDonald, 1994. *INLA: Deadly Divisions*. Dublin: Torc.

Iris, 1982. Dublin: Sinn Féin. November.

Maguire, Keith, 1993. "Fraud, extortion and racketeering: The black economy in Northern Ireland," *Crime, Law and Social Change* 20, pp. 273–292.

Maguire, Maria, 1973. *To Take Arms: A Year in the Provisional IRA*. London: Quartet.

Mallie, Eamonn, and David McKittrick, 1996. *The Fight for Peace: The Secret Story Behind the Irish Peace Process*. London: Heinemann.

McIntyre, Anthony, 1995. "Modern Irish republicanism: The product of British state strategies," *Irish Political Studies* 10, pp. 97–122.

McKeown, Michael, 1989. *Two Seven Six Three*. Lucan: Murlough Press.

Munck, Ronnie, 1995. "Irish republicanism: Containment or new departure?" pp. 159–172 in Alan O'Day (ed.), *Terrorism's Laboratory: The Case of Northern Ireland*. Aldershot: Dartmouth.

Nelson, Sarah, 1984. *Ulster's Uncertain Defenders: Protestant Political Paramilitary and Community Groups and the Northern Ireland Conflict*. Belfast: Appletree Press.

New Ulster Research Political Group, 1979. *Beyond the Religious Divide*. Belfast.

O'Brien, Brendan, 1995. *The Long War: The IRA and Sinn Féin from Armed Struggle to Peace Talks*. Dublin: O'Brien Press.

O'Duffy, Brendan, 1995. "Violence in Northern Ireland 1969–1994: Sectarian or ethno-national?" *Ethnic and Racial Studies* 18:4, pp. 740–772.

O'Leary, Brendan, and John McGarry, 1993. *The Politics of Antagonism: Understanding Northern Ireland*. London: Athlone Press.

O'Malley, Padraig, 1990. *Biting at the Grave: The Irish Hunger Strikes and the Politics of Despair*. Belfast: Blackstaff Press.

Sinn Féin, 1989. *The Sinn Féin/SDLP Talks*. Dublin. January.

———, 1992. *Towards a Lasting Peace in Ireland*. Dublin. February.

Sutton, Malcolm, 1994. *Bear in Mind These Dead . . . : An Index of Deaths from the Conflict in Ireland 1969–1993*. Belfast: Beyond the Pale Publications.

Toolis, Kevin, 1995. *Rebel Hearts: Journeys Within the IRA's Soul*. London/Basingstoke: Picador.

Ulster Defender, 1994a. Lisburn: Ulster Information Service. 1: 9. March.

———, 1994b. Lisburn: Ulster Information Service. 1:12. Circa November/December.

———, 1995. Lisburn: Ulster Information Service. 1:13. Circa March.

Ulster Political Research Group, 1987. *Common Sense: Northern Ireland—An Agreed Process*. Belfast.

3

Segmentation and the Social Structure

RICHARD BREEN AND PAULA DEVINE

This chapter is concerned with the social and physical segregation of Northern Ireland. When one thinks of the bases of social stratification in Northern Irish society, the division between the Protestant and Catholic communities is inevitably central. And, indeed, the sectarian divide has lain at the root of the conflict that was renewed in the late 1960s. However, it is not the only significant source of social differentiation within Northern Ireland. In particular, if our interest is in the physical segregation of Northern Ireland, then social-class differences also play an important role. Accordingly, in this chapter we examine not only the sectarian bases of social division in Northern Ireland but also those associated with social class.[1] As we shall see, much of what is distinctive in the patterns of segregation found in Northern Ireland arises from the interaction of class and religious boundaries.

The Sizes of the Protestant and Catholic Communities

As is well known, the salience of religious labels in Northern Ireland arises largely because of the identification of Catholicism with nationalism, on the one hand, and Protestantism with unionism, on the other. At first sight, then, it may seem paradoxical that the sizes of these two major sectarian groupings in Northern Ireland are not known with any degree of accuracy. However, on further reflection the unwillingness of people to state their religion in surveys such as the Census of Population might be seen as due precisely to the fact that religion is such a potent source of identity and identification in Northern Ireland.

In the 1981 census, 28 percent of the population stated that they were Catholic and 53.5 percent were of another religion of which the majority (45.9 percent) stated that they belonged to one of the three main Protestant denominations—Presbyterian, Church of Ireland, or Methodist. However, a considerable proportion of the population—18.5 percent, or 274,584 people—refused to state their religion. In the 1991 census the level of uncertainty was somewhat lower but still substantial: 38.4 percent of the population stated that they were Catholic and 50.6 specified another religion; of the latter, 42.8 percent belonged to one of the three main Protestant denominations. Among the remainder of the population, 3.7 percent stated that they had no religion and 7.3 percent refused to state a religion. The year 1991 was the first in which figures were available for those who said they had no religion.

The link between unionism or nationalism and religion is generally assumed to be a product of upbringing. Indeed, even among those who state they have no religion there is a good deal of interest in seeking to determine the religion into which they were born. A good deal of effort has thus been expended on allocating to one or the other of the main religious groups the 11.0 percent of respondents to the 1991 census who either stated no religion or refused to state a religion. The task is a difficult one, to say the least, and the various methods adopted have all been of a somewhat *ad hoc* nature, although this fact has not prevented various estimates of when Northern Ireland might see a Catholic majority. However, apart from the difficulty of assigning the 1991 population to the Protestant and Catholic communities, the census is the only source that can be used to estimate fertility rates and emigration rates for the different religious groups. Hence uncertainty in population projections is compounded: Not only the 1991 baseline figures, but also the rates at which the populations of the two groups might be expected to change, remain unknown.[2]

The results of the 1991 census generated a good deal of debate in Northern Ireland because they seemed (at least to some commentators) to imply that the number of Catholics would come to exceed the number of Protestants within the early part of the next century—a result that, it was argued, would have clear implications for politics in Northern Ireland and possibly for the province's constitutional position. But even aside from the demographic difficulties already referred to, this is an oversimplification on many counts. First, of course, if we are concerned with the political and constitutional consequences of a Catholic majority, the real focus of interest should be on the population of voting age. Given the age structure of Northern Ireland, a Catholic voting majority here would not be realised for a considerable time after Catholics had come to make up the majority of the whole population. And, secondly, the Catholic community itself is quite heterogeneous in its political and constitutional preferences—a point we take up later.

Social Class

Social divisions in Northern Ireland are based on other issues as well, such as social class. Data from the 1991 Census of Population show that 5 percent of households have a head of household in Registrar General's Social Class I (professional); 28.3 percent in Class II (managerial/technical); 13.7 percent in Class IIIn (skilled nonmanual); 29.1 percent in Class IIIm (skilled manual); 14.5 percent in Class IV (partly skilled); and 6 percent in Class V (unskilled). Forty seven percent of households are thus headed by someone in one of the nonmanual classes, whereas 49 percent are headed by someone in a manual class. Moreover, data concerning individuals aggregated by religion show that 49 percent of Protestants are in nonmanual classes, compared to 40 percent of Catholics.

Using data from the 1971 Census of Population, Edmund Aunger (1975) has calculated that 31 percent of Catholics, versus 41 percent of Protestants, were in nonmanual occupations. These figures show a rise in the percentage of both Protestants and Catholics in nonmanual occupations, although the Protestant increase is marginally smaller. Aunger suggested that the existence of a Catholic middle class was mostly due to the provision of separate professional services within each community; otherwise, the number of Catholics in nonmanual classes would be much smaller. As we shall see, the expansion of the Catholic middle class has been associated with the substantial weakening of this pattern: The "new" Catholic middle class is much more widespread, serving a much greater share of the community.

Residential Segregation

Data from successive censuses indicate that residential segregation in Northern Ireland according to religious community is, if anything, increasing. We can gain some insight into this phenomenon by looking at the religious composition of census wards. These are the smallest geographical units for which census data are available, and their boundaries are drawn so as to make them correspond, to the extent possible, to local communities. By examining the religious composition of the population of wards, we can get some idea of the religious makeup of the communities in which people in Northern Ireland live.[3] According to the census of 1981 (when there were 526 wards in Northern Ireland), 5.7 percent of wards had a population greater than 70 percent Catholic; by 1991 (when there were 566 wards) this proportion had increased to 21.9 percent.[4] Among Protestants, segregation is even more marked. In 1991, 35.7 percent of wards had a population that was more than 70 percent Protestant—a percentage that varied little from the 1981 figure of 35.9 percent. In short, 41.4 percent of wards in 1981 and 57.8 percent of wards in 1991 were segregated; that is, they had a population that was more than 70 percent Catholic or Protestant.

In part, this finding reflects segregation at a larger geographical level, such that Catholics are overrepresented in the west and south of Northern Ireland. Thus, for example, in Newry and Mourne District Council Area (located in the southeast of Northern Ireland and adjoining the Irish Republic), the population is 71.8 percent Catholic and 19.8 Protestant. It is not entirely surprising to find that, in this region, 63.3 percent of wards are more than 70 percent Catholic whereas no wards are more than 70 percent Protestant. Yet even in areas where the overall population is more nearly balanced, residential segregation may still be very high. For example, in the Belfast District Council Area (DCA), where Catholics constitute 39 percent and Protestants 47.6 percent of the total population, 25 percent and 39.2 percent of the wards are more than 70 percent Catholic or Protestant, respectively. As we might expect, people's perceptions of residential segregation accord very closely with such findings. Consider the study by David Smith and Gerald Chambers (1991: 335–337), based on data from the Continuous Household Survey in the mid-1980s, in which the authors found that 37 percent of all households were located in wards where 90 percent or more of the population was drawn from one religious grouping or the other. In a survey also undertaken by Smith and Chambers, 38 percent of respondents reported that they lived in neighbourhoods containing "nearly all Protestants" or "nearly all Catholics."

Patterns of segregation by social class are no less marked (e.g., Boal 1971). According to the 1991 census, 148,847 out of a total of 300,438 households (49.5 percent) were headed by a manual worker (i.e., an individual in Registrar General's Social Class IIIm or lower). Fifty-seven percent of such households were found in wards where more than 50 percent of households were headed by a manual worker. In other words, parallel to residential segregation by religious group is an equally marked segregation by class.

Patterns of residential segregation are more than the sum of the effects of religious and class divisions. Drawing on data relating to the Belfast DCA, A. M. Gallagher, R. D. Osborne, and R. J. Cormack (1994: 61) noted that the Catholic middle class is relatively dispersed. A quarter of middle-class Catholics live in North and West Belfast close to the major concentrations of working-class Catholics. By contrast, middle-class Protestants living in the Belfast DCA are not only fewer in number, but there is "no significant Protestant middle-class representation in Protestant working-class areas of North and West Belfast" (Gallagher et al., 1994: 61). In other words, class-based residential segregation appears—in Belfast, at least—to be more marked among Protestants than Catholics. Furthermore, although religious residential segregation is generally considered more marked among working-class communities, religious residential segregation among the middle classes also seems more marked among Protestants than Catholics. Indeed, as Gallagher and his colleagues have (1994: 61–62) observed: "The majority experience for middle-class Protestants in . . . [Belfast] is still one of segregated living. Only a minority of middle-class Protestants live in 'mixed' areas. . . . The majority experience of middle-class Catholics . . . is to live in mixed areas."

Gallagher and his colleagues attribute this difference to greater Catholic residential mobility, which, in turn, they view as deriving from upward social mobility. As we have seen, the class distribution of the Catholic community has changed quite drastically since the early 1970s, and the phenomenon of the "new Catholic middle class" has frequently been remarked upon (e.g., Cormack and Osborne 1994). Expanded educational opportunities are specified as having played a crucial role in the growth of this new middle class. It has been contrasted with the smaller, older Catholic middle class that primarily acted to service the needs of the Catholic community. And newly upwardly mobile Catholics are much more widely distributed across middle-class positions; in particular, "a substantial section of the Catholic middle class is now employed in the public services, a major change over the past 25 years" (Cormack and Osborne 1994: 79). A more contentious issue, however, concerns the political consequences of the growth of the Catholic middle class; some commentators argue that it will lead to a decline in support for nationalism. Cormack and Osborne (1994: 84) have outlined the argument, albeit sceptically. It has also been less cautiously advanced by some journalists (Brennock 1991; McKittrick 1991). This distinctively Northern Irish variant of what social scientists know as the "embourgeoisement thesis" will be examined in more detail later.

The Education of Catholics and Protestants

Although expanded educational opportunities have been presented as playing the main role in the recent growth of the Catholic middle class, the educational system in which these opportunities were made available continues to be starkly divided not only by religion but also by class. Northern Ireland has the dubious distinction of being the only part of the United Kingdom to retain a selective system of post-primary education, with pupils being allocated to grammar or secondary schools on the basis of an examination taken at the age of eleven. One obvious consequence is that post-primary education is characterised by very clear class divisions. A survey of pupils transferring from primary schools, undertaken in 1981 by the Northern Ireland Council for Education Research, showed that 48 percent of middle-class children transferred to a grammar school, compared to 18 percent of working-class pupils (NIEC 1995). The corresponding figures concerning transfers to a secondary school were 52 percent and 82 percent, respectively. By any standard, these figures represent a stark degree of class segregation.

Similarly, the educational system is divided by religion—except that there are separate Catholic and Protestant systems at both the primary and secondary levels. This division has arisen as a consequence of historical opposition to the state's attempts to establish a nondenominational system of schools. From this circumstance three types of school evolved: controlled, maintained, and voluntary, which differ in terms of management and financial structures (Darby and Dunn 1987). Controlled schools are funded by education and library boards, although Protestant Churches are guaranteed a majority on school management boards (Cormack, Miller, and Osborne 1987). In order to preserve a Catholic ethos, the Catholic Church refused to place its schools under such an arrangement with the government. Later, agreement was reached to enable Catholic schools to receive financial aid from education and library boards, with the government representing a minority on school management boards. The capital and running costs of voluntary nonmaintained schools are met by the Department of Education for Northern Ireland. Controlled schools are almost all Protestant, maintained schools are almost all Catholic, and voluntary schools are all grammar schools and can be either Catholic or Protestant. Official figures for 1993–1994 (PPRU 1995) indicate that 98.6 percent of pupils attended schools in the controlled, maintained, and voluntary sectors, whereas only 1 percent of pupils attended integrated schools. However, this picture is changing—albeit slowly—as more integrated schools are established.

At the tertiary level, the picture is dramatically reversed. None of the third-level institutions in Northern Ireland are religiously affiliated or segregated, and the percentage of working-class children continuing to some form of tertiary education is higher in Northern Ireland than elsewhere in the United Kingdom.

Occupational Segregation

It is now widely accepted that during the period when Northern Ireland had its own parliament (1922–1972) there was systematic discrimination against Catholics in three main areas:[5] the electoral system, the allocation of public housing, and the labour market (Smith and Chambers 1991: 14–22). Over the past two decades, discrimination in the first two areas has quite clearly been eradicated, but the extent of labour market discrimination that still exists has been hotly debated (see Cormack and Osborne 1991 for a review of this debate; see also Whyte 1990: ch. 3).

What is not in doubt is that Catholics experience much higher levels of unemployment than Protestants and that the magnitude of the difference between them has barely changed since 1971. The unemployment rate of Catholic men in 1991 was 2.2 times greater than that of Protestant men (28.4 percent versus 12.7 percent). This differential of 2.2 in 1991 compares with a differential of 2.6 in 1971. Among women the differential is smaller but still substantial: The unemployment rate of Catholic women in 1991 was 1.8 times greater than that of Protestant women (14.5 percent versus 8 percent). Among the range of explanations for the differential among males and its persistence, there is general agreement that at least some part of it is due to what are sometimes termed "structural" differences between the two communities—that is, differences in factors such as level of educational qualifications, geographical distribution, and age, all of which are related to the chances of having a job. Some of these accounts suggest (or imply) that discrimination also plays a significant role (Smith and Chambers 1991; Murphy and Armstrong 1994), whereas others maintain that discrimination accounts for relatively little of the differential (Gudgin and Breen 1996).

However, alongside sectarian differences in the risk of being unemployed there is comparable—indeed, greater—variation according to social class. For example, data from the Northern Ireland Social Attitudes survey aggregated over the years 1989, 1990, 1993, and 1994 show that rates of registered unemployment are very strongly linked to class. Of the respondents in Registrar General's Social Class I, none were registered as unemployed, compared with 3 percent in Class II, 8 percent in Class IIIn, 15 percent in Classes IIIm and IV, and 26 percent in Class V. It is easy to see that the ratio of unemployment rates between different classes is, in several instances, much greater than the

Catholic-to-Protestant ratio. Within each class, of course, the unemployment rate among Catholics is higher than that among Protestants—but equally, within each community group, there is substantial class-based variation.

In the area of employment, religious segregation—when measured at the level of gross occupational or industrial group—is relatively minor (e.g., PPRU Monitor 2-94). However, at the level of individual firms there remains a high degree of such segregation.

Mixing and Intermarriage

The picture drawn so far is of a society in which the two communities are educated separately and in which there is an unusually high degree of both residential and occupational segregation. From this scenario, certain other observations follow. For example, owing to segregation in education, work, and residence, social activities and social networks are largely confined to members of one's own social class and religious grouping (see Boal 1969; Darby 1986). One corollary of this trend is found in the low rates of inter-religious marriage in Northern Ireland. According to figures based on the 1991 census, only 2.3 percent of marriages involved partners of mixed religion (Compton 1995). (This statistic does not, however, account for people who have no religion or who did not specify a religion.) The 1983 Northern Ireland Fertility Survey (NIFS) indicates a rate of 3.6 percent. Data from four Northern Ireland Social Attitude (NISA) surveys—undertaken in 1989, 1991, 1993, and 1994—show that around 6 percent of respondents are of a different religion than their spouses. Although this figure may underestimate the rate of inter-religious marriage, inasmuch as the survey questions deal with current religion and do not identify those respondents who changed religion to that of their spouses when they married, the NIFS nevertheless calculated the rate of mixed marriage as being 6.0 percent when based on religion at the time of marriage—that is, on the respondents' religion of origin.

Intrasectarian Divisions

Sectarian divisions are deeply etched, but they are not the only source of segregation in Northern Ireland. One might therefore ask whether, and to what extent, these other sources have the capacity to weaken or cut across religious segregation. Of course, this is an argument often associated with Marxist accounts of Northern Ireland, where the working class is seen as the potential source through which sectarian divisions might be transcended (e.g., McGarry and O'Leary 1995: ch. 2). More recently, attention has shifted to the possibility of Catholic embourgeoisement, as noted above. More generally, we might anticipate that, although political and constitutional preferences as well as beliefs and attitudes about relations between the two communities in Northern Ireland are structured on sectarian grounds, the existence of intrasectarian structural divisions—particularly along class lines—will render the Catholic and Protestant blocs less monolithic than might otherwise be the case. In the remainder of this chapter we examine the extent of internal heterogeneity in these areas and the degree to which it reflects internal class divisions.

Perhaps the clearest intrareligious division is found in patterns of party political support. Using data from one of the aforementioned NISA surveys, Geoffrey Evans and Mary Duffy (1997) have examined the sources of intrasectarian party competition—in other words, the competition between Sinn Féin and the SDLP among nationalists/Catholics and between the DUP and the UUP among unionists/Protestants. They find that younger people on both sides of the sectarian divide tend to be more likely to support the less "moderate" parties and more likely to support Sinn Féin and the DUP, respectively. Social-class effects are also evident among both groups, such that support for Sinn Féin and the DUP is disproportionately voiced by those in the working class. But Evans and Duffy have also found that this effect is stronger among unionists/Protestants than among Catholics: In the latter group, constitutional cleavages (measured in terms of strength of nationalism) are a somewhat stronger predictor of party preference. The fact that this is not the case among unionists/Protestants reflects the lack of variation in constitutional preferences within the latter community.

This scenario is very clearly reflected in Table 3.1, which, again based on NISA data, reveals the very substantial homogeneity in views among Protestants concerning their preferences for long-term future constitutional arrangements for Northern Ireland. Protestants are overwhelmingly in favour of retaining the union with Britain: Only 10 percent, at most, are in favour of some other option, and support for a united Ireland never exceeds 5 percent. In contrast, Catholics are more divided on the question, with around half wanting a united Ireland but about one-third favouring the retention of the union with Britain. What is perhaps most surprising about intrasectarian constitutional preferences is that, although there is more variation within the Catholic than the Protestant community, socioeconomic factors such as social class, level of education, and household income explain much more of the variation in such preferences among the lat-

TABLE 3.1 Preferred Long-Term Policy for Northern Ireland, by Religion (%)

	1989	*1990*	*1991*	*1993*	*1994*
Protestants					
Remain part of U.K.	93	93	92	90	90
Reunify Ireland	3	5	4	5	6
Other option	2	1	1	4	3
Don't know	2	1	1	1	1
Not answered	0	0	1	0	0
Catholics					
Remain part of U.K.	32	33	35	36	24
Reunify Ireland	56	55	53	49	60
Other option	4	5	2	5	7
Don't know	7	6	7	10	8
Not answered	1	1	2	1	1
Others					
Remain part of U.K.	81	72	79	74	66
Reunify Ireland	13	19	13	13	15
Other option	4	5	4	6	14
Don't know	3	2	4	7	5
Not answered	0	2	0	0	0

Sources: Northern Ireland Social Attitudes Surveys (1989–1992 and 1993–1994).

ter than among the former (Breen 1996). An embourgeoisement thesis would lead us to expect that Catholics, who are inclined to support the continuation of the union, are disproportionately drawn from the middle class. But as this is not the case, the plausibility of that thesis is in doubt.[6]

This pattern—of greater heterogeneity of views among Catholics than among Protestants, whereby the variation is less strongly linked to socioeconomic factors among the former than among the latter—is, perhaps surprisingly, common across a range of areas. For example, questions concerning people's beliefs about the impartiality of the security forces in their treatment of Catholics and Protestants tend to elicit a similar pattern of responses: greater variation among Catholics, of which much less can be accounted for by the socioeconomic characteristics of respondents (Breen 1995).

Attitudes Toward Segregation

We have seen that Northern Ireland is characterised by a high degree of residential and other segregation. Although it would be valuable to

TABLE 3.2 Attitudes of Catholics and Protestants Toward Mixing of the Two Communities (%)

	Prefer much more or a bit more mixing	*Keep things as they are*	*Prefer a bit more or much more separation*
Where people work			
Protestant	79	20	2
Catholic	93	7	0
Where people live			
Protestant	73	24	3
Catholic	84	15	1
Marriage			
Protestant	38	47	15
Catholic	60	36	4

Note: Rows may not sum to 100 because of rounding.
Sources: Northern Ireland Social Attitudes surveys (1989, 1991, 1993, 1994).

know both the extent to which such segregation reflects a simple preference for being with "one's own kind" and the extent to which it arises out of a need to ensure personal security, the NISA data do not allow us to answer this question. They do, however, shed some light on people's attitudes toward the possibility of greater mixing of the two communities.

Table 3.2 shows the responses to three questions asking whether people would favour greater mixing of the two communities in areas where they work and where they live, as well as in marriage. What is quite noticeable from these responses is that, in terms of workplace and residential segregation, a majority of Catholics and of Protestants would like to see either a bit more or much more mixing, but in terms of the three questions overall, Catholics express a stronger desire for more mixing than do Protestants. Furthermore, although support for greater mixing at work is very high in both communities, it is somewhat lower for residential mixing and much lower for mixed marriages. In this last category, 62 percent of Protestants and 40 percent of Catholics wish either to keep things as they are or to increase the degree of separation.

But within each community there are also marked class differences. Though relatively weak in the case of attitudes toward greater mixing at work, these differences are more evident in relation to mixed neighbourhoods and mixed marriages. The general pattern is for the higher social classes (particularly members of Registrar General's Social Class I) to be much more strongly in favour of mixing than all other classes, with the manual classes (IIIm, IV, and V) most in favour of keeping things as they are or increasing the degree of separation. But, again, these class effects are stronger among Protestants than among Catholics. Particularly striking is the fact that, although there are class differences among Catholics with respect to views toward residential segregation, these disappear in the context of mixing through marriage. Thus, for example, 45 percent of Catholics in Class I (professional workers) want things to stay the same or to see more separation, compared with 41 percent of Catholics in Class IV (partly skilled workers) and 50 percent of Catholics in Class V (unskilled workers). Among Protestants the comparable figures are 38 percent for Class I and 69 and 72 percent for Classes IV and V, respectively.

Conclusion

Although sectarian differences do indeed form the basis for most social and physical segregation in Northern Ireland, a number of stylised "facts" about the situation are not borne out by empirical analysis. First, parallel to sectarian divisions are significant social-class effects of a kind that are perhaps more familiar for being similar to those found in societies in which sectarian conflict plays little or no role. Secondly, the nature of sectarian divisions is, to a considerable extent, shaped by class differences. So we find that religious residential segregation is more marked among the working class of both communities; yet, at the same time, residential segregation by social class is somewhat more pronounced among Protestants than among Catholics. The Catholic middle class, which has enjoyed very rapid rates of growth over the past two and a half decades, is particularly notable for being relatively widespread throughout Belfast. Hence we find enclaves of Catholic middle-class housing adjacent to predominantly working-class Catholic areas, but we also find them in areas traditionally considered Protestant.

Thirdly, the notion that the two communities in Northern Ireland are homogenous blocs, each a mirror image of the other, is quite false. Members of the Catholic community display a considerable degree of heterogeneity in attitudes toward community relations issues, political preferences, and constitutional preferences, whereas members of the Protestant community tend to share a greater commonality of outlook in such areas. But, contrary to what the embourgeoisement thesis might seem to imply, it is in the Protestant community that internal variation in attitudes can be linked to social class and other socioeconomic characteristics. Among Catholics, whose views are more diverse, the relationship between an individual's socioeconomic position and his or her views is, perhaps paradoxically, somewhat weaker.

References and Further Reading

Aunger, Edmund A., 1975. "Religious and occupational class in Northern Ireland," *Economic and Social Review* 7, pp. 1–17.

Boal, Fred W., 1969. "Territoriality on the Shankill-Falls Divide, Belfast," *Irish Geography* 6, pp. 30–50.

______, 1971. "Territoriality and class: A study of two residential areas in Belfast," *Irish Geography* 8, pp. 229–248.

Breen, Richard, 1994. "Over the horizon," *Fortnight* 325, February 1994.

______, 1995. "Beliefs about the treatment of Catholics and Protestants by the security forces," pp. 49–62 in Richard Breen, Gillian Robinson, and Paula Devine (eds.), *Social Attitudes in Northern Ireland, the Fourth Volume.* Belfast: Appletree Press.

______, 1996. "Who wants a united Ireland? Constitutional preferences among Catholics and Protestants," pp. 33–48 in Richard Breen, Lizanne Dowds, and Paula Devine (eds.), *Social Attitudes in Northern Ireland, the Fifth Volume.* Belfast: Appletree Press.

Brennock, Mark, 1991. "Guess who's coming to Belfast 9?" *Irish Times*, 23 March.

Compton, Paul, 1995. *Demographic Review, Northern Ireland 1995.* Northern Ireland Economic Council Research Monograph 1. Belfast: Northern Ireland Economic Council.

Cormack, Robert J., and Robert D. Osborne, 1991. "Disadvantage and discrimination in Northern Ireland," pp. 5–48 in Robert J. Cormack and Robert D. Osborne (eds.), *Discrimination and Public Policy in Northern Ireland.* Oxford: Clarendon Press.

______, 1994. "The evolution of the Catholic middle class," pp. 65–85 in Adrian Guelke (ed.), *New Perspectives on the Northern Ireland Conflict.* Aldershot: Avebury.

Cormack, R. J., R. L. Miller, and R. D. Osborne, 1987. "Education and policy in Northern Ireland," pp. 1–28 in R. D. Osborne, R. J. Cormack, and R. L Miller (eds.), *Education and Policy in Northern Ireland.* Belfast: Policy Research Institute.

Darby, John, 1986. *Intimidation and the Control of Conflict.* Dublin: Gill and Macmillan.

Darby, John, and Seamus Dunn, 1987. "Segregated schools: The research evidence," pp. 85–97 in R. D. Osborne, R. J. Cormack, and R. L Miller (eds.), *Education and Policy in Northern Ireland.* Belfast: Policy Research Institute.

Evans, Geoffrey, and Mary Duffy, 1997. "Beyond the sectarian divide: The social bases and political consequences of Nationalist and Unionist Party competition in Northern Ireland," *British Journal of Political Science* 27, pp. 47–81.

Gallagher, A. M., R. D. Osborne, and R. J. Cormack, 1994. *Fair Shares? Employment, Unemployment and Economic Status.* Belfast: Fair Employment Commission.

Gudgin, Graham, and Richard Breen, 1996. *An Evaluation of the Ratio of Unemployment as an Indicator of Fair Employment.* Belfast: Central Community Relations Unit.

Hewitt, Christopher, 1981. "Catholic grievances, Catholic nationalism and violence in Northern Ireland during the civil rights period: A reconsideration," *British Journal of Sociology* 32:3, pp. 362–380.

———, 1983. "Discrimination in Northern Ireland: A rejoinder," *British Journal of Sociology* 34:3, pp. 446–451.

———, 1985. "Catholic grievances and violence in Northern Ireland," *British Journal of Sociology* 36:1, pp. 102–105.

McGarry, John, and Brendan O'Leary, 1995. *Explaining Northern Ireland: Broken Images*. Oxford: Blackwell.

McKittrick, David, 1991. "Catholics find middle-class oasis in Belfast," *The Independent*. 11 January.

Murphy, Anthony, and David Armstrong, 1994. *A Picture of the Catholic and Protestant Male Unemployed*. Belfast: Central Community Relations Unit.

NIEC, 1995. Reforming the Education System in Northern Ireland, Occasional Paper 1. Belfast: Northern Ireland Economic Council.

Northern Ireland Social Attitudes Surveys, 1989–1992. Published by Blackstaff Press.

Northern Ireland Social Attitudes Surveys, 1993–1994. Published by Appletree Press.

O'Hearn, Denis, 1983. "Catholic grievances, Catholic nationalism: A comment," *British Journal of Sociology* 34:3, pp. 438–445.

———, 1985. "Again on discrimination in the North of Ireland: A reply to the rejoinder," *British Journal of Sociology* 36:1, pp. 94–101.

———, 1987. "Catholic grievances: Comments," *British Journal of Sociology* 38:1, pp. 94–100.

PPRU, 1995. Northern Ireland Annual Abstract of Statistics, Number 13—1995. Belfast: Policy Planning and Research Unit.

PPRU Monitor 2/94, 1994. *1993 Labour Force Survey: Religion Report*. Belfast: Policy Planning and Research Unit.

Smith, David J., and Gerald Chambers, 1991. *Inequality in Northern Ireland*. Oxford: Clarendon Press.

Whyte, John, 1983. "How much discrimination was there under the Unionist Regime, 1921–68?" pp. 1–35 in Tom Gallagher and James O'Connell (eds.), *Contemporary Irish Studies*. Manchester: Manchester University Press.

———, 1990. *Interpreting Northern Ireland*. Oxford: Clarendon Press.

4

The Electoral Systems

PAUL MITCHELL AND GORDON GILLESPIE

Electoral systems are an important part of the rules of the game of representative politics. Although all electoral systems convert the votes cast into seats in an assembly, they do so differently and with distinct consequences. The choice of electoral system is rarely technocratic or apolitical, since politicians and parties either make the choice directly or at least structure the alternatives that are placed before the electorate in referendums. It is hardly surprising that parties tend to advocate electoral systems that they believe will be in their own best interests. Certainly many such calculations, both by British governments and by the local parties, have influenced the choice of electoral systems used in Northern Ireland. The purpose of this chapter is to examine these electoral systems, to explain how they work, and to evaluate the political consequences of their selection and use.

In the first section we examine the political motivation and effects of the decision by the British government, as part of the process of partition, to adopt proportional representation (PR) for elections within Northern Ireland and, especially, the subsequent determination by the unionist government to return to plurality rule. Following the abolition of the regional (Stormont) parliament, the British government again adopted PR for local, regional, and European parliament elections. In the next section we focus on electoral malpractice, especially the gerrymandering of constituency boundaries and the personation of voters. We then explain how PR-STV (proportional representation by means of the single transferable vote) actually works and evaluate it as an electoral system. After that we consider the surprising decision to adopt a third, markedly different electoral system for the 1996 elections to the Northern Ireland Forum (proportional representation by list system). Finally, we explore the consequences of these different electoral systems, principally in terms of their effects on proportionality and the party system.

Why Different Electoral Systems in Northern Ireland?

In contrast to elections in other political jurisdictions, those in Northern Ireland have utilised both the Westminster plurality (or "first past the post") system and PR-STV. The Northern Ireland members of the Westminster parliament (like all other members) have always been elected by the plurality system, in which the candidate with the most votes in a single-member constituency takes the seat. Although the plurality system is the simplest to operate, a significant shortcoming is that the results are frequently "unfair" (disproportional), in the sense that the number of seats won by a party may not closely correspond to its share of the overall vote. Typically, the result is that larger parties receive a "bonus" (the difference between share of the seats and share of the votes), whereas smaller parties are underrepresented. One of the most dramatic cases of disproportionality in recent British electoral history occurred at the 1983 general election. The recently formed Liberal/Social Democratic Party (SDP) Alliance achieved an impressive 25.3 percent of the votes but was rewarded by the electoral system with only 3.5 percent of the seats. (If the electoral system had been perfectly proportional, the Liberal/SDP Alliance would have had 165 seats in the House of Commons rather than the 23 seats it actually received) (Bogdanor 1984:7–16). The main beneficiary of the underrepresentation of the Alliance was the incumbent Conservative Party, whose "overwhelming majority" (61.1 percent of the seats) was in reality an artefact of the electoral system (the Conservatives secured only 43.9 percent of the vote).

Given the probability that the plurality system tends to underrepresent minorities, the Government of Ireland Act of 1920, in addition to establishing separate parliaments in southern and northern Ireland, mandated that elections to them should be "according to the principles of proportional representation, each elector having one transferable vote" (quoted in Carstairs 1980: 203). Although the adoption of PR-STV was noncontroversial in Southern Ireland (see Sinnott 1993), many unionists in what became Northern Ireland were opposed to proportional representation and strongly favoured retaining the "traditional British" plurality system. Nevertheless, elections at the local government and regional parliament ("Stormont"[1]) levels were to take place by means of PR-STV. However, although the British government in 1920 had introduced proportional representation "as a safeguard to minorities north and south" (Whyte 1983: 5), one of the earliest acts of the new Northern Ireland government in 1922 was to abolish PR for local government elections and revert to the plurality system. Thus, starting in 1923, all local government elections were conducted according to the "first past the post" system until, in 1973, following the suspension of Stormont and the introduction of direct rule from Westminster, the British government once again chose PR-STV as a "fairer" system for all local government elections.

Although the Government of Ireland Act (1920) introduced PR-STV as the means of electing the regional Northern Ireland parliament, a surprising subclause stated that PR was guaranteed for only the first three years. Thereafter, the Northern Ireland parliament was free to change the electoral system, a power it utilised to abolish PR and return to the plurality system in time for the 1929 election.[2] Thus there were only two PR elections to this parliament (in 1921 and 1925), so from 1929 until Stormont was prorogued in 1972, elections were held according to the "first past the post" system.

Given the opposition of most unionist politicians to PR, they had been expected to revert to plurality elections at the earliest opportunity (in time for the 1925 elections) rather than in 1929. Brendan O'Leary and John McGarry (citing Mansergh 1936) argue that unionists would have abolished PR earlier "but for their fear that the British government might have responded to such behaviour by taking a repartitionist line in the boundary commission" (1993: 121). (On the boundary commission, see Chapter 1 of this volume.) A different but not contradictory interpretation is offered by Robert Osborne, who argues that the urgency for unionists of abolishing PR "was assuaged by the comforting results of the first Northern Ireland general election held in 1921" (1979: 43). High communal polarisation contributed to a secure unionist majority over nationalists and republicans of 28 in a 52-seat legislature (40 unionists, 6 nationalists, and 6 Sinn Féin members). However, the 1925 election in a somewhat less polarised environment led to a loss of 8 unionist seats to independent and Northern Ireland Labour Party (NILP) candidates, thus reducing their overall majority to 12 seats (nationalists and republicans again won 12 seats). Fearing the continuation of such a trend, unionists decided to revert to plurality rule. Although there is some unresolved debate concerning whether the change was principally designed to weaken Labour and independent candidates or to further undermine the strategic position of nationalists (Buckland 1979; Farrell 1976; Osborne 1979; Pringle 1980; O'Leary and McGarry 1993), there is no doubt that the reversion to plurality elections entrenched the dominance of the Ulster Unionist Party (UUP). Prime Minister James Craig was explicit about his motivation:

> What I want to get in this House, and what I believe we will get very much better in this House under the old-fashioned plain and simple [plurality] system, are men who are for the Union on the one hand, or who are against it and want to go into a Dublin parliament on the other. (NI Parliamentary Debates, House of Commons, Vol. 8, Col. 2276, 1927)

Nationalist leader Joe Devlin was of the opinion that "this thing [the change of electoral system] is not to wipe us out. It is to wipe out what are called the Independent and Labour members" (NI Hansard, Vol. 10, Col. 451, 5 March 1929). At the 1929 election, the Unionist Party recovered 5 seats and nationalists lost 1, whereas the number of independents and Labour candidates was cut in half, thus restoring a more comfortable Unionist Party majority of 22 seats. The more serious consequence of the change of system was that the "electoral institutionalisation of ethnic divisions" (O'Leary and McGarry 1993: 123) rendered the system profoundly uncompetitive. The re-adoption of plurality rule led directly to a sharp increase in the number of uncontested seats (42 percent of all seats in 1929, precisely double the number in 1925). Indeed, in the period from 1929 to 1965 (nine general elections) on average an astonishing 45.9 percent of all seats were not contested. Osborne refers to this outcome as a "parody of electoral competition in a democratic system," and argues that the 1929 change "corralled electors into neat areas of nationalist or unionist dominance" such that the new electoral system "provided a structural prop to the communal divisions of Northern Ireland" (Osborne 1979: 54–55). Craig had achieved his aim.

Electoral Malpractice

In addition to the abolition of proportional representation in favour of plurality rule, unionist electoral domination was reinforced by a ratepayer franchise,[3] by company votes (which gave directors multiple votes), and, especially, by the gerrymandering of constituency boundaries. Gerrymandering will be examined next, followed by discussion of a continuing form of electoral malpractice: the personation of voters.

Gerrymandering

Gerrymandering[4] was endemic during the Stormont period, although the practice related mostly to local government elections rather than to elections to the regional parliament. There are numerous methods of achieving a gerrymander, but the principle is the same in all: Waste the votes of your opponents. Single-seat districts are particularly prone to the gerrymander; under a PR electoral system, however, it is less likely because fewer votes are wasted and there are fewer constituencies.[5]

In single-seat districts, one method of implementing a gerrymander is to divide up the electoral stronghold of opponents into different constituencies, keeping them below 50 percent in each constituency and thus likely to win no seats under the plurality system (provided that one's own vote is not fragmented). Another device is to concentrate opposition votes in as few constituencies as possible. The opposition will win these seats with massive majorities in "overkill" victories; but in plurality elections, of course, all votes above one more than your nearest opponent are "wasted" votes (in the sense that the surplus votes cannot contribute to the election of a second member). If the gerrymander has been well designed, the other party will then win many more seats with slim but comfortable majorities. A third method (akin to Governor Gerry's classic gerrymander and still sometimes practised in American politics) is to construct bizarrely shaped constituencies that gather together outlying support so that seats can be won.

The practice of gerrymandering is best understood by examining an actual case—as discussed here, the one clear case of the gerrymandering of a constituency in Northern Ireland parliament elections. With the abolition of PR in 1929, and in the absence of an independent boundary commission, the new constituencies were created by Craig and his colleagues. A 3-seat constituency in Fermanagh was designed to return two unionists and one nationalist. The 1949 result is summarized in Table 4.1.[6]

As can be seen, the nationalist vote was concentrated into Fermanagh South, producing an "overkill" victory, whereas the remaining nationalist vote was evenly divided into the two remaining constituencies, thus allowing unionist victories in both. With 53 percent of the vote, nationalists received only 1 of the 3 seats.[7]

It should be stressed that such explicit gerrymandering was not widespread in elections to the Stormont parliament. As Osborne concluded: "Gerrymandering was undoubtedly a feature of the Fermanagh seat distribution and may also have been involved in Armagh. However, on the basis of this evidence it is hardly possible to call the 1929 redistribution a general exercise in gerrymandering" (1979: 53). The same cannot be said of local government elections, which were much more extensively gerrymandered. Although unionists constituted "at most 66 per cent of the population in the late 1920s they controlled 85 per cent of all local authorities" (O'Leary and McGarry 1993: 120). A

TABLE 4.1 Constituency Results for Fermanagh in the 1949 Parliamentary Election

	Nationalists			Unionists		
Constituency	*N*	*% of votes*	*seats*	*N*	*% of votes*	*seats*
Fermanagh South	6,680	72.0	1	2,596	28.0	0
Fermanagh Enniskillen	4,729	45.3	0	5,706	54.7	1
Fermanagh Lisnaskea	4,173	42.7	0	5,593	57.3	1
Total	15,582	52.9	1	13,868	47.1	2
Votes:Seats	15,582:1			6,934:1		

Source: Elliot (1973).

direct comparison of the local elections in 1920 (PR) with those in 1922 (plurality) shows that 13 councils held by nationalists under PR were captured by unionists (Whyte 1983: 6). The paradigmatic case was that of the city of Derry/Londonderry, where unionists maintained control through a combination of plurality rule, the ratepayer franchise, and a gerrymander, despite the fact that the adult population contained a large Catholic majority in a ratio of almost 2:1 (see Cameron Commission 1969; O'Leary and McGarry 1993: 121). More generally, "nationalists were manipulated out of control in a number of councils where they had a majority of electors. This is one of the clearest areas of discrimination in the whole field of controversy" (Whyte 1983: 7). The combination of the return to plurality rule and electoral malpractices further entrenched Northern Ireland's ethnic political parties and institutionalised the constitutional divide as the salient basis of party competition. The already limited opportunities for non-unionist and non-nationalist alternatives were thereby further undermined.

Personation

Personation has entered the folklore of electoral politics in Northern Ireland with slogans urging the faithful to "vote early and vote often," while jokes about the dead casting ballots from their graves are legion. Although it is widely believed that personation occurs, evidence of systematic abuse is not available. There are two principal "types" of personation. The first is the practice of using the vote of another person who either does not intend to vote or who cannot vote (e.g., the person may be deceased but still on the electoral register or simply absent from the home address). This type is sometimes known as "benign personation" and, though illegal, is widely believed to have been tolerated in Northern Ireland for decades. The second type of personation, of which Sinn Féin (SF) in particular is often accused, is the direct attempt to steal votes by using the votes of opponents before they can do so themselves—a process known as "malign personation" or simply vote stealing. The legitimate voter discovers upon arriving at the polling station that her or his vote has already been cast.

Unfortunately, given the nature of these practices, there is no quantifiable information concerning the extent to which they are used; thus most claims concerning personation are based on indirect information or anecdotal evidence. One indirect indication that widespread personation is a real danger is that the parties have their own personation agents in the polling stations, trying to prevent the personation of their voters by their opponents. As Desmond Neill commented in reference to the 1951 election: "It was thought essential for an efficient party machine to have sufficient workers not only to man the 'tally' rooms through which the faithful passed on their way to the polling-station, but also to have at least one officially approved 'personation' agent to each polling-booth within the precincts of the station" (Neill 1952: 224). Neill further reported that many presiding officers often advised personation agents to be cautious in making challenges since, if they were mistaken, they could be liable to claims for damages for wrongful accusation. He might have added that they could also be the targets of intimidation. Nevertheless, personation agents in some constituencies do help prevent vote stealing.

Some evidence of the existence—though not the extent—of personation is provided by the use of "tendered ballot papers," special ballot forms printed on pink paper that can be given to electors who discover when they get to the polling station that their votes have already been cast by someone else. The tendered ballot papers are not placed in the ballot box (and therefore are not included in the count) but are kept in a separate packet by the presiding officer. They may be used only if there is a subsequent inquiry into the election in the constituency. According to Douglas Hurd (then Secretary of State for Northern Ireland), at the 1982 Assembly and during the 1983 Westminster elections in Northern Ireland, the numbers of tendered ballot papers issued were 762 and 949, respectively (House of Commons Debates, 15 November 1984: 810). However, although tendered ballot papers provide some concrete evidence of the existence of personation, they are not a reliable indication of the extent of the practice. The reason is that many (perhaps most) electors, upon discovering that their vote has been stolen, do not cast a tendered ballot paper. Some may feel that there is little point since for all practical purposes they have already lost their vote, and others do not know that they can cast a "pink ballot" and election officials do not always inform them of this right. Thus, the number of tendered ballot papers issued is likely to represent only a fraction of the total amount of personation. (Attempts to estimate the latter are largely speculative.)

Certainly, in the context of Sinn Féin's electoral mobilisation in the early 1980s, the government believed that personation had become a serious problem. Introducing the second reading of the Elections (Northern Ireland) Bill, Douglas Hurd stated: "In the Government's view, the scale of the problem has changed so dramatically in recent years as to amount to a threat to the integrity of the electoral system . . . In the face of highly co-ordinated efforts to personate, it was not possible to prevent massive personation at last year's general election" (House of Commons Debates, 15 November 1984: 808). Although Hurd blamed Sinn Féin for most of the abuse, he offered no concrete evidence of the extent of personation. The principal change in the law effected by the 1985 legislation was that in future, and contrary to the situation in Great Britain, electors would be required to produce one of a range of approved documents before they could vote. However, as was pointed out by many unionist MPs in the 1984 parliamentary debate on personation, the new legislation would not eliminate the problem since these documents could be forged.

In the 1990s the controversy has returned with a vengeance, apparently fueled by what has been described as the electoral "second coming" (O'Leary and Evans 1997) of Sinn Féin. After the 1997 local government elections the Social Democratic and Labour Party (SDLP) alleged widespread electoral fraud by Sinn Féin (*Irish News,* 23 May 1997). Sinn Féin denied this and claimed that the SDLP had voiced these allegations without producing evidence, in an effort to explain why the Sinn Féin vote was increasing at their expense.[8] Certainly it is unlikely that most of Sinn Féin's recent electoral advances can be explained by more efficient personation.

In response to the continuing controversy, Secretary of State Marjorie Mowlam announced a review of the region's electoral system on 31 July 1997. Six weeks later, however, it was revealed that none of the main parties had presented evidence to the inquiry (*Belfast Telegraph,* 16 September 1997). However, unease has grown, leading to three separate investigations into electoral malpractice: by the Northern Ireland Office, by a committee of the Northern Ireland Forum, and by the Northern Ireland Affairs Select Committee of the Westminster Parliament. Past experience suggests that progress in this area will be slow, and personation is likely to remain a live issue, both because systematic evidence is so hard to come by and because the incentives to personate increase as the party system becomes more competitive.

Brief Guide to PR-STV

In the period since 1972 there have been at most four different levels of electoral representation in Northern Ireland.[9] Westminster seats continue to be allocated by the plurality system, but all other elections (local government, European parliament, and regional assemblies) have been conducted by PR-STV.[10] Whereas the operation of the plurality system is straightforward, PR-STV is a more sophisticated electoral system and requires further elaboration.

In the case of the "first past the post" system, the logic is easy to grasp: Each voter has one "X" vote in a single-member constituency and the seat is given to the candidate with the most votes, irrespective of their proportion of the total vote. As we have seen, this process can allow considerable anomalies such that larger parties are overrepresented whereas smaller parties fail to receive the "fair" share of the seats that their votes warrant. Because plurality and majority electoral systems allow highly disproportional overall results, most European countries have adopted proportional representation. The essential feature of all PR systems are multiseat constituencies. Seats are allocated to parties within each multiseat constituency in approximate proportion to the votes that each receives. Indeed, PR cannot be based on single-seat constituencies, since obviously there is no manner in which a single seat can be shared out proportionally.[11] The general rule is that the larger the district magnitude (the number of seats in each constituency), the more proportional the overall result is likely to be. There are two broad types of PR electoral system; these can be conveniently labeled as "list systems" and the "single transferable vote" (see Gallagher, Laver, and Mair 1995; Farrell 1997).

Most European countries use list system PR. Although there are important variations within the overall category of list systems, the general idea is that each party presents a list of candidates in each constituency. The seats are then distributed among the parties in broad proportion to the votes they win, according to a preselected electoral formula. Thus, votes are cast first and foremost for parties rather than for individuals.[12] This highlights a key difference associated with PR-STV: It does not require (though also does not prevent) party voting. Votes are cast for individual candidates in a rank order according to the preferences of the voter. Thus the ballot paper contains a list of all the candidates (usually) in alphabetical order. Instead of marking one "X" against the name of the voter's preferred candidate (as in the plurality system), the number 1 is entered, followed by a 2 beside the name of the voter's second choice, and so on. The voter can rank-order all of the candidates on the ballot paper or stop at any point and express no further preferences. It is important to realise, however, that each voter has one vote that is transferable, rather than multiple votes. Richard Sinnott (1993) stresses that, although the mechanics of the count under PR-STV are quite complex, from the voter's perspective the actual business of voting is simple and intuitive: "All that is needed in order to use the system to the full is an understanding of the notion of ranking a set of candidates according to one's preferences" (Sinnott 1993: 69).[13] Of course, others need to understand the mechanics and full implications of PR-STV, such as the returning officers and the central parties, if the latter want to attempt strategic vote management.

The first stage in the count (after determining the number of valid votes) is to calculate the quota, the number of votes that guarantees election. Any candidate who achieves a quota is deemed elected. The quota is calculated according to the following formula:

$$\text{Quota} = \frac{\textit{Total number of valid votes}}{\text{Number of seats} + 1} + 1$$

Thus, when there is only 1 seat, the quota is half the number of votes plus 1. In a 2-seat constituency the quota is a third plus 1, in a 3-seater it is a quarter plus 1, and so on. We can see, then, that as the number of seats in a constituency increases, the quota falls, making it easier for small parties or independents to win a seat (see Table 4.2). For example, in the local government elections of 1989 the district magnitude ranged from five to seven, whereas in the Northern Ireland Assembly elections of 1982 constituencies returned between five and ten members, the latter producing a very low quota of 9.1 percent.

The best way to grasp the mechanics of the system is to work through an actual count. Table 4.3 reproduces the count of the Cookstown (Ballinderry) constituency at the 1989 district council elections, selected simply because it demonstrates many of the features of PR-STV in a relatively small number of counts. This was a 6-seat constituency with a valid vote of 6,117. When the latter number is divided by the number of seats plus 1 (i.e., by 7) and, disregarding the fraction, 1 is added to the result, the quota is 874 votes—that is, one-seventh of the vote plus 1.

As shown in the table, the result of the first count was that two candidates (Duffy and McIntyre) exceeded the quota and were thus elected. The next stages involved the transfer of the surplus of the

TABLE 4.2 Quota by District Magnitude in PR-STV

District Magnitude (Seats per constituency)	*Quota (in percentages)*
1	50.0
2	33.3
3	25.0
4	20.0
5	16.7
6	14.3
7	12.5
8	11.1
9	10.0
10	9.1

Source: Adapted from Table 4.1 in Sinnott (1993).

elected candidates. Notice that Duffy, who topped the poll with 1,370 votes, exceeded the quota (874) by 496 votes. Duffy is therefore said to have had a "surplus" of 496 votes. The distribution of this surplus is an important feature of PR-STV. Since Duffy was guaranteed election by reaching the quota, if his surplus was not transferred, then these 496 votes would have been "wasted" votes inasmuch as they were unnecessary for Duffy's election and, if not transferred, could not have helped a party colleague to get elected. In short, if no transfer was made, those who voted for (in this case) the SDLP would not have gotten the full share of representation to which they were entitled. Hence, the second count involved the transfer of Duffy's 496 surplus votes. What happened in this count is that 408 of them (82.3 percent) transferred to Duffy's SDLP colleague, O'Neill, indicating strong party solidarity.

The principle involved in transfers is clear, but the mechanics are more complex, depending partly on the stage of the count at which the transfer is made. The simplest case is the one described above in which the surplus to be transferred was from a candidate elected on the first count and therefore consisted only of original votes. What happened at the second count is that the destination of the 496 surplus votes was determined by reexamining all of Duffy's 1,370 votes. These were then arranged into "sub-parcels" according to the second preferences indicated on them. Votes that did not indicate a second preference became "nontransferable" and were set aside. The total number of transferable votes was then used to calculate each remaining candidate's share of the transferable vote. Thus, if O'Neil obtained 82.3 percent of the transferable vote in the original 1,370 votes examined (as in fact he did), then he

TABLE 4.3 Counting and Transfer of Votes in Cookstown (Ballinderry): 1989 District Council Election

	First Count	Second Count: Transfer of Duffy's surplus		Third Count: Transfer of McIntyre's surplus		Fourth Count: Transfer of Forsythe's votes		Fifth Count: Transfer of McGahie's surplus		Sixth Count: Transfer of McCartney's surplus	
P. Duffy (SDLP)	*1370*	–496	874		874		874		874		874
N. Forsythe (UUP)	512	+3	515	+4	519	–519					
S. McCartney (DUP)	528	0	528	+121	649	+116	765	+324	*1089*	–215	874
V. McGahie (UUP)	781	+1	782	+30	812	+397	*1209*	–335	874		874
W. McIntyre (DUP)	*1039*		1039	–165	874		874		874		874
F. McNally (SF)	868	+53	*921*		921		921		921		921
S. McQuillan (SF)	617	+20	637	0	637	+1	638	0	638	0	638
J. O'Neill (SDLP)	402	+408	810	0	810	+1	811	+9	820	+69	*889*
Nontransferable		+12	12	+12	22	+4	26	+2	28	+146	174
Total	6117		6118		6118		6118		6118		6118

Note: Elected were P. Duffy (SDLP); W. McIntyre (DUP), F. McNally (SF); V. McGahie (UUP); S. McCartney (DUP); J. O'Neill (SDLP). The total number of electors was 7,775, and 6,117 valid votes were cast. The number of seats contested was 6, and the quota of votes required to win a seat was 874. Figures in italics indicate the point at which the candidate achieved a quota and hence was elected.

Source: Constructed from data in Elliott and Smith (1992).

was entitled to 82.3 percent of the 496 surplus votes (i.e., 0.823 × 496 = 408).[14] At the second count, although McNally received only 53 votes from Duffy's transfers, this was enough to give him a quota such that he was deemed elected at this point.

The third count involved the transfer of McIntyre's surplus (the second candidate elected on the first count). Notice again the strong communal polarisation and party discipline. All of McIntyre's (Democratic Unionist Party, or DUP) surplus of 165 votes transferred to the three remaining unionist candidates, including 73.3 percent to his DUP colleague. The two other candidates (one SDLP and one SF) received no transfers from the DUP. However, no one was elected on the third count, although McGahie (UUP) and O'Neill (SDLP) were close to a quota. Now we come to the fourth count. Logically, one would imagine that the next thing to do is to transfer McNally's surplus, the candidate elected on the second count. However, McNally had a surplus of only 47 votes, which is less than the difference between the two bottom-placed candidates at the end of the third count. These are Forsythe with 519 votes and McQuillan with 637 (637 − 519 = 118). Hence, at the end of the third count, McQuillan was 118 votes ahead of Forsythe, the lowest-placed candidate at that point. Thus, even if Forsythe received all 47 of McNally's surplus votes, he would still be behind McQuillan. Since the transfer of McNally' s surplus could therefore make no difference to the relative position of the two lowest candidates, the transfer was postponed. Of course, if the transfer of the surplus could have made any conceivable difference to their relative positions, then it must have proceeded immediately.

The result of all of this is that the lowest-placed candidate (Forsythe) was now eliminated and the fourth count involved transferring his "next available preferences." Let's say, for example, that on examination one of his ballot papers expressed a second preference for Duffy, a candidate who was already elected (and therefore not available). In this event, the third preference would become the operative one. Thus, in any case when the next preference examined lists an elected or eliminated candidate, the procedure is to move on and examine the "next available preference," which then becomes the operative one. At the fourth count 76.5 percent of Forsythe's votes transferred to his UUP running mate, McGahie—enough to elect him.

The fifth count involved the transfer of McGahie's surplus of 335 votes, an impressive 334 of which transferred to the only remaining unionist candidate, McCartney (DUP). Thus, in the sixth and last count there were only two remaining candidates: one SDLP and one SF. Given that the sixth count entailed the transfer of the DUP candidate's (i.e., McCartney's) surplus, 67.9 percent of his surplus became nontransferable at this point, and no votes at all went to the SF candidate. The 69 votes received by the SDLP's O'Neill were enough to give him a quota on the last count. However, even if O'Neill had not received the 69 transfers, he would have been elected at that point. Since only two candidates remained, there was no one else to eliminate, so O'Neill would have been declared elected without reaching the quota.[15]

Evaluation of PR-STV

The only countries that have adopted PR-STV for their lower chambers are the Republic of Ireland and Malta, suggesting a general lack of popularity in other European countries that have preferred to use list systems. Two main practical criticisms of STV have been put forth (for a review see Gallagher, Laver, and Mair 1995: 287–288; Farrell 1997).[16] The first is that some mainland Europeans do not endorse the opportunity for voters to cross party lines that STV allows, on the grounds that this could weaken political parties and encourage them to offer less distinctive choices to the electorate because of their pursuit of lower preferences. As Gallagher and colleagues (1995: 288) argue: "This might make the parties 'fuzzy at the edges' as candidates adopt bland positions for fear of alienating any voter who might possibly give them a lower preference." Too few countries use STV to properly evaluate this criticism, although Malta and Ireland certainly do not have weak political parties and Malta at least does not have "bland" consensual politics.[17] Unfortunately there is little prospect of consensual politics in Northern Ireland, so that even if STV *does* encourage less ideological distinctiveness, this tendency would be overwhelmed by sharp communal segmentation. The DUP does not expect to receive any transfers from SF, and vice versa.

The second criticism of PR-STV is that, in practice, it requires relatively small district magnitudes and therefore may be prone to disproportionality. This prospect does not appear to be a danger, however, since "election results in Ireland and Malta have been as proportional as those in other PR systems" (Gallagher, Laver, and Mair 1995: 288).

On the other hand, the advantages of PR-STV are considerable. The most obvious advantage of PR-STV, compared to the plurality system, is precisely that it involves a form of proportional representation and, hence, does not allow the sometimes massive disproportionality of the "first past the post" system. But STV also has advantages over list systems. First, STV is sophisticated in that it collects a lot of information about a voter's entire preference structure and allows voters to cross party lines if they wish (thus turning the above criticism into a virtue). Secondly, STV enables voters to vote sincerely without the risk of wasting their vote. Voters can choose their favourite candidate even knowing that he or she has no hope of being elected, secure in the knowledge that their vote will then be transferred to another candidate in line with their second preference.[18] The third principal advantage of STV is that voters have some control over the manner in which their votes will be used during the count. With STV, in contrast to all list systems, no vote can ever help a candidate unless it explicitly expresses a preference for him or her. "Under STV, voters can continue to give preferences after their first, knowing that doing this cannot possibly damage their favoured candidate. A lower preference given to a candidate can never help that person against a candidate to whom the voter gave a higher preference" (Gallagher, Laver, and Mair 1995: 287). Finally, a less serious, though not inconsequential, advantage of STV is that, compared with most other electoral systems, it is great fun for psephologists and the electorate at large.

Change to List System PR for the 1996 Forum Elections

For reasons that have never been adequately explained, the government chose to abandon STV for the election to the 1996 Forum and instead adopted a party list system in which the eighteen Westminster constituencies would each elect five members to the Forum from constituency lists (90 seats), and each of the "top ten" parties on a regional list would receive two additional seats (bringing the total to 110 seats). Having closely observed the election process, Michael Gallagher has commented: "The unique method of filling seats for the Forum elections should probably remain unique" (1996: 8). Given that this electoral system is unlikely to be used again—it has been almost universally condemned by politicians and political scientists—only a brief account of it will be given here.

Although the idea of holding such an election (rather than trying to immediately proceed to all-party negotiations) was controversial, with the UUP and the Alliance Party in favour of an election and the SDLP and SF against, once it became clear that there would indeed be a contest, most of the parties began to consider the type of electoral system that would maximise their representation. The DUP and SDLP wanted a party list system using the d'hondt (DH) divisor in one regional Northern Ireland constituency. Their calculation was that they would benefit from regional lists headed by their main electoral assets—namely, their party leaders, Ian Paisley and John Hume—as tends to happen in elections to the European parliament. Northern

Ireland's largest political party, the UUP, has usually languished in third place in the European elections and, therefore, was determined to prevent the adoption of a single constituency. The UUP and Alliance Party wanted STV, using the Droop quota (which involves the same formula as STV: valid votes divided by the district magnitude + 1), in eighteen 5-seat districts based on the Westminster constituencies. The result was that the government adopted a fudged compromise formula, motivated by the desire to "split the differences" between the parties (Evans and O'Leary 1997: 25). This formula was not well thought out or even properly understood by its architects.

Thus the eighteen-constituency option was chosen rather than a single regional poll (hence placating the UUP and Alliance Party), but election would be by party lists (as the SDLP and DUP wanted) rather than by STV. In addition to the eighteen constituencies there would be a regional list from which twenty more members would be elected. The regional list was primarily designed to ensure the election of minor-party candidates, especially the political representatives of the loyalist paramilitaries, the Ulster Democratic Party, and the Progressive Unionist Party. Given that the Droop quota in a 5-seat constituency is 16.7 percent (recall Table 4.2), these parties would be unlikely to win any constituency seats (at least by means of d'hondt allocation). Hence, by allocating two seats to each of the top ten parties, the regional list ensured the inclusion of a wider range of parties in the negotiating process.

The allocation of these seats in the eighteen constituencies caused considerable confusion and misinterpretation. Officially, in the first stage of the count, the Droop quota was used and parties were allocated seats based on how many quotas they achieved. Since it was unlikely that all seats would be distributed at the first stage, the second stage[19] was used to allocate partial quotas using d'hondt divisors (1, 2, 3). As Gallagher has pointed out: "The quotas were in fact an irrelevant distraction; the method used was the d'hondt method, pure and simple" (1996: 8).

The combination of small 5-seat constituencies and d'hondt allocation "is notorious for its tendency to favour the big battalions in any constituency" (Gallagher 1996: 8). And, indeed, the 1996 elections produced quite a large number of disproportional outcomes in individual constituencies. Most obviously, in West Belfast, Sinn Féin was allocated 4 of the 5 seats on only 53 percent of the votes. Likewise, in Lagan Valley, the UUP and DUP took all 5 seats with less than 60 percent of the vote. Hence minority communities in several constituencies were left entirely without local political representation, as a direct result of the electoral system chosen.

Perhaps surprisingly, and despite numerous local anomalies, the overall distribution of seats was not markedly disproportional. Indeed, the overall results of the Forum election indicate that it was one of the most proportional ever held in Northern Ireland, with a disproportionality score of 3.9. (In Table 4.4, this score is represented as a least squares index, or LSq.) The explanation for this surprising result is twofold. First, some of the disproportional constituency results canceled each other out at the aggregate level. Secondly, the regional list (the second-stage allocation in which the top ten parties received 2 seats each) rendered the outcome much more proportional than it would have been otherwise.[20] This however was a fortuitous outcome and there is little doubt that the electoral system used for the Forum elections could produce a highly disproportional overall result.

Disproportionality is not the only criticism of the Forum electoral system that can be sustained. One frequently overlooked aspect is that this system was entirely nonpreferential: Voters had no way of influencing which of a party's candidates would be elected (inasmuch as they had one "X" vote). The rank order of candidates on the lists was entirely determined by the parties themselves. Clearly, then, voters had no opportunity to cross party lines and vote according to other criteria, such as moderation or gender, as is possible with PR-STV.

In sum, this first experiment in any part of the United Kingdom with a version of list system PR was not a particularly happy one. Since many political scientists believe that PR-STV is the "best" electoral system (Taagepera and Shugart 1989: 27), the reasons for abandoning it should have been more clearly spelt out. And if the decision is made to use list system PR in the future, many improvements to the system used for the Forum elections can easily be made (some have already been suggested by Gallagher [1996]). Certainly, a hastily agreed-upon and rather incoherent compromise between the understandably instrumental calculations of political parties is not the best method of designing an electoral system that accurately reflects the electorate's will.

Consequences of Northern Ireland's Electoral Systems

Some of the standard methods of evaluating electoral systems, such as their effect on the stability of governments, do not apply—precisely because there is no government elected in the region. We can, however, consider the impact of the different electoral systems on the pro-

Table 4.4 Individual Party Seat "Bonuses" and Index of Disproportionality Arranged by Type of Election

	UUP			DUP			SDLP			SF			APNI			
	V (%)	*S (%)*	*S-V*	*V (%)*	*S (%)*	*S-V*	*V (%)*	*S (%)*	*S-V*	*V (%)*	*S (%)*	*S-V*	*V (%)*	*S (%)*	*S-V*	*Disproportionality LSq*[a]
Westminster (Plurality)																
1983	34.0	64.7	30.7	20.0	17.6	–2.4	17.9	5.9	–12	13.4	5.9	–7.5	8.0	0	–8.0	24.7
1987	37.8	52.9	15.1	11.7	17.6	5.9	21.1	17.6	–3.5	11.4	5.9	–5.5	10.0	0	–10.0	14.6
1992	34.5	52.9	18.4	13.1	17.6	4.5	23.5	23.5	0	10.0	0	–10	8.7	0	–8.7	17.0
1997	32.7	55.6	22.9	13.6	11.1	–2.5	24.1	16.7	–7.4	16.1	11.1	–5.0	8.0	0	–8.0	18.4
Average			21.8			1.4			–5.7			–7			–8.7	18.7
Local Govt. (STV)																
1981	26.5	28.9	2.4	26.6	27.0	0.4	17.5	19.6	2.1	–	–	–	8.9	7.2	-1.7	2.8
1985	29.5	33.6	4.1	24.3	25.1	0.8	17.8	17.8	0	11.8	10.4	–1.4	7.1	6.0	-1.1	3.3
1989	31.3	34.3	3.0	17.7	19.4	1.7	21.0	21.4	0.4	11.2	7.6	–3.6	6.9	6.7	-0.2	3.7
1993	29.4	33.8	4.4	17.3	17.7	0.4	22.0	21.8	–0.2	12.4	8.8	–3.6	7.6	7.6	0	4.0
1997	27.8	31.8	4.0	15.6	15.6	0	20.7	20.6	–0.1	16.9	12.7	–4.2	6.5	7.0	0.5	4.2
Average			3.6			0.6			0.4			–3.2			-0.3	3.6
European (STV)[b]																
1979	21.9	33.3	11.4	29.8	33.3	3.5	24.6	33.3	8.7	–	–	–	6.8	0	–6.8	12.5
1984	21.5	33.3	11.6	33.6	33.3	0.3	22.1	33.3	11.2	13.3	0	–13.1	5.0	0	–5.0	15.2
1989	22.2	33.3	11.1	29.9	33.3	3.4	25.5	33.3	7.8	9.1	0	–9.1	5.2	0	–5.2	12.9
1994	23.8	33.3	9.5	29.2	33.3	4.1	28.9	33.3	4.4	9.9	0	–9.9	4.1	0	–4.1	11.1
Average			10.9			2.8			8.0			–10.7			–5.3	12.9
Other																
1982 A (STV)[c]	29.7	33.3	3.6	23.0	26.9	3.9	18.8	17.9	–0.9	10.1	6.4	–3.7	9.3	12.8	3.5	6.1
1996 F[d]	24.2	27.3	3.1	18.8	21.8	3.0	21.4	19.1	–2.3	15.5	15.5	0	6.5	6.4	–0.1	3.9

[a]The measure of disproportionality used is the least squares index (LSq) devised by Michael Gallagher (1991). Disproportionality = $\sqrt{{}^1/_2\Sigma(Vi - Si)^2}$. Although there are a variety of different indexes for this purpose, Arend Lijphart regards the least squares method as "the most sensitive and faithful reflection of the disproportionality of election results"(1994: 62). "Others" and independents have been excluded from the calculations.

[b]For elections to the European Parliament, Northern Ireland serves as one constituency and returns three members ($M = 3$).

[c]Seventy-eight members were elected to the 1982 NI Assembly by single transferable vote from 12 constituencies ranging in district magnitude from 4 to 10 (average M = 6.5).

[d]The election to the 1996 Forum was by list system PR.

Source: Calculated by the author from information supplied by the Chief Electoral Office for Northern Ireland.

portionality of the relationship between votes and seats and their wider impact on the party system.

Consequences for Proportionality

The choice of electoral system has clear effects on disproportionality, as shown in Table 4.4, which uses data for the 1980s and 1990s. The final column lists the disproportionality scores for each election and the average scores by type of election according to the least squares index devised by Michael Gallagher (1991). A higher score indicates greater disproportionality. As we would expect, a comparison of the plurality system (in only seventeen to eighteen Westminster constituencies) with PR-STV across several hundred seats (in local government elections with district magnitudes of between five and seven) reveals a dramatic effect on disproportionality. The Westminster elections have an average disproportionality score of 18.7, compared with only 3.6 for the local government (STV) elections. In particular, the Ulster Unionist Party received a massive "seat bonus" in the Westminster elections, which, on average, amounts to 21.8 percent. In other words, during the four Westminster elections from 1983 to 1997, the UUP won on average just over one-third of the votes (34.7 percent), yet it was rewarded by the electoral system with well over half of the total seats (56.5 percent). By contrast, the use of proportional representation in local government elections significantly reduced—but did not entirely eliminate—this UUP seat bonus, which averaged 3.6 percent. The other parties, especially the SDLP, Sinn Féin, and the Alliance Party have been underrepresented in Westminster elections (with negative seat bonuses), but, as expected, have done better in PR elections. Nevertheless, it is apparent from Table 4.4 that Sinn Féin has been underrepresented in every election it has contested (the only exception being the election to the 1996 Forum), faring even worse than the Alliance Party. The Alliance Party and Sinn Féin both tend to be underrepresented in Westminster elections (Alliance never wins a seat), but Alliance has been more successful than Sinn Féin in converting its votes into seats in local government contests.

The European parliament elections appear to be anomalous in that disproportionality is high (12.9) despite their use of PR-STV. The explanation is the low district magnitude of these elections and the very small total number of seats (one constituency with only 3 seats). And since these 3 seats have always been taken (one each) by the DUP, SDLP, and UUP, votes for any other parties do not result in their winning a seat, thus leading to quite high levels of disproportionality. The effect in the Republic of Ireland has been quite similar. Whereas the disproportionality (LSq) score is 3.5 for Dáil elections, it is 10.8 for elections to the European parliament (Lijphart 1994: 161).

In summary, then, Westminster and European elections in Northern Ireland are very disproportional, whereas local government elections and elections to regional assemblies are much more proportional and thus more accurately reflect the range of votes cast. Nevertheless, as can be seen from Table 4.4, the UUP as the largest party has received significant to very dramatic seat bonuses from every electoral system that has been used. Given the added importance in divided societies of fairly representing communities and minority opinions, a strong case can be made for the adoption of some type of PR for *all* elections.

Consequences for the Party System

One of the traditional arguments against proportional representation, usually made by defenders of the plurality system, is that it leads to a fragmentation of the party system and an unwieldy proliferation of parties. Northern Ireland offers a unique opportunity to partially evaluate this proposition since it uses both electoral systems during the same time period.[21]

Any attempt to consider this question immediately raises the practical problem of deciding how to count the number of political parties. Simply counting the absolute number of parties that win votes, or seats, may not be very helpful if there are large differences in the sizes of the parties. For example, if three parties take almost exactly one-third of the vote each, most people would reasonably conclude that this is a three-party system. However, if two parties take 45 percent each and an additional five parties take 2 percent each, should this be regarded as a seven-party system? Or consider an example from Northern Ireland. Twenty-three parties contested the elections to the 1996 Forum and ten parties won seats: But does it make much sense to describe Northern Ireland as having either a twenty-three or a ten-party system? Most people would say that it does not. What we need, then, is some measure that takes account of both the absolute number of parties and their relative sizes. Fortunately, Markku Laakso and Rein Taagepera (1979) have proposed an index, known as the "effective number of parties," that does precisely this (see the last column of Table 5.1 for details). What it demonstrates is that over the period 1981–1997, the effective number of parliamentary parties in Northern Ireland was 4.0 (the average across all elections, excluding those to the European parliament). Comparatively, what this means is that the party system of Northern Ireland (measured by the effective number of parliamentary parties) is considerably bigger than that of Britain

(2.10) or the Republic of Ireland (2.79) and, indeed, close in size to the party systems in Belgium (4.63) and the Netherlands (4.60), both societies that at various times have had segmented party systems (data cited in Lijphart 1994: 160–162).[22]

Another important matter is that the choice of electoral system may affect the ability of small parties to be represented at all: In fact, the plurality system can squeeze out such parties with the result that fewer parties are represented. Consider the data in Table 4.5, which demonstrates the impact of the different electoral systems on the effective number of parliamentary parties. In this table, the average effective number of parties is arranged by type of electoral system in Northern Ireland. Note that the high effective threshold in Westminster elections sharply reduced the number of parties (an effective number of parties of 2.62), whereas proportional representation in all other elections significantly increased the number of parties that win seats. In short, all of the PR elections (both STV and list system) allowed a greater number of parties to be represented (between 4.2 and 5.3), both in local government and in the regional assemblies. Clearly, the conclusion to be drawn is that the electoral system in operation does influence the effective number of parties.

This electoral system has other important effects on the party system, particularly on the competitive dynamics in Northern Ireland's dual-party system. Since this topic is more extensively discussed in the next chapter, only a brief comment will be made here: Basically, the use of PR-STV allows for freer competition within the unionist and nationalist party systems, whereas the plurality system provides strong incentives for each segment of Northern Ireland's divided party system to attenuate competition if "vote-splitting" risks making a gift of the seat to the ethno-national rival. In other words, both plurality and list PR systems "force voters to choose sides by casting a ballot for one party or another" (Grofman and Bowler 1996/1997: 46; see also Horowitz 1991), whereas STV allows voters to cross party lines and vote for candidates of more than one party. Of course, this opportunity for voters in no sense guarantees that STV will lead to electoral bridge building and moderation in divided societies, but at least it does not prevent such outcomes.

Conclusion

There are debates in many countries concerning the choice of the "best" electoral system, but such controversies tend to assume an extra resonance in societies with sharp ethno-national divisions be-

TABLE 4.5 Effective Number of Parliamentary Parties Arranged by Type of Electoral System: 1981–1997

Type of Election	*Effective Number of Parties (period averages)*
Westminster (plurality)	
1983	2.17
1987	2.87
1992	2.71
1997	2.74
Average	*2.62*
Local government (PR-STV)	
1981	4.95
1985	4.50
1989	4.72
1993	4.87
1997	5.02
Average	*4.81*
1982 Assembly (PR-STV)	4.20
1996 Forum (list system PR)	5.29

Note: The "effective number of parties" is a measure that takes into account both the number of political parties and their relative sizes (Taagepera and Shugart 1989; see Table 5.1 in this volume). Here it is calculated on the basis of share of the seats rather than votes since we wish to examine the impact of the electoral systems on the number of parties in parliament.

Source: Calculated from Table 5.1 of the present volume and from electoral results.

cause the stakes are higher and minorities may find themselves underrepresented in parliament and excluded from power. As we have seen, Northern Ireland has not avoided these controversies. The early reversion to the plurality system in the 1920s, combined with a variety of electoral malpractices, contributed to the dominance of the Unionist Party during the Stormont years and helped undermine political alternatives to it.

Although Horowitz surely exaggerates when he states that "[t]he electoral system is by far the most powerful lever of constitutional engineering for accommodation and harmony in severely divided societies" (1991: 163), there is little doubt that the plurality system is likely to exacerbate divisions. Plurality rule focuses electoral competition on the main basis of ethnic division and polarisation—to the exclusion of other forms of competition—and thus tends to transform elections into ethnic head-counts. In addition, plurality elections are likely to exaggerate the representation of the largest community while accentuating the minority status of minorities by means of the seat bonuses that typically accrue to the largest party. And defenders of plurality rule often approve of these seat bonuses as a method of ensuring single-party government by manufacturing a decisive majority for the largest party. However, single-party government and the resultant exclusion of minorities is precisely what divided societies need to avoid. Proportional representation values votes equally and is more likely to facilitate the coalition politics and power sharing that such societies desperately require. The precise form of PR is a secondary matter, and opinions vary quite widely. PR-STV has worked well in Northern Ireland, and its supporters point to its sophistication and the maximum choice that it gives to voters. In turn, advocates of list system PR can respond that party lists may help to strengthen the party leaders, who are usually vulnerable in segmented societies, especially if they engage in meaningful negotiations with rival communities.

The choice of an appropriate electoral system will not, in itself, do much to end protracted ethno-national conflicts. Nevertheless, some version of proportional representation is an indispensable component of a settlement. Plurality rule in segmented societies is incompatible with the inclusion and fairness that are vital if democracy is to be substantive rather than merely formal.

References and Further Reading

Bogdanor, Vernon, 1984. *What Is Proportional Representation?* Oxford: Martin Robertson.

Bradley, Patrick, 1995. "STV and monotonicity: A hands-on assessment," *Representation* 33:2, pp. 46–47.

Buckland, Patrick, 1979. *The Factory of Grievances: Devolved Government in Northern Ireland, 1921–39*. Dublin: Gill and Macmillan.

Cameron Commission, 1969. Disturbances in Northern Ireland: Report of the Commission Appointed by the Governor of Northern Ireland. Belfast.

Carstairs, Andrew McLaren, 1980. *A Short History of Electoral Systems*. London: George Allen and Unwin.

Elliott, Sydney, 1973. *Northern Ireland Parliamentary Election Results 1921–1972*. Chichester: Parliamentary Research Services.

______, 1992. "Voting systems and political parties in Northern Ireland," pp. 76–93 in Brigid Hadfield (ed.), *Northern Ireland: Politics and the Constitution*. Buckingham/Philadelphia: Open University Press.

______, 1997. "The Northern Ireland Forum/entry to negotiations election, 1996," *Irish Political Studies* 12, pp. 111–122.

Evans, Geoffrey, and Brendan O'Leary, 1997. "Frameworked futures: Intransigence and flexibility in the Northern Ireland elections of May 30, 1996," *Irish Political Studies* 12, pp. 23–47.

Farrell, David, 1997. *Comparing Electoral Systems*. Hemel Hempstead: Prentice Hall/Harvester Wheatsheaf.

Farrell, Michael, 1976. *Northern Ireland: The Orange State*. London: Pluto Press. (2nd ed. published in 1980.)

Flackes W. D., and Sydney Elliott, 1994. *Northern Ireland: A Political Directory, 1968–1993*. Belfast: Blackstaff Press.

Gallagher, Michael, 1991. "Proportionality, disproportionality and electoral systems," *Electoral Studies* 10, pp. 33–51.

______, 1993. "The election of the 27th Dail," pp. 57–78 in Michael Gallagher and Michael Laver (eds.), *How Ireland Voted 1992*. Dublin: Folens and PSAI Press.

______, 1996. "Choose your leader?" *Fortnight* 351, pp. 8–9. Belfast.

______, 1996/1997. "The single transferable vote: An assessment," *Representation* 34:1, pp. 2–6.

Gallagher, Michael, and A. R. Unwin, 1986. "Electoral distortion under STV random sampling procedures," *British Journal of Political Science* 16:2, pp. 243–253.

Gallagher, Michael, and Lee Komito, 1993. "Dail deputies and their constituency work," pp. 126–149 in John Coakley and Michael Gallagher (eds.), *Politics in the Republic of Ireland*. Dublin: Folens and PSAI Press.

Gallagher, Michael, Michael Laver, and Peter Mair, 1995. *Representative Government in Modern Europe*. New York: McGraw-Hill.

Grofman, Bernard, and Shaun Bowler, 1996/1997. "STV's place in the family of electoral systems: The theoretical comparisons and contrasts," *Representation* 34:1, pp. 43–47.

Horowitz, Donald, 1991. *A Democratic South Africa: Constitutional Engineering in a Divided Society*. Berkeley: University of California Press.

Laakso, M., and Rein Taagepera, 1979. "Effective number of parties: A measure with application to West Europe," *Comparative Political Studies* 12, pp. 3–27.

Lijphart, Arend, 1994. *Electoral Systems and Party Systems: A Study of Twenty-Seven Democracies, 1945–1990*. New York: Oxford University Press.

Mansergh, Nicholas, 1936. *The Government of Northern Ireland: A Study in Devolution*. London: Allen and Unwin.

Neill, Desmond G., 1952. "The election in Northern Ireland," pp. 220–235 in David E. Butler (ed.), *The British General Election of 1951*. London: Macmillan.

O'Leary, Brendan, and John McGarry, 1993. *The Politics of Antagonism: Understanding Northern Ireland*. London: Athlone Press.

O'Leary, Brendan, and Geoffrey Evans, 1997. "The 1997 Westminster election in Northern Ireland: *La fin de siecle*, the twilight of the second Protestant ascendancy and Sinn Féin's second coming," *Parliamentary Affairs*, forthcoming.

O'Leary, Cornelius, Sydney Elliott, and R. A. Wilford, 1988. *The Northern Ireland Assembly 1982–1986: A Constitutional Experiment*. London: Hurst.

Osborne, Robert D., 1979. "The Northern Ireland Parliamentary electoral system: The 1929 reapportionment," *Irish Geography* 12, pp. 42–56.

Pringle, D. G., 1980. "Electoral systems and political manipulation: A case study of Northern Ireland in the 1920s," *Economic and Social Review* 11:3, pp. 187–205.

Riker, William H., 1986. *The Art of Political Manipulation*. New Haven: Yale University Press.

Sinnott, Richard, 1993. "The electoral system," pp. 67–85 in John Coakley and Michael Gallagher (eds.), *Politics in the Republic of Ireland*. Dublin: Folens and PSAI Press.

______, 1995. *Irish Voters Decide: Voting Behaviour in Elections and Referendums Since 1918*. Manchester: Manchester University Press.

Taagepera, Rein, and Matthew Soberg Shugart, 1989. *Seats and Votes: The Effects and Determinants of Electoral Systems*. New Haven: Yale University Press.

Whyte, John, 1983. "How much discrimination was there under the unionist regime, 1921–68?" pp. 1–35 in Tom Gallagher and James O'Connell (eds.), *Contemporary Irish Studies*. Manchester: Manchester University Press.

5

The Party System and Party Competition

PAUL MITCHELL

It is probably fair to say that most of us think of politicians, parties, and elections when we think about politics. However, individual parties do not operate independently of one another as autonomous organisations. Rather, it is the competitive interactions of the parties, in a wide range of electoral, parliamentary, and governing arenas, that generates much of the high drama at the heart of representative politics. In a competitive party system each party's behaviour is at least partially conditioned by the actions of its rivals as each seeks to position itself to its maximum advantage. Thus, it is the multiple interactions of individual parties that constitutes the *party system*.

The last thirty years of political conflict in Northern Ireland have generated an enormous volume of academic literature (in 1990, John Whyte estimated over 7,000 items); nevertheless, a relatively small proportion of this work has focused on the usual topics in liberal democracies: parties, elections, and resource allocation. Although most of the literature concerning Northern Ireland understandably concentrates on explaining or "solving" the conflict, the unfortunate result is that many central areas of political research have been neglected. For example, no up-to-date books on any of the political parties currently exist (although for less recent or partial treatments of some of the parties, see Harbinson 1973; McAllister 1977; Bruce 1986). Accordingly, this chapter examines the development of party competition in Northern Ireland by identifying three broad phases in which the patterns and extent of competition can be clearly distinguished. Closest attention will be paid to the third phase of competition, the modern party system since 1982, characterised by a highly mobilised electorate and sharply competitive party politics contained within an overall bipolar political cleavage. But, first, let us briefly consider the comparative context of Northern Ireland's "deviant" party system.

"Deviant" Party Systems in Ireland

The party systems in both Irish jurisdictions are deviant in comparison to most other European countries. Typically, we expect the main and enduring parties to derive their *raison d'être* from the principal social conflicts that structured party competition in the early decades of this century, when mass suffrage was first introduced (Lipset and Rokkan 1967). Thus, social cleavages derived from religious, regional, linguistic, and, especially, class conflicts, result in a familiar set of "party families" that now dominate politics throughout Europe. These include the Social Democrats, Christian Democrats, Conservatives, Liberals, and, more recently, the Greens and the extreme right. Not so in Ireland.

One of the principal respects in which Irish politics differs is that the parties do not easily fit into the main European party families.[1] In both Irish political systems, the largest political parties crystallised around a sharply defined *political* cleavage rather than around the *social* divisions that underpin most other European countries. The Government of Ireland Act of 1920 partitioned the island into two new political systems. In what later became the Republic of Ireland, partial "independence" from Britain led to a bitter civil war unleashed by an intra-nationalist conflict over the terms of the settlement with Britain. The pro- and anti-Treaty forces that prosecuted the civil war evolved, respectively, into Fine Gael and Fianna Fáil, the political parties that went on to dominate politics up to the present. Clearly, neither of these parties fits neatly into any of the party families found throughout the rest of Europe (Coakley 1993; Mair 1993).

If the party system in the Republic of Ireland is deviant by comparative European standards, then the system in Northern Ireland is wildly aberrant. Although an intra-nationalist cleavage continued to structure party competition in Southern Ireland, the dangerous anti-system component was *de facto* resolved in 1926–1927 when Fianna Fáil was formed by de Valera (part of the anti-Treaty faction of Sinn Féin) and, within months, had abandoned abstentionism and entered Dáil Éireann. The process of regime legitimation continued such that in 1932 Fianna Fáil became the largest party, and an orderly transfer of power took place. The contrast with Northern Ireland, in terms of legitimacy and alternation in power, is stark.

For reasons examined in greater detail in Chapter 1, the smaller state created by the 1920 partition failed to become widely legitimate or fully functional as a liberal democracy. Instead of a primarily internal cleavage (as in the Republic of Ireland), in Northern Ireland politics polarised around a profound constitutional cleavage: defenders of the new state (those supporting the union with Britain) against those who opposed its very existence (those supporting union with the rest of Ireland). Northern nationalists opposed the creation of Northern Ireland, regarded it as an illegitimate and artificial construction, and refused to participate in its institutions; unionists had incentives to regard the new state as a bulwark against absorption by a gaelicised catholic Ireland, and, perhaps not surprisingly, treated nationalists as a disloyal minority that had to be controlled. The result was extreme polarisation. Most aspects of social and political life ossified into largely segmented communities with very limited meaningful interaction.

At the party political level, this cleavage made it virtually impossible for parties to operate as agents of aggregation across the wider political spectrum, as (at least theoretically) is the case in stable liberal democracies. In Northern Ireland, party politics is dominated primarily by ethnic parties, which seek only the support of the electorate on "their side" of the big constitutional divide. Whereas parties are conventionally conceived as instruments of choice by voters, in an ethnic party system loyalties have a strongly ascriptive character. Although all parties clearly have incentives to appeal to particular groups, the nonethnic party has a strategic interest in "governing for the whole." As Giovanni Sartori puts it, "although a party only represents a part, this part must take a *non-partial* approach to the whole" (1976: 26; emphasis in original). A central problem in party systems like Northern Ireland is that ethnic parties tend to identify "narrow group interests with the totality of the common interest" (Horowitz 1985: 297). Northern Ireland party politics can only truly be understood as a dual-party system (Mitchell 1991, 1995). At each election, it is only a mild exaggeration to say that two simultaneous but largely separate elections take place. Each community holds its own discrete election to decide who will represent the community in dealings with the ethnonational rivals: Unionist and nationalist parties do not, thereby, meaningfully compete for each other's electorate since very few such "floating" voters exist. Elections are, in effect, indices of demographic change (colloquially, the "sectarian head-count") and of competitive mobilisation ("getting the vote out"). Thus, at least as far as the other community is concerned, political leaders talk past one another, so that the more significant competition takes place within rather than between each segmented community.

Although the nature of party competition in Northern Ireland appears unusual by liberal democratic standards, it is much less aberrational when compared to other party systems where the primary political cleavage is based on an ethno-national conflict. Indeed, one of the arguments of this chapter is that electoral behaviour in Northern Ireland is better understood as a rational response to the competitive dynamics of an ethnic party system than as a primordial reaction to ancient antagonisms.

Three Phases of Party Competition

Despite the pervasive and enduring nature of the Northern Ireland conflict, the 1920 partition did not completely "freeze" the political landscape. Certainly the patterns of party competition in the 1990s look quite different from those that prevailed in the 1920s. Of the parties fighting elections in the first decade of the new province, the Ulster Unionist Party (UUP) is the only survivor, and even it has undergone splits and transformations.[2] Of the five main political parties in the 1990s, four were formed as recently as 1970–1971 (namely, the Democratic Unionists, the Alliance Party of Northern Ireland, the Social Democratic and Labour Party, and Sinn Féin). In addition, a quite bewildering multitude of smaller parties and alliances have come and gone during the first eight decades of Northern Ireland's existence.[3] However, in order to avoid drowning in detail, one may identify three main phases in the evolution of the party system.

Ulster Unionist Party Hegemony: 1920–1969

The 1920 partition left the Ulster Unionist Party as the dominant party in Northern Ireland and the permanent party of government, whereas all nationalist forces were consigned to perennial opposition. Unlike Sinn Féin (SF) in Southern Ireland, the UUP did not split in acrimony, thus facilitating its hegemonic control of the new state.[4] Given the demographic construction of the state and the apparent political unity of unionists, the UUP "won" all elections in the half-century to 1969. It faced a small amount of opposition from unionist independents in parliament, occasionally from the "left" but more typically from the "right" (Whyte 1973). In addition to restricting the electoral franchise and gerrymandering the constituency boundaries (see Chapter 4), the Unionist government's reintroduction in 1929 of an electoral system based on plurality rule had the effect of institutionalising ethnic divisions. "The UUP obtained exactly what it wanted: a British voting-system which focused elections on a straight fight between nationalists and unionists, cemented its status as a hegemonic party, and disadvantaged all smaller electoral groupings which might have fragmented the unionist vote" (O'Leary and McGarry 1993: 125). Plurality rule weakened non-nationalist alternatives to the UUP—provided it maintained internal cohesion and discipline, which it was subsequently unable to do.

The prospects for nonethnic parties were (and remain) slim as long as the main basis of polarisation remained salient. The Northern Ireland Labour Party (NILP) was the main electoral threat to the UUP in the 1950s (though this threat is sometimes exaggerated), winning 4 seats at the 1958 election and forming the official opposition in a 52-seat parliament.[5] However, the electoral fortunes of bi-confessional or cross-community parties in ethnic party systems are, typically, slender. For example, the NILP's vote (much like that of the Alliance Party since 1970) "was a virtual barometer of communal tension" (McAllister and Nelson 1979: 293), falling off whenever communal pressure intensified. This experience is consistent with that in other ethnic party systems, where "the choice for a Left party is to adapt and become essentially an ethnic party or to wither and die" (Horowitz 1985: 338).[6] Although the NILP had been clearly pro-partition since 1949, the increasing polarisation of the late 1960s and early 1970s induced the party to adopt an increasingly unionist position at the expense of its bi-confessionalism.

The experience of "constitutional" nationalist political forces during this period was one of alienation from the new state, as expressed by partial participation in the electoral process and intermittent abstention from parliament. For example, Nationalist Party MPs abstained from 1921 to 1927 and from 1932 to 1945. Although the Nationalist Party issued nominal denunciations of periodic IRA violence, its opposition to physical-force nationalism was much more equivocal than that of its successor party, the Social Democratic and Labour Party (SDLP). The Nationalist Party, consigned to permanent opposition by the frontiers of the new state, in combination with gerrymandering, was an ineffectual, poorly organised cadre-party of local notables.

This was the Northern Ireland party system at its least competitive. Indeed, many parliamentary seats were such a foregone conclusion that they habitually went uncontested. For almost the entire period between 1920 and 1969, 40 to 50 percent of all seats were uncontested, reaching an astonishing peak of nearly two-thirds of all seats in 1933 (O'Leary and McGarry 1993: 123). Northern Ireland's lack of domestic and international legitimacy resulted in the UUP's prioritising of unity and eternal vigilance as bulwarks against the twin evils of internal insurrection by nationalists and "external" betrayal by perfidious Britain. Nationalists, opposed to the creation of Northern Ireland in the first place, were in a state of atrophy, disillusioned and largely defeated.

Fragmentation and Reconstruction: 1969–1982

The 1969 election to the Stormont parliament marked a watershed in the Northern Ireland party system as the once-monolithic UUP fragmented into several factions and the Nationalist Party was eclipsed by political developments. In addition to being the most violent years of the conflict, this period marked an interregnum between the old uncompetitive party system characterised by UUP dominance and the "modern" competitive five-party system that was fully mobilised by 1982. The party system in the 1970s is a confusing picture of fragmentation and party proliferation in which many "party" labels were convenient vehicles for what proved to be temporary alliances engendered by the decade's turbulent events.

The 1969 election was the first truly competitive election in Northern Ireland. Of all 52 seats only 7 (13.5 percent) were uncontested, by far the lowest number since 1921. In addition, with both communal groups fragmented, voters were offered an unprecedented degree of choice (twelve groups, excluding independents), albeit little expansion in the range of choice, since most of the groups taking part represented different shades of opinion along the still-dominant communal cleavage.[7] The contest, which Prime Minister Terence O'Neill described as the "cross-roads election," was called earlier than necessary in an effort to validate his reform programme (announced in November 1968) and to isolate his unionist critics both inside and outside of the UUP. The unionist vote split into a wide variety of groupings, simplified in terms of whether they supported or opposed O'Neill's reform programme. Although O'Neill was not routed in the election (pro-O'Neill unionists, official and unofficial, won 44 percent of the total vote), his failure to eclipse his unionist opponents led indirectly to his resignation two months later.

Whereas 1969 marks a convenient point of departure for charting party-system developments, the antecedents of unionist fragmentation can be found during the civil rights period in the battles between reformers and hardliners. The party political consequences of this internecine struggle, as measured by electoral challenges to the UUP, lagged behind wider transformations of the domestic and external environments. Brendan O'Leary and John McGarry enumerate a variety of exogenous and endogenous factors that combined during the 1960s to undermine the UUP's hegemonic control and to amplify intra-unionist divisions and rivalries (1993: ch. 4). First, amongst the exogenous factors was the realisation by Northern nationalists that they would not be rescued by external forces. The Republic of Ireland prioritised its own economic development ahead of the national question, so that any improvements in the position of Northern nationalists would have to be achieved within the British political system (O'Leary and McGarry 1993: 156). Secondly, one of the unintended consequences of the extension of the postwar British welfare state to Northern Ireland was the dimming of northern nationalists' enthusiasm for a united (and poorer) independent Ireland. Amongst the endogenous factors, two stand out. First, physical-force nationalism, exemplified contemporaneously by the disastrous 1956–1962 "border campaign," had palpably demonstrated its failure to achieve *any* nationalist goals. By the mid-1960s the IRA was disorganised and barely credible as an option. Secondly, partly because of new participatory attitudes amongst Catholics fostered by their educational inclusion, "abstentionist defeatism was no longer the minority's preferred option" (O'Leary and McGarry 1993: 161). For significant numbers of Catholics, the reform of Northern Ireland became an important goal for the first time.

This new demand for inclusion through a civil rights movement could not easily be ignored or suppressed in the manner that abstention and insurrection had been, and it created a divisive dynamic that destroyed UUP unity. Despite the multitude of unionist organisations during this period, unionism essentially fragmented into two broad political tendencies: those exemplified by O'Neill (and his later successor Brian Faulkner), who conditionally accepted reforms promoted by the British government; and those exemplified by William Craig's Vanguard Unionist Party (VUP) or Paisley's Democratic Unionists (DUP), who vociferously rejected the reforms as a form of "capitulation" to the civil rights movement, interpreted by them as a nationalist conspiracy. Accordingly, the UUP leadership faced fierce competition from a range of other unionist parties. For example, in one of its poorest electoral performances (to the 1975 Convention), the UUP managed only 25.8 percent of the total vote, whereas the DUP and VUP registered 14.8 percent and 12.7 percent, respectively. Table 5.1 demonstrates the electoral decline of the UUP in the period until 1977 and the concomitant growth in other unionist parties.

Nevertheless, despite a rapid procession of Unionist Party leaders, the UUP ultimately proved resilient, helped in no small part by internecine conflict amongst the party's unionist rivals. Most dramatically, the VUP leader William Craig committed political suicide in

TABLE 5.1 Party Support in Northern Ireland Elections: 1969–1997 (% of vote)

	Unionist Bloc			*Nationalist Bloc*			*Nonconfessional Bloc*				
Election	*UUP*	*DUP*	*Other*	*SDLP*	*SF*	*Other*	*NILP*	*APNI*	*WP*	*Other*	*Effective Number of Parties*[a]
1969 S	61.1	–	6.3	–	–	18.8	8.1	–		5.7	–
1970 W	54.3	–	4.5	–	–	23.3	12.6	–		5.1	3.07
1973 LG	41.4	4.3	10.9	13.4	–	5.8	2.5	13.7		8.0	4.58
1973 A	29.3	10.8	21.8	22.1	–	2.0	2.6	9.2		1.0	5.72
1974 W	32.3	8.2	23.7	22.4	–	4.5	2.4	3.2		3.3	4.70
1974 W	36.5	8.5	17.1	22.0	–	7.8	1.6	6.3		0.2	4.72
1975 C	25.8	14.8	21.9	23.7	–	2.2	1.4	9.8		0.4	5.65
1977 LG	29.6	12.7	8.5	20.6	–	4.1	0.8	14.4		8.3	5.87
1979 W	36.6	10.2	12.2	19.9	–	8.2		11.8		2.1	5.11
1979 E	21.9	29.8	7.3	24.6	–	6.7		6.8		2.9	4.24
1981 LG	26.5	26.6	4.2	17.5	–	5.3		8.9	1.8	8.2	5.50
1982 A	29.7	23.0	6.7	18.8	10.1	–		9.3	2.7	0.7	5.06
1983 W	34.0	20.0	3.0	17.9	13.4	–		8.0	1.9	1.6	4.69
1984 E	21.5	33.6	2.9	22.1	13.3	–		5.0	1.3	0.3	4.36
1985 LG	29.5	24.3	3.1	17.8	11.8	2.4		7.1	1.6	1.8	5.07
1987 W	37.8	11.7	5.4	21.1	11.4	–		10.0	2.6	0.0	4.44
1989 LG	31.3	17.7	4.6	21.0	11.2	0.1		6.9	2.1	5.1	5.17
1989 E	22.2	29.9	–	25.5	9.1	–		5.2	1.0	6.9	4.60
1992 W	34.5	13.1	2.7	23.5	10.0	–		8.7	0.9	6.6	4.70
1993 LG	29.4	17.3	2.7	22.0	12.4	0.3		7.6	1.0	6.8	5.37
1994 E	23.8	29.2	–	28.9	9.9	–		4.1	0.4	3.6	4.22
1996 F	24.2	18.8	9.3	21.4	15.5	–		6.5	0.5	3.8	5.84
1997 W	32.7	13.6	4.2	24.1	16.1	–		8.0		1.3	5.05
1997 LG	27.8	15.6	4.1	20.7	16.9	–		6.5		8.4	5.62

Key: S = Stormont; W = Westminster; LG = Local Government; E = European Parliament; A = Assembly; C = Convention; F = Forum

[a]The final column is a measure of the "effective number of parties" that takes into account the number of political parties and their relative weights. The calculation here is based on vote shares according to the formula: N_V = the sum of 1/p. Stated in words, N is "the effective number of hypothetical equal-sized parties that would have the same effect on fractionalization of the party system as have the actual parties of varying sizes" (Taagepera and Shugart 1989: 79). Data on independents have been excluded from the figures in this table.

Source: The format of this table is a slightly amended and updated version of a table that first appeared in O'Leary (1991).

1975 when he suggested that a temporary coalition with the SDLP might be possible (all the more surprising since Craig had been instrumental in overthrowing the 1974 power-sharing Executive). The VUP immediately split, and Paisley was able to mobilise the opposition to Craig's proposal in his successful bid to reorganise the "no-surrender" vote behind the DUP. Most of the Vanguard rump that stayed with Craig returned to the Unionist Party: "In that sense Vanguard groupings have represented challenges from within Unionism rather than from outside it (a contrast with Ian Paisley's movements)" (McAllister and Nelson 1979: 288). Craig's fate demonstrated that even hardline unionists can quickly be thrown overboard if they concede too much to their ethno-national enemies. By contrast, many of the pro-reform O'Neill unionists decamped from the UUP to join the new bi-confessional Alliance Party of Northern Ireland (APNI) founded in April 1970. Thus, by 1977 unionist fragmentation had decreased, leaving a streamlined choice between the UUP and the DUP (with the Alliance Party as a third possibility).

This was also a period of reconstruction for the political representatives of the nationalist community. The civil rights mobilisation of the 1960s caused as many problems for the conservative and increasingly moribund Nationalist Party as it did for the ruling unionists. Having barely changed from 1921 to the early 1960s, and opposed to street protests and marches, it was overtaken by events when the unionist government, unable to systematically respond to nonviolent protests with excessive force, acquiesced to some of the Northern Ireland Civil Rights Association's (NICRA) demands. In comparison to the dynamic of street protest, the Nationalist Party seemed ineffectual. Although the diverse coalition that composed NICRA did not itself contest the 1969 election, many of its prominent figures did so in other guises. The Nationalist Party leader, Eddie McAteer, was defeated by John Hume, later to become the most prominent Northern nationalist and leader of the SDLP,[8] founded by six MPs who had been active in the civil rights movement.

The SDLP marked an intergenerational change, with members by far the youngest, on average, relative to those in the parties represented in the 1973 Assembly: 42 percent were under age thirty-nine, compared to 18 percent of unionists (McAllister 1977: 68). Involvement in the civil rights movement was the main common characteristic of early SDLP members. As Ian McAllister argues, "participation in the civil rights movement makes it comparable as a route of entry to involvement in the 1919 to 1921 Anglo-Irish War for Dáil Deputies" (1977: 76). The importance of the SDLP is greater than the simple matter of replacing one nationalist party with another, since it signaled several significant changes in political strategy. The SDLP was the first "modern" political party in Northern Ireland—the first to create an extensive political organisation and to adopt a fairly coherent policy platform. Most significantly, however, the SDLP accepted that there would be no change in the constitutional position of Northern Ireland without the consent of the majority. This radical departure for a nationalist party meant that the SDLP was prepared to participate in the governance of the province. The SDLP's approach "has been to demand endogenous change and not to alter the [communities'] weights [by territorial change], but *the institutions within which the weights are applied*" (McAllister, 1977, 162; emphasis in original). Thus, in its formative years the SDLP demanded the reintroduction of proportional representation and, more important, a departure from executive-branch majoritarianism, so that SDLP participation in coalition governments would be mandatory. The frustration of this latter goal led to a change of policy emphasis in the late 1970s, with the SDLP increasingly focusing on the internationalisation of the conflict and a wider Anglo-Irish process rather than on internal reform (see Chapters 10 and 11).

The SDLP quickly managed to establish itself as the only credible electoral representative of the nationalist community during the 1970s. Indeed, in the 1973 Assembly and 1975 Convention elections, it was the only nationalist party to win any seats. With the resumption of political violence in 1969, no republican groups managed to mount a serious electoral challenge to the SDLP (until the republican hunger strikes of 1980–1981). During the 1970s, Republican Clubs (the political wing of the Official IRA) received only negligible electoral support (1.8 percent in the 1973 Assembly and 2.2 percent in the 1975 Convention elections), whereas Provisional Sinn Féin did not contest elections.

In summary, the pattern during this period is one in which the turmoil connected with a multistage regime transition and a recrudescence of violence led to extensive electoral challenges to the traditional political representatives of both ethno-national communities. The intense period of electoral volatility and party decomposition within each community gradually receded, leaving four of the five parties that now dominate Northern Ireland elections. Although independents and other small parties continue to exist (their success depending on the type of election and electoral system in operation), the choice within mainstream unionism was effectively streamlined down to just two parties, the UUP and DUP, and the SDLP emerged as the only significant electoral representative of the nationalist community.[9]

The Dual-Party System: Post-1982

In an ethnic party system there are two principal types of "competition": *between* and *within* the ethnic segments of the society.[10] First and foremost is the changing overall balance between the communal segments in terms of political representation. This is not "competition" in the conventional sense of one group actively seeking the votes of the other groups. Indeed, there is very little cross-segmental movement of votes in Northern Ireland, so that in electoral terms the segments are virtually exclusive groups. Elections in ethnic party systems have a census-type quality in which long-term trends are demographic. In Northern Ireland the main demographic trend (see Chapter 3) is the steady growth of the Catholic population, which is partially responsible for boosting nationalist voting. The most striking long-term trend in party support is the growth of the nationalist bloc relative to the unionist bloc, and the fact that the "Catholic population has become both absolutely and relatively more nationalist in its voting since 1969" (O'Leary 1991: 348). Table 5.2 clearly demonstrates this trend: An average nationalist vote of 25.8 percent in the 1970s grew to 31.3 percent in the 1980s and to 37.0 percent in the 1990s. Furthermore, there is no indication that this trend is tailing off: For the first three elections since the 1994 ceasefires, the average nationalist vote is 38.2 percent. Correspondingly, the unionist vote is in long-term decline, from an average of 59.4 percent in the 1970s to 56.2 percent in the 1980s and only 50.5 in the 1990s. The continuation of this trend will soon cause the unionist bloc's support to fall below 50 percent on a regular basis. The long-term trends for the bi-confessional bloc suggest a slow but steady decline with an average vote in the 1970s of 11.0 percent, falling to 9.4 percent in the 1980s and to 7.3 percent in the 1990s. The Alliance Party continues to be squeezed in a party system that remains highly polarised (see the last column of Table 5.2).

Apart from these long-term trends, there are significant questions of *competitive strategy* at stake for each segment: most significantly, mobilisation and vote management. In an ethnic party system there is little uncertainty about which bloc a voter will vote for *if* he or she votes. Very few votes float across the segmental boundary. What *is* uncertain "is *whether* a potential voter will vote" (Horowitz 1985: 332; emphasis in original). Hence the importance of turnout, the competitive effort to out-mobilise the other segment. And of course one of the most effective methods of mobilising supporters is to adopt a highly ideological and inflammatory language of appeal that suggests that the community's vital interests are at stake. In an ethnic party system

TABLE 5.2 Electoral Support by Bloc: 1969–1997

Election	*Unionist Bloc*	*Nationalist Bloc*	*Nonconfessional Bloc*	*Others*	*Polarised Bloc*
1969 S	67.4	18.8	8.1	5.7	86.2
1970 W	58.8	23.2	12.6	5.1	82.0
1973 LG	56.6	19.2	16.2	8.0	75.8
1973 A	61.9	24.1	11.8	1.0	86.0
1974 W	64.2	26.9	5.6	3.3	91.1
1974 W	62.1	29.8	7.9	0.2	91.9
1975 C	62.5	25.9	11.2	0.4	88.4
1977 LG	50.8	24.1	15.2	8.3	74.9
1979 W	59.0	28.1	11.8	2.1	87.1
1979 E	59.0	31.1	6.8	2.9	90.1
1981 LG	57.3	22.8	10.7	8.2	80.1
1982 A	59.4	28.9	12.0	0.7	88.3
1983 W	57.0	31.3	9.9	1.6	88.3
1984 E	58.0	35.4	6.3	0.3	93.4
1985 LG	56.9	32.0	8.7	1.8	88.9
1987 W	54.9	32.8	12.6	0.0	87.7
1989 LG	53.6	32.3	9.0	5.1	85.9
1989 E	52.1	34.6	6.2	6.9	86.7
1992 W	50.3	33.5	9.6	6.6	83.8
1993 LG	49.4	34.7	8.6	6.8	84.1
1994 E	53.0	38.8	4.6	3.6	91.8
1996 F	52.4	36.9	6.5	1.9	89.3
1997 W	50.5	40.2	8.0	1.3	90.7
1997 LG	47.5	37.6	6.5	8.4	85.1
Average:					
1970s	59.4	25.8	11.0	3.5	85.3
1980s	56.2	31.3	9.4	3.1	87.4
1990s[a]	50.5	37.0	7.3	4.8	87.5

Key: S = Stormont; W = Westminster; LG = Local Government; E = European Parliament; A = Assembly; C = Convention; F = Forum

[a]The figures for the 1990s represent the averages of the six elections held between 1992 and 1997.

Source: Calculated from election returns.

there is no electoral premium on moderation. Finally, in terms of between-segment competition, it is important that each segment is able to manage its vote in circumstances where internal division will benefit the ethnic rival. (The politics of vote-splitting will be analysed below.)

However, most of the rest of this chapter examines competition within each segment in the dual-party system. Apart from the overall standing of their bloc, one of the central concerns of Northern Ireland political parties is the battle to become the dominant party in their own communities. This internecine warfare is ever-present, but especially pronounced whenever an election approaches.

Competition in the Nationalist Bloc

Northern Ireland's dual-party system was fully institutionalised by the decision of Provisional Sinn Féin—in the wake of the 1980–1981 republican hunger strikes—to challenge the SDLP's right to speak for Northern nationalists by contesting elections. At each subsequent election, two largely separate contests have taken place within the ethno-national blocs, as each party endeavoured to project itself as the most effective advocate of its community's vital interests. Sinn Féin explicitly asserted this intention prior to the first election it contested in 1982: Its Belfast press officer stated that "we will not allow it [the SDLP] to go unchallenged and masquerade as the political voice of the nationalist people" (*Irish Times*, 9 April 1982: 5). Whereas the "unionist party system" had simplified by 1977 to a choice between two main parties, the emergence of Sinn Féin as an electoral force was the consequence not of a fragmentation of an umbrella party but of the successful mobilisation of a previously largely abstentionist republican section of the electorate.

Nevertheless, although the development of an electoral strategy by Sinn Féin brought new voters into the party system rather than primarily winning over SDLP partisans, Sinn Féin's electoral presence presented a clear threat to the SDLP's leadership of Northern nationalists. Indeed, at only its second election (to the Westminster parliament in 1983), Sinn Féin's share of the nationalist vote, at 43 percent, raised the alarming prospect (to the SDLP and the British and Irish governments) that the party might replace the SDLP as the largest nationalist party (see Table 5.3). Faced with such a serious prospect, the Irish and British governments came to the conclusion that "it might now be more dangerous to do nothing than to attempt an initiative aimed at stabilising the situation" (FitzGerald 1991: 497). The two governments responded with the Anglo-Irish Agreement (AIA) of 1985, motivated in part by the perceived need to bolster the SDLP and to insulate it from the centrifugal pull exerted by the necessity of competing with Sinn Féin. This short-term goal was partially fulfilled in that further Sinn Féin advances were stalled, but hopes of seriously undermining existing Sinn Féin support proved futile (FitzGerald 1991: 532). In the four elections that Sinn Féin contested before the AIA was signed, the party averaged 12.1 percent of the total vote, compared to an average

TABLE 5.3 The Intra-Ethnic Balance of Power: 1981–1997

DUP share of UUP + DUP vote (%)	*UUP share of UUP + DUP vote (%)*	*Election*	*SDLP share of SDLP + SF vote (%)*	*SF share of SDLP + SF vote (%)*
50	50	1981 Local Govt.	–	–
44	56	1982 NI Assembly	65	35
37	63	1983 Westminster	57	43
61	39	1984 European	62	38
45	55	1985 Local Govt.	60	40
24	76	1987 Westminster	65	35
36	64	1989 Local Govt.	65	35
57	43	1989 European	74	26
28	72	1992 Westminster	70	30
37	63	1993 Local Govt.	64	36
55	45	1994 European	74	26
44	56	1996 Forum	58	42
29	71	1997 Westminster	60	40
36	64	1997 Local Govt.	55	45

Source: Updated from a table in Mitchell (1995).

of 12.5 percent afterward (in the nine elections from 1987 to 1997). Although it is an exaggeration to say that the AIA "decisively restored" the SDLP's position within the nationalist bloc (O'Leary and McGarry 1993: 259), there is no doubt that the initiative provided the SDLP with some protective armour against Sinn Féin's charge that constitutional nationalism had achieved nothing of consequence.

Certainly, in the subsequent "talks processes"—notably, the initiatives chaired by two successive Secretaries of State, Peter Brooke and Patrick Mayhew (1991–1993)—the fact that the SDLP already had the limited "Irish dimension" contained in the AIA meant that the SDLP could take part in negotiations from a position of strength, since, if as expected nothing of substance emerged, a return to the full workings of AIA was an acceptable default option. The problem for British and Irish policymakers was that the limited redistribution of political support in favour of the more moderate parties, in part engineered by the AIA, was not sufficient to persuade these parties to embrace conflict-regulating outcomes. The dangers of ethnic out-flanking, in this case by the continued presence of Sinn Féin in the nationalist party system, constrained overly conciliatory behaviour by the SDLP. The SDLP's position in the nationalist community following the AIA did not make the SDLP more likely to agree to internal devolution. Indeed, the successful negotiation of the AIA made the SDLP even less likely to accept a purely internal settlement, since the AIA could be interpreted as a first step toward a more substantial institutional embodiment of the Irish dimension.

Since Sinn Féin's participation in the party system, the size of the nationalist bloc (the SDLP and SF) has steadily grown (see Table 5.2); from 1985 until 1996, however, most of this electoral growth benefited the SDLP more than Sinn Féin (see Table 5.3). Both parties continued to compete for the nationalist vote. The extent and intensity of intrasegmental competition are conditioned by the type of electoral system in operation. The single transferable vote (STV) used for all elections other than those to the Westminster Parliament and the 1996 Forum election allows freer competition, since the preference ordering and the transfer system permit a voter to express a sincere choice and still be effective at the same time (i.e., there are no "wasted" votes). However, in terms of the most important elections—those to Westminster—the plurality electoral system generates incentives to attenuate intrasegmental competition if this will result in the segment losing the seat. In other words, vote-splitting is one of the most important electoral dynamics in competitive ethnic party systems under plurality rule.

Clearly, the greater extent of vote-splitting amongst nationalists reflected deeper divisions between the SDLP and SF than among the unionist parties. The two nationalist parties are divided in their electorates, policies, and tactics. The polarisation of their electorates is revealed in STV elections by the very low transfer rates between the two parties. Indeed, "many SDLP supporters give their [lower] preference to the pro-union Alliance Party sooner than to Sinn Féin" (Whyte 1990: 74). In contrast, despite often fierce language, the unionist parties typically transfer to each other. For example, the DUP's return to the campaign themes of ethnic betrayal during the 1994 European elections, with Paisley describing the UUP leader as the modern "Judas Iscariot" of Ulster politics, did not prevent 69 percent of DUP voters from giving a second preference to the UUP. Moreover, significant differences exist in terms of the social bases of party support for the two nationalist parties. A recent multivariate analysis confirms the widely held observation that SDLP supporters are both older and more middle class than those supporting Sinn Féin (Evans and Duffy 1997: 71–72).

The nationalist parties are divided in terms of their policies by the SDLP's belief that changes in the constitutional status of Northern Ireland can realistically be achieved only with the consent of (some of) the unionist community. By contrast, Sinn Féin continues to regard unionists as an Irish national minority with minority rights. In terms of tactics, Sinn Féin's defence of the use of political violence has made it an unacceptable partner for even a tacit electoral alliance. On the rare occasions when the SDLP has not opposed a republican candidate—for example, in 1981, when Owen Carron (SF) was elected MP for Fermanagh-South Tyrone—a strong backlash has dented the SDLP's credibility as the party that provides a bulwark against physical-force nationalism. So long as SF has defended IRA violence, the nationalist bloc has continued to split its vote.

The most dramatic example of the politics of ethnic vote-splitting is the Westminster constituency of Mid-Ulster, which, despite an overall nationalist majority, usually elects a unionist member of parliament. In 1970 the seat was won by an independent nationalist, Bernadette Devlin, who took the seat with 53.5 percent because she was the only nationalist candidate. In February 1974 she was opposed by the SDLP, which was fighting its first Westminster election, so that the unionist candidate won with only 39 percent (the combined nationalist vote was undiminished at 54 percent). Thereafter, a divided nationalist vote allowed the election of a unionist at each contest by the nomination of a single agreed unionist candidate. That occurred until 1983, when fierce competition between the two main unionist parties meant that there was no agreed candidate. In the event, the Reverend William McRea of the DUP won the seat with only 30.0 percent, 78 votes (0.1 percent) ahead of Danny Morrison, the Sinn Féin candidate. (As usual, the combined nationalist vote—this time, 52.3 percent—represented an absolute majority.) Having looked into the abyss in 1983, only the DUP candidate contested the seat at subsequent elections, providing an easy victory as long as both the SDLP and Sinn Féin continued to field candidates. In 1997, having held the seat for fourteen years, McRea finally lost to Sinn Féin's Martin McGuinness, despite continued nationalist vote-splitting. Sinn Féin used McRea's apparent support for a loyalist (who was subsequently jailed) to mobilise support behind its chief negotiator, who was imported as their candidate. Indeed, Sinn Féin successfully created the impression that it was best placed to oust McRea so that the SDLP vote declined by 6.4 percent (relative to the 1996 Forum election) whereas Sinn Féin's grew by 10.5 percent. Thus, some probable tactical voting by SDLP supporters, combined with an 86 percent turnout (the highest in the U.K.), led to a nationalist victory without an agreed candidate.[11]

Following the IRA ceasefire of August 1994, considerable speculation arose as to whether nationalists would alter their candidate nomination strategies at the 1997 General Election, since agreed nationalist candidates would most likely result in two or three net gains. However, even while the ceasefire was intact, the prospect of an electoral alliance with Sinn Féin was highly problematic for the SDLP. At its 1995 Annual Conference the party was openly divided on the subject, with members in the areas suffering the most concentrated IRA violence (Belfast and the border counties) tending to be the most hostile to the idea of any electoral cooperation with Sinn Féin.[12] The IRA's return to violence in February 1996 precluded the possibility of an alliance, at least in the short term.

The "second" IRA ceasefire, which began on 20 July 1997, will (if sustained) reopen questions of competitive strategy amongst nationalists. Indeed, following the referendum on 22 May 1998 at which the electorate endorsed the Good Friday Agreement (see Epilogue), the president of Sinn Féin, Gerry Adams, proposed an electoral pact with the SDLP for the Assembly election held on 25 June. This proposal was, however, rebuffed by John Hume, the leader of the SDLP. Ultimately, the SDLP and SF may agree to some electoral cooperation unless the new British Labour Government makes this unnecessary by introducing proportional representation for all elections. Either way, the distribution of seats will be more proportional, with the result that the unionists will lose seats to nationalists.

Competition in the Unionist Bloc

Although the Anglo-Irish Agreement was welcomed by the SDLP and criticised by Sinn Féin, it was universally condemned by the unionist parties as a betrayal by Britain and a capitulation to nationalists. The period immediately prior to that of the AIA had been marked by fierce intra-unionist competition, as the DUP threatened to surpass the UUP as the leading voice of unionism. Although the DUP leader would always win this contest if the count was in decibels, in the early 1980s his party became a major electoral force within the unionist party system. Having won two more seats at the 1979 Westminster election, Paisley topped the poll at the first direct election to the European parliament, before marginally overtaking the UUP (for the first and only time at a non-European election) at the 1981 local government elections (see Table 5.1). Unionist party rivalry focused on who was best able to create the impression that they were most equipped to "smash Sinn Féin" and end summit meetings between the British and Irish governments. During the 1985 local government elections, the *Economist* commented: "[W]hich ever unionist party comes top this time will claim to speak for Protestant Ulster. They are using identical strategies and peculiar tactics. Both parties claim to be the biggest enemy of the IRA" (27 April 1985, 84). In fact, there is nothing "peculiar" about these tactics; if anything, they are instrumentally rational since there is no premium on moderation in an ethnically polarised dual-party system. The centrifugal dynamic inherent in ethnic party systems was readily apparent as each unionist party attempted to outdo the other in terms of ethnic intransigence. At this time the DUP was well placed to threaten the Ulster Unionist's position as the leading party defending the Union.

Despite the overall importance of the constitutional issue, there is also some social patterning to intra-unionist party competition, with class and left-right ideology playing a greater role than in the nationalist party system. Put broadly, DUP supporters tend to be younger, poorer, and less religious than UUP supporters (Diskin 1984; Evans and Duffy 1997).

The largely unforeseen party political consequence of the Anglo-Irish Agreement was to hamstring the DUP's competitive options and to re-consolidate the position of their rivals in the UUP (Mitchell 1995). As part of their response to the perceived Anglo-Irish threat to their constitutional position, the unionist party leaders agreed to a comprehensive electoral pact for the 1987 Westminster election, in order to prevent communal disunity and focus attention on their attempts to undermine the AIA. The result was demobilising for unionists in general and disastrous for the DUP in particular. Eliminating intra-unionist competition left very little at stake, so that overall turnout fell by 5.9 percent, and the combined vote of the DUP and UUP declined from 54 percent in 1983 to only 49.5 percent in 1987.

Of course, Westminster (plurality) elections tend to benefit the largest parties even in normal circumstances. The unionist "unity" strategy in 1987 compounded the DUP's disadvantage and firmly reestablished the Ulster Unionists as the dominant unionist party. The UUP had a clear positional advantage in the unity strategy as the party with the largest number of incumbents: It had eleven outgoing MPs at the 1987 election to the DUP's three and therefore benefited most from the mutual protection pact. The election proved debilitating for the DUP, with its total vote falling from 20 percent in 1983 to just 11.7 percent in 1987—a loss of more than 40 percent of DUP voters. The temporary cessation of hostilities between the unionist parties held firm at the 1987 election even though it obviously disadvantaged the DUP. This outcome reinforces the observation that, in times of crisis (specifically, the "threat" of the Anglo-Irish Agreement), the group leaders' primary loyalty is to the segment rather than to the party. Nevertheless, the imposition of the pact by the party leaders caused considerable acrimony within the DUP, especially in seats where they could credibly challenge the incumbent unionist. The best prospect for a DUP gain had been East Antrim, where Jim Allister (a former DUP press officer and personal assistant to Ian Paisley) had been only 367 votes behind the winning Ulster Unionist candidate at the 1983 election. The unionist pact denied Allister a probable victory in 1987 (the UUP candidate was elected with a 15,000 majority), and Allister withdrew from politics. The DUP remains vulnerable at Westminster elections to the charge of disloyal vote-splitting whenever it tries to position itself competitively. Thus, the DUP recovered only marginally at the 1992 election, taking 13.1 percent (to the UUP's 34.5 percent)—well behind the 20 percent it achieved in 1983. The DUP continues to be disadvantaged by the plurality electoral system that operates for Westminster polls, and it is left with only the European parliament elections as a context in which it can vanquish the Ulster Unionists, since Paisley is more popular than his party.

Whatever the merits and limitations of the Anglo-Irish Agreement, it proved resistant to unionist attempts to destroy it. Though vocal and at times dramatic, the unionist anti-AIA campaign proved ineffective and counterproductive, such that an Anglo-Irish intergovernmental approach to Northern Ireland has become the norm. Cooperation between the two main unionist parties gradually reverted to competition and then fierce hostility.

Competition Before and After the 'First' Ceasefire

The failure of the long-drawn-out talks of 1991–1993, with each side blaming the other for the collapse, led to a change of tack by John Hume, who now accelerated his discussions with the Sinn Féin president, Gerry Adams. The SDLP leader appeared to believe that the unionist parties had no intention of making the necessary compromises in any resuscitation of talks, and that it was therefore preferable to attempt to transform the context of any future negotiations by first achieving a republican ceasefire. Hume's dialogue with Adams ensured that there would be no unionist parties to talk to in the short term.

Unionist competition was exacerbated by the increasingly cosy relationship between James Molyneaux (the UUP leader) and John Major (British PM), facilitated by parliamentary developments at Westminster. The Conservative Party's slim 21-seat majority at the 1992 election increasingly seemed unlikely to be sufficient, given its haemorrhaging over European integration. Facing defeat in the House of Commons over the Maastricht Social Chapter amendment (July 1993), Major adopted the language of a born-again unionist. The prime minister told the House on 1 July 1993 that "the Union is vital for all parts of the United Kingdom. It has the democratic approval of the people of Northern Ireland and we in the Conservative and Unionist party" (Moore 1993: 13). There emerged a new "understanding" between Major and Molyneaux whereby the UUP would provide extra security for the Conservatives in parliament, in return for the implementation of part of the UUP's policy agenda, such as the new Northern Ireland Affairs Select Committee at Westminster (see Chapter 6). Although this "understanding" did not represent a departure from the British government's commitment to the Anglo-Irish process, it did imply greater sensitivity to the concerns of the UUP. Molyneaux's apparent inclusion in the British policymaking process only highlighted the DUP's isolation.

The DUP's total opposition to the Downing Street Declaration, signed by the British and Irish governments in December 1993, followed by the UUP's ambiguous response, marked the return of full hostilities between the two unionist parties. Whereas Paisley denounced the accord as further treachery, the UUP leadership "did not seem keen to conform to stereotype by joining in with the 'primal screams' being emitted from the mouths of DUP politicians" (Cochrane 1997: 319). The DUP tried to portray the 1994 European parliament elections as a referendum on the Downing Street Declaration and revived the ethnic themes of "betrayal" and "capitulation."

After the election Molyneaux looked increasingly like a leader caught in a trap. His attempts to maintain a relationship with the British government and hence validate the proposition that he had some influence over its actions set him up as a target for the DUP. The DUP continued to denounce Molyneaux for supporting the government and, even worse, ridiculed his belief that he had some real influence. The British and Irish governments' joint publication in February 1995 of the Framework Documents damaged Molyneaux's position and undermined his leadership of the UUP by demonstrating that he had no veto on the actions of the British government.

Although unionist politics in the mid-1990s amounted to new episodes in an old story, with the UUP and DUP claiming to be the best defences against the twin machinations of the two governments and the "pan-nationalist front," an altered strategy emerged in the nationalist party system that was to lead to an apparent breakthrough in the ongoing stalemate.

Despite nationalist vote-splitting, the SDLP's ascendant position in the nationalist community was symbolically reinforced during the 1980s and early 1990s by the increase in the size of its Westminster parliamentary party from a single MP in 1983 (John Hume) to four by 1992. The icing on the cake for the SDLP and a low point for Sinn Féin was the transfer of the West Belfast seat from Sinn Féin to the SDLP at the 1992 election. Although a constellation of forces explains the IRA ceasefire (O'Leary 1995; Mallie and McKittrick 1996; see also Chapter 2 of this volume), prominent amongst these was the realisation by the Sinn Féin leadership that the conflict was in stalemate: The IRA could not be defeated, but neither could it win. Apparently, the Sinn Féin leadership's assessment (by 1992–1993) was that "republicans at this time and on their own do not have the strength to achieve the end goal"(Mallie and McKittrick 1996: 318). In electoral terms the Sinn Féin vote was fairly stable but had made no further advances since the adoption of its "ballot and bomb" strategy in the early 1980s. Sinn Féin reevaluated its options and engaged with John Hume's attempts to find a formula that could result in a republican ceasefire and a political settlement. In danger of losing control of the process, the two governments eventually responded with what became known as the Downing Street Declaration of December 1993. This document challenged the British government's usual preference of trying to isolate the extremes and insulate the centre ground—a strategy that had never succeeded—and replaced it with an offer to Sinn Féin of participation in comprehensive negotiations in return for a ceasefire (Mitchell 1995). When on 31 August 1994 the IRA announced a "complete cessation of military operations," in excess of the British government's expectation of a more qualified ceasefire, there was widespread relief and hope of progress toward a settlement. However, all such hopes were dashed when almost no progress was made toward inclusive negotiations during the seventeen months of the republican ceasefire.

Contrary to Peter Brooke's promise as Secretary of State for Northern Ireland that the British government would make a "flexible and imaginative" response to a ceasefire, the government decided on a long game of continually pressuring republicans to prove their *bona fides* by making further concessions (Mallie and McKittrick 1996: 337–339). Despite initial euphoria about the ceasefires, a gulf quickly emerged between the two governments concerning the appropriate response to the new situation.

The British government, in an increasingly weak parliamentary position, established a series of pre-conditions to Sinn Féin's entry into all-party talks, ranging from initial insistence on a declaration that the ceasefire was "permanent" to the partial decommissioning of IRA weapons *prior* to negotiations, to an election to a forum that, in Mayhew's words, would not be "a hurdle but a door opening to the conference chamber." Although evidence exists that the British and Irish governments knew that there was no prospect of prior decommissioning—confirmed by the international body set up to examine the issue—the British government argued that the handing over of some arms was essential to ensure that the unionist parties participated in the negotiations. Republicans gradually came to believe that the British government was not serious about real negotiations, and the Sinn Féin leader referred to the new preconditions as "the ambush up the road" (Mallie and McKittrick 1996: 353). The ceasefire ended on 9 February 1996 with a massive bomb at Canary Wharf in London that killed two people.

Despite the return to violence, and the lack of enthusiasm by both nationalist parties for an election, Sinn Féin recorded its best result at the subsequent election to the 1996 Northern Ireland Forum with 15.5 percent (at 42 percent of the nationalist party vote, this was second only to Sinn Féin's 43 percent at the 1983 Westminster election; see Table 5.3). One interpretation of this outcome was that part of the nationalist community gave the British government an "electoral bloody nose" for its perceived failure to sustain the peace process; but it can also be interpreted more positively as an attempt to recommit the republican movement to a "peace" strategy, despite the IRA's return to violence.

What was not immediately apparent but became clear during 1997 was that the Sinn Féin surge of 1996 was not just a temporary blip caused by frustration with the British government but part of a broader process by which nationalist voters provided incentives for Sinn Féin to stick with a faltering "peace process." Described as Sinn Féin's "second coming" (O'Leary and Evans 1997), the party's performance in the Forum election was surpassed at the 1997 Westminster and, later, local government elections, achieving 16.1 percent and 16.9 percent, respectively. Thus, for the 1996–1997 period Sinn Féin averaged 16.2 percent of the total vote and 42 percent of the nationalist vote.[13] Moreover, the party picked up symbolically important seats when Gerry Adams retook West Belfast, Martin McGuinness won Mid-Ulster (see above), and Caoimhin Ó Caolain (SF) won a seat in the Irish parliament (Dáil Éireann) at the June 1997 election. Though clearly losing out to Sinn Féin (see Table 5.3), the SDLP also gained votes due to the overall demographic expansion of the nationalist bloc to a high point of 40.2 percent of the overall vote at the 1997 Westminster election (see Table 5.2). Nevertheless, the electoral threat to the SDLP posed by Sinn Féin was keenly felt by many SDLP party workers and second-rank leaders, even if John Hume prioritised the search for a settlement over his party's electoral well-being.[14]

In the unionist party system, Molyneaux (the UUP leader) had resigned in August 1995 and been replaced by David Trimble, the candidate with ostensibly the most intransigent reputation. Yet again, a politics of ethnic outbidding through the DUP's perennial incantation of communal fears helped pull the Ulster Unionists to a more uncompromising position. In the Forum election, with the UUP on the defensive, the DUP temporarily recovered some ground relative to the Ulster Unionists, winning 44 percent of the combined two-party (DUP and UUP) vote, its best in a non-European election since 1985 (see Table 5.3).[15] The 1996 election, with its strange electoral system (see Chapter 4), reflected a renewed fragmentation of the unionist vote: Three small parties—the United Kingdom Unionist Party (UKUP), the Progressive Unionist Party (PUP) and the Ulster Democratic Party (UDP)—collectively took 9.3 percent of the total vote. Whereas the UKUP is little more than a one-man show centred on Robert McCartney, the PUP and the UDP are more significant as the political representatives of the two main loyalist paramilitary groups, the Ulster Volunteer Force (UVF) and the Ulster Defence Association (UDA), respectively. Although the electoral impact of the PUP and UDP has been modest (3.5 percent in total at the 1997 local government elections), these parties are important for two principal reasons: whom they represent and their willingness to be more constitutionally creative than the main unionist parties. The UUP thus risks being outflanked on all sides, a position that does not aid it in entering risky negotiations with nationalists. In the short term the UUP won the intra-unionist battle with the DUP during 1997 (see Table 5.3), providing some respite from the elections in 1994 and 1995; nevertheless, the UUP's electoral future is likely to be focused more on slowing the process of gradual decline than on reversing its fortunes.

Conclusion

Party competition in Northern Ireland is not simply—or even primarily—a reflection of ineluctable ancient antagonisms. Indeed, it is better understood as an electorally rational contest for position within the constraints of a segmented dual-party system. Given a political system underpinned by a sharp constitutional cleavage and loyalties that are highly ascriptive in character, it is not fruitful to appeal for votes across the entire spectrum (witness the fate of a succession of parties in the bi-confessional bloc). And given the primary salience of the ongoing constitutional conflict, it is not surprising that the main parties are essentially ethno-national, irrespective of what some of them might officially claim.

In a fully functioning (nonsegmented) liberal democracy, parties with ambitions to govern have electoral incentives to moderate their appeals and ideologies. In particular, they attempt to strike a policy balance between retaining party loyalists and appealing for uncommitted voters. Moderation is rewarded and a competitive dynamic tends to push parties toward the centre of the party system, the best place to be for those parties hoping to govern. But in an ethnic party system this logic is all too frequently turned on its head. Since very few voters are not committed to one bloc or the other, there are fewer electoral reasons to be moderate. Indeed, extremist and emotive ethnic appeals that suggest that the group's vital interests are in mortal danger may be highly effective in mobilising supporters who are otherwise apathetic in a context of little change.

An intrinsic feature of ethnic party systems is the constant threat of a politics of ethnic outbidding by rival parties within each bloc. It is common for once-dominant parties (such as the UUP and SDLP) to be challenged by new parties within their own communities who allege "that the existing ethnic party has sold out group interests by its excessive moderation towards the other ethnic groups" (Horowitz 1985: 354). The respective parties in each bloc often attempt to outdo each other in terms of ethnic intransigence—and increased polarisation is the net result. Although some of this can be explained as ritualistic posturing for the purposes of electioneering, the more serious consequence of intra-ethnic competition is that it makes conflict resolution much more difficult. The enlightened compromises required to resolve ethno-national conflicts are less likely to be forthcoming when there are rival parties in each bloc ready to profit by denouncing any deal as a "sell-out."

Leadership is precarious in ethnic party systems, and party "leaders" tend to follow rather than lead their parties. In the unionist bloc, leaders such as O'Neill, Faulkner, and Craig were dispensed with due to conciliatory overtures, and even Paisley has had to be careful not to get too far ahead of his "followers." Prominent nationalist leaders such as Gerry Fitt and Paddy Devlin found themselves out of favour as the SDLP became more nationalist in tone. Indeed, John Hume is possibly the only leader who has been able to lead in directions that (like the Hume-Adams dialogue) are not always popular with his party colleagues.

Although the logic of electoral competition in an ethnic party system is unconducive to conflict resolution, productive inter-ethnic bargaining between elections is not ruled out. What such competition does mean is that talks excluding some of the key parties (either by self-exclusion or by exclusion on the governments' part) are less likely to result in meaningful reciprocal concessions because the participating parties usually cannot afford to have their intra-ethnic rivals outside of the process, denouncing the proceedings. Of course, the absence of an all-party process does not inevitably preclude progress. Negotiations (and any proposed settlement) may be feasible only among the more moderate representatives of each community. However, the political risks to the negotiating parties are increased and the stability of any settlement is diminished, though not doomed, by a partial process.

References and Further Reading

Bruce, Steve, 1986. *God Save Ulster: The Religion and Politics of Paisleyism.* Oxford: Clarendon Press.

Coakley, John, 1993. "The foundations of statehood," pp. 1–24 in John Coakley and Michael Gallagher (eds.), *Politics in the Republic of Ireland.* Dublin: Folens and Limerick: PSAI Press.

Cochrane, Feargal, 1997. *Unionist Politics and the Politics of Unionism Since the Anglo-Irish Agreement.* Cork: Cork University Press.

Diskin, Michael, 1984. "The development of party competition among unionists in Ulster 1966–82," *Studies in Public Policy* No. 129, Centre for the Study of Public Policy, University of Strathclyde.

Elliott, Sydney, 1992. "Voting systems and political parties in Northern Ireland," pp. 76–93 in Brigid Hadfield (ed.), *Northern Ireland: Politics and the Constitution.* Buckingham/Philadelphia: Open University Press.

Evans, Geoffrey, and Mary Duffy, 1997. "Beyond the sectarian divide: The social bases and political consequences of nationalist and unionist party competition in Northern Ireland," *British Journal of Political Science* 27, pp. 47–81.

FitzGerald, Garret, 1991. *All in a Life: Garret FitzGerald, An Autobiography.* London: Macmillan.

Gallagher, Michael, 1996, "Choose your leader?" *Fortnight*, pp. 8–9. July.

Harbinson, J., 1973. *The Ulster Unionist Party, 1882–1973: Its Development and Organisation.* Belfast: Blackstaff Press.

Horowitz, Donald, 1985. *Ethnic Groups in Conflict.* Berkeley/Los Angeles: University of California Press.

Lipset, S. M., and Stein Rokkan, 1967. "Cleavage structures, party systems, and voter alignments: An introduction," pp. 1–64 in S. M. Lipset and Stein Rokkan (eds.), *Party Systems and Voter Alignments.* New York: The Free Press.

Lustick, Ian, 1979. "Stability in deeply divided societies: Consociationalism versus control," *World Politics* 31, pp. 325–344.

Mair, Peter, 1993. "The party system and party competition," pp. 86–103 in John Coakley and Michael Gallagher (eds.), *Politics in the Republic of Ireland*. Dublin: Folens/Limerick: PSAI Press.

Mallie, Eamonn, and David McKittrick, 1996. *The Fight for Peace: The Secret Story Behind the Irish Peace Process*. London: Heinemann.

McAllister, Ian, 1977. *The Social Democratic and Labour Party*. London: Macmillan Press.

McAllister, Ian, and Sarah Nelson, 1979. "Modern developments in the Northern Ireland party system," *Parliamentary Affairs* 32:3, pp. 279–316.

McGarry, John, and Brendan O'Leary, 1995. *Explaining Northern Ireland: Broken Images*. Oxford: Blackwell.

Mitchell, Paul, 1991. "Conflict regulation and party competition in Northern Ireland," *European Journal of Political Research* 20, pp. 67–92.

______, 1995. "Party competition in an ethnic dual party system," *Ethnic and Racial Studies* 18:4, pp. 773–796.

Moore, Jonathan, 1993, "The blue card . . . ," *Fortnight*, No. 320, pp. 12–13.

O'Leary, Brendan, 1991. "Party support in Northern Ireland, 1969–1989," pp. 342–357 in John McGarry and Brendan O'Leary (eds.) *The Future of Northern Ireland*. Oxford: Oxford University Press.

______, 1995. "Introduction: Reflections on a cold peace," *Ethnic and Racial Studies* 18:4, pp. 695–714.

O'Leary, Brendan, and John McGarry, 1993. *The Politics of Antagonism: Understanding Northern Ireland*. London: Athlone Press.

O'Leary, Brendan, and Geoffrey Evans, 1997. "The 1997 Westminster election in Northern Ireland: *La fin de siècle*, the twilight of the second Protestant ascendancy and Sinn Féin's second coming," *Parliamentary Affairs*, forthcoming.

Sartori, Giovanni, 1976. *Parties and Party Systems: A Framework for Analysis*. Cambridge: Cambridge University Press.

Taagepera, Rein, and Matthew S. Shugart, 1989. *Seats and Votes: The Effects and Determinants of Electoral Systems*. New Haven: Yale University Press.

Whyte, John, 1973. "Intra-unionist disputes in the Northern Ireland House of Commons, 1921–72," *Economic and Social Review* 5:1.

______, 1990. *Interpreting Northern Ireland*. Oxford: Oxford University Press.

6

Regional Assemblies and Parliament

RICK WILFORD

Since the imposition of direct rule in 1972, attempts to restore a settled scheme of devolution to Northern Ireland have proceeded fitfully and unsuccessfully. Among other things, the elusiveness of this goal has meant that the U.K. parliament has been constrained to make wider provision for the handling of Northern Ireland matters at Westminster. This chapter explores the continuities and discontinuities involved in the attempts to construct a regional assembly and, more briefly, the procedures that have been developed to handle Northern Ireland matters within the Westminster parliament. Both issues bear directly on the constitutional status of the province, which, unlike that of Scotland and Wales, is a contingent one—resting as it does on majority consent.

The speed with which the Stormont regime was prorogued provided an object lesson in the subordinate nature of the Northern Ireland parliament. Although central government had intervened on a growing scale since 1968, direct rule meant that the province was placed unambiguously in a position subordinate to the metropolitan power in London. The invention of the post of Secretary of State (Bell 1987; Bloomfield and Lankford 1996), enjoying full cabinet status and supported by a team of junior ministers, has provided its incumbents with enormous powers and influence, akin to that of a governor-general of a former British colony (Prior 1986). All legislative and executive powers that had been bestowed upon the Northern Ireland parliament now reposed in one office. Thus, having been marginalised in the deliberations of central government for the greater part of a half-century,

Northern Ireland under direct rule became subject to close political and administrative control from London.

Yet, having asserted its authority, the then Conservative government, through the agency of the first Secretary of State, William Whitelaw, sought to rebuild a provincial assembly out of the debris of the old order—in short, to return power to local politicians. This apparently paradoxical motive was signaled by the instrument that instituted direct rule—namely, the Northern Ireland (Temporary Provisions) Act, which received Royal Assent on 30 March 1972: It was intended to create an interim set of political and administrative arrangements whilst efforts to restore regional government were taking place. Faced with the towering and uncertain seas of the province, British policymakers sought constitutional ballast in devolution, which promised some stability during the initial stormy period of direct rule.

The brainchild of Edmund Burke, devolution involves "the transfer to a subordinate elected body on a geographical basis, of functions at present exercised by Parliament" (Bogdanor 1979: 2). Whereas federalism divides power between a parliament and provincial bodies, devolution maintains the supremacy of the national parliament while at the same time providing a measure of autonomy to a region or regions of the national territory. Although this system of territorial management was considered preferable to other thinkable alternatives—including, for instance, some sort of federal arrangement or full integration into the U.K.—the decidedly political elements of any constitutional equation had to be reshaped. This objective required, perhaps above all else, that the U.K. government be perceived by the contending parties and interests to be dispassionate in its actions: to assume, in effect, the role of (benevolent) arbiter, itself a considerable undertaking (O'Leary and McGarry 1996). Given the speed with which direct rule was effected, none could doubt the capacity of central government to exercise its constitutionally superordinate power. Yet, rather than seeking to impose a "solution" on Northern Ireland in like manner, policymakers sought to create the basis for an agreement that could be built on by local politicians. In this way the role of arbiter would, the calculation ran, find its due reward.

Direct Rule: Phase One

The first attempt by the government to engage the region's political parties in roundtable talks occurred in September 1972 at the Darlington Conference. It was a dismal failure. Only three parties attended—

the Ulster Unionists, the recently founded and bi-confessional Alliance Party, and the NI Labour Party—and they failed to reach agreement on the future shape of government for the province. Undeterred, a month later the government published a discussion paper (HMSO 1972) that introduced three coordinate factors establishing the (variable) geometry of British thinking. First, it stated Britain's commitment to the Union for as long as the people of Northern Ireland (rather than a future parliament—this being the test in both the 1920 Government of Ireland Act and the 1949 Ireland Act) wished to remain within the U.K. Secondly, it indicated a preference for coalition government rather than for majority-rule: "[T]here are strong arguments that the objective of real participation should be achieved by giving minority interests a share in the exercise of executive power." Thirdly, prefiguring the later and decided emphasis on bilateralism, the discussion paper referred explicitly to the "Irish Dimension" of Northern Ireland.

Given the preference for a devolved institution, the onus was firmly placed on political leaders within Northern Ireland to not only consent to such fresh thinking but also to carry their supporters with them. For many unionist politicians, nourished by a history of majoritarianism, the prospect of power sharing was, to say the least, a challenging one. More particularly, the provision for some institutionalised involvement by the Irish Republic was anathema to most of them. In signaling its preference for power sharing, the British government could draw on a model of governing divided societies adumbrated by a Dutch political scientist, Arend Lijphart—namely, consociational democracy (Lijphart 1968, 1969), which provided the intellectual underpinning of attempts to build a devolved structure within Northern Ireland.

The lure of consociationalism rested on its four major institutional characteristics. First, it prescribed government by a power-sharing coalition: Elite accommodation was, therefore, a necessary component of this model. Secondly, it provided for segmental autonomy. Lijphart subscribed to the idea that high fences promoted good neighbourliness and thus proposed that each distinct segment of the wider community should enjoy the autonomy to administer those policies it considers to be central to its identity and well-being. Through such ring-fencing of sensitive issues, any perceived threat to a community's integrity is reduced, thus facilitating the stability of the wider political system. Thirdly, Lijphart proposed that the principle of proportionality should apply in the public sector through, for instance, the adoption of proportional representation (PR) at elections, as well as proportionality in executive bodies and legislative committees, in public employment, and in the allocation of public expenditure. Through the use of PR and the application of ratios to the allocation of public resources, any sense that a particular section of the society is advantaged over others is removed, thus eliminating a material source of grievance and potential conflict. The final element of the model concerns the procedure employed by political leaders to make their decisions. Exemplifying its emphasis on the politics of accommodation, consociationalism relies upon unanimity among elites and therefore endorses a mutual veto or concurring majority principle in relation to their decisions. This device enables the representatives of the relevant communities to protect their most deeply felt interests simply by saying "No."

This "off-the-shelf" model was not intended by Lijphart to be an end in itself but, rather, was a somewhat confected means of enabling effective government to proceed in divided societies in the shorter run. In the longer run it could, *ceteris paribus*, supply the route toward a more competitive political system by establishing mutual trust and confidence among previously conflictual communities—or at least among their leaders. In effect, the British government in the early phase of direct rule was seeking to provide a set of principles and the institutions through which they could be enacted in order to restore a devolved system of government. This objective became clear with the publication in March 1973 of a White Paper (HMSO 1973), whose proposals were subsequently embodied in the NI Assembly Act and the NI Constitution Act of 3 May and 18 July, respectively.

The flurry of legislative activity at Westminster succeeded the referendum (promised by Prime Minister Edward Heath when Stormont was prorogued) held on 8 March to determine the preferred constitutional position of Northern Ireland. Colloquially termed the "border poll," this referendum offered the electorate two alternatives: Either the province was "to remain part of the UK" or it was "to be joined with the Republic of Ireland outside the UK." The poll was boycotted by most nationalists; turnout fell below 60 percent, resulting in a walkover for those endorsing the first option.

The White Paper, which was published twelve days after the poll, demonstrated the government's zeal for devolution. The proposals provided for a new, unicameral Assembly, not a bicameral parliament as was the case with Stormont. The latter, standing prorogued, was subsequently abolished by the Constitution Act of 1973, as was the office of governor. Their demise, as Brigid Hadfield (1992: 8) observes, meant that "the trappings of the mini-state were dismantled." Consistent with the consociational formula, the new Assembly was to be elected by the STV system of proportional representation (see Chapter 4).

The fingerprints of consociationalism were also evident in the proposal that the Secretary of State would play a key role in the formation of, not a cabinet, but an Executive, whose members had to reflect wide support throughout the community: In essence, then, the Secretary of State was empowered to create a power-sharing coalition, led by a chief executive and not a prime minister. The Executive, in turn, would be advised by a system of consultative committees, which themselves were to reflect the party balance in the Assembly. Legislative proposals (termed *measures* rather than *acts*) emanating from the latter were to be subject to scrutiny and approval by the Secretary of State. This policy effectively placed the prospective Executive and Assembly on a very short leash, thereby providing a safeguard against any potential abuse of powers. Control was also exercised by voiding any measures that discriminated on the grounds of religious belief or political opinion. As a means of copper-fastening the safeguards, the Constitution Act (like the 1920 Government of Ireland Act) maintained the right of the Westminster parliament to legislate on any matter for Northern Ireland.

The legislative remit of the Assembly was defined by the Constitution Act of 1973, which sustained the tripartite distinction among transferred, excepted, and reserved matters drawn by the Government of Ireland Act of 1920 (Elliott and Wilford 1987). It was the transferred matters—including agriculture, economic development, education, environment, and health and social services—that fell within the legislative competence of the Assembly, whereas responsibility for excepted matters (including the Crown, defence and foreign affairs, and issues relating to citizenship) would remain with the U.K. parliament. The reserved matters were, potentially, a moveable feast. These—including police, prisons, the Supreme Court, postal services, and a variety of fiscal policies—would normally be the responsibility of Westminster but could be transferred to a devolved Assembly if future political conditions were adjudged to be appropriate. In the first instance, however, they were to remain within the scope of Westminster since the reserved matters were highly divisive.

These proposals were thus the blueprint for a devolved, power-sharing institution, overseen by a patrician arbiter personified in the considerable bulk of William Whitelaw. Although subsequent initiatives changed in matters of detail, the consociational template struck in the first phase of direct rule has remained largely intact. Power sharing marked a clear departure from the discredited *ancien régime* and was a difficult pill for unionists to swallow. However, what stuck in the throat of most was the inclusion of a North-South Irish dimension in the form of a Council of Ireland. The 1920 Government of Ireland Act, which provided the constitution of Northern Ireland during the Stormont era, had included provision for a Council of Ireland, which, due to trenchant opposition by unionists, never met and was rendered defunct in 1925. The reappearance in 1973 of such a proposed body—a precondition of the Social Democratic and Labour Party's participation in the power-sharing Executive—aroused even greater hostility among a new generation of unionist politicians and was to provoke a near insurrection in the form of the Ulster Workers' Council (UWC) strike of May 1974 (Fisk 1975; Anderson 1994; Gillespie 1994).

This new Council of Ireland emerged from negotiations at the Sunningdale Conference held between 6 and 9 December 1973. The talks involved representatives of the British and Irish governments and members of the Northern Ireland Executive designate, chosen from among the pro-power-sharing Assembly members who had been elected on 28 June. In effect, only three of the province's parties were represented fully at Sunningdale: Ulster Unionists, Alliance, and the SDLP. Attempts by the unionists present to persuade the Irish representatives to propose the removal of the territorial claim to Northern Ireland failed; instead, Liam Cosgrave (*An Taoiseach*) offered a declaration—namely, "that there could be no change in the status of Northern Ireland until a majority of the people of Northern Ireland desired a change in that status" (Bew and Gillespie 1993: 73).

The proposed composition and role of the Council and its advisory body, the Consultative Assembly, fractured unionism (see Chapter 5). The Executive coalition, which took office on 1 January 1974, was assailed by loyalists and those unionists who detected in the institutionalised North-South relationship an embryonic all-Ireland parliament. Consequently, the Sunningdale Agreement was never implemented. The chief executive, Brian Faulkner, was forced to resign his leadership of the Ulster Unionist Party on 4 January and, later, in September 1974, would try to resuscitate his following by establishing the Unionist Party of Northern Ireland (UPNI). Within a month of his resignation, the pro-power-sharing unionists were routed in the surprise general election called by Edward Heath. Politically hobbled, the Executive stumbled on until it was brought down by the tumult of the UWC strike of the 14–28 May. Thus ended the one brief interlude in direct rule. At the end of May, the Assembly was prorogued and the U.K. government restored direct rule on an interim basis until 17 July 1974. Thereafter, the Northern Ireland Act of 1974 set out new arrangements for the governance of the province, based upon the NI Temporary Provisions Act of 1972.

Although the first attempt to restore a devolved institution to Northern Ireland ended in failure, it did set a pattern for future British thinking. The terminology has varied, but the principle of power sharing has remained a *sine qua non*. Its constancy has not, however, been matched by provision for the Irish dimension. The British government declared in 1969 that Northern Ireland was purely a matter of concern to them, and by the early 1970s a successor administration had recognised and legitimised a potential role for the Irish government in its affairs. The conversion to an institutionalised Irish involvement was sustained by the Labour government elected in February 1974 which, in July of the same year, produced its own proposals (HMSO 1974), committing it to introduce legislation for the election, via the single transferable vote (STV), of a "Constitutional Convention."

Direct Rule: Phase Two

As recommended by Labour's first Secretary of State, Merlyn Rees, the Convention's task was "to consider what provisions for the government of Northern Ireland would be likely to command the most widespread acceptance throughout the community there." The seventy-eight members of this body would, the government stated, have to recognise three "realities" in bringing forward its proposals: the principle of power sharing, the Irish dimension, and the requirement that its proposals would necessarily have to satisfy the Westminster parliament. In effect, there was policy continuity between the preceding Conservative government and the new administration regarding the essential contours of any proposed devolved body. There was, however, one important difference in Labour's proposals. Whereas the earlier scheme had elaborated a key, controlling role for the Secretary of State, on this occasion the government was to remain, if not at arm's length, then at wrist's length from any ensuing discussions and negotiations. As the then–prime minister was to state in his memoirs: "The initiatives taken at Darlington and Sunningdale, the policies of the Heath Government and of our own, had reached a dead end. No solution could be imposed from across the water. From now on, we had to throw the task clearly to the Northern Ireland people themselves" (Wilson 1979: 78).

At one level this policy signified a more supple approach by the British government. Local politicians would themselves be enabled to design the architecture of a devolved structure, aided by an independent chairman of "high standing and impartiality" (rather than by the Secretary of State), who would officiate at the Convention. With the benefit of hindsight—always a cheap commodity—such a loosening of the government's grip on the discussions may be interpreted as a retrograde move: It soon became apparent that, alone, the parties could not agree to a voluntary consociation.

After some delay, punctuated by a general election in October 1974 (at which anti-power-sharing unionists—UUP, DUP, and Vanguard—won 10 of Northern Ireland's 17 parliamentary seats) and the announcement on 9 February 1975 of an indefinite IRA ceasefire (which itself fanned unionist apprehensions that some sort of deal had been struck between the government and republicans), the Convention began its proceedings on 8 May 1975, a week after its election. However, the writing was clearly on the wall. None of the parties within the warring "unionist family" accepted the inclusion of an Irish dimension, including the UPNI led by Brian Faulkner. But unlike its unionist opponents, who had combined to form the United Ulster Unionist Council (UUUC), the UPNI did endorse power sharing, as did the Alliance Party, whereas the SDLP saw each element as integral to any settlement. Sinn Féin, de-proscribed in April 1974, boycotted the election on the basis that any internal solution trammeled the right of the Irish people to govern themselves.

The UUUC's common platform was for the restoration of the "traditional British democratic parliamentary system"—that is, majority rule. Having emerged as the single largest bloc in the Convention, the UUUC effectively halted any progress—although one member party, Vanguard, did subsequently propose a temporary emergency coalition that led to its expulsion from the Council. After ten months of formal and informal talks and discussions, the Convention's majority endorsed a call for the restoration to a new devolved government of the powers bestowed on Stormont by the 1920 Act. Failing the criteria of the White Paper, this proposal was rejected by parliament. Merlyn Rees did, however, recall the Convention and invited it to rethink its proposals. In the process, he made it clear that cross-border cooperation did not necessarily involve the creation of a Council of Ireland, thereby signaling that the Irish dimension did not have to be formalised. This carrot was insufficient to tempt the majority in the Convention toward an agreement that was acceptable to Westminster, and in March 1976 it was dissolved.

Thus, within four years of the introduction of direct rule, two concerted attempts by successive British governments to engineer the return of devolution had foundered. Moreover, original British thinking had changed to the extent that the institutionalised involvement of the Irish government *à la* Sunningdale had changed, indicating the variableness of the policy geometry. It was also apparent that the British Labour Party had come to the view that any scheme had to be worked out by the province's political leaders. Straddling the efforts of both governments was an adherence to what Christopher McCrudden (1994) has termed "procedural idealism," which provides the institutions, processes, and methods through which an agreed scheme for devolution could be realised. However, such apparent sweet reasonableness did not commend itself to the majority of unionists, who, by the mid- to late 1970s wanted either a majoritarian government or full integration into the Union. Certainly, the Irish dimension seemed at that stage to be less salient in British thinking, which, inevitably, alienated the SDLP.

When Roy Mason succeeded Merlyn Rees as Secretary of State in September 1976, even the procedural approach to institution building appeared to have been abandoned. At his first press conference (Bew and Gillespie 1993: 114), Mason stressed that the task of revitalising Northern Ireland's economy would be his first priority, achieved by improving the security situation and thereby creating a climate that was more attractive for potential external investors. "Positive direct rule" became the hallmark of Mason's tenure, although like his predecessors—and each of his successors—he was unable to resist a political initiative in the form of a five-point plan for partial devolution that was unveiled in November 1977 (Flackes 1980: 297–298). Significantly, though, his tentative proposals entirely omitted the Irish dimension. The initiative petered out in early 1978, and for the remainder of his period in office Mason focused his energies on seeking to implement direct rule—which he apostrophised as "positive, compassionate and caring."

By the time the Conservatives were returned to office in May 1979, the party under Margaret Thatcher's leadership had come, or so it appeared, to eschew any grand designs for returning devolved government to Northern Ireland. Instead, its general election manifesto proposed the creation of "one or more regional councils with a wide range of powers over local services"—in effect, revitalising local government. The idea was rejected by the SDLP on the grounds that it would entrench unionist political control within the province. Within five months the new Secretary of State, Humphrey Atkins, abandoned the proposal and announced his intention to embark on a new initiative, a "Constitutional Conference." Its purpose was defined in a consultative document (HMSO 1979) published in November as seeking to achieve "the highest level of agreement . . . which will best meet the needs of Northern Ireland."

Acknowledging the unsatisfactory nature of direct rule, the government endorsed the restoration of devolution but omitted the Irish dimension from its proposals and discounted discussion of the constitutional status of the province. The proposed agenda for the Conference caused a split in the SDLP, occasioning the resignation of its leader, Gerry Fitt, who was prepared to engage in talks with unionists despite the exclusion of the Irish dimension. His successor, John Hume, took a contrary position and succeeded in persuading the government that relations with the Republic be discussed in parallel talks. However, the Ulster Unionists refused to participate in the Conference, which began in January 1980 attended by the SDLP, Alliance, and the DUP. They got nowhere. The DUP wanted a majority-rule Stormont and the other two parties, a power-sharing administration, whereas the UUP decried the talks as reneging on the government's manifesto commitment and as providing a means to institutionalise a minority veto on any proposals. Inside the talks, the DUP refused to participate in the parallel discussions concerning the Irish dimension. Toward the end of March the initiative fizzled out.

At this stage, the institutionalisation of the Irish dimension was not an element in the British government's calculations. "Unilateral containment" (O'Duffy 1996) seemed to characterise the period from the mid-1970s until the early 1980s, whereas bilateral conflict management by London and Dublin was the hallmark of the Sunningdale initiative. Although Atkins was to try (and fail) again in July 1980 to resuscitate talks on the basis of either a power-sharing Executive or a majority-rule Executive with entrenched safeguards for the minority community, he also ruled out provision for an Irish role. Indeed, in May of that year Mrs. Thatcher had told the House of Commons that the "constitutional affairs of Northern Ireland are a matter for the people of Northern Ireland, this government and this Parliament and no-one else" (HC Debs., vol. 985, col. 250: 20 May 1980). Yet, amid the ruins of these failed unilateral efforts by London, bilateralism was beginning to emerge Phoenix-like. A series of Anglo-Irish summits began in May 1980, leading ultimately to the Anglo-Irish Agreement (AIA) of November 1985 and a new era of joint attempts to fashion a climate for a political settlement (Kenny 1986; O'Leary 1987; McGarry 1988, 1990; Aughey 1989; Hadden and Boyle 1989; Arthur 1993; Fitzgerald 1991, 1993; Cox 1996; O'Leary and McGarry 1996).

However, concurrent with the resuscitation of bilateralism, the British government launched another devolution initiative (HMSO 1982), which, paradoxically, neglected provision for an integral Irish dimension. The scheme for "rolling devolution"—the handiwork of James Prior, who had been reshuffled rather reluctantly into the NIO in September 1981 (Prior 1986)—was announced in April 1982 (O'Leary, Elliott, and Wilford 1988). Modeled closely on its parent Constitution Act of 1973, the White Paper was wedded to power sharing and proposed that a newly elected seventy-eight-member advisory and consultative Assembly should embark on a two-stage process designed to usher in a new political order.

The first stage would involve the creation of a system of scrutiny committees, modeled on the new generation of select committees inaugurated at Westminster in 1979–1980 (Engelfield 1984; Drewry 1985). At one level, these committees would provide a local and potentially effective means of improving the accountability of the blunt direct-rule regime. At another level, the hope in government was that, by working alongside one another in the task of examining the expenditure, administration, and policy of the six local departments (Agriculture, Economic Development, Education, Environment, Finance and Personnel, and Health and Social Services), the members of the committees could develop an *esprit* that would prove conducive to the progression to the second stage—namely, agreement on a scheme for the restoration of devolution. However, failure to agree to such a scheme was not, in the government's view, sufficient to wind up the Assembly before its initial four-year term had expired.

Again, the government refrained from imposing its own blueprint for the return of a provincial Assembly to Northern Ireland—short of the requirement that it had to be founded on a power-sharing basis—instead insisting that local politicians had an "inescapable responsibility" to fashion proposals that would be likely to command "widespread acceptance" throughout the community. Moreover, rather than charging those elected to devise a plan for the wholesale return of transferred matters to a local Assembly and Executive, it provided that devolution could occur in stages, one department at a time—hence the concept of "rolling devolution." The speed and scope of devolution would, in effect, be governed by the spread of cross-party cooperation and the capacity of the parties to carry their respective electorates with them.

This rather novel idea, designed to help build mutual trust and confidence among the parties, was not the only piece of original thinking in the Prior scheme. Its other fresh feature lay in the tests it established for the submission of devolution proposals by the planned Assembly. Whereas in 1973 the Secretary of State used his subjective judgement to evaluate the merits of any such proposal, on this occasion two explicit tests were built into the legislation. First, if a scheme secured the support of at least 70 percent of Assembly members, it would automatically be referred to the Westminster parliament for approval. Secondly, if it was endorsed by a majority of less than 70 percent, the Secretary of State could exercise his discretion by laying the proposal before parliament if he was persuaded that it was capable of mustering widespread acceptance throughout the community. In either case, it would be the national parliament that would take the final decision and not the Secretary of State as was the case in 1973.

The legislation creating the proposed Assembly was enacted on 23 July 1982, and the Assembly itself was duly elected in the following October, convening for the first time on 11 November. However, it was hamstrung from the outset. Bereft of an Irish dimension, the SDLP boycotted the Assembly; so did Sinn Féin, which had reentered the electoral fray at the Assembly election, causing shudders of apprehension not only in Northern Ireland but also in both London and Dublin about the level of support it attracted (see Chapter 5). At the election the Ulster Unionists opted for either integration or the implementation of the Convention report, whereas the DUP opposed power sharing. This left only the Alliance Party committed to the proposals. In the event, the Assembly staggered on until 1986 but never moved beyond the first stage of scrutinising the agencies of direct rule. In short, this initiative also ran into the sand that had piled up in the wake of the Anglo-Irish Agreement (O'Leary, Elliott, and Wilford 1988). Even without the AIA, which undoubtedly hastened its demise, the scheme was destined to fail.

The Prior proposals continued a pattern of incremental policymaking that had become evident since the demise of the Executive in 1974. Some details were altered—the tests of acceptability, the allocation of responsibility for devising a scheme for the restoration of a local Assembly, the pace of the return of legislative and executive powers to local politicians—but the proposals held fast to the essential devolved, power-sharing requirement. That said, the apparent demise of an institutionalised Irish dimension marked a more radical departure from the initiative fashioned at Sunningdale and was virtually guaranteed to antagonise the SDLP, which, since the later 1970s, had turned its face against an internal "solution." In effect, constitutional policy had become more disjointed than neatly incremental. Yet, against a background in which British attempts at internal and unilaterally inspired institution building lay in tatters, and amid a growing chorus of international dismay and disapproval, bilateralism was renascent (see Chapters 10 and 11).

Direct Rule: Phase Three

The renaissance of bilateralism exerted a profound shock on unionists. The AIA's creation of an Intergovernmental Conference (IGC) tasked to deal with political, security, and legal matters and cross-border cooperation, serviced by a Belfast-based "Secretariat" staffed by civil servants from both jurisdictions, was perceived by unionists as a stalking horse for, at the least, the imposition of joint authority over Northern Ireland by the British and Irish governments. Enabling the Irish government to be consulted about a host of matters internal to Northern Ireland without providing a reciprocal arrangement was interpreted by unionists to mean that British sovereignty had been conceded.

Interpretations of the AIA varied widely (see O'Leary and McGarry 1996: 221–241), but regardless of whether one sees it in a positive or a negative light, it ushered in a new era of Anglo-Irish relations. Notwithstanding the fact that it recommitted both governments to search for a consociational formula for Northern Ireland, the Agreement marked a radical departure from the approach adopted since 1974. The refurbished bilateral approach, unlike Sunningdale, set in place an institutionalised Irish dimension not alongside but *before* there was any agreement among indigenous politicians about a formula for devolution. By confining relations to the ministerial and civil service personnel of each state, the AIA also proofed its institutions and procedures against a boycott by dissenters. Perforce, opposition to the Agreement was voiced on the streets and through a variety of other tactics designed to subvert the AIA and all its works, whether real or imagined.

The muscular reinsertion of the Irish dimension into the dynamics of constitutional policy did not impose a *de jure* role for Dublin, although, as Brendan O'Leary and John McGarry (1996: 224) comment, it did represent "*de facto* concessions on how Westminster's sovereignty would be exercised." The affirmation by both governments that "any change in the status of Northern Ireland would only come about with the consent of a majority of the people of Northern Ireland," together with their shared recognition that "the present wish of a majority of the people of Northern Ireland is for no change in [its] status," did nothing to assuage opposition. The accompanying declaration—"if in the future a majority of the people of Northern Ireland clearly wish for and formally consent to the establishment of a united Ireland, they will introduce and support in the respective Parliaments legislation to give effect to that wish"—made it clear that the U.K. Parliament would not act as the safety net for the Union: The contingent status of Northern Ireland was, in effect, writ large.

Despite the shared purpose of restoring devolution to Northern Ireland based on the familiar tests of power sharing ("the co-operation of constitutional representatives . . . of both traditions") and reinstating cross-community support (such that any devolved arrangement would be able to "secure widespread acceptance throughout the community"), this reassurance fell on deaf unionist ears. Moreover, the commitment that the remit of the IGC would be governed by the scope of any agreed scheme for devolution was an offer that its opponents could and did refuse. Indeed, for the next five years there was an impasse: Perfidious Albion, represented by a Conservative government, so alienated unionist and loyalist political leaders that any meaningful talks were stymied.

The hostility of the unionists did not, however, shake the resolve of the governments to engage in bilateral initiatives to manage the situation in Northern Ireland, with London and Dublin acting as proxies for the two respective communities. Initiatives by Peter Brooke, who became Secretary of State in July 1989, to sustain talks were tried, but with no tangible success. Yet, behind-the-scenes efforts by the British government and the SDLP's John Hume to encourage the participation of Sinn Féin in inclusive dialogue were also taking place. In public, Brooke acknowledged that the IRA could not be defeated militarily and promised an "imaginative" response if the violence ceased. Moreover, in stating that Britain had "no selfish strategic or economic interest" in Northern Ireland, Brooke made plain its neutrality on the province's constitutional future—a view later restated by Brooke's successor, Sir Patrick Mayhew.

Brooke initiated a three-stranded formula for interparty talks that has remained intact. The strands to the conflict were defined as (1) that between the two communities within the province, (2) that between the North and the South, and (3) that between Britain and Ireland—with the rider that nothing could be agreed until everything was agreed. What was, and is, missing from this agenda was the Northern Ireland–British strand: In effect, the Union—the constitutional status quo—was ruled out of the proposed talks. Britain's role, in conjunction with Ireland, was henceforth "to help, enable and encourage" the realisation of, to use the terms employed by the AIA, peace, stability, and reconciliation in the province, throughout Ireland, and between the peoples of Britain and Ireland. Furthermore, Brooke recognised the legitimacy of the peaceful and democratic pursuit of a united Ireland and opened the door to participation by Irish republicans in inclusive talks if they renounced violence: "In Northern Ireland," he stated "it is not the aspiration to a sovereign united Ireland against which we set our face, but its violent expression" (Cox 1996: 197).

This posture of studied neutrality by the British government was music to the ears of John Hume, who since 1987–1988 had been seeking to convince republicans that the AIA itself had signaled Britain's neutrality. Hume's task had been to persuade republicans to adopt an unarmed strategy and Brooke's speech appeared to endorse these efforts. In December 1992, Mayhew reiterated Brooke's position by stating that the aspiration to achieve a united Ireland was no less legitimate than that of seeking to retain the Union. What was clear was that Britain and Ireland would not dismantle the intergovernmental institutions embodying the Irish dimension even if an agreed internal devolved settlement could be fashioned.

Although the Irish government does not enjoy an executive role in relation to matters within Northern Ireland (Fitzgerald 1991), that it is routinely consulted about a wide range of issues, as defined by the AIA, represents a sea-change in the *de facto* status of the province. Due to the secrecy surrounding the activities of the IGC and the Secretariat, it is impossible to state with any certainty exactly what input successive Irish governments have had into policy measures implemented within Northern Ireland. However, since 1985 there have been a number of reforms that have the ostensible purpose of improving the social and economic condition of the province.

Whether in relation to fair employment law, educational reform, the targeting of social needs, or community relations, a series of policy initiatives have been undertaken, designed to promote mutual accommodation and understanding among and between Northern Ireland's divided communities. In that respect, the AIA appears to have been the engine driving attempts to improve relations at the grassroots level, despite its failure to secure any tangible forward movement among political elites. This dual strategy—seeking to foster talks among the political leaders along consociational lines while concurrently attempting to improve community relations at less elevated levels—has been described as "inverting consociationalism" (Wilford 1992). The thinking in both governments appears to be that by building trust, confidence, and mutual respect at ground level, the soil in which any agreed devolution package might be planted would prove to be, if not wholly receptive, less hostile than in 1973–1974 when the Sunningdale Agreement was undermined through a popular revolt by the majority.

Realistically, in Northern Ireland community relations are likely to improve only at a glacial pace. This is not to diminish the nature and worth of the reforms that have been put in place. However, as both governments recognise, a balanced political settlement founded upon the inclusive agreement of all parties committed to democratic and peaceful means of conflict resolution—underpinned by majority consent—is the surest guarantee of stability. Hence the Downing Street Declaration of 15 December 1993, which, after further clarification, helped to pave the way toward the ceasefires of August and October 1994 (Rowan 1995; Coogan 1995).

The Joint Declaration for Peace, its official title, gave formal expression to the peace process. Restating that Britain had no selfish strategic or economic interest in remaining in Northern Ireland, it authenticated the right of self-determination by the people of the North and the South to secure unification "on the basis of consent, freely and concurrently given" if that was their wish. Majority consent in Northern Ireland was underwritten by the Irish government, which also undertook to remove those aspects of Irish public life that were perceived to pose a threat to unionist traditions and, as part of an overall settlement, to promote changes to the 1937 constitution embodying that commitment.

The Joint Declaration did not set out a scheme for a political settlement but, rather, defined the terms by which inclusive dialogue among the parties could proceed. In the context altered by the ceasefires of August and October 1994, the governments published their two "Framework" documents in the following February; these elaborated their joint proposals both for the internal governance of Northern Ireland (Brooke's strand one) and relationships between North and South and Britain and Ireland (strands two and three). The former was addressed solely by the British government in *A Framework for Accountable Government in Northern Ireland* and the latter in the bilateral document *A New Framework for Agreement*. Designed to set the agenda for all-party talks, these documents were eloquent testimony to a bilateral approach toward, if not conflict resolution, then at least conflict management, and they indicated that an Irish dimension was integral to any agreement struck by politicians in the province.

In relation to strand one, the relevant document recommended the election of a unicameral Assembly of approximately ninety members empowered to legislate on transferred matters, with the caveat that controversial legislation could be secured only by means of a weighted majority, thereby building in a minority safeguard. The precise extent of devolution would, however, be the subject of negotiations during planned all-party talks. In addition, a system of Assembly committees would be created and charged to oversee the work of the six departments that administer transferred matters, recalling the scrutiny committees established in the 1982–1986 Assembly.

In addition, the document proposed to restore executive authority to local politicians, but in a form radically different from that in 1973–1974. A system of legislative committees was proposed whose chairs would also become the political heads of the departments, thereby conflating law and decisionmaking responsibilities in the one role. Both the chairpersons and their deputies would, consistent with consociational thinking, be ratified by Assembly members in proportion to their respective party strengths. To ensure a system of checks and balances, the document also proposed that an executive Panel, probably three-strong, should be separately elected via STV and, therefore, be free-standing. By deriving its legitimacy from the electorate, the Panel could thereby be inured from becoming a hostage of the Assembly. This body would operate on the basis of unanimity—thus risking the permanent exercise of a mutual veto—and be able, among other things, to reject legislation from the Assembly, with the attendant danger of creating an impasse between the two.

The tracery of earlier devolution proposals is apparent in the document. Although it encompasses some original ideas, its subtext, as O'Leary and McGarry (1996: 338) pertinently observe, is "squarely consociational in nature." The three wise chairpersons on the Panel—likely (based on past province-wide electoral performance) to represent the DUP, UUP, and the SDLP—were to be elected by proportional representation, as were the Assembly members. Moreover, the committees of the Assembly, as well as their chairs/heads of departments and deputy chairs, would be nominated by the Panel according to relative party strengths and thence ratified by the Assembly. The scheme did not entail the creation of a formal power-sharing Executive as in 1973–1974, but it was nevertheless redolent with the notion of a coalescent if not strictly coalitionist style of decisionmaking. The various provisions for checks and balances, including the unanimity rule within the Panel and the weighted majority required for controversial proposals within the Assembly, would operate to prevent simple majoritarianism from subordinating minority rights and interests.

Strands two and three, the exogenous aspects of the proposals, envisaged a cross-border institution or institutions—established by the two national parliaments, not by the proposed Assembly—that in the first instance would be delegated a series of functions by both governments that could be extended through negotiation by departmental heads/committee chairs in the province and government ministers from the Irish Republic. The only constraint on the range of these functions was that supplied by limiting the Assembly's scope to transferred matters. Thus, the extent of future cross-border cooperation would be negotiable and could embrace "consultative," "harmonising," and "executive" functions.

The British-Irish strand would see, via a new joint agreement, the continuance of the IGC whose writ would be circumscribed by the powers devolved to the proposed Assembly. Moreover, as a means of carrying indigenous, especially unionist, politicians along, local politicians would be able, on a permissible basis, to attend and be consulted by the IGC, whereas previously they enjoyed no rights of access to its meetings. Underlining bilateralism, the document committed both governments to act in concert in order to achieve a common position on matters within the purview of the IGC, including arrangements designed to protect civil, social, cultural, and political rights in both parts of the island. The explicitly constitutional provisions of the proposals included the British government's preparedness to modify the 1920 Government of Ireland Act, upon which its sovereignty in Northern Ireland is based, whereas the Irish government undertook to introduce and support changes to Articles 2 and 3 of the Irish Constitution, which express the formal territorial claim to the province—although any such change would require popular consent by way of a referendum.

Although the documents bore the hallmarks of a difficult process of negotiations between the two governments—the prose style of *A New Framework for Agreement* is tortuous—they were designed to produce an agreement among local political parties that involved a "balanced accommodation of the differing views of the two main traditions on the constitutional issues in relation to the special position of Northern Ireland." To reassure any who might anticipate an imposed set of arrangements, both governments reiterated that any agreement as might emerge from all-party talks would have to secure majority consent within Northern Ireland. However, any lingering belief that the third strand could be negotiated away, finessed, or superseded was dispelled. If negotiations failed to produce an agreed devolved scheme, or the Assembly collapsed, or it failed to discharge its functions, the Anglo-Irish nexus, including the development of cross-border relations (albeit at ministerial and official levels) would proceed as indicated by the Downing Street Declaration of 1993. In effect, the offer was clear: Agree upon a devolved structure that included both North-South and East-West institutions or Northern Ireland would be subjected anew to direct rule buttressed by a more sophisticated Irish dimension.

In the event it was an offer that unionists, scenting joint authority, did refuse. Despite the readiness of both governments to consider alternative proposals from the region's parties, thereby lending the documents a certain inherent flexibility, they found favour only with the SDLP and the Alliance Party. Moreover, the growing insistence by the British government that the IRA had to make its ceasefire permanent before Sinn Féin could participate in all-party talks shifted attention to the decommissioning issue, occasioning a crisis in Anglo-Irish relations. Resolution came only with the joint announcement in November 1995 of a twin-track approach: a round of preparatory meetings with the parties designed to revive all-party talks, and the creation of an international and advisory commission tasked to recommend the means by which decommissioning could be implemented and to assess the commitment to decommissioning by the paramilitaries.

The impasse created by the reception to the Framework Documents took a decided turn for the worse when the IRA breached its ceasefire on 9 February 1996. The intention announced just two weeks earlier by the British prime minister that an election to a Northern Ireland Forum would take place thus placed the first region-wide elected body since the 1982 Assembly in a markedly different context. Representatives from the Forum, elected on 30 May 1996, were to attend all-party talks designed to break the deadlock. In reality, they became multiparty talks, since Sinn Féin was excluded until the declaration of a renewed ceasefire by the IRA. This outcome lent asymmetry to the talks, which quickly encountered a range of problems concerning the agenda, procedures, and chairmanship of the proceedings. With no new proposals from either government, the Framework Documents were in effect the baseline for the talks, at least in the sense that they described how the necessary three strands of the Northern Ireland issue could, rather than should, be woven into the fabric of a political settlement.

The renewal of the IRA's ceasefire in July 1997 facilitated the entry of Sinn Féin into the talks some six weeks later. Yet, as the republican negotiating team entered, two of the unionist parties—the DUP and the UK Unionists—exited in protest, thereby changing the balance of political forces around the negotiating table. The absence of these two parties denies the possibility of unanimity, but it does not compromise the safeguards built into the process that are designed to secure consent for any agreed settlement. In addition to generating agreement around the table, the proposals will have to pass two tests: popular consent within Northern Ireland via a referendum, and endorsement by the British parliament. Since the early 1990s MPs have become better acquainted with Northern Ireland matters as a result of numerous procedural reforms that have integrated the province more fully into the parliamentary process. Although there are doubts about the motives that inspired the reforms (Wilford and Elliott 1995), not least the view that they were introduced in an effort to ensure that the Conservative government's increasingly slender majority was bolstered by the support of unionist MPs, they nevertheless have meant that Northern Ireland business is more solidly grounded in the parliamentary firmament.

Northern Ireland at Westminster

Although the geometry of constitutional policy has proved variable, the regime of direct rule, whether or not embellished by the Irish dimension, required that new procedures be put in place at Westminster to deal with all the functions previously carried out by the Northern Ireland parliament. Both the bluntness and remoteness of these procedures have attracted widespread criticism. As one expert in constitutional law has put it: "[T]heir consequences . . . are at best disquieting and at worst deplorable" (Hadfield 1992: 6).

With the exception of the brief Executive interlude in 1974, the vast majority of legislation for Northern Ireland since 1972 has taken the form of Orders in Council, a type of delegated legislation (Punnett 1987). Once laid before parliament by the Secretary of State as Draft Orders, they are unamendable. They come into effect in one of two ways: either by means of the negative procedure, whereby they have the immediate force of law and remain in force unless "negatived" within a period of forty days, or via the positive procedure, whereby both houses of parliament must approve the Drafts, also within forty days. In addition, they must be either accepted in full or rejected in full, whether they represent measures that make the law in Northern Ireland the same as that in Britain or are tailor-made for the province.

To ameliorate this procedure, measures have been taken to enable consultation to take place with local and affected interests (Birrell 1990). This pre-legislative phase involves the publication of a Proposal for Draft Order—accompanied by an explanatory document that sets out the government's thinking behind the Order—and responses to the Proposal are invited within a specified period. One such means of consultation was the practice of laying Proposals before the six scrutiny committees established in the 1982–1986 Assembly (O'Leary, Elliott, and Wilford 1988).

Though something of an improvement, the forms of consultation that have been introduced are no substitute for the normal passage of bills through the legislative process. Apart from anything else, the time allowed for the debate of Orders pales in comparison to that allocated to bills, which are, of course, amendable. Some legislation for Northern Ireland is subject to these normal procedures—notably, "excepted" matters as defined by the 1973 Constitution Act. Other measures are deemed to be of such national import and interest as to merit the full rigour of parliamentary debate—one recent example being the revised legislation on fair employment enacted in 1988 (McCrudden 1990; Jay and Wilford 1991). Indeed, it has always been the case that the government of the day could choose to legislate for Northern Ireland entirely by the usual methods, although doing so would clutter an already overburdened parliamentary timetable.

Of late, there has been something of a growing trend toward inclusive legislation, which is extending law to Northern Ireland on a parity basis with Britain and thereby subjecting it to the normal legislative process, including policies that formally lay within the field of transferred matters (Birrell 1990). At the parliamentary level this trend represents an integrationist development that, at face value, seems at odds with the pattern of constitutional policy. Equally, the creation in 1993 of a Northern Ireland Affairs Select Committee (NIASC), long sought by the UUP (Wilford and Elliott 1995), also bolted Northern Ireland more tightly to Westminster and put it on a par with Scotland and Wales, each of which has had its own Select Committee since the 1979–1980 parliamentary session (Jones and Wilford 1986).

Prior to the establishment of NIASC, and with the exception of the period 1982–1986 when the Assembly possessed its own system of scrutiny committees, the parliamentary scrutiny of government activities in the province was achieved through debates, Parliamentary Questions, other departmental Select Committees, and the Public Accounts Committee. The introduction of the new departmental Select Committee system in 1979–1980 was an important reform enabling backbenchers to examine whatever aspects of the expenditure, administration, and policy of their respective departments they chose. Unlike Wales and Scotland, Northern Ireland was denied such a committee; instead, the Select Committees that were created were enabled to include matters that were the responsibility of the Secretary of State within their remit, insofar as they impinged on their own target departments. In addition, the Select Committees could take evidence from individuals and organisations from within Northern Ireland if it was germane to a particular enquiry. In great measure, though, the opportunity to scrutinise the Northern Ireland Office (NIO), the six local departments, and their associated bodies—all of which fell within the scope of the Select Committees—was, as Derek Birrell (1990: 442–443) implies, largely foregone.

This unsatisfactory situation was remedied in 1993 with the creation of NIASC, which enjoyed the same powers as other departmental Select Committees. Its remit embraces all matters that are the responsibility of the Secretary of State, with the exception of legal matters that are the responsibility of the province's Director of Public Prosecutions. As yet, NIASC has not tackled any sensitive issue likely to cause divisiveness among its thirteen members. However, NIASC's significance lies in its very existence, since it too could be interpreted as an integrationist measure at the parliamentary level. Similarly, the creation of the Northern Ireland Grand Committee at Westminster in the autumn of 1996 (like its existing Scottish and Welsh equivalents, this committee takes Second Readings on legislative proposals, debates the Estimates, and engages in general debates on territorial matters) further dovetails the province into the wider parliamentary system.

These new reforms, required to ensure the proper scrutiny of Northern Ireland matters, were long overdue. Bereft of regional government, the province—under direct rule—experienced a yawning democratic deficit that left much of the day-to-day administration of key services largely unaccountable to both politicians and people.

Conclusion

In retrospect, high policy relating to the restoration of devolved powers to the province has developed through three phases distinguished not least by the provision for an institutionalised Irish dimension. The first, from 1973 until 1976, included that provision; the second, between the demise of the Convention and the Anglo-Irish Agreement of 1985, omitted it; and the third, since November 1985, has elevated the Irish dimension in two respects: (1) through the emergence of a process of bilateral initiatives (which have gained widespread international approval), and (2) by the insistence upon the creation of some form of North-South strand that is capable of securing the consent of a majority. Thus, although the detailed formula concerning how cross-border institutions may be established and what functions they should discharge are left, ideally, to a fully inclusive talks process, political leaders in Northern Ireland know that they must seek to integrate an all-island element into their calculations.

This is not to imply that the wheel has turned full circle since the earliest direct-rule phase. The rigidities of the more nearly stereotypical consociational model of 1973 have been dissolved, but its imprint is still apparent. Moreover, the attempts to invert consociationalism mentioned earlier fly in the face of Lijphart's insistence upon high fences between neighbouring communities. If anything, the efforts to improve mutual understanding and respect for different traditions, to accord them "parity of esteem," implies that in time the fences should be dismantled rather than reinforced. Legitimising the peaceful and democratic pursuit of a united Ireland, together with a stated position of "rigorous impartiality" in relation to the future of Northern Ireland, also denotes substantive changes in the trajectory of British thinking since the tumult of the 1970s.

The reforms enacted within parliament to deal with Northern Ireland matters, though welcome, may seem to run counter to the protracted search for an agreed devolution scheme; but not so. A new Assembly, even one that encompassed North-South linkages, would not dispense with the need for parliamentary oversight of both reserved and excepted matters, neither of which are planned to be devolved in the foreseeable future. Westminster would, in fact, redefine its role in terms of the powers transferred to such a body: As parliament proposes, so too it disposes. Devolution, plus an institutionalised Irish dimension, would not of itself sever the parliamentary Union of the U.K.

References and Further Reading

Anderson, Don, 1994. *14 May Days: The Inside Story of the Loyalist Strike of 1974.* Dublin: Gill and Macmillan.

Arthur, Paul, 1993. "The Anglo-Irish Agreement: A device for territorial management?" pp. 208–225 in Dermot Keogh and Michael H. Haltzel (eds.), *Northern Ireland and the Politics of Reconciliation.* Cambridge: Cambridge University Press.

_____, 1996. "Northern Ireland 1968–72," pp. 11–19 in Arthur Aughey and Duncan Morrow (eds.), *Northern Ireland Politics.* London: Longman.

Aughey, Arthur, 1989. *Under Siege: Ulster Unionism and the Anglo-Irish Agreement.* Belfast: Blackstaff Press.

Bell, Peter, 1987. "Direct rule in Northern Ireland," pp. 189–226 in Richard Rose (ed.), *Ministers and Ministries: A Functional Analysis.* Oxford: Clarendon Press.

Bew, Paul, and Gordon Gillespie, 1993. *Northern Ireland: A Chronology of the Troubles 1968–1993.* Dublin: Gill and Macmillan.

Birrell, Derek, 1990. "The Westminster Parliament and Northern Ireland Business," *Parliamentary Affairs* 43, pp. 435–447.

Bloomfield, David, and Maeve Lankford, 1996. "From Whitewash to Mayhem: The state of the Secretary in Northern Ireland," pp. 143–161 in Peter Catterall and Sean McDougall (eds.), *The Northern Ireland Question in British Politics.* London: Macmillan.

Bogdanor, Vernon, 1979. *Devolution.* Oxford: Oxford University Press.

Coogan, Tim Pat, 1995. *The Troubles: Ireland's Ordeal 1966–1995 and the Search for Peace.* London: Hutchinson.

Cox, W. Harvey, 1996. "From Hillsborough to Downing Street—and after," pp. 182–211 in Peter Catterall and Sean McDougall (eds.), *The Northern Ireland Question in British Politics.* London: Macmillan.

Drewry, Gavin (ed.), 1985. *The New Select Committees: A Study of the 1979 Reforms.* Oxford: Clarendon Press.

Elliott, Sydney, and Rick Wilford, 1987. "Administration," pp. 285–304 in R. H. Buchanan and B. M. Walker (eds.), *Province, City and People: Belfast and Its Region.* Antrim: Greystone Books.

Engelfield, Dermot, 1984. *The Commons' Select Committees—Catalysts for Progress?* London: Longman.

Fisk, Robert, 1975. *The Point of No Return: The Strike Which Broke the British in Ulster.* London: Andre Deutsch.

Fitzgerald, Garret, 1991. *All in a Life.* Dublin: Gill and Macmillan.

_____, 1993. "The origins and rationale of the Anglo-Irish Agreement of 1985," pp. 189–202 in Dermot Keogh and Michael H. Haltzel (eds.), *North-*

ern Ireland and the Politics of Reconciliation. Cambridge: Cambridge University Press.

Flackes, William, 1980. *Northern Ireland: A Political Directory*. London: BBC Publications.

Gillespie, Gordon, 1994. "Loyalist Politics and the Ulster Workers' Council Strike 1974." Unpublished Ph.D. thesis, Queen's University, Belfast.

Hadden, Tom, and Kevin Boyle, 1989. *Anglo-Irish Agreement: Commentary, Text and Official Review*. London: Sweet and Maxwell.

Hadfield, Brigid, 1992. "The Northern Ireland Constitution," pp. 1–12 in Brigid Hadfield (ed.), *Northern Ireland: Politics and the Constitution*. Buckingham: Open University Press.

HMSO, 1972. *A Paper: The Future of Northern Ireland for Discussion*. London: HMSO.

______, 1973. *Northern Ireland Constitutional Proposals*, Cmnd. 5259. Belfast: HMSO.

______, 1974. *The Northern Ireland Constitution*, Cmnd. 5675. Belfast: HMSO.

______, 1979. *The Government of Northern Ireland: A Working Paper for a Conference*, Cmnd. 7763. Belfast: HMSO.

______, 1982. *Northern Ireland: A Framework for Devolution*, Cmnd. 8541. Belfast: HMSO.

Jay, Richard, and Rick Wilford, 1991. "An end to discrimination? The Northern Ireland Fair Employment Act of 1989," *Irish Political Studies* 6: pp. 15–36.

Jones, Barry, and Rick Wilford, 1986. *Parliament and Territoriality*. Cardiff: University of Wales Press.

Kenny, Anthony, 1986. *The Road to Hillsborough*. Oxford: Pergamon Press.

Lijphart, Arend, 1968. *The Politics of Accommodation: Pluralism and Democracy in the Netherlands.* Berkeley/Los Angeles: University of California Press.

______, 1969. "Consociational democracy," *World Politics* 21, pp. 207–225.

McCrudden, Christopher, 1990. "The evolution of the Fair Employment (Northern Ireland) Act in Parliament," pp. 244–264 in Robert Cormac and Robert Osborne (eds.), *Discrimination and Public Policy in Northern Ireland*. Oxford: Clarendon Press.

______, 1994. "Northern Ireland and the British Constitution," pp. 323–378 in Jeffrey Jowell and Dawn Oliver (eds.), *The Changing Constitution*, 3rd ed. Oxford: Clarendon Press.

McGarry, John, 1988. "The Anglo-Irish Agreement and the prospects for power-sharing in Northern Ireland," *Political Quarterly* 59, pp. 236–250.

______, 1990. "A consociational settlement for Northern Ireland?" *Plural Societies* 20, pp. 1–21.

O'Duffy, Brendan, 1996. "The price of containment: Deaths and debate on Northern Ireland in the House of Commons 1968–94," pp. 102–128 in Peter Catterall and Sean McDougall (eds.), *The Northern Ireland Question in British Politics*. London: Macmillan.

O'Leary, Brendan, 1987. "The Anglo-Irish Agreement: Folly or statecraft?" *West European Politics* 10:1, pp. 69–74.

O'Leary, Brendan, and John McGarry, 1996. *The Politics of Antagonism: Understanding Northern Ireland*, 2nd ed. London: Athlone Press.

O'Leary, Cornelius, Sydney Elliott, and R. A. Wilford, 1988. *The Northern Ireland Assembly 1982–1986: A Constitutional Experiment*. London: Hurst.

Prior, James, 1986. *A Balance of Power*. London: Hamish Hamilton.

Punnett, Malcolm, 1987. *British Government and Politics*, 5th ed. Aldershot: Gower.

Rowan, Brian, 1995. *Behind the Lines: The Story of the IRA and Loyalist Ceasefires*. Belfast: Blackstaff Press.

Wilford, Rick, 1992. "Inverting consociationalism? Policy, pluralism and the post-modern," pp. 29–46 in Brigid Hadfield (ed.), *Northern Ireland: Politics and the Constitution*. Buckingham: Open University Press.

Wilford, Rick, and Sydney Elliott, 1995. "The Northern Ireland Affairs Select Committee," *Irish Political Studies* 10, pp. 216–224.

Wilson, Harold, 1979. *Final Term: The Labour Government 1974–1976*. London: Wiedenfeld and Nicolson.

7

Policymaking

ALAN GREER

This chapter concentrates on the structures and processes of policymaking and administration within Northern Ireland since 1972. It begins with a description of the formal institutional structures of policymaking and service delivery and then discusses the nature of the policymaking system using the themes of policy variation and accountability. (For more theoretical accounts of public policy, see, for example, Parsons 1995; Ham and Hill 1993; Hill 1993). Finally, the future development of the policy machinery and processes is considered in the light of proposals for greater cooperation between Northern Ireland and the Republic of Ireland.

The Machinery of Policymaking

Northern Ireland's policymaking machinery reflects both the territorial location of the regional polity within the British state and the legacy of devolution. Despite the absence of a devolved parliament, the formal structures of policymaking still embody the interrelationship among national, regional, and local tiers of government that developed after 1921. Since direct rule, the governance of Northern Ireland has become increasingly complex, involving not just relationships between government institutions but also a weakening of the boundaries among the public, private, and voluntary sectors.

The Government of Ireland Act (1920) laid down a threefold division of functions among excepted matters such as defence, reserved matters such as major taxes, and transferred matters including agriculture, education, and economic development (see Birrell and Murie 1980, Buckland 1979, and Chapter 6 of this volume). Whereas Westminster retained responsibility for excepted and reserved matters, the Northern Ireland parliament was endowed with considerable legislative and administrative autonomy. Since 1972, however, constitutional changes have attenuated the range of transferred matters, particularly in the area of law and order.

The administrative and policymaking system in the province embraces four main institutional elements—the Northern Ireland Office, Northern Ireland departments, local government, and nonelected bodies—which encompass territorial and functional divisions. We now turn to a discussion of each of these elements.

The Northern Ireland Office

During the devolution period the Home Office was the formal point of contact between Northern Ireland and Whitehall, and the relationship between them was, for the most part, conducted at arms-length. The creation of the Northern Ireland Office (NIO) in 1972, necessitated by the introduction of direct rule, meant that Northern Ireland matters gravitated to the heart of government at Whitehall. Although Richard Rose has argued that in "every political sense, the territorial ministries are much more part of Whitehall than they are part of Scotland, Wales or Northern Ireland" (1982: 103), departments such as the NIO have a clear territorial orientation. Indeed, for Rod Rhodes the key feature of territorial ministries is "their *dual* character; they are simultaneously in the centre and for a territory" (1988: 144).

The NIO is responsible for a range of specific functions, many of a "high" policy nature. These include law and order, prisons, political and constitutional policy, and international matters affecting Northern Ireland, including relations with the Republic of Ireland. The NIO is headed by a Secretary of State of cabinet rank who is answerable to the Westminster parliament. Constitutionally the Secretary of State is sovereign, but in practice operational responsibility is delegated to four or five junior ministers who oversee both the NIO and individual departmental functions. Portfolios are allocated amongst the ministerial team, and it is customary for individuals to be responsible for more than one department. In addition to its important specific functions, the NIO provides general advice and support to the Secretary of State. However, owing to the broad nature of the role, the Secretary of State's responsibilities extend into departmental matters such as finance and economic development.

Northern Ireland Departments

The key constituent components of the Northern Ireland Civil Service (NICS) established in 1921 were six functional ministries plus a prime minister's department. Subsequently the original dispensation has been modified to cope with the changing nature of government. A trend toward fragmentation had resulted in some nine separate departments by 1972, increasing to thirteen in 1974 to accommodate the political requirements of the power-sharing Executive; however, a fundamental rationalisation of the administrative structure has since taken place.

In 1982 a sixfold functional division of departments was restored: Finance and Personnel, Agriculture, Economic Development, Education, Environment, and Health and Social Services. Three of these departments—Agriculture, Education, and Finance—have an unbroken lineage dating from 1921, but important administrative reforms have been introduced, particularly since 1979. Innovations such as the Financial Management Initiative, Next Steps, Market Testing, and Competing for Quality have all been applied to the Northern Ireland administration to promote greater efficiency, effectiveness, and economy. Under the Next Steps reforms, for example, a number of executive agencies such as the Prison Service and the Social Security Agency have been established. By 1995 such agencies accounted for 41 percent of the 25,000-strong Northern Ireland civil service, and planned developments will increase this figure to 79 percent (NIO 1996: 298–299).

Under devolved government the Northern Ireland departments were headed by a locally elected minister, responsible to the regional parliament. Direct rule has removed the ministerial head but left the administrative body intact. Grafted somewhat imperfectly onto this body has been the political structure of the NIO. As a result, formally independent individual departments report directly to the Secretary of State but have their own departmental minister who is constitutionally part of the NIO, as reflected in the arrangements for monitoring and control of public spending. Whereas the Treasury treats the NIO like other Whitehall departments, the regional Department of Finance and Personnel (DFP) acts as a mini-Treasury and oversees the spending of the Northern Ireland departments (Thain and Wright 1995).

The complex interweaving between the NIO and the six departments, and between Belfast- and London-based civil servants, places a premium on effective coordination, achieved in part through the control of resources exercised by the DFP and also through the operation of a Policy Coordination Committee (PCC). The PCC comprises the Permanent Secretaries of all the Northern Ireland departments and

NIO representatives, and advises the Secretary of State on policy issues and resource allocation. However, although Michael Connolly and Andrew Erridge argue that there is "little doubt about the influence of the PCC on policy-making" (1990: 27–28), Peter Bell emphasises the fact that the Secretary of State "delineates clear political and strategic guidelines for the resource allocation exercise after consulting his Ministerial colleagues" (1987: 212).

Local Government

Prior to direct rule, county councils were responsible for the provision of major services such as education and health, and borough and district councils were responsible for housing, refuse collection, and recreation. Two basic criticisms have been made of local government during the devolution period. First, efficiency and effectiveness were hampered by the existence of far too many small authorities (some seventy-three elected local councils) with insufficient financial resources. Secondly, political manipulation, particularly anti-Catholic discrimination, undermined the legitimacy of the whole local government structure.

By the 1960s a radical overhaul of the local government system was given added urgency by the outbreak of violence and the British government's desire to promote social and administrative reforms. A series of policy proposals culminated in the publication of the Macrory Report in 1970 and led to a streamlined structure of twenty-six elected district councils with greatly reduced functional responsibilities (Birrell and Murie 1980: 167–171). As a result, district councils now have executive responsibility for relatively minor environmental and recreational matters, often described as "burying the dead and emptying the bins." Nonetheless, the representative and consultative functions of local councils give them an opportunity to influence regional services and participate in a wider policy process (Connolly 1990).

In recent years, local councils have been rehabilitated to some extent as service deliverers—for example, in the area of community relations (Knox and Hughes 1995). Since 1992, moreover, councils have been permitted to spend up to five pence in the pound from rate receipts for the specific purpose of economic development, which in 1995–1996 amounted to a total of £9 million. Setting party differences aside, councils have been energetically employing these funds to improve their local economies. Such cross-party cooperation has been facilitated by the advent of "responsibility-sharing" within councils, whereby mayors and council chairs are rotated among the parties—a trend begun by the Dungannon District Council in 1989. Since 1990 some dozen councils have embraced such responsibility-sharing, and there is a likelihood that it will soon extend to Belfast City Council, which in 1997 elected SDLP councillor Alban Maginness as its first nationalist mayor.

Nonelected Bodies

Nonelected bodies have always been used to facilitate the making and implementation of public policy in Northern Ireland. Even during devolution there was a growing trend toward the use of nominated bodies to administer services that were the responsibility of local government elsewhere in the United Kingdom. The local government reforms of the 1960s, rooted in the conviction that "regional" functions should be provided by larger administrative units under the direction of the Northern Ireland parliament and government, led to the creation of a centralised Housing Executive, four area boards for health and personal social services, and five for education and libraries.

Approximately one hundred of what Whitehall calls "non-departmental public bodies" (NDPBs) operate in Northern Ireland. Stephen Livingstone and John Morison (1995: 15) claim that service delivery boards together account for some 50 percent of public spending in Northern Ireland, around 53 percent of public-sector employment, and about 21 percent of total employment. Important executive NDPBs, of which there were fifty-six in 1996, include the Police Authority and the Fair Employment Commission. Advisory bodies such as the Northern Ireland Economic Council and the Standing Advisory Commission on Human Rights may also play an important role in the policy process.

The official definition of NDPB has some notable exclusions. Public bodies such as the education boards and the Housing Executive are excluded from the official NDPB count on the spurious grounds that they fulfil functions carried out by local government in Great Britain. There are also what the Nolan Committee terms "local public spending bodies." These are organisations such as housing associations that "are neither fully elected nor appointed by Ministers, but which provide public services, often delivered at the local level, which are wholly or largely publicly funded. . . . [T]heir decisions are in many respects part of public policy" (Committee on Standards in Public Life 1995: 5). In 1996, for example, there were forty-four housing associations in Northern Ireland (funded to the tune of £33.5 million) and fifteen health trusts, as well as numerous grant-maintained integrated schools, further- and higher-education institutions, and the Laganside Corporation (see NIO 1996; Weir and Hall 1994).

The growth of, and reliance upon, such bodies is justified in part on the grounds of administrative efficiency. More to the point, their responsibility for contentious areas of public affairs (such as policing and housing) has facilitated a distancing from the sectarian politics that disfigured the performance of local government before direct rule. However, the use of nonelected bodies does raise the issue of political accountability.

Political Accountability

Although Northern Ireland shares the generic problems of accountability, under direct rule there are specific features of the regional political system that make the proper exercise of accountability even more problematic than usual. These include the widespread use of nonelected bodies, the relative influence of civil servants *vis-à-vis* elected politicians, and the shroud of secrecy that envelopes the machinery of consultation established by the British and Irish governments since 1980.

Nonelected Bodies and the "Democratic Deficit"

The widespread use of appointed bodies has been the subject of much criticism, especially concerning their lack of accountability. Moreover, there is a widely held public perception that policymaking is remote and that local people have relatively little influence over the decisions taken in their name. Unionist politicians in particular are trenchant critics of what is variously referred to as the "democratic deficit" or "NIO diktat." Thus the Ulster Unionist Party's 1997 general election manifesto argued for "a new and more accountable democratic system in Northern Ireland which will ensure that 'faceless bureaucrats' and their unrepresentative Quango nominees will no longer rule us from behind closed doors."

Accountability is a multifaceted concept (see Stewart 1992; Day and Klein 1987). For instance, a distinction can be drawn between "giving an account"—which depends upon the openness of government—and "being held to account," whereby sanctions can be applied if there is dissatisfaction about actions taken. In addition, political accountability refers to the relationship between public servants and the people. Though typically thought of as upward accountability toward elected bodies, it can also extend downward to communities and the users of services. Managerial accountability, on the other hand, concerns the requirement that tasks are performed according to agreed criteria of performance—a more technical process that can be conducted by impartial experts such as auditors.

The trend throughout the United Kingdom in recent years has been for political accountability to be replaced by more managerial forms such as public audit, performance indicators, and Citizens' Charters. Northern Ireland has not escaped these changes. Most nonelected bodies in Northern Ireland are encouraged to use performance indicators where appropriate, and to apply the principles of the Citizens' Charters (so far, seven charters and twenty-five charter statements have been adopted). Many are also subject to the scrutiny of the Northern Ireland Audit Office and the Northern Ireland Commissioner for Complaints (NIO 1996; Weir and Hall 1994), but these are clearly no substitute for proper procedures of political accountability.

Much of the criticism concerning the "democratic deficit" centres on the prolonged period of "temporary" direct rule and the so-called Macrory gap (the term refers to the absence of a top-tier regional parliament, which the 1973 reforms assumed would be the locus of upward political accountability for those services removed from local control). Although Northern Ireland elects eighteen Westminster MPs, the accountability problem is exacerbated by the fact that people in Northern Ireland have little or no opportunity to vote for the main British political parties from which the NIO ministers are drawn. Hence the electorate cannot hold to account, via the ballot-box, those responsible for administration of the services that impact directly on their lives.

In addition, an element of political accountability is attained through the representative role of local councils, which provide, for example, 40 percent of the members of education and library boards and 30 percent of the members of health boards. Nonetheless, such individuals have only limited influence, for two reasons: They are in a minority, and the autonomy of boards is severely constrained by policy guidelines and funding mechanisms set by their parent departments. More recent research into education boards, however, indicates that "district councillors wielded considerably more influence than their minority position might suggest" because of their elected legitimacy and awareness of feelings on the ground (Salters and McEwen 1993: 48).

Political accountability can also extend downward toward local communities. Of great significance, aside from the issue of whether board members should be elected, is the extent to which they are accessible and responsive to service users. Ministers can use their power of appointment to create a board that, by including service users and by being more representative in terms of gender and ethnicity, is better balanced than one resulting from the electoral process. Evidence indicates, however, that the majority of board members, whether in public or voluntary agencies, still tend to be drawn from a narrow socioeconomic, age, and gender profile (Heenan and Gray, forthcoming). Although board members are believed to be less representative than locally elected councillors, this description overstates the extent to which local councils mirror the community they represent. Downward accountability can be frustrated by the unrepresentative nature of the boards themselves, by formal upward accountability, and by the operation of powerful professional networks. Indeed, the proposed rationalisation of the structure of education boards, along with increased regional centralisation, seems to reaffirm the view that considerations of managerial efficiency still outweigh those of public accountability.

There is little doubt that criticisms of the undemocratic nature of policymaking and administration do have some validity. Connolly remarks that the depoliticisation of public policy management in Northern Ireland "has perhaps gone further than elsewhere in the United Kingdom" (1990: 79), but concerns about unaccountable nonelected bodies are not unique to Northern Ireland. Equally valid criticisms have also been levied against the reforms made to structures of administration and service delivery in Great Britain. Indeed, in many respects, service provision in Northern Ireland is subject to greater political accountability than that in England and Wales, where locally elected representatives have been removed from many of the boards responsible for service delivery (Greer and Hoggett 1996: 154).

Public Officials and Policymaking

The nature of devolved government provided public officials with both the strategic opportunity and the space to influence public policy. The influence of civil servants in the policy process was strengthened by the weakness of parliament, the relative absence of sources of specialist advice, and the tendency for ministers to work on a part-time basis, particularly before the 1960s (Buckland 1979; Oliver 1978).

At the same time, however, there were important countervailing factors on bureaucratic government. In particular, Patrick Buckland notes a "disregard of civil service advice and bureaucratic processes" during the interwar years (1979: 25). This disregard is partly attributable to the politicisation of administration by one-party government. As Derek Birrell and Alan Murie observe, senior civil servants were "continually in contact with ministers who had broadly the same ideas and points of view, and they were not required to consider alternative policies or to adapt to different political perspectives on problems" (1980: 142). Powerful interest groups such as the Orange Order and the Ulster Farmers' Union could also exert substantial pressure on ministers and policymaking. One result was that discretion varied according to policy sector and in areas "of the greatest political sensitivity, such as education or home affairs, civil servants appear to have had less influence and less scope for initiating new policies" (Birrell and Murie 1980: 144).

If anything, direct rule and the depoliticisation of administration have increased the influence of public officials. And it is not just that civil servants are insulated from local political influence. All NIO ministers have represented constituencies in Great Britain and have had at best tenuous connections with Northern Ireland, with the exception of Ulster-born and educated Brian Mawhinney. On appointment, most NIO ministers have relatively little firsthand knowledge and appreciation of Northern Ireland, although some have had family connections. Although much has been made of the local knowledge of Dr. Marjorie Mowlam, who was appointed Secretary of State in May 1997, most ministers are heavily reliant on the advice and expertise of civil servants—at least in the early stages of their tenure. Opinions vary about the extent to which Northern Ireland is an official-led administrative system (Connolly and Erridgc 1990: 25; Birrell and Murie 1980: 153). In a BBC interview in June 1997, Baroness Denton, an unelected former minister, complained bitterly about the autonomy of the NICS. Accusing it of making decisions without the involvement of elected politicians, she described the NICS as "the ultimate closed shop." Her successor, Adam Ingram, took a contrary view, complimenting his civil servants for the high standards of advice, help, and cooperation he had received since taking office (*News Letter,* 6 June 1997; *Irish News,* 6 June 1997).

Policymaking, Secrecy, and Anglo-Irish Cooperation

In formal terms the role of public officials is to advise ministers on policy formulation and to put policy into effect. This constitutional position has been buttressed by the conventions of anonymity and official secrecy. The cloak of anonymity traditionally worn by civil servants has in some measure been discarded. John Oliver comments that, after the local government reforms, officers in the field were encouraged "to make themselves known to their public so that the public would feel they were dealing with named individual men rather than with faceless officials" (1978: 174).

Open government may be central to the proper exercise of accountability, but official secrecy continues to characterise the work of government, justified on the grounds that it is essential to effective and efficient policymaking. Public right of access to information about the operation of public agencies in Northern Ireland is minimal (Weir and Hall 1994: 95–96; HC Debs., vol. 292, cols. 822–828, 20 March 1997, and vol. 292, cols. 928–930, 21 March 1997). Although they publish annual reports and accounts, most nonelected bodies, including the Fair Employment Commission and the Housing Executive, do not allow members of the public to inspect minutes of meetings, to see policy papers or documents, to attend board or committee meetings, or to inspect registers of members' interests. The health boards allow public access to minutes, hold open meetings (a statutory requirement), and publish a register of members' interests; the education boards voluntarily publish minutes of meetings but do not allow access to agendas or registers of interest. There have been some modest but encouraging signs of a move toward increased openness. In April 1997, for example, the Police Authority, long criticised for its secrecy and resistance to widespread consultation, announced its intention to hold at least one annual public meeting to encourage the public to participate in the policing debate. It also decided to compile a register of members' interests (open to public inspection), provide attendance records, and publish the agenda and minutes of its meetings with the Chief Constable. The Labour government elected in May 1997 has also made clear its commitment to greater openness and the democratisation of unelected bodies providing public services, such as hospital trusts.

The exercise of accountability is further complicated by the influence of external policy agents including the European Union (EU) and the European Court of Human Rights. Even more politically controversial is the increased influence wielded by the government of the Republic of Ireland, particularly since the signing of the Anglo-Irish Agreement in 1985. The Intergovernmental Conference (IGC) of British and Irish ministers enables the Irish government to put forward views and proposals on legislation and policy matters for which the NIO and departments are responsible, particularly where the interests of the minority community are significantly affected. In addition, Article 6 of the Anglo-Irish Agreement gives the Irish government an input into the role and composition of nonelected bodies including those concerned with fair employment, human rights, and the police. This arrangement ensures that the Irish government "has been formally and informally consulted both on the work of these agencies and has vetted the personnel appointed to salient positions within them" (O'Leary and McGarry 1996: 227).

The IGC is supported by a permanent Secretariat of British and Irish civil servants, located at the Maryfield offices in Belfast. For unionists, the operation of this Secretariat is one of the most objectionable aspects of Anglo-Irish cooperation and stands as yet another element in unaccountable government—what DUP leader Ian Paisley often refers to as the "Anglo-Irish diktat." Such emotive language should not be allowed to obscure the kernel of truth in the observation. Kevin Boyle and Tom Hadden, for example, assert that one of the main problems with the working of the IGC machinery has been "the atmosphere of secrecy and intrigue which has surrounded its operations" (1989: 78). To help dispel this atmosphere, they have made a number of recommendations, including the advance publication of agendas and creation of a mechanism for inviting submissions from interested parties. To date, however, little has been accomplished in this respect: The British government has shown a marked reluctance to reveal any information that might shed more light on the role being played by the Irish government within the IGC.

This secrecy inhibits an informed evaluation of the role and impact of the Secretariat in the policy process. In an essentially formal account, Brendan O'Leary and John McGarry argue that the IGC has "no executive authority or capacity, no recognisable instruments of state, such as taxation, expenditure or coercive powers, and has no formal policy implementation function" (1996: 226). The establishment of the Secretariat has institutionalised Anglo-Irish cooperation, but the IGC "fundamentally is no more than a policy-formulation forum which the Secretary of State for Northern Ireland can choose to take into consideration, concur with or ignore" (O'Leary and McGarry 1996: 226).

Other interpretations stress the informal dynamic of the IGC. John Loughlin comments, for example, that the IGC does "exercise an important influence over policy" (1992: 71), and Joseph Ruane and Jennifer Todd remark that it gives the Irish government "a role in policy-making" that, although imprecise, was, as Garret FitzGerald claimed, "more than consultative but less than executive" (1996: 134–135). Nevertheless, Loughlin stresses the IGC's concern with "high" politics and sees "no evidence that it affects the running of the Northern Ireland departments or the other administrative agencies in Northern Ireland" (1992: 73). However, it is difficult to sustain this distinction in practice because apparently low-salience issues may have important implications for "high" politics. In addition, there are some more recent indications that the government of the Republic interprets its role much more widely to encompass, for example, public expenditure (*Belfast Telegraph*, 9 April 1997). On the other hand, a certain nationalist disillusion, borne from a feeling that the Anglo-Irish Agreement has not had the expected impact on specific policy issues such as religious discrimination, may indicate that important political factors constrain the extent to which the Irish government can influence policy through the IGC.

If it is accepted that the mechanisms of political accountability in Northern Ireland need to be strengthened, the question is how best this can be achieved. In the absence of an overall political accommodation, the restoration of powers to local councils would risk a repeat of the pre-1972 experience, when democratic local government in Northern Ireland was notable by its absence. Ad hoc adjustments have been made to the administrative system in an attempt to render it more accountable and responsive—for example, through the creation of the Northern Ireland Select and Grand Committees at Westminster (see Chapter 6). But the paradox is that the integration of Northern Ireland into the Whitehall system tends to institutionalise the accountability gap at the regional level. Downward accountability could also be strengthened by making nonelected boards more representative and responsive to those whom they serve. Modern governance, given the increasingly blurred boundaries among the public, private, and not-for-profit sectors, requires new thinking about how those responsible for public services relate to local communities and civic associations. Ultimately, however, the development of a proper system of political accountability for Northern Ireland depends upon the restoration of devolved regional government. Political accountability would then extend upward from the service delivery agents to a regional assembly elected by the people of Northern Ireland.

Policy Variation

In addition to the case made for accountability, it is often argued that more responsive government is one of the chief advantages to be gained from devolution. The conviction is that devolution will permit the formulation and sympathetic implementation of policies designed to suit regional needs. Conditions in Northern Ireland are in many respects different from those in Great Britain. And these basic constitutional and political differences give rise to regionally specific problems such as religious discrimination. Different socioeconomic conditions, such as the relatively higher incidence of poverty and unemployment in Northern Ireland, and the predominance of relatively small family farms there, may also require different policy prescriptions.

It does not follow, however, that the flexibility and responsiveness needed to cope with such differences require legislative devolution (see Buckland 1979: 277–280). The critical question in policymaking terms is to what extent the structures and processes of policy formulation and implementation, whether under legislative devolution or administrative decentralisation, can reflect and incorporate territorial differentiation. Opinions are divided, for example, regarding the scope for variation that legislative devolution provided in practice. Nevil Johnson (1975: 4) opts for a centrifugal view, arguing that the clout of central government ensured broad uniformity in services and standards, whereas Birrell and Murie (1980: 266) stress centripetal pressures and claim that the practice of devolution entailed substantial variations from the legislation and standards operating "across the water."

Direct rule has also affected the range of policy variation, although there is some dispute about the impact. Birrell and Murie, for example, argue that direct rule has not meant an "end to variations in social and economic policy" (1980: 296), whereas Rose (1982: 113–115) has stressed a trend to uniformity with Britain. Capacity for variation is also linked to the existence of territorial policy networks that attempt to defend and promote regional interests (Rhodes 1988). This capacity may mean either the development of policies designed particularly for Northern Ireland or the adoption of uniform policies for the United Kingdom as a whole. The operation of regional policy networks is constrained, however, by national-functional networks of which regional organisations may form a part. Moreover, Northern Ireland's policy agenda is governed in large measure by the wider national interests of the United Kingdom.

Explanations of policy variation in Northern Ireland, whether under direct rule or devolution, need to take account of the heterogeneity of policy sectors and issues (see Greer 1994; Connolly and Loughlin 1990; Birrell and Murie 1980). The notion of a policy continuum is helpful here. At one end there is minimal variation from national policies (what has been referred to as "parity" or "adoption"); at the other extreme there is considerable scope to formulate policies to suit local conditions ("particularity" or "adaptation"). Policy variations can best be demonstrated by a brief examination of specific case studies. These must necessarily be selective, but in this chapter the concern is with public expenditure, fair employment/fair treatment, and EU issues.

Public Expenditure Planning and Priorities

Under direct rule, Northern Ireland has been included within the Whitehall public expenditure process, although its arrangements remain distinctive in many respects. Financial resources for Northern Ireland are allocated according to a percentage formula that is related to British expenditure on equivalent programmes (Thain and Wright 1995: 307–313; Heald 1994: 148). This arrangement provides a block grant that the Secretary of State for Northern Ireland can distribute, within constraints, to mould public expenditure priorities to local needs.

In the context of policy variation, therefore, the key consideration is the extent of flexibility in resource distribution. Discretion in expenditure has advantages for both the territory and the Treasury. For the Treasury it encourages departments to make efficiency savings that can then be diverted to other spending priorities, whereas the system gives the territorial departments some flexibility to allocate resources to local priorities (Thain and Wright 1995: 326–327).

There are a number of constraints on this freedom. First, only around 90 percent of government expenditure in Northern Ireland comes under the control of the Secretary of State. Excluded, for example, are national agricultural programmes and resources obtained from a variety of EU-funded programmes. Secondly, significant spending programmes are determined in Whitehall—notably, social security, which accounts for more than 30 percent of public expenditure. Thirdly, political factors and the Treasury's overall control of the system acts as a brake on discretion, ruling out, for example, spending allocations that run counter to overall government policy. What remains is a relatively small sum, estimated by Colin Thain and Maurice Wright at approximately £30 million in 1992, that can be distributed in line with local priorities and be used incrementally to build up an innovative and distinct territorial programme (see Thain and Wright 1995).

Under direct rule, the level of identifiable general government expenditure (per capita) in Northern Ireland has consistently been higher than that in other parts of the United Kingdom (see Table 7.1). Though striking, such disparities may reflect more intractable social and economic problems, a previous pattern of the relative underfunding of public services in relation to needs, and the costs of security.

Spending patterns in Northern Ireland reflect the nature of the salient political, economic, and social problems facing the region. There are three main public expenditure priorities: preserving law and order, promoting self-sustaining economic growth, and "targeting social need." It is not surprising, given the scale of political violence, that expenditure on law and order has been a relatively heavy drain on public funds, accounting for some 11 percent of the more than £8 billion of planned public expenditure for 1996–1997 (excluding expenditure on the army, which is borne by the Ministry of Defence). With the paramilitary ceasefires in 1994, the tantalising prospect was that

TABLE 7.1 Identifiable General Government Expenditure (per capita)

	£ per capita	*Relativities*	
	1994–95	*1986–87*	*1994–95*
U.K. average	3760	100	100
Northern Ireland	4976	147	132
Scotland	4505	124	120
Wales	4208	109	112
England	3614	96	96

Sources: Treasury (1996); Heald (1994).

significant resources—estimated at nearly £300 million from the 1994 and 1995 expenditure surveys—could be redirected into other spending programmes. However, the breakdown of the IRA ceasefire, and other major public-order problems such as those surrounding Orange Order parades, entailed the reallocation of resources back to the law-and-order budget (HC Deb. 292, cols. 531–532, 18 March 1997).

In the area of economic development, Northern Ireland has continued to operate some significant policy variations since 1972. Institutions such as the Industrial Development Board have persisted, despite the downgrading of the notion of active regional policy in the United Kingdom after 1979. Programmes for inner-city regeneration, such as Making Belfast Work (MBW) and the Londonderry Initiative, allow some resources to be targeted to areas of greatest need (see Gaffikin and Morrisey 1990: 140–149). However, although there is clearly some scope within which to attune programmes to local needs, regional policy is formulated and implemented within the overall context of macro-level ideological and political changes. One result has been that the emphasis in economic development has moved from a concentration on attracting inward investment to more supply side–oriented strategies such as deregulation, development of an indigenous enterprise culture, and improvement of competitiveness. Initiatives such as the Community Economic Regeneration Scheme and the creation of Area Partnerships, which promote collaboration among public-, private-, and voluntary-sector interests, are also clearly influenced by national developments.

In 1991, Targeting Social Need (TSN) was announced as a third public expenditure priority that would apply across all departments and programmes (Osborne 1996; Quirk and McLaughlin 1996). Clearly the need to tackle problems of social deprivation did not just suddenly emerge in the late 1980s. Rather, the importance of TSN lies in the way in which social need has been reconceptualised within the general context of the development of religion-specific policies that "seek to redress socio-economic inequities between the two ethno-religious communities" (Osborne 1996: 181). However, the TSN initiative is shrouded in confusion. It is unclear, for example, whether the aim is to tackle social need generally or to promote the reduction of Catholic disadvantage in particular. Indeed, Pádraic Quirk and Eithne McLaughlin argue that TSN is "a principle awaiting definition, operationalisation and implementation" (1996: 183). Experience to date indicates that TSN has had little impact on public spending and departmental policy formulation. One key factor is that the desire to maintain parity of provision with Great Britain constrains significant policy innovation and change, especially in the short term, and hinders the implementation of TSN as a public expenditure priority. Nevertheless, its introduction does indicate the importance attached by government to ensuring the equitable distribution of public spending between the two communities. The subtext of TSN, and of measures designed to tackle religious discrimination in the employment process, appears to be a determination to ensure fairness and social justice in the allocation of resources throughout Northern Ireland, including opportunities for work.

Fair Employment and Fair Treatment

The issue of fair employment is inextricably bound up with more general Catholic feelings of alienation and with the fundamental political problems in Northern Ireland. Reliable data, drawn from census returns and other sources, show that Catholics in Northern Ireland are still more than twice as likely to be unemployed than Protestants, although the differentials are greater for men than for women (see Osborne 1996; Cormack and Osborne 1991b; Smith and Chambers 1991). Much more controversial are the imputed causes of such differentials, and debates still rage about direct discrimination, education, attitudes toward work, and the nature of the labour market. Finally, the question remains as to whether disadvantage should be tackled through the use of specific public policy instruments to create equal employment opportunities and stamp out discriminatory practices.

A body of fair employment legislation has developed, somewhat incrementally, since the report of the van Straubenzee working party in 1973 (Rose and Magill 1996; Cormack and Osborne 1991a; Jay and Wilford 1991; McCrudden 1988). It is clear that the 1976 Fair Employment Act, which established a Fair Employment Agency (FEA) to tackle discrimination and promote equality of opportunity, failed to produce a significant reduction in the extent of Catholic disadvantage. The relative ineffectiveness of the policy was central to the decision to reform the legislation; but also crucially important were the criticisms voiced by influential external actors such as the Irish government, especially through the Anglo-Irish Conference. In addition, the Irish-American lobby has linked fair employment to U.S. investment through its campaign on the MacBride Principles, which stress, for example, increased representation in the workforce of individuals from underrepresented religious groups, protection of minority employees in transit and at place of work, the outlawing of provocative emblems, special training programmes for employees from minorities, and the development of assessment and recruitment procedures aimed at those with the potential for advancement (Cormack and Osborne 1991a: 16).

Robert Cormack and Robert Osborne argue that there is little doubt that the reforms owe "much to the international context of the Northern Ireland problem" and comparatively little to the government's "commitment to promoting equal opportunities" (1991a: 46). Internal political considerations have also been a factor. The reform debate took place in the context of a phase of "positive direct rule," during which the senior civil service was "far more vigorous, interventionist and anxious to modernise both itself and Northern Irish society at large" and recognised thc need for more radical action to tackle Catholic disadvantage (Jay and Wilford 1991: 20–21).

The 1989 Fair Employment Act, intended as a new improved model of anti-discrimination law, transformed the Fair Employment Agency into a better-resourced Fair Employment Commission and a separate Fair Employment Tribunal. Positive discrimination and quotas were again deemed inappropriate, but employment equality law was substantially strengthened. For example, there was a significant move toward mandatory affirmative action to achieve "fair participation," encouragement of targets and timetables, stricter contract compliance, and improved monitoring, registration, and enforcement measures. In addition, the Fair Employment Act made indirect discrimination illegal. The result is arguably "not only the most stringent anti-discrimination legislation in the UK but also in Europe" (Osborne 1996: 185). However, Cormack and Osborne (1991a: 38) caution that "only relatively small changes in the broad socio-economic profiles of the two communities can be expected. It is almost inevitable, therefore, that demands for the further strengthening of the legislation towards a 'quotas' policy will continue."

Undoubtedly, the fair employment legislation represents a specific and innovative response to particular regional conditions, evidenced by the willingness of the government to consult widely and take on board suggestions for the improvement of the legislation. Of particular strategic importance was the bipartisan agreement in parliament on the necessity for exceptional treatment to cope with specific territorial conditions. In part, this agreement was dictated by the need to justify state intervention in the employment market at precisely a time when neo-liberal suspicion of labour market regulation was dominant.

Of perhaps much greater long-term significance is the broadening of the fair employment approach from a narrow concern with employment disadvantage into a general strategy whereby equality of opportunity influences the whole range of social and economic policy. Policy developments since the late 1980s have illustrated the influence of arguments that all government policies "should be subjected to the test of whether their effect furthers or retards equality of opportunity" (McCrudden 1991: 263–264). First, in 1987 a Central Community Relations Unit was established to "ensure that policy decisions within government are informed by an evaluation of their possible effect on community relations" (Gallagher 1995: 37). The result was that community relations were placed at "the heart of the government's decision-making process within the civil service" (Knox and Hughes 1995: 46). Secondly, in 1990 "equal opportunity proofing" of all government policy and legislation was introduced to ensure that they do not contribute to discriminatory practices. Thirdly, Targeting Social Need is intended to guide policy formulation and priority setting within departments. Fourthly, in 1994 equal opportunity proofing was revamped through the introduction of Policy Appraisal and Fair Treatment (PAFT) guidelines designed "to secure 'equitable' public policy making and implementation" (Osborne 1996: 181). Although they have no statutory basis, these guidelines stress that policy formulation and implementation at all levels of government activity must take account of the need to promote equality and equity.

Although the fair employment legislation has been influenced by contemporary British laws on race and gender equality, the initiative demonstrates a high degree of variation and reflects the need to formulate policies to suit particular local conditions. Conversely, the parity concept is clearly much less useful as an explanation of policy developments both in the specific area of fair employment and in the general approach to equality of opportunity.

The Influence of the European Union

Coinciding almost directly with direct rule, the United Kingdom's entry into the European Community (now the EU) in 1973 has had a crucial impact on Northern Ireland. The EU influences the policy process in Northern Ireland in two related ways. First, it is an important actor and resource in the wider political and constitutional process; and, secondly, the role of the EU is significant in particular policy areas where it has competence—for example, in regional development, agriculture, and fisheries.

At the level of "high" politics, Northern Ireland's membership in the EU, and the potential constitutional implications of same, has generated much controversy. Whereas many unionists have always been sceptical of the benefits of EU membership, nationalists such as SDLP leader John Hume have regarded increasing European integration as a means of promoting greater links, if not eventual unification, between the two parts of Ireland (see McGarry and O'Leary 1995: 279–282). EU institutions, particularly the parliament, have provided a forum where the political problems of Northern Ireland can be discussed. However, there is fundamental disagreement about EU intervention in the internal affairs of member states and the extent to which such intervention can contribute directly to a resolution of the political problems in Northern Ireland (Moxon-Browne 1992; Hainsworth 1990). This disagreement was demonstrated by the differing responses to the 1983 investigation by the Danish MEP Niels Haagerup, which was sponsored by the Political Affairs Committee of the European parliament on the initiative of John Hume. Unionists not only rejected many of the recommendations of the report (including increased cross-border cooperation), but they also questioned whether the European parliament had any competence on a matter that they regarded as an internal United Kingdom matter.

EU competence on specific policy issues is much less likely to lead to disputes between the political parties in Northern Ireland. Indeed, unionist and nationalist politicians often cooperate to secure European funding for regional policy sectors. Although there has been some debate about to what extent Northern Ireland benefits financially from EU membership, even as an Objective 1 region, several policy programmes and sectors are clearly advantaged. Agriculture, for example, receives substantial sums from the Common Agricultural Policy's (CAP) price and structural support mechanisms. Structural funds have also been used to improve the industrial and transport infrastructure. And specific programmes, such as Links Between Actions for the Development of the Rural Economy (LEADER) and A Community Initiative to Assist Border Areas (INTERREG), have provided funding for rural regeneration and border areas. The EU also funds programmes under the Special Support Programme for Peace and Reconciliation (also known as the "Delors package"), which was agreed upon in July 1995 in the wake of the paramilitary ceasefires. Assessment of the scale and importance of EU funding is complicated by the vexed issue of additionality. EU financial support is intended to supplement that provided by national governments, but there is a strong suspicion that it is often used to offset national funding. A definitive judgement on the additionality issue in the Northern Ireland context is difficult to make, but it would be very surprising if the British government did not take EU contributions into account when considering the level and nature of public spending (see Hainsworth 1990; O'Leary, Elliott, and Wilford 1988: 143–144).

In terms of the policy process, the removal of the locus of responsibility for many important policy matters from London to Brussels has altered the roles and behaviour of the territorial policy actors. For example, pressure groups such as the Ulster Farmers' Union, often in cooperation with their counterparts in Britain and other EU states, try to influence policy directly through lobbying in Brussels. Groups also work indirectly through national governmental channels. In agriculture, for instance, demands may be communicated to Brussels through the regional Department of Agriculture (DANI) and the NIO, or via the Ministry for Agriculture, Fisheries, and Food (MAFF) in London. On important issues, however, policy is negotiated by British ministers at the European Council level, and there is only limited scope for regional interests to influence the outcome. The absence of a direct regional input has generated strong criticism from both unionists and nationalists and prompted demands for improved links between Northern Ireland and the EU (Greer 1996; Hainsworth 1990).

The EU influences some policy sectors and issues more than others. In some cases it has promoted parity throughout the United Kingdom in both policy formulation and implementation; in other cases EU membership has permitted the development of a specific regional approach (Hainsworth 1990: 77). In agriculture, participation in the CAP has increased the scope for particularity in the implementation of certain schemes, including the sheepmeat regime. Some EU schemes are unique to Northern Ireland; others operate throughout the island in order to avoid border complications. In addition, CAP may reinforce policy uniformity and make the formulation of a distinctive regional policy even less likely. In the policy disputes about milk quotas in the mid-1980s, and in the actions taken to counteract bovine spongiform encephalitis (BSE) in the 1990s, farmers in Northern Ireland sought adaptations to take account of regional conditions. Although some variation was possible, there was much criticism of the inadequacy of the milk quota arrangements, and policy continued to be guided by the need for sympathetic implementation within the overall parity approach (Greer 1996). Similarly, during the BSE crisis, proposals for separate treatment for the regional beef sector were generally supported within Northern

Ireland (and, indeed, throughout Europe), but wider political considerations within the U.K. restricted the scope for variation.

Overall, therefore, the EU has had a differential impact on public policy in Northern Ireland. Although it is important in some areas, such as agriculture, it has left sectors such as education relatively untouched. And even in agriculture, the extent of EU influence varies according to the nature of the issue. In terms of parity and particularity, the policy process in some areas mirrors that in the United Kingdom as a whole; in others, specific territorial conditions have been acknowledged and incorporated into policy development. Moreover, although EU funding is undoubtedly significant in some sectors, the fact remains that the total of EU support for Northern Ireland is dwarfed by the British subvention.

The Policy Process and Political Developments

From this examination of specific policy sectors it seems clear that variety is the defining characteristic of the nature of regional policy development. Each of the above examples illustrates that policy reflects a basic tension between parity and particularity. A definitive judgement about which of these pressures best encapsulates the nature of the policy process in general, or even that of specific policy sectors, is difficult to make. But the fundamental point is that the extent of policy variation that is possible differs not only between sectors but also between programmes within sectors, both concurrently and over time. In some programme areas, such as social security, there is a high degree of uniformity across the United Kingdom, whereas in others there has been some scope for sympathetic implementation, both during the devolution period and since EU entry. Where finance is less crucial and where specific territorial factors are important, the Northern Ireland departments have relatively more autonomy and the policy pattern may be characterised much more by adaptation to local circumstances.

Although finance is of fundamental significance, it is important not to see it as a unicausal factor determining the capacity for policy variation. Indeed, several other factors also influence the nature of policy development, including the salience of the issue (whether "high" or "low" politics), the existence of regional policy networks, the distinct regional political and social context, constraints (both formal and informal) imposed on and from the centre, and the political ideologies, choices, and imperatives generated both in the centre and in Northern Ireland itself. Since 1979, much policy development has been strongly influenced by the wider project of successive Conservative governments, designed to expose large areas of public life to market forces. This helps to explain the parity approach in Northern Ireland on matters such as Sunday trading and licensing laws. However, although parity has been the dominant force in policy development, Northern Ireland does not always react to external forces. Some argue that Northern Ireland has been used as a test-bed for programmes that are subsequently extended to Great Britain, including the emasculation of local authority power and the development of rigorous law-and-order policies.

"Fair treatment" has recently become a buzz-phrase in the Northern Ireland context. What it signifies is precisely what the parity approach has always been about—namely, equity of treatment for all within the United Kingdom. Different needs and different structures may justify different treatment, but this fact should not unfairly disadvantage, or advantage, one area of the United Kingdom over another. The key question is whether the requirement for fair treatment in the Northern Ireland context is compatible with the parity principle. Some argue that the broadening of the fair employment approach in Northern Ireland toward a more all-encompassing concern with fair treatment seems to provide the grounds on which a greater variation across the whole range of public policy might be justified. According to Cormack and Osborne, for example, measures such as equal opportunity proofing have the "potential to open up a major new dimension to the development of public policy in Northern Ireland" in that it threatens to displace parity as a "new guiding system for policy" (1991a: 35). However, there are still significant constraints on the development of innovative policies in the overall United Kingdom context. Thus Osborne notes that it is "not difficult to see a considerable resistance from the Home Office to Northern Ireland developing a suite of religion specific policies because of the potential 'read-across' to Britain in relation to gender, race and ethnicity" (Osborne 1996: 197).

North-South Frameworks

One way such constraints might be overcome is through the recasting of the political relationships between Northern Ireland and Great Britain as part of an overall constitutional settlement. In the Framework Documents of February 1995, the British and Irish governments agreed on the need to establish "new institutions and structures to take account of the totality of relationships and to enable the people of Ireland to work together in all areas of common interest while fully respecting their diversity" (*Frameworks for the Future, Part II,* 1995: para. 5). A North-South Body, drawn from the Irish government and from new democratic institutions in Northern Ireland, would carry out delegated functions over a range of designated matters in which there was a common interest, such as the mutual benefits to be gained from cooperation, the achievement of economies of scale, and the avoidance of unnecessary duplication of effort. In principle, any responsibilities transferred to a Northern Ireland assembly could be designated to the North-South Body, which would have an important role in developing an agreed all-island approach on EU matters.

The prime candidates for designation to the North-South Body were sectors such as tourism, economic development, and agriculture. First, on *executive* matters, including sectors involving a natural or physical all-Ireland framework and EU programmes, the North-South Body would be directly responsible for the formulation and implementation of agreed policies. Clearly this arrangement opened the way for the joint implementation of a CAP regime for Ireland. Secondly, on *harmonising* matters—for example, transport, energy, trade, health, social welfare, education, and economic policy—both sides would be obliged to seek agreement on common policy, although implementation might be undertaken separately. Thirdly, the North-South Body would be a *consultative* forum with a duty to consult about policy and exchange information, but with no formal requirement for agreement, policy harmonisation, or joint implementation. Designated matters could be moved on the scale among consultation, harmonisation, and executive action. But downgrading would not be likely, given the express intention that the "remit of the body should be dynamic, enabling progressive extension by agreement of its functions to new areas" (*Frameworks for the Future, Part II,* 1995: para. 38).

Such institution building would clearly have a significant impact on the structures and processes of policymaking and implementation, on mechanisms of accountability, and on the nature and extent of policy variation. Bear in mind, however, that the proposals in the Framework Documents are primarily motivated not by considerations of policy but by fundamental political and constitutional factors. This is precisely why the proposals are controversial. Unionists, for example, are hostile to the idea that the envisaged cross-border institutions should be dynamic because they fear the constitutional implications much more than any impact on policy.

Disadvantages in respect of efficiency, effectiveness, and accountability, as well as practical problems of implementation, might be regarded by many, including the British and Irish governments, as a small price to pay if the overall result were to be a comprehensive and agreed political settlement. Yet the important implications for the policy process should not be overlooked. In terms of accountability, there is a danger that the political role ascribed to cross-border bodies might lead to a further entrenchment of technocratic policymaking. The desire to insulate North-South institutions against criticism and obstructionist tactics by hostile elements should not prevent openness and proper political accountability. Care needs to be taken to ensure that any such bodies are made amenable to democratic control, perhaps achieved in part through the strengthening of the institutions of civil society (Anderson and Goodman 1997).

Implementation of the proposals for all-Ireland institutions would also have an important effect on the capacity for, and nature of, policy variation. Indeed, it would completely recast the traditional parity dynamic. Since the creation of Northern Ireland in 1920, developments in Britain have been the benchmark against which territorial policymaking has been considered. For many unionists, parity was a political imperative. Nationalist critics of the parity approach demanded regional policies that would stress the differences between Northern Ireland and Britain, and emphasise the similarities with the rest of Ireland. The effect of the introduction of dynamic all-Ireland institutions with executive powers would be to lessen the influence of the United Kingdom on policy formulation whilst correspondingly increasing that of the Republic of Ireland and the EU. Similarly, the harmonisation of policies and programmes is likely to mean that the benchmark for policy in Northern Ireland will increasingly become the Republic of Ireland, not Great Britain. What is envisaged in the framework proposals seems to be the incremental development of parity within Ireland as a whole. It would be a mistake, however, to replace parity in a United Kingdom frame of reference with parity in an Irish context. Harmonisation should not prevent variation as there will be a continuing need for Northern Ireland to formulate policies to take account of its specific conditions and problems.

Conclusion

The distinctive form of the policymaking and administrative process in Northern Ireland has been shaped by wider historical, political, and constitutional forces. The legacies of direct rule and of devolution, itself the result of an earlier attempt at constitutional change and institution building, have had a profound influence on structures of policy and administration, on patterns of political accountability, and on the extent of policy variation. Although Great Britain has traditionally provided the standard against which policy development in Northern Ireland has been judged, other external actors such as the Republic of Ireland and the EU have become increasingly important. There is also a high degree of consensus regarding the nature of constitutional change amongst political elites in both the United Kingdom and the Republic of Ireland, and alternation of political parties in government is unlikely to have much impact on policies toward Northern Ireland. Indeed, both of the new governments elected in 1997 made it clear that they will continue to follow the general lines of policy set by their predecessors. To some extent the outcome of political negotiations has been prejudged. In the future, therefore, it is likely that the structures and processes of policymaking in Northern Ireland will be recast along the lines envisaged in the Framework Documents to reflect the basic compromises involved in a resolution of fundamental political problems.

References and Further Reading

Anderson, James, and James Goodman, 1997. *North-South Integration in Ireland: The Rocky Road to Prosperity and Peace.* Submission to the Forum for Peace and Reconciliation, Dublin.

Applebey, George, and Evelyn Ellis, 1991. "Law and employment discrimination: The working of the Northern Ireland Fair Employment Agency," pp. 217–243 in Robert J. Cormack and Robert D. Osborne (eds.), *Discrimination and Public Policy in Northern Ireland.* Oxford: Clarendon Press.

Bell, Peter N., 1987. "Direct rule in Northern Ireland," pp. 189–226 in Richard Rose (ed.), *Ministers and Ministries: A Functional Analysis.* Oxford: Clarendon Press.

Birrell, Derek, and Alan Murie, 1980. *Policy and Government in Northern Ireland: Lessons of Devolution.* Dublin: Gill and Macmillan.

Boyle, Kevin, and Tom Hadden, 1989. *The Anglo-Irish Agreement: Commentary, Text and Official Review.* London: Sweet and Maxwell.

Buckland, Patrick, 1979. *The Factory of Grievances: Devolved Government in Northern Ireland, 1921–39.* Dublin: Gill and Macmillan.

Cabinet Office, 1993. *Public Bodies 1993.* London: HMSO.

Committee on Standards in Public Life, 1995. *Local Public Spending Bodies: Issues and Questions.* London: HMSO.

Connolly, Michael, 1990. *Politics and Policymaking in Northern Ireland.* Hemel Hempstead: Philip Allan.

Connolly, Michael, and Andrew Erridge, 1990. "Central government in Northern Ireland," pp. 19–34 in Michael Connolly and John Loughlin (eds.), *Public Policy in Northern Ireland: Adoption or Adaptation?* Queen's University of Belfast/University of Ulster: Policy Research Institute.

Connolly, Michael, and John Loughlin (eds.), 1990. *Public Policy in Northern Ireland: Adoption or Adaptation?* Queens University of Belfast/University of Ulster: Policy Research Institute.

Cormack, Robert J., and Robert D. Osborne, 1991a. "Disadvantage and discrimination in Northern Ireland," pp. 5–48 in Robert J. Cormack and Robert D. Osborne (eds.), *Discrimination and Public Policy in Northern Ireland*. Oxford: Clarendon Press.

______, 1991b. "Religion and the labour market: Patterns and profiles," pp. 49–71 in Robert J. Cormack and Robert D. Osborne (eds.), *Discrimination and Public Policy in Northern Ireland*. Oxford: Clarendon Press.

Day, Patricia, and Rudolf Klein, 1987. *Accountabilities*. London: Tavistock Publications.

Dunn, Seamus (ed.), 1995. *Facets of the Conflict in Northern Ireland*. Basingstoke: Macmillan.

Fitzpatrick, Barry, Angela Heggarty, and Patricia Maxwell, 1996. "A comparative review of Fair Employment and Equality of Opportunity Law," pp. 151–174 in Denise Magill and Sarah Rose (eds.), *Fair Employment Law in Northern Ireland: Debates and Issues*. Belfast: Standing Advisory Commission on Human Rights.

A Framework for Accountable Government in Northern Ireland, 1995. London/Belfast: HMSO.

Gaffikin, Frank, and Mike Morrisey, 1990. *Northern Ireland: The Thatcher Years*. London: Zed Books

Gallagher, Anthony M., 1995. "The approach of government: Community relations and equity," pp. 27–42 in Seamus Dunn (ed.), *Facets of the Conflict in Northern Ireland*. Basongstoke: Macmillan.

Gallagher, Anthony, Robert Osborne, and Robert Cormack, 1993. "Community relations, equality and education," pp. 177–195 in Robert D. Osborne, Robert J. Cormack, and Anthony Gallagher (eds.), *After the Reforms*. Aldershot: Avebury.

Greer, Alan, 1994. "Policy networks and state-farmer relations in Northern Ireland, 1921–72," *Political Studies* 42, 396–412.

______, 1996. *Rural Politics in Northern Ireland*. Aldershot: Avebury.

Greer, Alan, and Paul Hoggett, 1996. "Quangos and local governance," pp. 150–169 in Lawrence Pratchett and David Wilson (eds.), *Local Democracy and Local Government*. Basingstoke: Macmillan and CLD Ltd.

Hadfield, Brigid (ed.), 1992. *Northern Ireland: Politics and the Constitution*. Buckingham: Open University Press.

Hainsworth, Paul, 1990. "The European Community as a policy arena in Northern Ireland," pp. 77–97 in Michael Connolly and John Loughlin (eds.), *Public Policy in Northern Ireland: Adoption or Adaptation?* Queen's University Belfast/University of Ulster: Policy Research Institute.

Ham, Christopher, and Michael Hill, 1993. *The Policy Process in the Modern Capitalist State*. Hemel Hempstead: Harvester Wheatsheaf.

Heald, David, 1994. "Territorial public expenditure in the United Kingdom," *Public Administration* 72, 147–175.

Hill, Michael (ed.), 1993. *The Policy Process: A Reader*. Hemel Hempstead: Harvester Wheatsheaf.

Jay, Richard, and Rick Wilford, 1991. "An end to discrimination? The Northern Ireland Fair Employment Act of 1989," *Irish Political Studies* 6, 15–36.

Johnson, Nevil, 1975. "Editorial: The Royal Commission on the Constitution," *Public Administration* 52, 1–12.

Knox, Colin, and Joanne Hughes, 1995. "Local government and community relations," pp. 43–60 in Seamus Dunn (ed.), *Facets of the Conflict in Northern Ireland*. Basingstoke: Macmillan.

Livingstone, Stephen, and John Morison, 1995. *An Audit of Democracy in Northern Ireland*. Fortnight Educational Trust and Democratic Audit of the United Kingdom.

Loughlin, John, 1992. "Administering policy in Northern Ireland," pp. 60–75 in Brigid Hadfield (ed.), *Northern Ireland: Politics and the Constitution.* Buckingham: Open University Press.

McCrudden, Christopher, 1988. "The Northern Ireland Fair Employment White Paper: A critical assessment," *Industrial Law Journal* 17, 162–181.

______, 1991. "The evolution of the Fair Employment (Northern Ireland) Act 1989 in Parliament," pp. 244–264 in Robert J. Cormack and Robert D. Osborne (eds.), *Discrimination and Public Policy in Northern Ireland*. Oxford: Clarendon Press.

McGarry, John, and Brendan O'Leary, 1995. *Explaining Northern Ireland*. Oxford: Blackwell.

Moxon-Browne, Edward, 1992. "The impact of the European Community," pp. 47–59 in Brigid Hadfield (ed.), *Northern Ireland: Politics and the Constitution.* Buckingham: Open University Press.

NIO (Northern Ireland Office/Treasury), 1996. *Expenditure Plans and Priorities: Northern Ireland* (Cmnd. 3216). London: HMSO.

O'Leary, Brendan, and John McGarry, 1996. *The Politics of Antagonism: Understanding Northern Ireland* (2nd ed.). London: Athlone Press.

O'Leary, Cornelius, Sydney Elliott, and Rick Wilford, 1988. *The Northern Ireland Assembly 1982–1986: A Constitutional Experiment* (London/Belfast: C. Hurst & Co./Queen's University Bookshop.

Oliver, John, 1978. *Working at Stormont*. Dublin: Institute of Public Administration.

Osborne, Robert, 1996. "Policy dilemmas in Belfast," *Journal of Social Policy* 25, 181–199.

Osborne, Robert, Robert Cormack, and Anthony Gallagher (eds.), 1993. *After the Reforms: Education Policy in Northern Ireland*. Aldershot: Avebury.

Osborne, R. D, R. J. Cormack, and R. L. Miller (eds.), 1987. *Education and Policy in Northern Ireland*. Belfast: Policy Research Institute.

Parsons, Wayne, 1995. *Public Policy: An Introduction to the Theory and Practice of Policy Analysis*. Aldershot: Edward Elgar.

Quirk, Pádraic, and Eithne McLaughlin, 1996. "Targeting social need," pp. 155–185 in Eithne McLaughlin and Pádraic Quirk (eds.), *Policy Aspects of Employment Equality in Northern Ireland*. Belfast: SACHR.

Rhodes, Rod, 1988. *Beyond Westminster and Whitehall: The Sub-Central Governments of Britain*. London: Unwin/Hyman.

Rose, Richard, 1982. *Understanding the United Kingdom: The Territorial Dimension in Government*. London: Longman.

Rose, Sarah, and Denise Magill, 1996. "The development of Fair Employment Legislation in Northern Ireland," pp. 1–25 in Denise Magill and Sarah Rose (eds.), *Fair Employment Law in Northern Ireland*. Belfast: Standing Advisory Commission on Human Rights.

Ruane, Joseph, and Jennifer Todd, 1996. *The Dynamics of Conflict in Northern Ireland: Power, Conflict and Emancipation*. Cambridge: Cambridge University Press.

Salters, Matthew, and Alex McEwen, 1993. "Public policy and education in Northern Ireland," pp. 45–57 in Robert D. Osborne, Robert J. Cormack, and Anthony Gallagher (eds.), *After the Reforms*. Aldershot: Avebury.

Smith, David J., and Gerald Chambers, 1991. *Inequality in Northern Ireland*. Oxford: Clarendon Press.

Stewart, John, 1992. *Accountability to the Public*. European Policy Forum.

Thain, Colin, and Maurice Wright, 1995. *The Treasury and Whitehall: The Planning and Control of Public Expenditure, 1976–1993*. Oxford: Clarendon Press.

Treasury, 1996. *Public Expenditure: Statistical Analyses 1996–97*. London: HMSO.

Weir, Stuart, and Wendy Hall, 1994. *Ego Trip: Extra-Governmental Organisations in the UK and Their Accountability*. Democratic Audit, University of Essex, and Charter 88 Trust.

Wilford, R. A, 1992. "Inverting consociationalism? Policy, pluralism and the post-modern," pp. 29–46 in Brigid Hadfield (ed.), *Northern Ireland: Politics and the Constitution*. Buckingham: Open University Press.

8

Policing and Security

RONALD WEITZER

Policing in communally divided societies is organised around the defence of a sectarian regime and the preservation of a social order based on institutionalised inequality between dominant and subordinate ethnic, racial, or religious groups. To a greater extent than in more integrated societies, the police in divided societies are politicised, tend to be biased against the subordinate group, are unencumbered by effective mechanisms of accountability, wield extensive powers over civilians, and are responsible for both ordinary crime and security problems. The combination and magnitude of these features is such that policing in divided societies differs substantially from that in more integrated societies (Brewer 1991; Weitzer 1985, 1995).

Research on policing during the period of unionist rule (Farrell 1983; Weitzer 1995) indicates that it closely resembled the divided society model. The new police force, the Royal Ulster Constabulary (RUC), was unlike other police forces in Great Britain in several respects. It was responsible for both ordinary crime and internal security; it was armed and militarised; it was insulated from British traditions of minimum force, policing by popular consent, and political independence; it was overwhelmingly Protestant and showed bias against Catholics; it was unchecked by neutral, independent mechanisms of accountability; it enjoyed exceptional police powers in the areas of security and public order, as reflected in the draconian Special Powers Act of 1922; and it had significantly more police officers per capita than the rest of the United Kingdom (in 1924 the ratio of police to population was 1:160 in Ulster, compared to 1:669 in England and Wales) (Farrell 1983: 218). The force was closely tied to the Ministry of Home Affairs, whose top officials were strident defenders of Protestant interests and whose policies with regard to law and order were sometimes purely political and prejudiced against Catholics (Buckland 1979). Supporting the RUC was another paramilitary force, the Ulster Special Constabulary (USC), which was formed at the end of 1920. The USC provided assistance to the RUC during public disturbances, staffed checkpoints on roads, and was involved in border patrols and other, more mundane tasks. It developed a reputation as a fiercely sectarian force and was despised by Catholics.

In certain respects, contemporary policing in Northern Ireland resembles these traditional patterns, but there are also some important differences between the periods of unionist rule and British rule and thus some divergence from the divided-society type of policing described above.

Police Reform After 1969

The civil rights movement of the late 1960s was a major watershed in Northern Ireland, and the events of this period had a profound impact on policing. The RUC's crowd control methods, its apparent bias with respect to Catholic and Protestant civilians, and the casualties resulting from aggressive policing of the demonstrations generated critical media coverage, a crisis for the unionist state, and rising concern in London over the security situation and the integrity of the forces of law and order. Several commissions of inquiry were established to examine the causes of the disturbances and the problems in the security forces.

The most influential inquiry with regard to policing was that chaired by Lord Hunt in 1969. In particular, the commission objected to the militarised style and security role of the RUC and USC: "[T]he protection of . . . the state against armed attacks is not a role which should have to be undertaken by the police, whether they be regular or special." A counterinsurgency police force adversely affected police-community relations: "[A]ny police force, military in appearance and equipment, is less acceptable to minority and moderate opinion than if it is clearly civilian in character" (Hunt Committee 1969: 21, 41). The Hunt Committee recommended that the RUC abandon its "warlike" armoured cars, be relieved of most security duties, and be disarmed since firearms were "inappropriate" for a civil police force. Other important recommendations included the following:

- disbandment of most of the USC, to be replaced with a military regiment under the command of the British army chief stationed in Ulster;
- repeal of the Special Powers Act;

- a major increase in RUC personnel;
- a programme to recruit Catholics;
- expansion of community relations programmes;
- more training in crowd control;
- creation of a Police Authority, whose members were representative of the society, to administer the RUC and to which the police chief would be accountable; and
- investigation of civilian complaints by officers stationed outside where the complaint originated.

Many of the Hunt Committee's proposals were offensive to the Unionist government, but it felt compelled to accept certain recommendations in the context of growing public disorder and pressure from the British government. Some reforms were rather quickly implemented (e.g., creation of a Community Relations Branch, a Police Authority, and screening mechanisms for new recruits, as well as dismantling of the USC), but other proposals were delayed, watered down, or not implemented at all.

Elsewhere (Weitzer 1987, 1990) I have argued that the resilience of traditional policing arrangements during this period was largely due to Northern Ireland's political environment, especially to the intractability of a unionist regime that had little interest in reforming the institutions of law and order. With the termination of the old regime in 1972 and the beginning of direct rule by Britain, there was greater potential for meaningful reforms. In fact, significant changes have occurred under direct rule, but they have been conditioned and constrained by some strong countervailing factors, such as police resistance to reform, opposition from influential conservative groups (i.e., the unionist parties), continuing political instability and ethnic strife, and a high level of political violence, including frequent attacks on the security forces.

Fortification and Militarisation

From 1970 to 1976 the British army replaced the RUC as the premier security force in Ulster. It was responsible for conducting street patrols, house searches, arrests of suspected insurgents, intelligence gathering, riot control, and undercover operations. The army was primarily deployed in Catholic areas, where it frequently acted harshly and indiscriminately toward residents, who, in turn, were seen as the enemy. The police were largely relegated to duties of ordinary crime control in less disturbed Protestant and mixed areas (Boyle, Hadden, and Hillyard 1975).

The policy of military primacy came under review by a new Labour government, which appointed the Gardiner Committee (1975) to assess the security situation. It concluded that the military approach had failed to curb political violence and that the very use of the military gave the impression that a war was being fought. Hence it recommended a shift of responsibility to the now "rehabilitated" RUC, which would result in more selective and sensitive operations and thus lessen the disturbance to Catholic communities. In addition, insurgents were no longer to be detained indefinitely without trial, nor were convicted terrorists to enjoy special privileges in prison because of their political status.

The government accepted the logic of the Gardiner Committee's arguments and subsequently implemented major changes that would become the pillars of security policy, in place to this day. Under the "criminalisation" strategy, the political motives of terrorists were denied (with their special-prisoner status phased out) and the conflict was recast as strictly a law-and-order problem to be handled by the police and the courts. Under the "Ulsterisation" strategy, indigenous forces (RUC and UDR) were given primary responsibility for internal security and British army involvement was reduced. The police resumed their senior role in the security field, and both the number of soldiers and their visibility declined: Between 1972 and 1990 the strength of the army fell by 50 percent, from 22,000 to 10,500 troops, although by 1994 it had increased to 17,600. Only in the most dangerous areas does the army play a major role; elsewhere it provides support to the police when called upon. Essentially, the RUC now performs both counterinsurgency and ordinary policing roles (as it did prior to 1970), although one style prevails in any given locale depending on its security profile.

As the role of the British military decreased, and in a context where political violence remained serious, it was inevitable that the RUC would be militarised and galvanised. Since 1976 the police have frequently been involved in managing public order situations (demonstrations, riots, traditional marches, political funerals, sectarian fighting) and in security duties such as conducting undercover surveillance operations, manning vehicle checkpoints, stopping and searching pedestrians, arresting persons for purposes of intelligence gathering, and executing house searches—all of which occur much more frequently now than they did during the period of unionist rule. These counterinsurgency duties tend to invite police aggression and abrasive encounters with citizens, continually reinforcing resentment in the communities most affected, as the army learned in the early 1970s. Less frequent but even more controversial are incidents resulting in fatalities, including deaths caused by plastic bullets during public disturbances and killings of suspected insurgents by members of the security forces.

Today, the RUC is one of the most formidable militarised police forces in the world. Heavily armed units patrol on foot and in armoured Land Rovers. Police stations are fortresses, built to withstand attacks by the Irish Republican Army (IRA). The force commands the most advanced computer system in the United Kingdom, and it is heavily involved in surveillance of political activists, known terrorists, and ordinary citizens. With 8,493 officers in the RUC and 4,690 in the RUC Reserve in 1994 (Chief Constable 1995), Northern Ireland has more than three times as many police officers per capita as England and Wales (a ratio of 1:135 in Ulster, 1:445 in England and Wales). The police budget has skyrocketed—from £16 million in 1972 to £610 million in 1995—and per capita expenditure in Northern Ireland is three times higher than that in England and Wales. Much of the expenditure is naturally driven by the security situation, as reflected in the Chief Constable's disclosure that terrorism and public order duties consume 80 percent of police time (*Irish Times*, 24 June 1985). Ordinary crime has been a much lower priority.

The police also wield an arsenal of exceptional powers under the emergency laws. The 1922 Special Powers Act was repealed in 1973, only to be immediately replaced with the Emergency Provisions Act (EPA), which has been renewed annually by Westminster with little debate. In 1974 Parliament passed the Prevention of Terrorism Act (PTA). Together the two acts allow for the following:

- house searches for weapons, explosives, and other contraband;
- stopping, questioning, and searching civilians in public, powers that do not require suspicion and thus may be exercised indiscriminately (the security forces are permitted to ask for a person's name, age, destination, and knowledge of terrorist activities, but interrogations sometimes cover personal or other matters unrelated to security);
- arrest, detention, and interrogation of a person for up to seven days, the first forty-eight hours of which a person may be denied access to a lawyer;
- banning of organisations connected with terrorism, such as the IRA, the Ulster Volunteer Force, and the Ulster Freedom Fighters;
- exclusion from Britain and Northern Ireland of individuals thought to be connected to paramilitary or terrorist groups; and
- nonjury Diplock courts for terrorist cases, with more elastic rules of evidence than in ordinary criminal cases.

Until 1987 when the EPA was amended, the security forces were not required to have "reasonable suspicion" that an offence had been committed to justify stops, searches, seizures, or arrests.

These broad powers are clearly vulnerable to abuse by the police and army. Arrest and interrogation, for example, can be used for harassment or intelligence gathering. Many of the persons arrested have been pressured to provide information about their associates or others in their community or to become informers; relatively few have been arrested in regard to a specific offence with a view toward prosecution. From 1978 to 1986 only 13.7 percent of the persons arrested under the EPA were charged with offences. Under the Prevention of Terrorism Act, only 10 percent of the 7,052 persons detained in Britain from 1974 to 1991 were charged with offences (Hillyard 1993: 11), whereas the figure is closer to 30 percent in Northern Ireland (Helsinki Watch 1991). The vast majority of detainees have been interrogated and released without charge (under the ordinary criminal law in Britain, 80–90 percent of those arrested are charged). Since 1973, more than 60,000 people have been arrested, interrogated, and released without charge. Moreover, a 1980 study of detentions in Northern Ireland found that only 28 percent of those arrested were questioned about a specific offence (Walsh 1983). Instead, interrogators asked detainees about their associates, family members, and political sympathies.

Virtually the entire population of Northern Ireland has been stopped on the street at some time by the security forces. One study (McVeigh, 1994) found that 96 percent of the population had been stopped at a vehicle checkpoint and 25 percent had been stopped and searched while on foot. According to the Community Attitudes Survey (CAS 1993–1994), an extraordinary number of Protestants (49 percent) and Catholics (58 percent) stated that they had been stopped on foot or in a vehicle within the past month, whereas one-fourth of the Protestants and one-third of the Catholics had been stopped in the previous week. Many of these stops are routine, albeit inconvenient for the people involved; but when they occur repeatedly and involve police incivility or abuse, the recipients naturally feel resentful and bitter toward the security forces. Residents of republican and some loyalist neighbourhoods have been especially critical of stops that they define as harassment and oppression by the police and army (Hamilton, Moore, and Trimble 1995; McVeigh 1994; Sluka 1989; Weitzer 1995).

Another major aspect of the RUC's security role involves house searches for arms, ammunition, and explosives. Warrants are not mandatory, but the EPA requires a senior police officer's determination that reasonable grounds exist before attempting to discover whether contraband is present. In republican and some loyalist areas, early morning raids are frequently conducted on one or more houses. Some of these operations yield illegal material; others produce nothing except property damage. Many searches include partial removal of walls, floor boards, and ceilings. Figures regarding the proportion of successful raids are scarce, but in 1990 only 5 percent of the army's house searches found weapons, ammunition, illegal radio equipment, or hiding places (Helsinki Watch 1991: 23). This low success rate suggests that many of the searches are not based on reasonable suspicion, as the law requires. The impact of these operations on the affected communities is reflected in their sheer magnitude: Between 1971 and 1988 the army and police carried out 330,000 house searches. Though less frequent in recent years, the raids are no less disturbing to the inhabitants, whose privacy is invaded and whose property is often damaged during the searches.

The RUC's pronounced counterinsurgency role has had negative effects on police officers as well as on civilians. First and foremost, it places officers in extreme danger. RUC officers perform one of the most dangerous policing jobs in the world. From 1969 to 1994, 297 RUC officers were killed and more than 7,300 were injured in attacks. Neither armoured Land Rovers nor fortified police stations are safe havens; both arc frequently blasted with rockets and mortars, and a substantial proportion of the 2,554 attacks on police stations from 1969 to 1991 caused significant damage. Police officers have seen many of their colleagues wounded or killed or have been attacked themselves. Frustration with this situation is reflected in the repeated complaints of the Police Federation (which represents 95 percent of RUC officers) concerning the erosion of normal policing and the hardening of officers due to their counterinsurgency duties and decades of exposure to hostile citizens and attacks by armed insurgents. These conditions help to explain why officers act overzealously or violently toward civilians, particularly in communities typified as "enemy territory."

As Table 8.1 shows, Protestants and Catholics perceive counterinsurgency policing quite differently. In particular, Protestants are consistently more likely to endorse stiff security measures. The primary reason is that, over the years, Catholics have received the lion's share of abuse at the hands of the police and army.

Of course, the RUC is also involved in ordinary law enforcement, particularly in communities that experience little or no political violence and subversive activity. Survey data suggest that there is greater public satisfaction with the RUC's handling of its ordinary duties than with that of its security duties, but satisfaction is much less common among Catholics than among Protestants (again, see Table 8.1). Partic-

TABLE 8.1 Attitudes Toward Counterinsurgency Policing

	Protestants	*Catholics*
Confidence in RUC's ability to provide ordinary policing (1996)		
Total or lot of confidence	61	23
Some confidence	30	36
Little or no confidence	9	40
Confidence in RUC's ability to police parades, demonstrations, and public order situations (1996)		
Total or lot of confidence	40	10
Some confidence	33	24
Little or no confidence	26	63
All parades and demonstrations should be banned for a time (1996)	29	74
Police do a bad job in controlling sectarian crime (1990)	12	40
Vehicle checkpoints are used too much		
1990	8	40
1993–94	6	26
Vehicle checkpoints are used too little		
1990	34	9
1993–94	36	17
Random searches of pedestrians are used too much		
1990	3	41
1993–94	6	43
Random searches of pedestrians are used too little		
1990	32	6
1993–94	50	18
House searches are used too much		
1990	3	35
1993–94	4	35
House searches are used too little		
1990	26	3
1993–94	42	17
Police should need a warrant to search a suspect's house (1990)	53	79
Police should always carry guns		
1990	86	37
1995	50	18

(continues)

TABLE 8.1 *(continued)*

	Protestants	*Catholics*
Persons who kill police officers should get death penalty (1990)	76	19
Use of plastic bullets during riots should be increased (1985a)	86	9
Undercover intelligence operations should be increased (1985b)	90	25
Shoot-to-kill action against terrorist suspects is acceptable (1985b)	61	7

Sources: 1985a poll (*N*=955): Northern Ireland Consumer Panel Poll (1985); 1985b poll (*N*=1,008): Ulster Marketing Survey (1985); 1990 poll (*N*=324 Catholics, 436 Protestants): Social Attitudes Survey; 1993–94 poll (*N*=783 Catholics, 1,261 Protestants): Community Attitudes Survey; 1995 poll: NIOS (1995); and 1996 poll (*N*=439 Catholics, 673 Protestants): NIOS (1996).

ularly in neighbourhoods where ordinary crime is flourishing, mostly working-class Catholic and Protestant areas, there is discontent with the RUC's performance (Hamilton et al. 1995; Weitzer 1995). A report of community workers in Protestant neighbourhoods included this comment: "The police are not fulfilling their role in crime prevention and are more interested in anti-terrorist work" (quoted in Weitzer 1995: 166). The RUC's performance in the area of ordinary crime control is conditioned, first, by legitimate concerns about officers being set up for ambush when responding to calls from citizens and, secondly, by the existence of strong pressures in certain communities against contacting or reporting crimes to the RUC due to generalised suspicion of the force and fears that police officers might attempt to recruit people as informers or engage in other intelligence gathering when they are called in to deal with ordinary crimes.

Composition and Impartiality

The composition of the RUC has changed in some respects but not in others. Only a sixth of the current force are officers who served under the Stormont regime. This change may be a progressive one, but it is diluted by the fact that the serving officers have grown accustomed to policing under abnormal circumstances and, consequently, may have become hardened by the threat of violence and insensitive to civilians. Moreover, the RUC is still largely Protestant (approximately 93 percent) and Catholics have shown little interest in joining the force since the beginning of the troubles. On the question of whether it would be better for Northern Ireland if the RUC employed more Catholics, 63 percent of Catholics and 54 percent of Protestants agreed (SAS 1990). Another poll found that 72 percent of Catholics and 48 percent of Protestants believe there are too few Catholics in the RUC (CAS 1993–1994). It appears that more Catholics would consider a police career were it not for the IRA's standing threat to kill Catholic officers, among other countervailing factors. The reasons most frequently cited to explain the low numbers of Catholics include fear of intimidation or attacks on officers (71 percent of Protestants, 72 percent of Catholics), expected loss of contact with family and friends (50 percent of Protestants, 54 percent of Catholics), pressure from Catholics not to join the force (49 percent of Protestants, 40 percent of Catholics), and alienation from the state (26 percent of Protestants, 20 percent of Catholics) (CAS 1993–1994).

It is commonly assumed that a substantial increase in the number of Catholic police officers would help to bolster popular confidence and legitimation of the RUC. For the past two decades the RUC has attempted to attract Catholic recruits, with little success, and the Police Authority and Northern Ireland Office (NIO) consider the need to attract applicants from the Catholic population to be of central importance in the future reform of the force. However, such a change would be welcomed by only a section of the Catholic population. Most politically moderate Catholics (67 percent of SDLP supporters) would indeed like to see more Catholic recruits, but the same is true for only 23 percent of Sinn Féin supporters (SAS 1990). In-depth interviews in republican communities in Belfast (Weitzer 1995) indicate that the residents would not be impressed by a greater ethnic balance in the RUC. More Catholic police officers would not be symbolically important (signifying a "desectarianisation" of the RUC), nor would they be expected to behave any differently than Protestant officers. Catholic police officers are seen by many residents of republican communities as traitors to their own people. And far from behaving more sensitively toward civilians, Catholic officers allegedly act more aggressively than Protestant officers: "Your own are the worst," as the saying goes. Some support for this view can be found in a survey of part-time RUC Reserve members, which found that Catholic officers took a much harder line on law-and-order issues than either the Catholic population or, on some of the issues, their Protestant colleagues (Mapstone 1992). Research on other societies suggests that police officers from a minority ethnic group do not necessarily act with more sensitivity toward minority-group civilians, because of strong organisational pressures to conform to their colleagues' expectations, and there is no reason to think that Northern Ireland is different on this score.

Has the RUC become more impartial, overall, in its dealings with Protestant and Catholic civilians? The ideal of universalistic law enforcement is frequently trumpeted by RUC chiefs, and, at least to some extent, it has penetrated the organisational culture of the force. RUC officers today pay greater attention than in the past to Catholic sensitivities and show less favouritism toward Protestants. Moreover, although both republican and loyalist paramilitaries are vigorously pursued, during the 1980s loyalist paramilitaries were *much more likely* than their republican counterparts to be apprehended for their respective terrorist offences—largely because it was more difficult for the police to gather incriminating evidence on the republicans (Weitzer 1995: 134–135). The RUC has also aggressively confronted Protestant rioters. And since the mid-1980s the police have rerouted or banned a number of Orange Order marches that wanted to pass through Catholic areas. Others, however, have been permitted, sparking verbal and physical confrontations among police, residents, and marchers.

Research on other countries shows that the values championed by senior officers are often subverted by lower-ranking officers, whose daily experiences tend to neutralise the lofty ideals of the "top brass." Indeed, at least two subcultures may be found in any police force: that of managers and that of street cops (Reuss-Ianni 1983). In Northern Ireland some long-serving officers and some of their younger counterparts continue to harbour strong unionist sympathies. It may be the case that only a minority of these officers allow their attitudes to affect their treatment of Catholics, but we lack observational research on the behaviour of officers while on patrol. And whatever their personal attitudes, it is likely that officers stationed in areas with the most belligerent populations and the highest incidence of political violence will be inclined to disregard formal norms of impartiality and minimum force.

Protestants and Catholics differ in their views about how the RUC fares on this score. As indicated by the survey data summarized in Table 8.2, the vast majority of Protestants believe the police are fair and treat both communities equally. Catholics are split on the question of whether the police are fair, and they are less inclined to believe the police act in an even-handed manner; the majority believe Protestants are treated better.

Other measures of police impartiality include questions about how police deal with inter-ethnic attacks and whether Catholic and Protestant demonstrators are treated similarly by police. As shown in the table, most Protestants think that the police try hard to stop Protestant attacks against Catholics, but only a minority of Catholics agree.

TABLE 8.2 Attitudes Toward Police Impartiality (% in agreement)

	Protestants	*Catholics*
Police are fair (1985)	96	47
Police treat Protestants and Catholics equally (1990)	75	38
Police treat Protestants better (1990)	12	55
Police try hard to stop Protestant attacks (1986)	86	46
Police try hard to stop Catholic attacks (1986)	74	82
Police act fairly in dealing with terrorist and sectarian crime (1993–94)	86	62
During public disorders, plastic bullets are used: (1996)		
more against Catholics	14	65
more against Protestants	6	2
against both equally	72	24
Controls on Catholic demonstrations are used too much (1990)	6	42
Controls on Catholic demonstrations are used too little (1990)	24	6
Controls on Protestant demonstrations are used too much (1990)	13	7
Controls on Protestant demonstrations are used too little (1990)	13	34

Sources: 1985 poll (*N*=955): Northern Ireland Consumer Panel Poll (1985); 1986 poll (*N*=594 Catholics, 1,059 Protestants): Smith (1987); 1990 poll (*N*=324 Catholics, 436 Protestants): Social Attitudes Survey; 1993–94 poll (*N*=783 Catholics, 1,261 Protestants): Community Attitudes Survey; 1995 poll: NIOS (1995); and 1996 poll (*N*=439 Catholics, 673 Protestants): NIOS (1996).

Protestants and Catholics are in closer agreement regarding police action against Catholics who attack Protestants. Regarding restrictions placed on demonstrations and parades, Catholics are far more likely than Protestants to say that police impose controls too often on Catholic demonstrations whereas controls on Protestant demonstrations are imposed too infrequently. Similarly, during public disturbances in which plastic bullets are fired, police are seen as having one trigger finger for Catholics and another for Protestants; two-thirds of the Catholics believe plastic bullets are used most against them, whereas most Protestants believe they are used equally against both sides.

It should be noted that sensitivity training for RUC recruits is a very recent development. Only since 1994 has the force included a six-day Community Awareness module in its twenty-five-week training course. The module involves workshops on ethnic identity, prejudice, religious traditions, socioeconomic inequality, and policing in divided societies. Even this relatively minor innovation met with stiff resistance from the top echelon of the RUC and from training officers. The recency of such sensitivity training is especially remarkable in a divided society like Northern Ireland. The head of the RUC's training centre told me in July 1995 that, in the past,

> [w]e paid lip-service to community awareness, but it wasn't part of training. This was partly because the RUC code says you can't talk about religion or politics. And the old-style thinking was that "we police the whole community, the public". We denied the differences in society, the religious differences. Now the view is that only if we accept our differences can we move forward.

There is considerable popular support for more sensitivity training. In a 1995 survey, of those who thought police training should be improved, 62 percent of Protestants and 69 percent of Catholics thought there should be more training in "dealing with people" (NIOS 1995).

Accountability

The problem of police accountability became especially controversial in the late 1960s when Northern Ireland was torn by political instability, growing public disorder, and repeated instances of police misconduct on the streets. Over the years, several oversight agencies have been created, although controversy persists over the effectiveness of these bodies. Some have opposed the new mechanisms of accountability on the grounds that they hinder police efforts to fight insurgency; others have criticised the changes as insufficient or cosmetic.

Police Authority for Northern Ireland

In 1970 the Police Authority was created to administer the RUC in a more neutral fashion than the politicised and discredited Ministry of Home Affairs. Members of the Authority are not elected, unlike their Scottish equivalents and two-thirds of police authority members in England and Wales, because of the concern that elected members might politicise the agency or be in a position to place partial demands on the RUC. In Ulster, the Secretary of State appoints the members in accordance with the 1970 Police Act, which stipulates that the membership should be representative of Northern Ireland. The measure allowing the Secretary of State to appoint these members helps to minimise sectarian influences on the Authority, but it can also be used to ensure that the Authority will be supportive and deferential toward the RUC.

The Police Authority is responsible for administering the RUC's finances, personnel, buildings, and supplies, and it has standing committees that address matters of general policing policies, public order problems, the handling of complaints, and police-community relations. The implication is that the Authority could play an important policymaking role with respect to the proper handling of demonstrations, marches, and riots; police-community problems and programmes; undercover units; weapons; and public complaints. But, until recently, it has devoted most of its time to technical and administrative matters. Controversial incidents have received little attention, and the root causes of recurrent policing problems have not been a major concern.

The Authority's performance as the leading police oversight body has been unsatisfactory, and it has thus had difficulty convincing the public that the RUC is truly under control. There are two basic reasons for this unsatisfactory performance: (1) the strong pro-police orientations of members and (2) its limited power, either on paper or in practice, over RUC chiefs. A member who served on the Authority in the late 1970s told me of the pro-police orientation:

> The predilection was to not upset the *status quo*. The Police Authority's orientation was as a sympathetic vote of confidence in the RUC. . . . There was always the view that we had to balance our criticisms of the police with praise. . . . Most members of the Authority would say that we . . . have to trust the police. And they wouldn't believe the police were acting in a partial manner. Members had a great disinclination to believe that the police were acting in a manner that kept the tensions going with the community.

A conservative bias persists to the present day. Recently, some relatively progressive members, such as former Chairman David Cook and Chris Ryder, encountered opposition from other members when they attempted to raise sensitive issues. Following a February 1996 vote of no confidence by their colleagues on the Authority, Cook and Ryder were sacked by the Secretary of State.

In theory, the Police Authority has important powers over the RUC, but in practice these powers seem illusory. On those few occasions when the Authority has pressed for a larger remit or asserted itself against the Chief Constable, it has usually encountered stiff resistance. In 1976 it was denied a request to attend security meetings at the NIO; it was also refused access to files on complaints against police officers; in the late 1970s it had difficulty getting information on police treatment of detainees at interrogation centres; and in 1992, when it called for expansion of the lay-visiting system to include visits to persons detained for terrorist crimes, it was snubbed by the RUC.

The Authority has assumed a low profile since its inception, neither publicising its work nor criticising the police in public. Recently, however, it has taken a more visible role on policing issues. It has pushed for expansion of Police-Community Liaison Committees (see below), and in 1995 it embarked on a massive public consultation process, including public meetings and a mass mailing to 600,000 homes to elicit written submissions on people's ideas for police reform and priorities (8,000 responses were received). Analysis of the submissions resulted in the identification of thirty topics (Police Authority 1996). The most frequently mentioned issues, however, are not necessarily the most important. For example, more than half of the writers mentioned the RUC's name, whereas only 1 percent mentioned police control of marches and 3 percent mentioned police powers. Such sensitive issues as police undercover operations, militarised patrols, and other aspects of counterinsurgency policing did not figure among the list of topics.

The Authority's consultative effort was a genuine attempt to inject popular input into the policing debate, but it was also motivated by the Authority's felt need to publicise *itself*. In recent polls, a quarter of the Protestants and a third of the Catholics said they had never heard of the Police Authority (NIOS 1995); and of those who had heard of it, a majority in each community believed it was part of the RUC (CAS 1993–1994). Only 1 percent of Protestants and Catholics selected the Police Authority (out of eight choices) as the agency they would contact to express views regarding a "general change in the way the police do their job" (CAS 1993–1994). It appears that the public doubts not only the Authority's capacity to shape change but also its very status as an independent oversight agency.

Police Complaints

The way in which citizens' complaints against police officers are handled is another important aspect of police accountability. Traditionally, the RUC handled all complaints internally. Partly in response to pressure from Catholics and various independent bodies and partly to bring Northern Ireland into conformity with earlier changes in England and Wales, an independent Police Complaints Board (PCB) was formed in 1977. The PCB reviewed allegations of misconduct by officers, but it had no role in the investigation of complaints. Its involvement did not begin until after the police investigation was completed, and then its main function was to decide whether a charge was warranted. If the board disagreed with the RUC's decision not to prefer disciplinary charges, it could recommend or direct that specific charges be made.

The PCB consistently expressed confidence in the thoroughness of police investigations and rarely saw fit to use its statutory power to insist on charges against accused officers. It disagreed with the RUC and recommended or directed disciplinary charges in well under 1 percent of the cases it reviewed between 1977 and 1987, and only 3 percent of complaints were substantiated between 1981 and 1987 (Weitzer 1995). This record discredited the PCB. Hoping to bolster public confidence, the government replaced the board in February 1988 with the Independent Commission for Police Complaints (ICPC), which has some powers the PCB lacked. Specifically, the ICPC must supervise police investigations of all complaints regarding death or serious injury; it may supervise other investigations if deemed to be in the "public interest"; it may inquire into exceptional, controversial matters where no complaint has been made; and it must review the reports of all investigated complaints, on the basis of which it may override the Chief Constable's decision not to charge an accused officer. If the Commission overrides the Chief Constable and directs that disciplinary charges be brought, the case must then be heard by a tribunal consisting of two Commission members and the Chief Constable.

Technically confined to supervising police investigations rather than conducting its own investigations, the Commission maintains that its actual role is greater than passive supervision. It can insist that additional witnesses be interviewed, that specific questions be asked of accused officers, and that accused officers be re-interviewed if the ICPC is not satisfied with their initial responses.

Has the ICPC been successful in ensuring that officers guilty of misconduct are identified and punished for their acts? The Commission's annual substantiation rate is no higher than the PCB's. Moreover, substantiation rates in Northern Ireland are consistently and significantly lower than in England and Wales. The mean substantiation rate in Northern Ireland during the 1980s (3.2 percent) was about one-third that of England and Wales (8.9 percent) (Weitzer 1995: 192–193).

Complaints related to counterinsurgency policing (i.e., most of the allegations of assault, harassment, unlawful arrest, and improper house search) account for a substantial proportion (more than half) of all complaints investigated in Northern Ireland. Very few of these complaints are substantiated. Moreover, complaints regarding the most serious offences, such as assault, are less likely to be investigated and substantiated by the RUC than are allegations of more minor offences such as incivility, neglect of duty, and procedural irregularity (Weitzer 1995). A huge proportion of assault complaints are withdrawn by complainants and never investigated. Of those assault cases that are investigated, the mean substantiation rate was 1.9 percent for 1981–1989, half the rate of all other complaints (3.9 percent).

Also noteworthy is the lack of action on the complaints of individuals arrested under the security laws, many of whom claim they were assaulted during interrogation at holding centres such as Castlereagh. Between 1988 and 1994 the ICPC reviewed 2,377 such cases, of which 1,623 were dispensed with because the complainant "failed to co-operate" with the investigating officer; 72 others withdrew their complaints. Remarkably, only *one* of the 682 remaining cases was substantiated (ICPC 1988–1994).

Catholics historically have been suspicious of agencies involved in policing matters, including those that handle police misconduct, and that suspicion has not lessened over time. Nearly three-quarters of SDLP supporters and nine out of ten Sinn Féin supporters agreed with the statement "When the police or army commit an offence in Northern Ireland, they usually get away with it" (SAS 1990). These opinions may reflect either general impressions or more specific perceptions of the ICPC (and its low substantiation rates as reported in the press) or the courts (and acquittals in controversial cases). Most Protestants, by contrast, are not of the opinion that police or soldiers usually get away with crimes: Only 10 percent of UUP supporters and 17 percent of DUP supporters took this position (SAS 1990).

Although the ICPC's power to supervise investigations is more extensive than the powers of most civilian oversight bodies elsewhere in the world, the actual investigative work is done by RUC officers—but the credibility of their procedures is problematic. Fifty percent of Catholics and 37 percent of Protestants believe that the police "cannot be trusted" to investigate complaints against police officers, and 56 percent of Catholics and 35 percent of Protestants believe complaints should be investigated by civilians, not police officers (ICPC 1995).

At the same time, public awareness of the ICPC is limited. Only 41 percent of Catholics and 52 percent of Protestants are aware of the Commission's existence (ICPC, 1995), and only about a quarter of the Catholics and Protestants identified the ICPC as the body responsible for reviewing complaints against police officers (CAS 1993–1994). Of those who are aware of the Commission, 56 percent of Protestants but only 38 percent of Catholics believed it was an agency independent of the police, whereas two-thirds of Protestants but only 27 percent of Catholics have confidence in the Commission's handling of complaints (ICPC, 1995). Clearly, the ICPC needs to work harder at publicising its existence and role and at convincing the public that it is an impartial and effective watchdog.

Police-Community Liaison

There is one other mechanism of accountability that deserves examination here. Police-Community Liaison Committees (PCLCs), which are linked to district and city councils in Northern Ireland, have existed since the 1980s. By 1995 all twenty-six councils had a liaison committee, but most restricted membership to police and elected councillors. A study of the PCLCs (Weitzer 1992) found that most were dominated by unionists (boycotted by Sinn Féin and the SDLP); detached from ordinary people and more closely linked to political and business elites; and preoccupied with fairly mundane problems (such as street lighting, graffiti, underage drinking) rather than with major issues such as local police policies and practices, police relations with residents, sectarian attacks, provocative marches, and so forth. In addition, most had very little impact on police practices, police-community relations, and meaningful accountability to the local population.

Although the Police Authority wishes to make the PCLCs more representative and has encouraged them to deal with more important matters, the problems identified here continue to dilute the impact of these committees in the areas of accountability and police-community relations. As a high-ranking member of the Police Authority told me in 1995, "The PCLC's are not worth the paper they are written on." Moreover, there does not appear to be significant public interest in this kind of contact with the police. When asked whether they would be interested in joining a local group that would meet regularly with police to discuss policing issues, 62 percent of Protestants and 65 percent of Catholics said "No" (CAS 1993–1994). This widespread unwillingness to participate on such a body may be driven by apathy, personal alienation from the RUC, or a desire not to be seen associating with the police. Political conditions will have to change before there is greater public involvement in these bodies.

Policing During and After the "First" Ceasefire

The seventeen-month ceasefire from September 1994 to February 1996 presented the authorities with a unique opportunity to begin to consider reforms in policing and security arrangements. Knowing that the ceasefire might not be permanent, the authorities entertained only those proposals consistent with the "principle of reversibility"—namely, that any change must be readily reversible in the event of a resurgence of political violence. Another factor was the need to maintain police morale. These considerations meant that far-reaching reform of the RUC was simply not on the agenda during the ceasefire.

A strikingly *minimalist* approach is evident in the recently published reviews of policing by the Police Authority (1996) and the Northern Ireland Office (1996). Neither report says much about the low proportion of Catholics in the RUC, possible changes in the legal and organisational pillars of security policing, or the serious problem of public alienation from the police in hard-core republican and loyalist communities. The Police Authority shows great reluctance to intervene meaningfully in the policing debate, proffering few recommendations of its own. It leaves the issue of arming police officers to the Chief Constable as part of his operational responsibility, and it defers to government on questions of whether the Union flag should be flown at police stations, whether the complaints commission should be empowered to conduct its own investigations of cases independent of the police, and whether a two-tiered police force should be created (with one tier dealing with local policing and the other with serious crime and national-level problems). In areas where the Police Authority does take a clear position, it usually advises against change. Specifically, the Authority has rejected as unnecessary and/or inefficient the proposals of certain political parties (SDLP and Alliance) and civic organisations to create regionally based police departments to supplant the centralised RUC, to alter the RUC's badge and uniform to symbolise its new identity, and to engage in more foot patrols.

The NIO's report is even more limited, making no mention whatsoever of possible changes in the RUC—with the exception of its name, badge, and uniform, which the report says should not be changed at this time. Consistent with recent reforms in Britain, the report does, however, advocate transferring control over the RUC's budget from the Police Authority to the Chief Constable. It also suggests that the force should be more accountable to the Authority and Secretary of State, but the proposed mechanisms for ensuring this outcome are essentially the same as at present.

A number of changes took place during the ceasefire: Police shelved their bullet-proof flak jackets, rifles, and machine guns; Land Rovers were gradually replaced on the street with police cars, though the former remained available for deployment in public order situations; the British army withdrew its patrols from the streets of West Belfast and the border areas; emergency powers were used less often for arrests, house searches, and so forth; and the number of vehicle checkpoints was greatly reduced. Many of these security measures were restored after the IRA resumed its offensive in February 1996. Nevertheless, the ceasefire demonstrated just how quickly certain aspects of the counterinsurgency enterprise could be suspended, a situation that was applauded by many Catholics and Protestants alike.

But the two populations continue to hold rather different views on the future direction of the RUC. A 1996 poll (*Belfast Telegraph,* 18 January) uncovered polarised opinions on the question "Are changes in the RUC necessary?" Three-quarters of the Catholics answered "Yes," whereas nearly the same number of Protestants said "No." Ninety percent of Sinn Féin supporters and 75 percent of SDLP supporters thought changes were necessary, whereas 80 percent of DUP supporters and 78 percent of UUP supporters rejected the idea of change. The vague wording of the question makes it difficult to judge the respondents' interpretation of *changes,* but it very likely means some kind of liberalisation to most Catholics, whereas most Protestants probably define it in terms of erosion of the RUC's capacity to do its job or appeasement of unwarranted Catholic demands. A somewhat more specific question in the 1995 Omnibus Survey found that 71 percent of Protestants and 28 percent of Catholics felt that in the future the RUC should be "allowed to carry on exactly as it is now"; 23 percent of Protestants and 38 percent of Catholics thought the RUC should be "reformed"; and 4 percent of Protestants and 31 percent of Catholics thought it should be replaced by an entirely new police force (NIOS 1995).

The 1995 Omnibus Survey also revealed polarised attitudes on several symbolic matters. Half of the Catholics surveyed want the name of the RUC changed—they dislike the British *Royal* and the loyalist *Ulster*—but only 8 percent of Protestants favour this outcome. One-third of the Catholics think the Union flag should never be flown at police stations and 42 percent would restrict its flying to designated days when it is flown on all Crown buildings. Half of the Protestants want the flag flown without restrictions, whereas a third would restrict it to designated days. The arming of RUC officers traditionally has had both a symbolic dimension, distinguishing them from police elsewhere in the United Kingdom, and practical consequences, in terms of the discharge of firearms, sometimes in disputed circumstances. Fifty percent of Protestants but only 18 percent of Catholics felt the police should always carry guns; two-thirds of Catholics thought the police should be armed only when engaged in high-risk duties, and 14 percent think they should never carry guns.

The idea of "community policing" has attracted much public attention since the beginning of the ceasefire.[1] The 1995 Omnibus Survey found that two-thirds of the Catholics and three-quarters of the Protestants favoured more "community policing" (left undefined in the survey). In troubled neighbourhoods, however, there is lingering distrust of the RUC's ostensibly benign practices, such as contacts with community groups, programmes for youth, and foot patrols. My in-depth interviews in these areas in 1990–1992 (Weitzer 1995) and in 1995 help to explain this continuing suspicion. For instance, in 1995 a community worker in a republican neighbourhood in Belfast stated:

> The RUC are trying to be too nice too soon. You don't shoot plastic bullets one day and come and give sweets to kids the next day. It's premature for them to be doing community relations work. They have to get their own house in order first. . . . It's the RUC's own fault, presenting themselves as a "nicey-nice" police force, the local bobby, as if they never did anything wrong before.

A community worker in another Republican area echoed this sentiment: "People here don't want more foot patrols. . . . A community affairs officer has been trying to get involved [with residents] but local people say it is too early. People feel police shouldn't push too quickly. Officers working with youth in schools or through the community centre—people think it's not time for that yet." My interviews in some staunchly loyalist neighbourhoods also suggest that residents may not be ready to welcome community constables, for the same reasons as in republican areas.

Even in the event of a lasting cessation of political violence, therefore, a rapid switch from counterinsurgency to community policing would be premature. Certain neighbourhoods are simply not receptive to any form of community policing, even during a ceasefire in the armed conflict. Moreover, the entrenchment of a security orientation among RUC officers increases the difficulty of making any switch to a more benign role, as a former Chief Constable admitted: "We'd have a stupendous job of reorienting the whole force to a community service role. . . . [Each officer] would have to become almost an entirely different sort of policeman" (quoted in Hart 1990: 30). It seems necessary for the RUC first to *expand its conventional law enforcement activities*, thereby gradually building citizen support and laying the foundation for community policing sometime in the future. Indeed, significant numbers of Catholics and Protestants have long felt that more priority should be given to ordinary crimes, such as burglary, drugs, and car theft (NIOS 1995; Weitzer 1995).

Reducing counterinsurgency actions and expanding ordinary policing will improve police-community relations, but another factor has perhaps a stronger influence on these relations. In the absence of a political settlement, that is, we should not expect substantial improvement in police relations with citizens, especially in militant republican and loyalist communities. In republican neighbourhoods the RUC has long been branded as "unreformable," and in the debate over reform during the 1994–1996 ceasefire, anti-RUC graffiti proliferated in these communities. The extent of such sentiment is evident in the 1995 Omnibus Survey's finding that nearly 33 percent of Catholics (but only 4 percent of Protestants) want the RUC dismantled and replaced by a new police force.

Conclusion

The connection between policing and the state is very much in the foreground in Northern Ireland. Popular legitimation of the police is ultimately contingent on the larger national question, and the British government's political initiatives since 1972 have influenced perceptions of the RUC for both Catholics and Protestants. Ever since the beginning of British rule, Protestants have worried about whose interests the police would protect. In the past decade they have increasingly questioned the RUC's leanings, sometimes labeling police as tools of the British state or even as anti-Protestant. Such suspicions have only *intensified* since the beginning of the ceasefire; many Protestants believe that political concessions are being made to Catholics alone, and a diffuse sense of being "sold out" by the British government is further undermining their confidence in the RUC. As community workers in two Protestant neighbourhoods told me, "The ceasefire has deepened hostility to the police," and "relations have worsened, gotten sharper—a feeling of betrayal among ordinary people, betrayal by the police and the state."

The breakdown in the IRA's first ceasefire in February 1996 encouraged caution among those formally responsible for the formulation and implementation of policing policy in Northern Ireland. The optimism for the future that greeted the first cessation of hostilities has not been emulated since the second one announced in July 1997, thus affecting the likelihood of RUC reform for the foreseeable future. There have been changes that bear on police-community relations—most notably, the announcement of a Parades Commission to arbitrate decisions on planned marches and parades, thereby taking the RUC out of the first line of decisionmaking on what has proven to be an increasingly contentious issue. However, the planned legislation to create the statutory framework for the Parades Commission and the code of conduct governing public processions will also empower the Chief Constable to refer decisions made by this commission to the Secretary of State at times when she is concerned about possible public disorder. In addition, the legislation provides for the exercise of police discretion on the day of a march at times when there is a concern to preserve public order. In effect, the RUC will be placed at wrist's length, rather than arm's length, in the decisionmaking process. On a broader front, the current Chief Constable, Ronnie Flanagan, has argued that the RUC is "opposed to change for change's sake" and that the collapse of the first ceasefire means "it is much too soon to contemplate structural changes to the force" (*Belfast Telegraph,* 23 October 1997).

As Flanagan himself has acknowledged, policing reforms in the absence of accompanying changes in the political system will have limited influence on popular attitudes. However, renewed efforts are to be made in the direction of changing the ethnic balance of the RUC and creating a neutral working environment within the force—achieved, in part, through the possibility of creating a register for officers who are affiliated with external organisations such as the Orange Order, membership of which requires some sort of oath. In addition, at the end of November 1997 Secretary of State Dr. Marjorie Mowlam launched the first-ever set of policing objectives for Northern Ireland, delineating six priorities for the RUC during the year 1998–1999:

- to counter the terrorist threat on behalf of the community and bring to justice those responsible for terrorist crime;
- to maintain public order, thereby providing for the protection and security of the public;
- to reduce violent crime in Northern Ireland and increase the proportion of violent crimes detected;
- to reduce burglaries in Northern Ireland and increase the proportion of domestic burglaries detected;
- to reduce the numbers of those killed and seriously injured in road traffic accidents; and
- to target the supply of illegal drugs and to work in partnership with other agencies in tackling the problem of drug misuse.

Similar objectives, with their attendant performance indicators, have become routinised by the British police forces, and their extension to Northern Ireland represents the attempt, in Dr. Mowlam's words, "to make the police service more efficient, effective and accountable"

(Northern Ireland Information Service, 25 November 1997). Indeed, the Secretary of State went to some lengths to present this initiative as an integral "part of a new framework of police accountability" that heralds "a new era in the field of policing" (Northern Ireland Information Service, 25 November 1997). Such objectives are necessary elements of a new policing regime in Northern Ireland. Ultimately, however, any major transformation of policing structures is contingent upon an overall political settlement acceptable to all parties.

References and Further Reading

Boyle, Kevin, Tom Hadden, and Paddy Hillyard, 1975. *Law and State: The Case of Northern Ireland.* Amherst: University of Massachusetts Press.

Brewer, John, 1991. "Policing in divided societies," *Policing and Society* 1, pp. 179–191.

Buckland, Patrick, 1979. *The Factory of Grievances: Devolved Government in Northern Ireland.* New York: Barnes and Noble.

CAS (Community Attitudes Survey), 1993–1994. Policy, Planning, and Research Unit. Belfast: Northern Ireland Office.

Chief Constable, 1995. *Annual Report, 1994.* Belfast: Police Authority.

Farrell, Michael, 1983. *Arming the Protestants: The Formation of the Ulster Special Constabulary and the Royal Ulster Constabulary.* London: Pluto.

Gardiner Committee, 1975. *Report of a Committee to Consider, in the Context of Civil Liberties and Human Rights, Measures to Deal with Terrorism in Northern Ireland,* Cmnd. 5847. London: HMSO.

Hamilton, Andrew, Linda Moore, and Tim Trimble, 1995. *Policing a Divided Society: Issues and Perceptions in Northern Ireland.* University of Ulster: Centre for the Study of Conflict.

Hart, William, 1990. "Waging peace in Northern Ireland," *Police Magazine* 3, May, pp. 23–30.

Helsinki Watch, 1991. *Human Rights in Northern Ireland.* New York: Helsinki Watch.

Hillyard, Paddy, 1993. *Suspect Community.* London: Pluto.

Hunt Committee, 1969. *Report of the Advisory Committee on Police in Northern Ireland,* Cmnd. 535. Belfast: HMSO.

ICPC (Independent Commission for Police Complaints), 1988–1994. *Annual Reports.* Belfast: HMSO.

______, 1995. *Northern Ireland Social Omnibus Survey.* Belfast: Research and Evaluation Services.

Mapstone, Richard, 1992. "The attitudes of police in a divided society," *British Journal of Criminology* 32, pp. 183–192.

McVeigh, Robbie, 1994. *"It's Part of Life Here": The Security Forces and Harassment in Northern Ireland.* Belfast: CAJ.

NIOS (Northern Ireland Omnibus Survey), 1995. Policy, Planning, and Research Unit. Belfast: Northern Ireland Office.

______, 1996. Northern Ireland Statistics and Research Agency report, reprinted in Police Authority, *A Partnership for Change*. Belfast: Northern Ireland Office.

Northern Ireland Consumer Panel Poll, 1985. *Belfast Telegraph*. February 6.

Northern Ireland Office, 1996. *Foundations for Policing*, Cmnd. 3249. London: HMSO.

Police Authority, 1996. *"Everyone's Police": A Partnership for Change*. Report on a Community Consultation Exercise. Belfast: Police Authority for Northern Ireland.

Reuss-Ianni, Elizabeth, 1983. *Two Cultures of Policing*. New Brunswick: Transaction.

SAS (Social Attitudes Survey), 1990. Social and Community Planning Research, London.

Sluka, Jeffrey, 1989. *Hearts and Minds, Water and Fish: Support for the IRA and the INLA in a Northern Irish Ghetto*. Greenwich, Conn.: JAI Press.

Smith, David, 1987. *Equality and Inequality in Northern Ireland*. London: Policy Studies Institute.

Ulster Marketing Survey, 1985. *BBC Spotlight Report*, British Broadcasting Corporation.

Walsh, Dermot, 1983. *The Use and Abuse of Emergency Legislation in Northern Ireland*. London: Cobden Trust.

Weitzer, Ronald, 1985. "Policing a divided society: Obstacles to normalisation in Northern Ireland," *Social Problems* 33, pp. 41–55.

______, 1987. "Contested order: The struggle over British security policy in Northern Ireland," *Comparative Politics* 19, pp. 281–298.

______, 1990. *Transforming Settler States: Communal Conflict and Internal Security in Northern Ireland and Zimbabwe*. Berkeley: University of California Press.

______, 1992. "Northern Ireland's police liaison committees," *Policing and Society* 2, pp. 233–243.

______, 1995. *Policing Under Fire: Ethnic Conflict and Police-Community Relations in Northern Ireland*. Albany, N.Y.: State University of New York Press.

9

Women and Politics

RICK WILFORD

Despite periodic efforts to forge a common front, the women's movement has foundered over the mutually reinforcing cleavages of nationality and religion that structure Northern Ireland's political alignments (Ward 1987; Loughran 1990; Evason 1991; McWilliams 1991, 1995).[1] Feminism, which everywhere is best comprehended as a broad church, has proven to be no less susceptible to sectarianism than other social movements in the province. That said, the cessation of violence following the ceasefires of 1994 raised the spectre of a more stable polity within which "normal" politics could develop.

That altered, though fragile, situation created the opportunity for strategic coalitions of women to campaign on issues previously marginalised by constitutional policy. The election to the Northern Ireland Forum held on 30 May 1996 provided the opening for just such a grouping to emerge in the shape of the hastily improvised Northern Ireland Women's Coalition (NIWC). A determinedly cross-community organisation, the NIWC sprang something of a surprise by securing a sufficient number of votes to return two members to the Forum; hence it was assured of a role in the multiparty talks,[2] including those begun in September 1997, following the IRA's renewal of its cessation of violence (Wilford, forthcoming).

The relative success of the Coalition was consistent with the findings of a major research project (Miller, Wilford, and Donoghue 1996) that suggested there was support, if not for a women's party, then certainly for increased representation by women within the public realm. This support was in part buoyed by the belief that, if elected in sufficient numbers, women could make a difference to politics in the province—a view also held by the region's women councillors (Wilford, Miller, Bell, and Donoghue 1993). Moreover, there was a widespread perception among women of all religious and political persuasions that the existing political parties in Northern Ireland had failed them, as well as broad support among women (and men) for a liberal feminist agenda. This support, however, fell short of the endorsement of a pro-choice position on the abortion issue: On matters of body/sexual politics, women in Northern Ireland generally embrace more conservative attitudes than do their cohorts in the more secular climate of Britain (Montgomery and Davies 1991).

Findings from the study of women's political participation by Robert Lee Miller and his colleagues (1996) also indicate that, although gender gaps do exist, women and men in the province are more alike than they are different (see also Donoghue and Devine, forthcoming), at least in terms of their rates of participation. This observation is consistent with the "revisionist" theory of political participation delineated by Pippa Norris (1991). In addition, there is evidence indicating that women do not participate (significantly) less than men, but also that their modes and arenas of political activity are somewhat different from men's. In that respect there is support for the "radical" theory of participation, which contends that women are active in relatively unstructured, fragmented, and transitory groups that, as Norris (1991) observes, are normally neglected by mainstream studies of political participation. Before we examine such findings in depth, however, a brief survey of the historical and cultural context of Northern Ireland will help to situate women in the public realm.

Unhappy Liaisons

Perhaps one of the less remarked-upon features of Northern Ireland is that its contingent place within the U.K., coupled until 1998 (see Chapter 12) with the irredentism of the Republic of Ireland, has infused the terms of political debate in the province with martial and, thereby, primarily "manly" virtues, embodied in republicanism's "ballot and bullet" strategy and loyalism's resolute slogan "Not an inch, no surrender." The dominance of these competing nationalisms has inhibited other more or less subtle distinctions of identity and leant a zero-sum character to its politics: "If they win, we lose." Such "either/or-ism" has yielded little to women of whatever tradition. Whether nationalist, republican, loyalist, or unionist, women in general—and feminists in particular—have discovered that the debate about citizenship has revolved around national identity, leaving little room for contemplation of its gendered dimensions.

Armed patriarchy[3] in Northern Ireland has been attenuated by the active involvement of women in paramilitary organisations, especially within the republican movement, but it has not resolved an historically unhappy relationship between feminism and Irish nationalism. Indeed, although the formal claim to socialist credentials espoused by Irish republicanism creates the ideological space for a commitment to gender equality, not all women in the contemporary republican movement are persuaded that this goal is a constituent element of its project. Similarly, the status of women within the unionist tradition has been an historically subordinate one. Its conservatism, expressed most obviously in terms of the determination to maintain the constitutional status quo, has spilled over into the realm of gender relations. In policy terms, the province's unionist parties have until recently paid scant attention to women, and loyalist paramilitarism has remained an exclusively male activity.

Despite the active involvement of women in the struggle for Irish independence, feminists were particularly ill-served by the nationalist movement. The foundation of the unhappy relationship between feminism and nationalism and, latterly, republicanism, was laid well before partition. Encouraged by the apparent promise of the Easter Rising of 1916 to deliver equality for all, feminists quickly recognised that Irish nationalism was inhospitable to their demands. As Margaret Ward (1983) observes, its "rigidly masculine" character subjugated the needs of women, while feminists were criticised for their "lack of commitment to the nationalist cause." The subsequent "reward" of independence was the Irish Constitution of 1937, celebrating Eamon De Valera's vision of a Catholic, predominantly rural, and decidedly patriarchal state.

The legacy of that experience endures. Although both the Provisional IRA and Sinn Féin accorded full equality to the women in their ranks during the early 1970s, the underlying tension between feminism and republicanism surfaced in a publication from the Women's Department of Sinn Féin commemorating the twenty-fifth anniversary of the renewed "troubles" (Sinn Féin 1994). One contributor, reflecting on the mobilisation of women during the hunger strikes of 1980 and 1981, notes that the "sense of purpose, of solidarity and common cause" that they generated was swiftly dissipated: "The failure to recognise women's particular abilities, to provide the means to allow women to function, meant that their cohesion faded" (McCrory 1994: 16). More pointedly, she observes that whereas women in the republican movement "always fought alongside our brothers without preconditions, men's support for women's demands has always been conditional. If we don't move forward together," she concludes, "we won't move forward at all" (McCrory 1994: 16).

These sentiments are echoed by a former Sinn Féin councillor: "[E]quality within our republican communities is still something that politically active women have yet to achieve" (Gillespie 1994: 17). Acknowledging the key priority to be the unification of Ireland, she insists, nevertheless, that "gender-based inequality must also be fought against now; we must recognise that the struggle for women's liberation is an integral part of that overall struggle against oppression" (Gillespie 1994: 17). Such admonitions belie the unreflective faith of an earlier nationalist leader (and the first woman to be elected to the Westminster parliament), Countess Markievicz: "[F]ix your minds on the idea of Ireland free, with her women enjoying the full rights of citizenship in their own nation" (quoted in Beale 1986). Later generations of feminist republicans are not prepared to wait on their "brothers" and risk the same fate as their predecessors: consigned, via a patriarchal constitution, to subordination.

The historic, secondary status of women in the nationalist and republican movements is mirrored within the unionist/loyalist tradition—as exemplified by events surrounding the passage of the third home-rule bill in parliament, when the Irish Unionists demonstrated their willingness to engage in rebellion by devising the Ulster Covenant. Its male signatories committed themselves to defend the union by force, whereas women were permitted to sign not the covenant but, rather, the Women's Declaration—itself drafted by two men—which obliged them to support the "uncompromising opposition of the men of Ulster." This helpmate role was consistent with the constitution of the Ulster Women's Unionist Council established in 1911. Its primary objective was "the maintenance of the Legislative Union between Great Britain and Ireland [to which] all other questions in which individual members may be specially interested shall be subordinated" (Kinghan 1975). Included among these subordinated questions was the issue of female suffrage, which effectively marginalised the gendered dimension of citizenship (Miller et al. 1996, 12–15).

The general lesson for women throughout Ireland was that the events of the decade or so leading to partition rendered their rights secondary to the imperatives of territorial politics. Although women in Northern Ireland were spared the formally subject status imposed by the Irish Constitution of 1937 (Galligan 1993), they, too, have faced formidable obstacles preventing their full enjoyment of equal citizenship. In the labour market they were confronted by a marriage bar in the public service that persisted until the late 1960s, their participation in the workforce has been subject to wearyingly familiar patterns of occupational segregation, and their rates of economic activity have been historically low and still lag approximately 10 percent behind those of women in the U.K. Additionally, the double burden carried by women is clear from evidence demonstrating the inequitable division of domestic labour, influenced in part by the fact that Northern Ireland, although it has among the highest birthrates in the European Union, also suffers one of the lowest levels of publicly funded childcare provision (EOCNI 1991; Turner 1993).

In the province, the unresolved national question, the readiness to resort to political violence, the doctrinal and institutional patriarchy of the Catholic Church, and the resilience of a "traditional model of gender relations" (Morgan and Fraser 1994) within the Church of Ireland and the Presbyterian Church, together with the inclement attitude of both nationalism and unionism toward feminism: All combine to create a formidable set of hurdles in the path of women seeking entry to the public realm. One index of these obstacles is the dismal record of women in elected office.

Women and Public Office

Elections

Between 1921 and 1969, there were 12 general elections to the local 52-seat parliament (Stormont), attracting a total of 1,008 candidacies, of which 37 (4 percent) were female. Together with a further 6 candidacies at by-elections, over the course of almost a half-century there was a total of merely 43 candidacies shared among 20 women, 9 of whom were elected.[4] Never constituting more than 6 percent of candidates, no more than 4 women were returned to any one of the dozen parliaments. At the final election in 1969 the proportion of female candidates dwindled to 2 percent, matching the paltry level achieved at the first one held almost fifty years before. When sectarian tension and conflict escalated, as was the case at both Stormont's birth and its eventual demise, the virtual male monopoly of the Northern Ireland parliament was all the more apparent.

Following the imposition of direct rule in 1972, successive British governments have pursued the goal of a devolved consociation (see Chapter 6). To that end, three attempts at creating region-wide institutions either founded upon, or seeking to promote, the principle of power sharing have been tried. Each of these failed institutions—the Assembly of 1973–1974, the Constitutional Convention of 1975–1976, and the Assembly of 1982–1986—had seventy-eight members elected by single transferable vote, and each boasted only four women members.

The paucity of women in the local parliament and the other regional assemblies is only modestly bettered at the local authority level. In the wake of direct rule the discredited local government system was subjected to wholesale reform, leaving the councils with a residue of only minor and uncontroversial functions. STV elections to the twenty-six District Councils, first contested in May 1973, are held every four years. As summarised in Table 9.1, the total number of women contesting local elections has shown a gentle upward trend since 1977, when wholly reliable data on the sex of candidates first became available.

The increased representation by women in local government cannot be explained in terms of the adoption of women-friendly selection procedures by the parties (see below). According to the 1989 intake of female councillors (Wilford et al. 1993), the emasculated role of local government has (appropriately enough, perhaps) deterred men from seeking candidacy—a perception that is confirmed by the fact that party competitiveness at local elections between 1977 and 1997 declined from 1.9 to 1.7 candidates per seat. In consequence, the parties have, the councillors believe, turned to women merely to complete their slates.

In relation to Westminster elcctions the picture is even gloomier. At the seven general elections held during the interwar period there were no female candidates for Northern Ireland's twelve Parliamentary seats, whereas at the fifteen postwar general elections only sixty-seven women have stood for Westminster constituencies, thirty-nine of whom (58 percent) contested the elections of 1992 and 1997. In all, just three have been elected: Patricia Ford, Ulster Unionist, Down North (1953–1955); Patricia McLaughlin, Ulster Unionist, West Belfast (1955–1959, 1959–1964); and Bernadette Devlin, Unity candidate, Mid-Ulster (1969–1970, 1970–February 1974). Furthermore, until 1994, when there were five female candidates, only one woman had previously fought for one of the province's three seats in the European parliament.

Appointment

The bleakness of this record is redeemed to some extent by the exercise of patronage. As Robert Darcy, Susan Welch, and Janet Clark (1994) have noted, appointment as a method of selection for public office does tend to favour women—partly because it has become increasingly difficult for those dispensing patronage to rationalise the exclusion of women, and partly as a result of the social utility gained by achieving gender balance in public appointments. However, although

TABLE 9.1 Women in Local Government Elections in Northern Ireland: 1977–1997

Year	Seats N	Total Candidates N	Women Candidates N	Women Candidates %	Women Elected N	Women Elected %
1977	526	1002	95	9.5	38	7.2
1981	526	982	107	10.9	42	8.0
1985	566	994	109	11.0	55	9.7
1989	566	905	128	14.1	64	11.3
1993	582	933	132	14.1	70	12.0
1997	582	975	167	17.1	83	14.1

Note: At the 1997 local government elections, the proportion of female candidates for each of the five major parties was as follows (1993 proportions are in parentheses): Ulster Unionist Party (UUP) 14 percent (14 percent); Democratic Unionist Party (DUP) 14 percent (10 percent); Social Democratic and Labour Party (SDLP) 26 percent (16 percent); Sinn Fein 17 percent (12 percent); and Alliance Party 29 percent (31 percent). The proportion of seats won by women on behalf of these five parties in 1997 was as follows (again 1993 proportions are in parentheses): UUP 14 percent (11 percent); DUP 11 percent (7 percent); SDLP 17 percent (16 percent); Sinn Fein 12 percent (16 percent); and Alliance Party 34 percent (25 percent). The modesty of the increase in number of women candidates between 1993 and 1997 (n=35) becomes even more apparent in light of the fact that 20 of them ran on behalf of the NIWC, which was formed in 1996.

Source: Calculated by the author from data supplied by the chief electoral officer for Northern Ireland.

Darcy and his colleagues (1994: 17) suggest that women are better represented in appointed bodies because they are "usually less politically important than elected positions," this general proposition applies less well in Northern Ireland.

The demotion of local government required the creation of a wide array of nominated bodies to administer services formerly provided by local councils (see Chapter 7). Expressly designed to be free of sectarianism and to ensure the efficient administration of, *inter alia*, public housing, education, health, and the personal social services, such bodies—besides monitoring the implementation of legislation to combat sex and religious discrimination—are invested with immense symbolic and practical significance. Their membership is determined by the Northern Ireland Office (NIO), whose successive ministerial teams have used their powers of patronage to the relative advantage of women. Between 1991 and 1995, for instance, the proportion of women serving on the province's 128 nominated bodies increased from 25 percent to 32 percent.[5] In the province, appointment, rather than election, has proved a surer route to numerical representation by women.

Political Participation

Women have not, of course, had to rely on appointed office to make their presence felt in the public realm; indeed, they have also proven adept at movement politics, whether as "deliberate" or "accidental" activists (McWilliams 1995). Before the renewal of violence in the late 1960s, for example, women were prominent in the Campaign for Social Justice formed in 1964; the NI Civil Rights Association established in 1967; and People's Democracy, the radical, student-led group formed in 1968. Since the outbreak of the troubles, women have also been active in organisations that constitute a response to certain of the pathologies of Northern Ireland. For instance, they were instrumental in launching the campaign for religiously integrated schools and in establishing groups opposed to the so-called punishment beatings and shootings meted out by both republican and loyalist paramilitaries. But the most pronounced, if fleeting, impact made by women *en masse* was that associated with the Women's Peace Movement—subsequently dubbed the Peace People—which emerged in 1976.

Prompted by the deaths of three children in a troubles-related incident, one of its founders, Mairead Corrigan, struck the feminised note that became the movement's theme: "I believe it is time for the women to have a go and see what the women, of both sides, working together, can do" (Bew and Gillespie 1993: 113). The campaign swiftly attracted international recognition, culminating in 1977 with the award of the Nobel Peace Prize to its co-founders. Here, it seemed, was the effective answer to conflict and, moreover, one that prized an essentialist association of women with nonviolence. Within three years, however, the movement was in disarray. Accused by republicans of being effectively pro-British because of its refusal to condemn the violence of the security forces, riven by internal disputes over policy, and beset by widespread criticism over the allocation of the monetary award accompanying the Nobel Prize, the movement witnessed the ebbing away of its support.

The circumstances of its decline are, though, perhaps less significant than the gender stereotype it perpetuated. The close identity of women with the Peace People stoked the image of them as peace makers—or at least as peace seekers. Yet, although the link between women and nonviolence implies an apparent moral strength, it can also be interpreted as a measure of powerlessness. Given that women have been bereft of all but a virtually token presence in elected office, the later observation by Eilish Rooney and Margaret Woods (1992: 24) seems pertinent: "We should be cautious about placing the burden of peace on women without the power of peacemaking."

Less dramatic than the emergence of the Peace People has been the quiet growth of a wide range of voluntary bodies organised by and for women (Taillon 1992; Smyth 1995). Many, in plugging the gaps of an inadequate welfare regime, have an ostensibly instrumental purpose—rape crisis centres, legal advice centres, refuges, and mother and toddler groups, to name just a few examples. But they also serve expressive and communitarian functions. Evidence from the survey of women's political participation in Northern Ireland (Miller et al. 1996) demonstrates that women are significantly more likely than men to be actively involved in a wide range of charitable, communal, voluntary, and church-related organisations that "can be seen as political since . . . they address policy issues of public concern" (Norris 1991), even if they do so in an indirect way. That women are engaged in such half-hidden arenas of activity does tend to legitimate the proposition that they participate differently from, and not less than, men. Furthermore, although men are, voting turnout excepted, more likely than women to engage in both conventional forms of political activity (party membership, pressure group membership, employment-related organisations, contacting behaviour) and unconventional forms (petitioning, letter writing, various forms of protests, boycotts), such differences are not statistically significant.

Gender in Northern Ireland does not, in fact, emerge as a reliable predictor of political participation; neither does one's religious affiliation nor one's felt national identity. Indeed, the findings of Miller and his colleagues (1996) are consistent with the revisionist theory of political participation: Women and men are more alike than they are different. In short, irrespective of sex, religious beliefs, or stated national identity, people who are politically active and politically interested tend also to be highly educated, to have a high occupational status, and to be in their middle years.

The definition of political participation employed in the study by Miller and his colleagues was an expansive one; encompassing activities in both the domestic and the public realms, it thereby incorporated direct as well as indirect attempts to influence policymakers. The inclusion of the domestic realm created the opportunity to explore its interactions with the public realm, rather than resulting in the treatment of each as a discrete arena. Hence the family emerged, especially among women, as a primary and safe venue for discussions and arguments about politics. Another family-based index of political participation employed by the study concerned the socialisation of children, especially in relation to the promotion of civic (or uncivic) virtues. On this series of measures, women emerge as moral arbiters, particularly in terms of the transmission of religious beliefs and attitudes concerning both sexual equality and behaviour. Men, however, appear to vacate these areas, concentrating instead on imparting their preferred partisan identity to their children.

In these explorations of the family as a site of political activity, a model of mutuality was seen to prevail among the most participative. The most politically active within the population, whether female or male, are commonly the partners of equally participative individuals: In effect, like attracts like. This resource of mutuality lends another dimension to the aphorism "The personal is political," as does the finding that the presence of children in the household can act as a spur, rather than an impediment, to participation by women—especially in relation to activities concerning the secular and religious education of children.

Communitarianism

Qualitative data from the study of participation also show that women's greater involvement in voluntary, charitable, and church-related groups is motivated primarily by two factors: personal fulfilment and the desire to be "socially useful." The latter is consistent with the communitarian motive identified by Geraint Parry, George Moyser, and Neil Day (1992: 12–13)—namely, that "where people are highly integrated into the local community and where they identify strongly with it, participation would be greater." Underlying this motive are feelings of interdependence, neighbourliness, and an awareness of shared needs believed to be characteristic of small, tightly knit societies.

Northern Ireland is, in both geographic and population terms, a small society within which political identities remain sharply drawn. Although mutual suspicion has tended to accentuate difference and insularity, among highly participative women irrespective of their national and/or religious identity there is an acknowledgement of a nascent community of interests that straddles the sectarian divide. Even "die-hards" find little difficulty in asserting the existence of a "sisterhood" within the province, albeit one that chimes with notions of female essentialism and with traditional assumptions about gendered family roles. A self-ascribed "dyed-in-the-wool" unionist captures the belief in a shared identity among women thus: "There is a sisterhood here, just by being a woman even. Women don't ask other women who they are and where they're from, they mix better: men don't" (quoted in Miller et al. 1996: 109). Such sentiments are echoed by a loyalist whose inclusive, gendered sense of community extends across even the political boundary: "While the south should have no say in Ulster, we could have a great relationship in that the women's groups there and here could meet and help each other. Both parts of the island could benefit" (quoted in Miller et al. 1996: 110).

A self-defined nationalist from North Belfast also voices a sense of sisterly solidarity, in the process finding no difficulty in identifying differences between the sexes:

> The women have the most experience of the troubles, the effects of the troubles and probably have the solution to its problems. Men have dominated for so long and have one-track minds on politics. I think women would be more open about it; they're more peaceful because of the maternal thing. . . . The troubles unite women, they come off worse because they are the ones that have to worry. Women can identify with the other side whereas men can only see their own side, one faction against another. The sisterhood isn't political like brotherhood is with men: it's to do with grief, bereavement and children. (Miller et al. 1996: 113)

Among other things, this quotation appears consistent with the portrayal of the dualism of women's culture—an "invisible sphere suppressed in the world of men [which] carries a potential for change and liberation that affects the entire society" (Hedlund 1988: 13). On the one hand lies the culture's negative dimension, implied by the image of a keening mother Ireland shouldering the miseries inflicted by men. On the other is its more positive guise: Unencumbered by sectarianism, women are believed to possess a clearer vision of a "solution," focused both by their oppression and by the experience of motherhood. Though it may seem something of a caricature, the prevalence of motives such as personal fulfilment and the desire to be socially useful among activist women suggests that they are able to negotiate, if not shed, the divisions of a segmented society. Whereas male activists tend to engage in intracommunal activities and to express a more insular sense of identity, female activists—in their dovetailing of self and other-directedness—are more likely to voice and enact an inclusive, woman-centred grasp of the concept of community (Miller et al. 1996: 107–120).

The finding that women activists tend to occupy a civic space poised between the formal realms of politics and the domestic arena might be interpreted as a means of rationalising their absence from elected office: necessity proving, as it were, the mother of political invention. This, though, would be to devalue the positive orientations that many bring to the more submerged arenas of political participation. Equally, such marginal terrain may seem to be safer ground upon which to become engaged in Northern Ireland's public realm. But though activist women tend to regard female identity as conferring the advantage of relative physical safety, at the same time they do not believe that it provides a badge of immunity against violence, either for themselves or their families.

Women and Party Offices

Nor are they deterred by any perceived risks of a more formal involvement in politics, even though most have experienced "the troubles" firsthand. Among activists and within the general population there is a demand for an increase in numerical representation by women. Almost two-thirds of all female respondents wish to see more women both in parliament and in local councils—views that are shared by half of all men (Miller et al. 1996: 189).

Within the general population there is also widespread evidence of disillusionment with the parties. In the same survey, for instance, when asked which of the parties "best serve the interests of women," 62 percent of all female respondents answered "none" (as did 46 percent of all men). Among party identifiers, a majority of the men (57 percent) and half of the women also stated the belief that no party represents women's interests. Furthermore, 62 percent of all the women and 51 percent of all the men agreed that the region's parties "do not give women the opportunity to enter politics." Such findings direct attention to party strategies concerning the selection of candidates and the extent of office holding by women within each of the parties.

With the exception of the Alliance Party of Northern Ireland (APNI), which has just one spokesperson on women's issues, each of the major parties from which I obtained information has a dedicated women's section. The oldest of these is the Ulster Unionist Party's Ulster Women's Unionist Council (UWUC), which is organised on a constituency basis and delegates members to the Ulster Unionist Council (UUC), the party's approximately 800-strong plenary body. The key policymaking agency within the UUC is the 120-strong Executive Committee (elected by members of the party's eighteen constituency associations); 18 of these 120 (15 percent) are women. In 1995 there were 120 constituency offices within the party, of which 27 (22.5 percent) were held by women, including two constituency association chairpersons. More indicative of the role of women within the UUP was the fact that, in 1996, each of the party's fourteen full-time officers were male, although one of its elected vice-chairpersons is female. The Ulster Unionist Party has also established an eight-strong Women's Affairs Committee (WAC) that was largely responsible for framing its 1997 manifesto proposals on "women's issues" (see below).

The APNI is one of the two major parties that has been chaired by a woman (the other is the SDLP). In 1995 four women sat on its twelve-member Executive, including the vice-chair of the party. Six of its twenty-three local associations (based on district electoral areas) were chaired by women, and ten each of the treasurers and secretaries of the associations were female. Like the UUP, the Alliance Party makes no provision for positive discrimination on behalf of women for either party offices or election candidacy. However, unlike the UUP, which restricts itself to a strategy of exhortation, the APNI does embrace positive action in the form of training seminars for potential female candidates.

The SDLP has six full-time party officers, only one of whom is female. Additionally, in 1995 there were six women on its fifteen-strong Executive, including the chairperson of its newly reorganised Women's Group and one of the vice-chairs of the party. Among other things, the Women's Group provides training and development courses for women interested in standing for election to public and/or party office. Thus, it too embraces a positive action strategy that has recently been complemented by the introduction of a quota system for party office. At its 1994 Annual Conference the SDLP adopted the following motion: "Conference . . . calls on the Party to adopt an affirmative action programme with the goal of women filling 50 per cent of all levels in the party." At a special delegate conference held in June 1995, the outcome of the motion was agreement to guarantee at least 40 percent of places on its Executive Committee to women, and to reserve at least two places for female councillors on a new General Council that will be responsible for developing and implementing party policy.

Until the SDLP's adoption of an internal quota, Sinn Féin was the only party to employ such a device for the election of its National Executive and other party committees. The result was that in 1995 there were nine women on its twenty-four-member Executive. Two of Sinn Féin's five members who were engaged in post-ceasefire negotiations with the NIO were women (including the party's general secretary, Lucilita Bhreatnach), as were two of its five delegates/alternates to the Dublin-based Forum for Peace and Reconciliation. The entry of Sinn Féin into the talks process in September 1997 led to the inclusion of one woman (Bhreatnach) in its negotiating team, where she joined the two women at the talks table representing the NIWC and, of course, the first woman to hold the post of Secretary of State, Dr. Marjorie Mowlam. Women are well represented within the organisational structure of Sinn Féin, holding six of the nine directorships of its departments.

In Northern Ireland, as elsewhere in Western Europe (see Lovenduski and Norris 1993), parties with at least nominally socialist credentials are the ones that have made the greatest provision for women in relation to party offices. The extent to which the varying levels of such provision is substantive or merely symbolic is difficult to gauge with precision. However, a brief overview of party policies on gender issues suggests that greater numerical representation does not necessarily entail a more sensitive approach to the representation of what might loosely be termed "women's interests."

Policy Issues

As guides to party thinking, manifestos have to be treated with some caution since they are invariably strong on slogans and weak on detail. Nevertheless, textual analysis of party manifestos and related documents suggests that parties tend to converge toward what Pru Chamberlayne (1993: 172) defines as a "gender recognition strategy" by focusing upon "the particular obstacles impeding women's equality." However, the attention devoted to gender issues by the parties shows considerable variation.

After 1976, and before 1997, the SDLP did not produce a discrete policy document on women, and its manifestos for the 1992 Westminster and 1994 European parliamentary elections offered few concrete proposals for the achievement of equal rights for women. In its Euromanifesto, for example, the party couched its appeal to women in a brief statement on "Equality" in which it reiterated the commitment to pursue the equal rights agenda for women adopted by the Parliamentary Group of the Party of European Socialists. This agenda included the strict application of the principle of equal pay for equal work; equal treatment within the social security system; equality of opportunity in education, training, and employment; and the availability of child care "to all those who need it."

The SDLP's 1997 publication, *Half the Future,* was couched in the same equality-of-opportunity terms. Though relegated to the status of a discussion document when it first appeared, it proved influential in shaping the SDLP's general election manifesto just three months later. The manifesto embraced the recommended overhaul of the existing legislation on equal pay and sex discrimination to provide for class actions and the adoption of affirmative action in employment practices (i.e., targets and timetables, not quotas), and it proposed the appointment of a "minister for equality" in government to oversee employment law and procedures. To enable women to enter the labour market it urged "investment in adequate child-care facilities," greater access to training and retraining courses, and an increase in the scale of publicly financed loans available to female entrepreneurs. It also recommended the introduction of an improved parental-leave scheme and, consistent with the policy of its sister parties in the European parliament, endorsed the Social Chapter, the implementation of a minimum wage, and guaranteed minimum rights for all workers, regardless of contractual status—a measure of particular interest to women employed on a part-time basis.

The SDLP's reform of its policies in regard to women, though belated, overshadows the record of the region's largest single party, the UUP. For instance, the UUP's *Policy Statement on Women's Issues* (produced for the 1992 General Election), which was less than two pages long, affirmed its support for existing legislation directed against sex discrimination and endorsed the principle of equal pay for equal work as well as the statutory provision of pregnancy and maternity rights consistent with Article 119 of the Treaty of Rome. In addition, it proposed the extension of tax concessions to encourage child-care facilities in the workplace and endorsed improved educational access designed to "encourage girls to achieve in areas which have traditionally been male-dominated." Such proposals were entirely consistent with its belief in "a society of equal opportunity" and its explicit rejection of positive discrimination, which it regards as unethical and ineffective. By the time the 1997 General Election took place, little had changed.

Drawing on *Women in the Nineties,* produced by the UUP's Women's Affairs Committee (WAC), the manifesto restated a commitment to the equal opportunities strategy. It favoured equal access to the job market where women, having secured *"training compatible with family responsibilities"* (my emphasis) should receive "equal pay for equal work" rather than for work of equal value. The manifesto acknowledges the effects of the "glass ceiling" on women's employment prospects, and, striking a utilitarian note, it recognises that impediments to women's upward mobility robs society of a pool of talent. Further, it argues that such impediments can be overcome through the adoption by employers of "family friendly management practices," including the widespread adoption of flexible working arrangements, nursery facilities at the workplace, and the extension of tax concessions to provide for workplace child care. At the same time the WAC also insists that "the UUP places considerable emphasis on the value of the family unit . . . and on the unique role of the mother, especially in a child's early years" (WAC 1996: 4).

The party's 1997 general election manifesto restated its adherence to the "merit principle," eschewing all forms of positive discrimination in employment. It then concluded by proposing the simplification of arrest, charge, and prosecution procedures in cases involving violence against women and by endorsing more extensive provision for rehabilitation and support centres for the victims of sexual violence. The UUP, via the WAC, also addressed a number of health and care issues on behalf of women, including better diagnostic and screening facilities, improved access to maternity units, and a more integrated community care service designed to support both patients and carers who, it recognises, are mostly female. The UUP's policies are directed primarily toward the reinforcement of women's roles, although it does flirt with a reformulation of gender roles by arguing that the responsibilities associated with caring, whether for the young or old, should be shared by men. The family-centredness of the UUP is apparent, and unapologetically so. The party accepts as axiomatic that women's place is tucked into the folds of the domestic realm where they can enact their caring tasks.

Between the 1992 and 1997 general elections, the Democratic Unionist Party (DUP)—judging from its manifestos—appears to have regressed. In 1992 it included a brief (eighty-six-word) statement on "women's issues" in which it acknowledged that "women are a majority and should no longer bc treated as a minority." To that end, and alone among the parties, the DUP called for the creation of a Ministry for Women whose remit included the promotion of equal pay and pensions, improved maternity rights, a parental leave scheme, and expanded child-care provision facilitated by tax relief. More a clutch of headlines than a detailed set of policy proposals, this particular manifesto gave equal prominence to the "fight for family and moral values"—a fight that was focused on its (failed) campaign to prevent the opening of a Brook Advisory Centre[6] in Belfast on the grounds that it would "undermine parental authority and family values." These proposals, though limited, surpassed the party's position in 1997 when its manifesto was exclusively concerned with constitutional matters.

However, a separate policy paper—*Women's Issues* (1997)—did address the numerical majority, albeit in rather patrician terms: "The women of Ulster deserve our best efforts on their behalf." Those efforts included support for state-subsidised workplace crèche facilities and flexible working arrangements designed to ensure that mothers are available to their children at the end of the school day. There is an air of reluctance enveloping these proposals, as evidenced by the remark in the policy paper that "many more women are in the position of having to work" than have the opportunity of choosing to do so. This rather grudging tone also applies to the party's views on single mothers. Regarding the increase in their numbers as "alarming" and extolling "the importance of the family unit and the institution of marriage," it nevertheless concedes that "we cannot ignore the hard realities of life" and recognises that single mothers, especially those in their teens, present "a vast area of need." This recognition reinforces the party's support for affordable workplace child care so that lone mothers can "hold down a job and raise their children."

In addition, the policy document addressed the crimes of rape, sexual abuse, domestic violence, and "the fight against pornography." The DUP favours an increase in the length of custodial sentences for all convicted of sexual offences as well as the prevention of those so convicted from living and working in the vicinity of their victims upon release. Indicating a belief in female essentialism, it also recommends that more women be appointed to the judiciary since they "could bring to their job an extra dimension of sensitivity and understanding."

The elision of "woman" and "wife" and "mother" is apparent in the DUP's platform, signaling its unreflective tendency to reinforce traditional gender roles. One of its loyalist opponents, the Ulster Democratic Party (UDP), took a more developed line in its 1997 manifesto, arguing, for instance, in favour of the widespread availability of free, comprehensive family planning services and, alone among all the parties, for the extension of the 1967 Abortion Act, as amended, to Northern Ireland. It shared the DUP's support for subsidised workplace child care and flexible working arrangements for working mothers, and leant support for increased employment opportunities for single mothers. It also expressed opposition to the reductions in social security payments to lone mothers proposed by the Major government's 1996 budget and, more broadly, proposed the introduction of paid leave from work to provide care for sick and/or elderly relatives. The manifesto of the other loyalist party, the Progressive Unionist Party, paled by comparison, confining itself to a rhetorical flourish by stating that "women have an equal role to play at all levels of political activity" and encouraging women to come forward as electoral candidates. The latter manifesto—like that of the DUP—concentrated on constitutional matters, simply appending a list of "other equally important issues"—including "women's rights"—that were left unstated.

Sinn Féin's paper record in relation to women is the most expansive of all the parties, as illustrated by its lengthy list of proposals in *Women in Ireland,* a publication that was prepared prior to the 1992 General Election and addressed both parts of the island. It was sustained both by a concern to empower women in the public and private realms and by its belief that "gender and social class are the two most important determinants of a person's life-chances." At first sight, the document appeared to be impeccably woman-centred. Yet, on closer inspection, it inclined clearly toward a maternalist perspective: "Present economic and social structures . . . are," it stated, "built around the life-cycles of men. Women's life-cycles are different; changes will have to reflect the needs of women as mothers, within the family, as well as their right to participate fully in all the economic, social and political aspects of society." To that end it proposed a statutory minimum wage, equal pay for work of equal value, the abolition of mandatory retirement ages, the extension of maternity leave on full pay, the provision of free comprehensive child care, and the introduction of positive action programmes "to enable women to get access to education and retraining, especially in non-traditional occupations." Consistent with its wider project, "the rights of women to full equality" will, it asserted, be secured only by the ending of partition and the creation of a "32-County Socialist Republic."

In 1997 Sinn Féin included a brief section on women in its general election manifesto and, alone among the parties, also carried its proposals in its local government manifesto published a few weeks later. The tone of its approach to gender issues was set by the statement that "women in Ireland suffer from systematic and institutionalised sexual discrimination," and its goal was expressed as the achievement of "equality of citizenship" for women. In relation to employment this meant the adoption of the model of affirmative action introduced by the 1989 Fair Employment Act—namely, the application of goals and timetables by employers to the hiring of women rather than to the sanctioning of job quotas. At the same time, however, Sinn Féin endorsed the stricter application of the principle of equal pay for work of equal value and embraced more flexible and extensive training schemes for women as well as the incorporation of child-care provision for women engaged in training or retraining. The one area in which Sinn Féin sanctioned preferential treatment was the provision of permanent state funding for women's organisations and community-based women-only educational courses. Such a limited flirtation with positive discrimination, together with the historically chequered relationship between republicanism and feminism, helps to explain the doubts expressed by female republicans about the commitment of Sinn Féin to women's equality that were noted earlier.

Like the SDLP, Sinn Féin sought the extension of the legal definition of rape alongside a more multifaceted approach to the eradication of violence against women, statutory funding for rape crisis centres, and better training for legal and medical personnel concerning the effects of rape. Another area of convergence related to health matters: Like the UUP, Sinn Féin argued for the adequate provision of health services for expectant mothers and for enhanced resources to be directed toward health education and preventative medicine.

The APNI's policy paper devised for the 1992 General Election (also entitled *Women's Issues*) and its 1997 manifesto were steeped in an equal rights philosophy and endorsed the EU's directives on social and economic equality for women. But as the party devoted just half of one page in its nineteen-page manifesto to "women's issues" (the same amount of space accorded to overseas development), the manifesto was woefully short on detail. Its commitment to the expansion of nursery and child-care provision and support for equal pay for equal work was undiminished, although the manifesto also implied a belief in interest representation by noting that women's rights are neglected "because they are not represented in the places where they can argue for them." This was a view shared by the SDLP, which, in its 1997 manifesto, insisted that the absence of women from public office meant "the omission of their priorities and world view from the processes of legislation and administration." Yet, like all the other parties, the APNI opposed gender-based positive discrimination (whether in relation to electoral candidacy or employment), opting instead for the vague statement that "positive steps should be taken to encourage women to take their place in leadership positions." Ultimately, however, such haziness—in combination with the historic record of the parties concerning both the numerical and the interest (under)representation of women—proved increasingly unacceptable to a number of women's community groups and led to the creation in 1996 of the Northern Ireland Women's Coalition (NIWC) (McWilliams and Kilmurray 1997; Wilford, forthcoming).

A little over a year old by the time of the 1997 General Election, the NIWC had already manifested its exasperation with the timidity of the region's parties in promoting women as electoral candidates by fielding seventy of its own at the 1996 Forum Election. On that occasion it secured a notable, if numerically modest, success by achieving its goal of seeing two of its number returned to the Forum and the consequent multiparty talks. This achievement owed much to the NIWC's success in mobilising its supporters across Northern Ireland in order to exploit the opportunity provided by the regional list employed as the second stage of the election (see Chapter 4).

At the 1996 Forum Election, the 1997 General Election (where the NIWC fielded three candidates, each of whom lost her deposit), and the 1997 District Council Election (where one of its twenty candidates was elected), the Coalition exhibited its belief in both interest representation and self-empowerment by running all-female tickets. On each occasion it framed its appeal to voters in the same terms—

namely, that the pursuit of "inclusion and accommodation," "equity," and "human rights" required, as its General Election manifesto stated, "new voices" and "new choices," and that these were provided by "women for a change." Freed from a fixed position on the constitutional question,[7] the NIWC portrayed itself as a vehicle for an inclusive approach to a political settlement. In this attempt at feminising politics, it effectively argued that change—the leitmotif of its appeal—would be assisted by "making women's voices heard," even though its women-specific policies were limited. It also insisted that "many issues of concern to women are ignored" (the examples it gave included domestic violence, sexual abuse, rape, and cancer screening) and pointed out that they affected everyone, not just women.

This stance was interesting inasmuch as it signaled a refusal by the Coalition to be ghettoised into an exclusive concern with the euphemistically termed "women's issues." At the same time it implied a certain female essentialism, but not in the unreflective (and untrue) sense that only women are concerned about achieving peace. Rather, the NIWC presented itself as an exemplar of the need for inclusiveness and pluralism in seeking a political settlement, reflecting the fact that the wider women's movement has successfully accommodated diversity in seeking equal status for women. In effect, the Coalition's platform drew inspiration from the shared and sometimes difficult experiences of ideologically distinctive feminists who have reconciled their doctrinal differences in pursuit of a common good. Yet, in the context of a divided society, such a position may find few friends—or at least electors. As the post-Forum Election results indicate, the ground that the NIWC identified for itself proved narrowly, if clearly, drawn.

A Women's Culture?

The shared sensitivity among the leading parties to the constraints impeding women's enjoyment of equal rights—notably, those associated with parenthood—is consistent with the gender recognition strategy identified by Chamberlayne (1993). Although none of the parties ignore the specificity of women's roles by adopting a "gender neutral" approach, there is little to indicate their awareness of a "gender reconstruction" strategy that stresses the need to change men's roles. The clear tilt of the parties toward gender recognition is, however, tempered by lingering evidence of a more conservative "gender reinforcement" approach. The common emphasis on maternity rights, the Alliance Party's stress on "value and respect for those who work in the home," the UUP's emphasis on the family unit, and the DUP's tren-

TABLE 9.2 "Which Party in Northern Ireland Best Represents the Interests of Women?" (% female party identifiers, $N = 1,174$)

	Party Identifiers Nominating:		
Party Identity	*Own Party (%)*	*Other Party (%)*	*No Party (%)*
UUP	27.2	13.5	59.3
DUP	21.5	19.1	59.4
APNI	36.9	8.6	54.5
SDLP	32.9	14.9	52.2
SF	10.5	31.2	58.3

Source: Miller, Wilford, and Donoghue (1996).

chant defence of family values, together with more than a hint of mother-centredness in Sinn Féin's proposals, are each symptomatic of a more traditional, pro-family view of women's roles.

The study by Miller and his colleagues (1996) also disclosed high levels of support for a gender recognition strategy, indicating a broad congruence between female voters and their preferred parties. This finding, however, raises an apparent anomaly. If there is a symmetry between the stated policy preferences of the parties and popular attitudes concerning women's rights, why do a significant majority of women believe that no party adequately represents their interests? (See Table 9.2.)

The affinity between the parties and the various blocs of female voters concerning the endorsement of gender recognition policies suggests that the failings of the parties are seen to reside elsewhere, notably in relation to the constitutional issue. In particular, the participation study demonstrates that it is the perceived unwillingness of male politicians to reach a political settlement that creates a sense of unrepresentation among women. This is not to say that women believe themselves to be less, or men more, principled on this first-order priority; rather, the perceived "ruthlessness" and "ambition" of male political leaders are understood to frustrate the achievement of compromise. The disposition to seek consensus is regarded by both sexes within the general population to be characteristic of female, not male, politicians.

There is also evidence indicating the existence of a shared agenda among women in the province, the neglect of which contributes to disillusion with the parties. Women of all political persuasions—and none—were critical of the tendency of male politicians to ignore "everyday problems," commonly citing education, the health service, child care, unemployment, and care of the elderly as issues that languished below the high politics of the constitutional question. The frequency with which politically active women are clustered into voluntary bodies involved with health, education, and welfare tends to confirm the salience of such issues for them. On the one hand, this clustering could be construed as the exercise of self-interest, whereby women are seeking to ameliorate the inadequacies of the welfare regime for instrumental reasons. On the other, it could be rationalised as an instance of *faut de mieux:* Women participate in such organisations simply because they have nowhere else to go. But each interpretation diminishes the motives that underpin such activities. The reward of self-fulfilment, allied to the desire to be socially useful, is consistent with Gun Hedlund's (1988: 13) delineation of the positive aspects of women's culture: an emphasis on connectedness, on care for others, and on a behavioural style that is cooperative and unaggressive, suggesting that women are not wholly powerless but, rather, enact distinctive values "that are independent of the male world and not merely compensatory to it."

Conclusion

I do not mean to imply that women, unlike men, have the future in their bones, nor that they are more likely to regard the past as a foreign country. The prospect that women in Northern Ireland—like those in Scotland, for instance (Brown 1996)—can combine to ensure parity of representation in a new regional Assembly is, if not entirely idle, rather more remote: The weight of history still bears heavily on the present among both women and men. There are, however, increasing signs that parity of esteem for women is being actively pursued by new organisations, notably the NIWC, seeking to ensure that they are included fully in any talks designed to secure a political settlement.[8]

The question of whether or not more women would make a positive difference remains untested. But the combined effect of three factors—the popular belief in Northern Ireland that female politicians are inclined toward compromise, the frequency with which communitarianism informs women's motives for political participation, and the desire for more women in public office—offers a challenging vision (Wilford 1996b). Moreover, as the aforementioned participation study shows, the belief among both sexes within the wider population that women typically possess attributes that are desired in politicians—including honesty, the capacity for hard work, approachability, and the disposition to care—suggests that any lingering voter hostility is eclipsed by more positive characterisations of female politicians (Miller et al. 1996).

Whether defended in terms of fairness, social utility, or interest representation, attempts to increase women's presence in elected office will, as Joni Lovenduski (1993) reminds us, rest largely on their own efforts. The record of its parties to date suggests that Northern Ireland is no exception to this general rule.

References and Further Reading

Beale, Jenny, 1986. *Women in Ireland: Voices of Change*. Dublin: Gill and Macmillan.

Bew, Paul, and Gordon Gillespie, 1993. *Northern Ireland: A Chronology of the Troubles 1968–1993*. Dublin: Gill and Macmillan.

Brown, Alice, 1996. "Women and politics in Scotland," *Parliamentary Affairs* 49, pp. 26–40.

Chamberlayne, Pru, 1993. "Women and the state: Changes in roles and rights in France, West Germany, Italy and Britain," pp. 170–193 in Jane Lewis (ed.), *Women and Social Policies in Europe*. Aldershot: Edward Elgar.

Darcy, Robert, Susan Welch, and Janet Clark, 1994. *Women, Elections and Representation*, 2nd ed. Lincoln: University of Nebraska Press.

Donoghue, Freda, and Paula Devine, forthcoming. "The battle of the sexes in Ireland, North and South: Is there a gender gap?" in Yvonne Galligan, Eilis Ward, and Rick Wilford (eds.), *Contesting Politics: Women in Ireland, North and South*. Boulder: Westview Press.

EOCNI (Equal Opportunities Commission for Northern Ireland), 1991. *Where Do Women Figure?* Belfast: EOCNI.

Evason, Eileen, 1991. *Against the Grain*. Dublin: Attic Press.

Galligan, Yvonne, 1993. "Party politics and gender in the Republic of Ireland," pp. 147–167 in Joni Lovenduski and Pippa Norris (eds.), *Gender and Party Politics*. London: Sage.

Gillespie, Una, 1994. "Women in struggle," pp. 17–19 in Sinn Féin Women's Department, *Women in Struggle: 25 Years of Resistance*. Dublin: Sinn Féin.

Hedlund, Gun, 1988. "Women's interests in local politics," pp. 79–105 in Kathleen Jones and Anna Jonasdottir (eds.), *The Political Interests of Gender: Developing Theory and Research with a Human Face*. London: Sage.

Kinghan, Nancy, 1975. *United We Stood: The Story of the Ulster Women's Unionist Council 1911–1974*. Belfast: Appletree Press.

Loughran, Christine, 1990. "Armagh and feminist strategy," pp. 170–183 in Terri Lovell (ed.), *British Feminist Thought*. Oxford: Blackwell.

Lovenduski, Joni, 1993. "Introduction: The dynamics of gender and party," pp. 1–15 in Joni Lovenduski and Pippa Norris (eds.), *Gender and Party Politics*. London: Sage.

Lovenduski, Joni, and Pippa Norris (eds.), 1993. *Gender and Party Politics*. London: Sage.

McCrory, Maura, 1994. "Women took the lead," pp. 15–16 in Sinn Féin Women's Department, *Women in Struggle: 25 Years of Resistance*. Dublin: Sinn Féin.

McWilliams, Monica, 1991. "Women in Northern Ireland," pp. 81–100 in Eamon Hughes (ed.), *Culture and Politics in Northern Ireland: 1960–1990*. Milton Keynes: Open University Press.

______, 1995. "Struggling for peace and justice: Reflections on women's activism in Northern Ireland," *Journal of Women's History* 6, pp. 13–39.

McWilliams, Monica, and Avila Kilmurray, 1997. "Athene on the loose: The origins of the Northern Ireland Women's Coalition," *Irish Journal of Feminist Studies* 2, pp. 1–21.

Miller, Robert Lee, Rick Wilford, and Freda Donoghue, 1996. *Women and Political Participation in Northern Ireland*. Aldershot: Avebury.

Montgomery, Pamela, and Celia Davies, 1991. "A woman's place in Northern Ireland," pp. 74–95 in Peter Stringer and Gillian Robinson (eds.), *Social Attitudes in Northern Ireland 1990–1991*. Belfast: Blackstaff Press.

Morgan, Valerie, and Grace Fraser, 1994. *The Company We Keep: Women, Community and Organisations*. University of Ulster: Centre for the Study of Conflict.

Norris, Pippa, 1991. "Gender differences in political participation in Britain: Traditional, radical and revisionist models," *Government and Opposition* 26, pp. 56–74.

Parry, Geraint, George Moyser, and Neil Day, 1992. *Political Participation and Democracy in Britain*. Cambridge: Cambridge University Press.

Pankhurst, Sylvia, 1977. *The Suffrage Movement*. London: Virago.

Rooney, Eilish, and Margaret Woods. 1992. *Women, Community and Politics in Northern Ireland: A Research Project with an Action Outcome*. Jordanstown: University of Ulster.

Sinn Féin, 1994. *Women in Struggle: 25 Years of Resistance*. Dublin: Sinn Féin Women's Department.

Smyth, Marie, 1995. "Women, peace, community relations and voluntary action," pp. 145–160 in Nick Acheson and Arthur Williamson (eds.), *Voluntary Action and Social Policy in Northern Ireland*. Aldershot: Avebury.

Taillon, Ruth, 1992. *Directory of Women's Organisations in Northern Ireland*. Belfast: Women's Support Network.

Turner, Irene, 1993. "Childcare," pp. 151–174 in John Kremer and Pamela Montgomery (eds.), *Women's Working Lives*. Belfast: HMSO.

WAC (Women's Affairs Committee), 1996. *Women in the Nineties*. Belfast: Ulster Unionist Party.

Ward, Margaret, 1983. *Unmanageable Revolutionaries: Women and Irish Nationalism*. London: Pluto Press.

______, 1987. *A Difficult, Dangerous Honesty*. Belfast: Women's Book Collective.

Wilford, Rick, 1996a. "Representing women," pp. 48–55 in Kate Fearon (ed.), *Power, Politics, Positionings—Women in Northern Ireland*. Belfast: Democratic Dialogue.

______, 1996b. "Women and politics in Northern Ireland," *Parliamentary Affairs* 49, pp. 41–54.

______, 1997. "The Northern Ireland Women's Coalition: A biographical survey." Women and Politics in Ireland Conference, Trinity College Dublin, April.

______, forthcoming. "Women's candidacies and electability in a divided society: The Northern Ireland Women's Coalition and the 1996 Forum Election," *Women and Politics*.

Wilford, Rick, Robert Lee Miller, Yolanda Bell, and Freda Donoghue, 1993. "In their own voices: Women councillors in Northern Ireland," *Public Administration* 71, pp. 341–355.

* Start to finish *

10

Northern Ireland and the Republic

BRIAN GIRVIN

Prior to the referendum on 22 May 1998 that endorsed the reformulation of Articles 2 and 3 of the its constitution, the Republic of Ireland was the only state in the European Union with a territorial claim over part of another member state.[1] Partition and this irredentist claim have been the main points of contention between the two sovereign governments, but they have also reinforced the polarisation of the political culture in Northern Ireland itself (Rose 1971). Until recently, neither traditional diplomacy nor conflict resolution has been successful in addressing the problems central to this polarisation; yet, in common with other liberal democratic states (Kant 1795; Doyle 1986), the conflict between Britain and Ireland has not escalated to a military level. The relationship between the Republic of Ireland and Northern Ireland has been even more complex than that between the two states. Irish nationalists have rejected the legitimacy of Northern Ireland ever since the Government of Ireland Act of 1920, whereas the unionist majority in Northern Ireland rejected the nationalist claim and repressed the nationalist minority within Northern Ireland (Kennedy 1988; Phoenix 1994; Follis 1995).

In turn, every Irish government has insisted on the integrity of the island as a political unit, holding the view that the only solution to conflict is a united Ireland under Dublin control. The nationalist case was based on the assumption that partition was imposed by Britain for imperial reasons, that it was unjust, and that all those who lived on the island formed a "natural" national community (Whyte 1990: 117–145). The logical consequence of this view was that Northern

Irish unionists had no right to self-determination, even if they themselves demanded it—a view still maintained by some writers (Anderson 1980; Adams 1986). The same view has been well represented in the literature of the anti-partitionist movement since the 1920s. For example, a government publication argued that,

> Ireland is by natural design a complete geographical entity. This natural design enforced on the political life of Ireland at a very early date the ideal of national unity, and it is doing violence, not only to nature, but to the whole trend of the political life of the island to divorce politically at this late date in her national existence a considerable section of the northern part of the country from the motherland. (*Handbook of the Ulster Question* 1923: 91)

The same general position was maintained by each of the Irish prime ministers since 1923—even one usually associated with reform, such as Seán Lemass (Lemass 1959). However, policy toward Northern Ireland was not a seamless garment. The Cumann na nGaedheal government (1923–1932) sought to secure gains from Britain through conventional diplomatic means, in some cases with considerable success (Harkness 1969). The Boundary Commission, which, it was hoped, would reduce the northern state to territorial absurdity, did not fulfil nationalist expectations, and its failure contributed to criticism of the government and the rise of a new and more radical nationalist party, Fianna Fáil. The alternative view is that there is no single nation on the island, though the consequence of accepting the multinational position is not always spelt out (Heslinga 1971; Gallagher 1990). In a recent review of the literature, Michael Gallagher (1995) has suggested that there may be three nations on the island or, at the very least, "two nations and part of another nation."

Fianna Fáil and the Constitutional Claim

The first item in the Fianna Fáil Constitution was and remains a commitment "[t]o secure the Unity and Independence of Ireland as a Republic." After that party came to power in 1932, a more vigorous approach was taken regarding the existence of Northern Ireland. In the 1937 Constitution, largely written by Eamon de Valera himself (Keogh 1994), the claim to Northern Ireland was made explicit in a number of articles, including the following:

- Article 2: The National territory consists of the whole island of Ireland, its islands and the territorial seas.

- Article 3: Pending the re-integration of the national territory, and without prejudice to the right of the Parliament and Government established by this constitution to exercise jurisdiction over the whole of that territory, the laws enacted by that Parliament shall have the like area and extent of application as the laws of Saorstát Éireann and the like extra-territorial effect.

Taken together, these articles provided a powerful ideological challenge to the existence of Northern Ireland. In March 1990 the Irish Supreme Court upheld the view that those who live in Northern Ireland are, in fact, citizens of the Republic of Ireland. Various interpretations of these articles have been offered, but, despite recent suggestions to the contrary, they were seen at the time as real claims to territory and, until 1998, as ones that Irish governments maintained subsequently (Girvin 1994: 10–12; O'Halloran 1987; Lee 1989).

The republicanisation of Irish society, which took place between 1932 and 1948, was a product of de Valera and the Fianna Fáil Party, but it was endorsed by most sections of nationalist opinion (Keogh 1994; Girvin, forthcoming). The Dáil was outraged by the U.K.'s decision in 1949 to introduce the Ireland Act, which, *inter alia*, reasserted British sovereignty in Northern Ireland—a decision made in response to the declaration of a Republic. The Anti-Partition campaign organised by de Valera, once he was out of office in 1948, pressured the 1948–1951 interparty coalition government to hold firm to the Fianna Fáil's position on Northern Ireland—or on the "Six Counties," as Irish diplomats, journalists, and politicians insisted on describing the state. The IRA border campaign, which started in December 1956, increased tension between North and South and between nationalists and unionists in Northern Ireland. Unionists continued to believe that, notwithstanding the decision of the Dublin government to intern IRA activists, there was a common interest between the aims (if not the methods) of the two.

A Change of Emphasis

Between 1932 and 1966 the de Valera view of partition remained dominant, but by the end of the 1950s the irredentist position began to appear increasingly outmoded even though the rhetoric was maintained for some time thereafter (Lemass 1959). Some writers began to question the traditional approach to the North and argued for a more nuanced and realistic set of policies (Barrington 1957; FitzGerald 1991: 64). But perhaps the most important contribution to this new mood came from the new Taoiseach, Seán Lemass, after he assumed the office in 1959. He quickly discarded the ritualistic condemnation of Northern unionism and sought to build bridges to the political elite there. This is not to say that Lemass relinquished the historic objective of achieving a united Ireland; rather, he believed it was possible to engage in dialogue with unionists and to achieve some semblance of normality in relations between the two parts of Ireland. The change in emphasis did not pass without criticism from nationalists, but it was an important point of departure for Irish nationalism. What it signaled was the recognition for the first time that if unity was to be achieved, then the Irish government would have to persuade unionists of this prospect rather than, as had been the case with de Valera, imposing unity on Northern Ireland in cooperation with the British government.

Lemass spelt out what this objective would entail for Irish nationalism when in 1966 he claimed that,

> [w]e recognise that the government and the parliament there (in Northern Ireland) exist with the support of the majority of the people of the six counties area—artificial though that area is. . . . Recognition of the realities of the situation has never been a difficulty with us. . . . [T]he solution of the problem of partition is one to be found in Ireland by Irishmen. (cited in Herz 1986: 147)

The recognition that partition was an Irish problem implied that the traditional view of it as the creation of the imperial power had been mistaken. In this light, consideration was given to revising the claim to Northern Ireland contained in Articles 2 and 3 of the constitution. One suggested revision affirmed the belief in unity, but framed it in terms of an aspiration: "The Irish nation hereby proclaims its firm will that its territory be reunited in harmony and brotherly affection between all Irishmen" (*Report of the Committee on the Constitution* 1967: 5). Despite the promise contained in this proposal and the commitment among sections of the political elite in the Republic to reform the constitution and normalise relations with Northern Ireland, it was not realised. There are a number of reasons for this outcome. By 1968 normalisation had become an elite activity that did not penetrate the mass of the population in the South. Also by that time, Lemass had retired as Taoiseach to be succeeded by Jack Lynch, an individual without the same republican credentials as his predecessor. This successor generation in Fianna Fáil was, as Conor Cruise O'Brien (1994: 160–167) points out, at an ideological disadvantage when conflict broke out in Northern Ireland in 1968 and 1969. It is possible that the elite in the Republic could have moved faster and with greater confidence in the absence of violence; it was, after all, operating in an environment that was both stable and legitimate. In Northern Ireland the unionist elite was seriously divided on policy and, in 1969, was opposed by the most effective anti-unionist movement since the establishment of the state. In these circumstances the return of violence in 1969 and the reorganisation of the IRA in the early 1970s polarised opinion in both parts of Ireland.

The Impact of the North on Policy

The response among the political elites in the South after 1969, in keeping with mass opinion, was to move toward a more confrontational and traditional position on Northern Ireland. This was most apparent among Fianna Fáil supporters, who identified strongly with the objective of a United Ireland; but it was also shared by significant sections of other parties. In addition, there is evidence that sections of Fianna Fáil cooperated in the establishment of the Provisional IRA and may have been involved in gun smuggling at this time. Although these allegations led to the dismissal of some government ministers and to their trial on gun-smuggling charges, Fianna Fáil itself continued to stress the traditional positions on unity (Joyce and Murtagh 1983: 87–91; Keogh 1994: 307–314).

As the conflict intensified, opinion in the South began to divide. There was widespread sympathy for northern Catholics in the Republic, but also some ambiguity about what policy to pursue. In May 1970, 17 percent of those interviewed in a survey believed it would be necessary to send Irish troops into Northern Ireland if violence on the scale of 1969 were to return. The intense reaction to "Bloody Sunday" in 1972, however, did not lead to intervention by the Irish army—and this was probably the moment when pressure to act in such a fashion was at its strongest. Survey evidence suggests that fewer than 20 percent of the people in the Republic embraced what might be described as a militant nationalist position, including support for the use of violence by the IRA in Northern Ireland. At the other end of the scale, a survey carried out in Dublin between 1972 and 1973 suggested that the violence in Northern Ireland was having an effect on opinion. Nearly 43 percent of those interviewed believed that Northern Ireland and the Republic constituted two separate nations, whereas 55 percent disagreed with this view. Over a third of those interviewed gave qualified support for the use of violence in Northern Ireland, whereas more than 50 percent considered that Northern Protestants had more in common with Britain than with the Irish people (Mac Greil 1977: 375–399; Davis and Sinnott 1979).

These surveys indicate that some rethinking was under way in the Republic, but it would have been difficult to detect at the level of policy or among the major political parties. The only politician to break decisively with the nationalist consensus at this time was Conor Cruise O'Brien, who challenged the main elements of nationalist thinking between 1973 and 1977 when he was a minister in the Fine Gael-Labour Party coalition government. Although some elements within the government were sympathetic to his views, the government adopted a law-and-order approach to the question without challenging in any fundamental way the claims contained in the constitution (O'Brien 1974; Akenson 1994: 385–425). Garret FitzGerald, foreign minister in the coalition government, was also engaged in a process of rethinking the relationship between the two parts of Ireland; but, unlike O'Brien, he remained within the nationalist consensus (FitzGerald 1991: 196–263).

The Sunningdale Agreement of 1973 provides a useful example of the limitations of policy on both sides of the border at this time. This arrangement secured Irish recognition of the constitutional status of Northern Ireland, as some unionists formed an unprecedented coalition government with the Social Democratic and Labour Party (SDLP) and other parties. However, the insistence by the Irish government and the SDLP on a Council of Ireland provided the means for unionist opponents of the arrangements to undermine the power-sharing Executive during the Ulster Workers Council strike in 1974. O'Brien (1994: 165–167) has argued that the Irish government did not appreciate the strength of feeling among unionists in respect of all-Ireland institutions and that the insistence on a Council of Ireland condemned power sharing to failure (cited in Girvin 1986: 123–124).

Haughey and Traditional Nationalism

The failure of the power-sharing Executive to gain legitimacy from both communities, the continuing violence, and the return of Fianna Fáil to power in 1977 reaffirmed the traditional nationalist position. The latter was reinforced after 1979, when Charles Haughey became leader of the Fianna Fáil party and articulated a fundamentalist position on Northern Ireland. For him the problem was one of the British presence in Northern Ireland, and in 1980 he openly called for British withdrawal as the only solution—a view most forcefully expressed by the SDLP. By this stage the real difference between Fianna Fáil and the

SDLP, on the one hand, and the Provisional IRA, on the other, was one of methods rather than objectives (Girvin 1994). The IRA believed that Irish unity could be achieved through the continuation of violence and that this outcome would force the British government to withdraw from Northern Ireland. Fianna Fáil and the SDLP did not embrace violence, but they shared the underlying assumption that the real problem was the presence of Britain in Northern Ireland. Despite the intervention of O'Brien, FitzGerald, and other liberal elements in the Northern debate, by the end of the 1970s Fianna Fáil and the SDLP were reasserting a traditional nationalist position on the North. Whereas government action was generally based on security considerations, this was not true of the political parties. Richard Sinnott (1986) notes the policy differences among the parties in the Republic, with Fianna Fáil identifiers adopting a traditional nationalist position.[2]

The importance of Charles Haughey should not be underestimated. In a very short period of time he imposed his political vision on Fianna Fáil, despite considerable opposition from the moderate elite within the party. The divisions that polarised the party for a decade were a consequence of Haughey's reassertion of traditional aspects of party policy. Peter Mair (1987: 217) has suggested that strategic and electoral considerations might have been involved at this time, but there also existed the ideological bias necessary for the strategy to be successful. Although this bias affected all aspects of party policy, it was more apparent in Northern Irish policy than elsewhere. Haughey consistently denied any distinct identity to the unionist population, arguing that partition had been imposed and was opposed by a majority of Irish people. For Haughey the question was a colonial one, similar to that of Hong Kong or other outposts of the British empire. Two sovereign governments could negotiate a settlement that would involve the orderly handover of power in Northern Ireland to the Irish government. However, much of this policy was based on wishful thinking. Haughey convinced himself that he had established a special understanding with Mrs. Thatcher in December 1980, but the British prime minister offered no public confirmation of this. Nor, despite his claims, did Haughey appreciate the sensitivity of unionist fears. When Robert McCartney, a prominent liberal unionist, argued that change in the Republic would help achieve reconciliation in the North (a view also actively promoted by FitzGerald), Haughey responded that this was not necessary because the problem rested with unionism rather than with nationalism: "[T]he whole problem of Northern Ireland arises from the refusal of the unionists in Northern Ireland to accept the democratic logic that they are part of a minority on this island." (See Mansergh 1986: 573–581 for the full text of Haughey's statement.)

The evidence suggests that for Haughey, and for a majority of his party, traditional policy objectives retained their saliency. Nevertheless, changes were taking place in the Republic. Between 1977 and 1982 Fianna Fáil's electoral support had weakened, and that of Fine Gael had strengthened. After a period of instability between 1981 and 1982, Garret FitzGerald was able to form a stable government in coalition with the Labour Party. Fine Gael had emerged as a liberalising party under FitzGerald's leadership, and he was especially anxious to distinguish his moderate and reasonable constitutional nationalism from that associated with traditional republicanism—especially that of Haughey. Though a nationalist in sentiment, FitzGerald took seriously the unionists' claim that they were British and considered that it was more important to end the violence and to promote reconciliation in the North than to seek unity as a short-term objective.

The years between 1982 and 1987 were of particular importance to the formulation of Irish government policy toward Northern Ireland. Although the hunger strikes by the Provisional IRA generated considerable sympathy among nationalists, the main political impact was Sinn Féin's electoral mobilisation in Northern Ireland. In the short term, FitzGerald's policy was motivated by a fear that the SDLP would find itself under electoral pressure from Sinn Féin. This fear led to the establishment of the New Ireland Forum, the objective of which was to promote the constitutional nationalist cause and to marginalise Sinn Féin. The most important long-term aim of FitzGerald's strategy was to challenge the traditional *methods* of pursuing Irish unity, though not the objective itself. Indeed, the logic of FitzGerald's position was that Irish unity would not be possible while IRA violence continued; nor did he believe that the constitutional claim helped in the process of reconciliation, although he did not actively campaign for the articles' deletion. Therefore, reconciliation and peace took precedence for FitzGerald over the territorial claim (FitzGerald 1991: 462–493).

Divisions Within Nationalism

At first, FitzGerald's attempt to change the nature of the political agenda failed in the face of Haughey's reassertion of nationalist orthodoxy. Within the Republic, FitzGerald's "constitutional crusade,"—initiated in the belief that constitutional reform would allay unionist fears concerning the power of the Catholic Church and nationalism—failed to realise his intentions. Ironically, his campaign led to the strengthening of Catholic and nationalist power during the referendums on moral issues in 1983 and 1986 (Girvin 1993: 389–390). Furthermore, the New Ireland Forum, though it held out the promise of a new beginning on the Northern question, led to the reassertion of the orthodox position in its May 1984 report. Although three alternatives were included in this final Forum Report, FitzGerald effectively conceded priority to the traditional nationalist objective of a united Ireland (FitzGerald 1991: 491–492). Moreover, Haughey politically outmanoeuvred FitzGerald subsequent to the publication of the report, giving the impression publicly that the united Ireland option was the one most favoured by the Forum. FitzGerald had sought nationalist consensus in the Forum and was not prepared to break decisively with this in response to Haughey.

Opinion polls reflected the divisions between nationalists and unionists on the Forum Report. In the Republic of Ireland 50 percent endorsed the unitary state view, whereas in Northern Ireland 87 percent of Sinn Féin and 62 percent of SDLP supporters endorsed this view. Nearly two-thirds of Protestants rejected the Forum Report, and 90 percent of those who identified with the Democratic Unionist Party (DUP) and the Ulster Unionist Party (UUP) opposed the idea of a unitary state (*Irish Times*/MRBI Poll, May 1984).[3] John Whyte (1990: 140) provides a more nuanced interpretation, suggesting that the Forum Report was not simply a "restatement of the old nationalist attitudes" but a more innovative attempt to break with the past. Subsequently, FitzGerald (1991) noted in his memoirs that, despite the weakness of the report, it allowed him to prepare the political ground for negotiations with the British government. This view is not convincing, however. It was the failure of the Forum to elicit a positive response, and especially the recognition that it was not possible to maintain a moderate constitutional consensus, that prompted FitzGerald to work toward an intergovernmental arrangement with Britain (Mair 1987b; O'Leary 1987).

In contrast, the 1985 Anglo-Irish Agreement (hereafter referred to as the Agreement) marks a major point of departure for Irish policy and "signifies the end of a united front amongst constitutional Irish nationalists" (O'Leary 1987: 15). It involved a defeat for the unionist position, giving Irish governments considerable policy input into Northern Ireland for the first time through the Intergovernmental Conference, as specified in Articles 4 and 5(c). Although Article 1 explicitly recognises the sovereignty of Northern Ireland, FitzGerald linked the text of this article to the view that "Britain has no interest in the continuing division of this island," arguing that partition "continues solely because this is the wish of a majority of the people of that area, and will not continue beyond the point where that consent is changed into consent for Irish unity" (quoted in Girvin 1986b: 160).

The Agreement highlighted growing divisions among Irish nationalists. Fianna Fáil and Sinn Féin believed that the Agreement involved conceding to unionist and British demands, and that it contradicted the recommendations of the Forum Report as well as being contrary to the constitutional claim on Northern Ireland. The concession on sovereignty was taken as the main source of criticism, and Haughey appeared to rule out the idea of consent in the relationship between the two parts of Ireland: "Does this mean that if the British government decided to legislate for Irish unity, Irish Nationalists would not accept it unless the unionists consented?" (quoted in Mansergh 1986: 1012–1026). This is the meaning clearly implied in Article 1 of the Agreement, but it was also the logic of the FitzGerald position. Haughey rejected the Agreement as the foundation for change, asserting that "[n]o government, no temporary majority has the right to sign away the rights of the Irish people." Haughey's invocation of de Valera in this quote reflects his weakness by this time. In contrast with his standing in 1983–1984, he was no longer the dominant force in Irish politics. His own party was divided on the issue: Two senior members, Desmond O'Malley and Mary Harney, were expelled for opposing policy and went on to form the Progressive Democrats, which supported the FitzGerald government on the Agreement.

The shift in Irish public opinion was appreciable, and its long-term impact was greatest in the Republic. Not only was there widespread support for the Agreement in the Republic and among Northern nationalists, but Fianna Fáil's opposition to it became an issue in the 1987 General Election. Although the popularity of FitzGerald and his government was low, some 44 percent of respondents believed that Fine Gael had the best policy on Northern Ireland, whereas only 29 percent considered that Fianna Fáil had the best policy. In addition, only 56 percent of Fianna Fáil supporters thought their own party had the best policy (*Irish Political Studies* 1988: 139). The new consensus on the North is evident in Fianna Fáil's change of policy during the election campaign: It reluctantly agreed to maintain the Agreement (Girvin 1987), thus confirming that Haughey had seriously miscalculated the extent of support for traditional territorial nationalism.

When Haughey formed a minority government after the election, he was faced with a pro-Agreement majority in the Dáil. In these circumstances he maintained the Agreement but applied the arrangements in a conservative fashion. The nature of the change in public opinion is highlighted in a December 1988 poll. It found that 74 percent of respondents wanted discussions with unionists; 15 percent believed that the purpose of the talks should be to achieve an internal settlement; a further 24 percent believed the purpose should be achievement of an all-Ireland settlement; and 49 percent considered that the object should be to "improve north-south relations, that is, the day-to-day relationships between the north and the south of the country." Although these views are not unproblematic, they highlight an increased sophistication in Irish opinion and the recognition that a "solution" would be complex (*Irish Political Studies* 1989).

As a consequence of the Anglo-Irish Agreement and the response to it, Articles 2 and 3 of the constitution entered the debate. For some time unionists had been arguing that these articles constituted a claim to control Northern Ireland, whereas Conor Cruise O'Brien and others in the South had been arguing for their deletion. Meanwhile, Haughey had argued that the Agreement contravened the articles and was unconstitutional. This claim was tested in the Irish Supreme Court by the McGimpsey brothers, moderate unionists who sought a ruling that the Agreement was contrary to the constitution. The Supreme Court rejected the McGimpsey case, holding,

> [t]hat in so far as the Anglo-Irish Agreement provided a means whereby the re-integration of the national territory might be achieved by a process of consultation and discussion, it would never be inconsistent with the constitution which is expressly devoted to peace and co-operation in international relations. (*Irish Law Reports* 1990)

The Supreme Court also found that re-integration was a "constitutional imperative" and that the claim in Article 2 to jurisdiction over the whole island was a "legal right." The Court concluded that the Agreement promoted Irish unity and was therefore not in conflict with the constitution. It then took the further step of invoking Article 9.2 of the constitution (which demands "fidelity to the nation and loyalty to the state"), claiming that the plaintiffs were citizens of the Irish state and were obliged to conform with this article (*Irish Law Reports* 1990).

The Supreme Court decision established the legal and constitutional limits of Irish nationalism by 1990. This formal reiteration of the traditional claim did not reflect the differences of opinion among the political parties, where considerable change was under way. In December 1990 these divisions were highlighted in a Dáil debate on a motion to amend Articles 2 and 3. Fianna Fáil defended the articles and cited the Supreme Court decision in their defence. All other parties gave qualified support for an amendment. The most radical contribution was made by John Bruton, the new leader of Fine Gael, who linked IRA violence to the claims in the constitution. Although the motion was defeated, the nature of the debate highlighted the changes taking place among the parties.

The resignation of Haughey in January 1992 and the election of his successor Albert Reynolds in February did not change the Fianna Fáil position on Northern Ireland. Indeed, Reynolds initially adopted a strong position on the so-called Brooke initiative launched in 1990 (see Chapter 6). Following the collapse of these discussions late in 1992, the Progressive Democrat and Alliance Party members who were involved accused the Taoiseach, Fianna Fáil, and the SDLP of intransigence and of refusing to conclude an agreement when one was possible. By the end of 1992 the nationalist position had become further hardened, in both the Irish government and the SDLP. A leaked position paper of the Irish government indicated that the latter would continue to insist on North-South institutions and a deepening of the process put in place by the Anglo-Irish Agreement (*Irish Times*, 11 November 1992).

Changing Opinion in the Republic

The collapse of the Irish government around this time, which led to general election in November 1992, highlighted considerable divisions within the nationalist community. During the election campaign Reynolds called John Bruton "John Unionist," an indication that for Fianna Fáil at least, Fine Gael had moved well beyond the nationalist consensus. There was also considerable disquiet among the SDLP leadership over the fact that a significant section of the political elite in Dublin was distancing itself from Articles 2 and 3 and, less explicitly, from anti-partitionism. As reflected in the MRBI surveys a complex position was emerging during the early 1990s. Over 80 percent of respondents believed a united Ireland was something to hope for, but some 40 percent believed that it would never happen or that it would take a hundred years. Male respondents, those over fifty, those living in rural areas, and Fianna Fáil supporters adopted the more traditional positions on these questions, whereas female respondents, the young, and those living in urban areas proved to be more sceptical in respect of traditional nationalist objectives (*Irish Times*/MRBI Polls, various dates).

On the question of whether Articles 2 and 3 should be retained, the MRBI surveys reveal a mixture of realism and ideological sentiment, but also a willingness to change opinion in the light of changing circumstances. Table 10.1 summarizes the evolution of opinion on this question between 1991 and 1995.

The dramatic change in opinion shown in this table can be attributed to a number of factors. One of these is the changing nature of the debate about Northern Ireland and the emergence of a more sophisti-

TABLE 10.1 Evolution of Opinion on the Question of Retaining Articles 2 and 3 of the Irish Constitution: 1991–1995

	1991	*1992*	*1993*	*1995*
Retain articles	58	41	28	20
Change articles	25	39	51	60
No opinion	17	20	21	20

Note: The wording of this survey question varied from one year to the next, as discussed in the text.

Source: Irish Times/MRBI Polls, 1991–1995.

cated view of what is involved, including a growing sensitivity toward the aspirations of unionists as well as nationalists. A second factor is the relative success that the realist political elite has had in negotiating with Britain and in insisting that any change will have to be consensual. Another factor is the nature of the questions asked. In the 1991 poll the question was posed in stark terms between retention and deletion, whereas thereafter respondents were offered the possibility of changing the claim to an aspiration.[4]

The change in the wording had a subtle effect on the way in which people responded to the question. When offered a stark alternative in 1991 between retaining or deleting Articles 2 and 3, there was considerable resistance to change. When, in contrast, the choice was between retaining the articles intact or amending them, there was increased support for an amendment. All of the questions in the MRBI surveys (*Irish Times*/MRBI Polls, 1993, 1995) offer a choice between aspiration and retention, but they also connect this choice with consent in Northern Ireland. This wider choice linked to the evolution of the peace process contributed to the increased willingness on the part of those polled to support change in the constitution.

The readiness to support constitutional change has been reinforced by a parallel development among the political parties in the Republic. The resignation of Charles Haughey as leader of Fianna Fáil, his replacement by Albert Reynolds as Taoiseach, and Fianna Fáil's poor election performance in the 1992 General Election provided the background for further change. The formation of a Fianna Fáil/Labour Party coalition in January 1993 and the appointment of Dick Spring as minister of foreign affairs marked a further erosion in Fianna Fáil's dominance in this policy area. On numerous occasions during 1992 and 1993, tension emerged between the Labour Party and Fianna Fáil in respect of Northern questions. These tensions were exacerbated by the Hume/Adams discussions, which required a response from the Irish government. Spring's speech to the Dáil on 27 October 1993 made clear that the Irish government wanted to distance itself from the Hume/Adams talks, and to provide an alternative momentum toward an agreement with the British government. The relevant section of Spring's "six points of principle" reads as follows:

> [N]o agreement can be reached in respect of any change in the present status of Northern Ireland without the freely expressed consent of a majority of the people of Northern Ireland—free as I have said of coercion or violence.
>
> Let us once and for all accept here that if we talk about the freedom of unionists to give their consent to constitutional change, we must also recognise the freedom of unionists to withhold their consent from such change, unless and until they are persuaded by democratic political means only. (*Irish Times,* 28 October 1993)

In a subsequent poll 81 percent of those questioned agreed explicitly with the sentiments outlined by Spring, whereas 13 percent disagreed. When asked about Articles 2 and 3 on this occasion, 51 percent supported change and 28 percent opposed it, with a large minority not having an opinion (*Irish Times*/MRBI Poll, November 1993). In this case, respondents were asked whether they would support change even though there was concern "about the impact this might have on Nationalists in Northern Ireland." This finding is of interest because, for some time, the SDLP had been arguing that unionist concern on the question was a "smokescreen." Although it is important not to read too much into a single poll finding, such a response does show that public opinion in the South was becoming more sensitive to unionist concerns (*Irish Times,* 23 March and 16 April 1993).

From the Downing Street Declaration to Ceasefire

The publication of the *Joint Declaration for Peace* (also known as the *Downing Street Declaration*) by the two governments in December 1993 advanced this process further. Representing an attempt to reclaim the initiative from the Hume/Adams discussions, the Declaration allowed the Dublin government to insist that it had achieved a considerable amount and advanced the peace process. It also provided the basis for serious criticism of Sinn Féin/IRA by the Dublin government and members of the SDLP. The continuation of violence, urged the Dublin government and the SDLP, could not be justified now that the Downing Street agreement had been signed and the British openly accepted that they "have no selfish strategic or economic interest in Northern Ireland." The *quid pro quo* for this was the full acceptance that the consent of the people of Northern Ireland was to be the central element in future developments. During the first half of 1994, the main aim of the Dublin government was to persuade the IRA to give up its campaign of violence. Following the Declaration, advocates of constitutional nationalism insisted that there was no justification for it. Seamus Mallon stated: "If the difference between what is contained in the *Joint Declaration* and the Hume/Adams document is the reason the IRA are continuing to kill people, then it is spurious and cynical in the extreme" (*Irish Times,* 31 December 1993). This sentiment was echoed by Albert Reynolds in his speech to the Irish Association in Dublin Castle in January 1994. Reynolds reinforced the view expressed in Spring's six points of principle and the *Joint Declaration* that there could be no coercion of the Northern population, and that if the IRA ended its violence the loyalist paramilitaries would also do so. In what has proved to be the most explicit recognition of partition and its internal Irish logic, Reynolds went on to state: "[I]t would be wrong to impose a united Ireland, in the absence of the freely-given consent of a majority of the people of Northern Ireland. Likewise, the democratic right of self-determination by the people of Ireland as a whole must be exercised with, and subject to, the agreement and consent of a majority in Northern Ireland" (*Irish Times,* 11 January 1994).

Sinn Féin and the IRA rejected both the principle of consent and the *Joint Declaration,* although for tactical reasons they were reluctant to come out openly against it. In criticising Sinn Féin, Mallon argued that it was quite possible to reject a "unionist veto" on developments, while at the same time accepting that the consent of the majority was necessary for any such developments. He added, significantly, that "[w]e, the nationalist people of Northern Ireland, who know what it is to be governed without our consent, should not, in any way, contemplate imposing that on anyone else" (*Irish Times,* 9 February 1994). Sinn Féin refused to accept the consent argument, which was now central to the constitutional nationalist position. Sinn Féin distinguished between the Hume/Adams document, which it claimed was not partitionist, and the *Joint Declaration,* which was.

Tom Hartley, national party chairperson of Sinn Féin, criticised Mallon on the grounds that the use of consent was simply a more attractive term for veto: "[C]onsent," Hartley said, "sentimentalised and seeks to legitimise the siege mentality of the unionist community." According to this view, "consent guarantees no change" (*Irish Times,* 15 February 1994). In a sharp retort, Pat Farrell, the general secretary of Fianna Fáil, argued that it was not necessary to support partition while accepting the need for consent within Northern Ireland for change. In addition, Farrell warned Sinn Féin that the consent of the

Republic would be necessary as well: "The overwhelming majority of the people of the Republic, whose consent is also required, want Irish unity achieved only by agreement and consent." Although Farrell did not spell out the consequences of this view, he seemed to be suggesting that the patience of the public was now short (*Irish Times,* 26 February 1994). The results of the MRBI Polls suggest that Mallon and Farrell reflected the majority of nationalist opinion North and South. Specifically, a poll carried out in February 1994 on an all-Ireland basis found that overwhelming majorities in both parts of the island favoured the consent principle; the only exception was found among Sinn Féin supporters, a majority of whom rejected consent (*Irish Political Studies* 1995: 319). Nor were Sinn Féin supporters prepared to support a cessation of violence in response to the *Joint Declaration,* whereas every other party and social grouping that was polled endorsed this view overwhelmingly. Of direct interest to Sinn Féin was the view among those in the Republic that there should be a security crackdown by the British and Irish governments against the paramilitaries if violence did not end (74 percent in favour). In the Republic, opinion shifted between January and March 1994 as a consequence of Sinn Féin's effective rejection of the *Joint Declaration:* In January only 36 percent of those questioned thought Sinn Féin/IRA should be excluded from a "talks process" if they did not end violence, but by March those in favour of exclusion had increased to 46 percent whereas those opposed had declined to 36 percent (*Irish Political Studies* 1995: 298, 319).

The IRA ceasefire in August 1994 cannot be disassociated from the changing nature of opinion in the South. Although it was not the only factor accounting for the ceasefire, the Irish public had become noticeably distanced from the aims articulated by Sinn Féin/IRA. Without a ceasefire there was a distinct possibility that future violence would be met by repression on both sides of the border. During past IRA campaigns, joint repression has been very successful in undermining the ability of the paramilitaries to continue—as could be seen most clearly in the weeks prior to the August ceasefire. At the end of May, at the Oxford Union, Reynolds stressed that the *Joint Declaration* gave him a mandate "to insist that the paramilitaries stop their campaigns, whether they want to or not" (*Irish Times,* 28 May 1994). Following Adams' effective rejection of Reynolds' call to end the violence, Reynolds in turn rejected the Sinn Féin demand for "self-determination" on the grounds that it would be coercive inasmuch as it ignored the unionist rights contained in the *Joint Declaration.* In a speech in July, Spring outlined what he deemed to be the need for an economic partnership between North and South, but he observed that the conditions for such a partnership could not emerge without an end to the violence. Furthermore, he insisted that Dublin was not attempting to rule Northern Ireland:

> What we are seeking is, first, political arrangements for the government of Northern Ireland which would command the support of the great majority of both traditions in the divided community in Northern Ireland. Side by side with that, we want the closest possible links between a Northern Ireland administration and the Irish Government in the interests of the people on the island as a whole. (*Irish Times,* 7 July 1994)

Reynolds later spelt out some of the implications of this thinking when he called on unionism to create the conditions whereby nationalists would no longer withhold consent to the British connection. He expressed the view that a recognition of identity, equal citizenship, and equal treatment was essential to achieving that aim. He added, significantly: "If unionists as a majority of the people of Northern Ireland insist that it must be their acknowledged right to remain under British jurisdiction rather than join a united Ireland, then they have a duty to consider the implications of that position for the nationalist community" (*Irish Times,* 13 July 1994).

Increased pressure was brought to bear on the IRA and Sinn Féin during August. Seamus Mallon insisted there was no reason why violence should continue, arguing that either Sinn Féin and the IRA could accept the wishes of the majority of Irish people or "they are removed from any further involvement in the process of creating peace and a new political dispensation on the island of Ireland" (*Irish Times,* 19 August 1994). The following day, Dick Spring reiterated this theme at a formal level by rejecting any talks with Sinn Féin prior to the ending of violence. Shortly after this, the Taoiseach was reported as being impatient with the refusal of the IRA to end the violence. These pressures from leading constitutional nationalists contributed significantly to the paramilitaries' decision to call a ceasefire (O'Leary 1995a).

Conclusion

The "first" ceasefire changed the nature of the Northern Irish situation beyond recognition. Many nationalists believed that this cessation of violence involved a permanent end to the use of physical force, though unionists were less optimistic. In response to this belief, the Forum for Peace and Reconciliation was established by the Irish government to promote the peace process. The unionist parties declined to attend because of Sinn Féin's participation. Nevertheless, the primary purpose of the Forum was to integrate Sinn Féin into normal democratic politics and secure its commitment to ending violence. In his opening statement to the Forum, Reynolds claimed that peace could be assured only if Northern Ireland was "equally owned for the first time by unionist and nationalist," and only if there were "substantial links" between the two parts of Ireland (Forum for Peace and Reconciliation 1995: 13). However, he did not elaborate on how either of these objectives could be achieved. The collapse of the Reynolds government in November 1994 did not change the direction of policy. The new government, comprising Fine Gael, the Labour Party, and the Democratic Left, remained committed to maintaining the Northern policy of the previous government. John Bruton, the new Taoiseach, in striking contrast to his predecessor, did claim that "normal life in Northern Ireland is our first national aim" (*Irish Times,* 16 December 1994). Although the change in government did not lead to a change of direction, Bruton's view entailed a subtle shift in emphasis.

The new government moved cautiously in the early months of 1995 to consolidate Sinn Féin's commitment to the peace process and to finalise a new joint document with the British government. The publication of *Frameworks for the Future* in February advanced this process, constituting evidence of the continuing diplomatic success of the Irish government (O'Leary 1995b). There are two documents involved: *A Framework for Accountable Government in Northern Ireland,* authored by the British government, and a joint document entitled *A New Framework for Agreement,* authored by the British and Irish governments. In the joint document it is Britain that makes the main concessions—in terms of (1) its neutrality between the two sides in Northern Ireland (Articles 15–20), (2) its stance regarding North/South institutions (Articles 24–29), and (3), more generally, its tone and emphasis throughout the document. Both governments agree, in the event of a political settlement, to amend respectively Articles 2 and 3 of the Irish Constitution and the Government of Ireland Act of 1920. The effect of the Framework Documents, if fully implemented, would be to provide a type of joint sovereignty for Northern Ireland, thereby appreciably increasing Irish government involvement.

The impact of the Framework Documents increased the possibility of a settlement to the conflict. The British government shifted from active support of the union to a more passive defence. The Irish government is now more intent on attaining stability and conflict resolution in Northern Ireland than on pursuing an irredentist claim, a view shared by a majority of people in the Republic (*Irish Times*/MRBI Poll, June 1996). The Irish government's diplomatic strategy had been successful in its twin objectives: to bring about a ceasefire and to persuade the British government to act in an innovative fashion (O'Leary 1995b: 863; O'Leary and McGarry 1993). This successful strategy was put under considerable pressure after February 1995, and it collapsed in 1996. One problem concerned the question of how to achieve the twin objectives of the Framework Documents: on the one hand, new institutions in Northern Ireland that would receive support from both communities and, on the other, new North-South institutions that would give nationalists a real influence within Northern Ireland, but without alienating unionists. Nationalists continued to be suspicious of the detail of the former, whereas unionists were fearful of the latter. These difficulties were further exacerbated by the divisions over the decommissioning of paramilitary armaments. The Irish government believed that all party negotiations should take place prior to decommissioning, whereas the British government and the unionists refused to accept this proposition. The decision in November 1995 to appoint an "International Body on Arms Decommissioning," chaired by former Senator Mitchell, postponed the question. The publication of the International Body's report in January 1996 polarised the two governments, leading to a deteriorating diplomatic situation. The Irish government believed that the Mitchell report vindicated its position, whereas the British government emphasised the need for elections in Northern Ireland before any further progress could be achieved (*Irish Times,* 25 January 1996).

The end of the IRA ceasefire came as a shock to both governments. The Irish government was badly affected by this development, as it had ignored the evidence that the more militant wing of the IRA had regained control of policy by the end of 1995, and continued to believe that the ceasefire was permanent. The government, and people in general within the Republic, blamed the British rather than the IRA for the end of the ceasefire, and this subsequently affected the judgement of the Irish government. Although a more cooperative approach to diplomacy has been restored between the two governments, considerable disagreement and suspicion characterised relations throughout 1996. Irish policymaking concentrated on attempting to secure another ceasefire, but without making any demonstrable impact on the IRA. By the beginning of 1997 this policy appeared to be the only one being pursued by the Irish government, especially after its failure to persuade John Major to adopt its position on the conditions considered necessary to agree to a ceasefire (*Irish Times,* 29 November 1996). By this time, opinion in Irish government circles was extremely pessimistic, one consequence of which was the government's decision to end all political contacts with Sinn Féin. Following changes of government in both London and Dublin in the early summer months of 1997, however, the prospects of a "second" ceasefire greatly improved and resulted in the IRA's renewal of its ceasefire on 31 July. Nevertheless, many of the problems associated with the "first" ceasefire are likely to re-emerge.

The difficulties associated with decommissioning draw attention to the complex and difficult conditions surrounding attempts to resolve ethnic conflicts even when the sovereign governments are in broad agreement. The publication of the Framework Documents in February 1995 was the high point of Irish diplomatic success and of cooperation between the governments. Events in 1996 demonstrated the limits to successful diplomatic initiatives in such circumstances. In a region where the two governments have limited influence over their ethnic "clients," it has proved extremely difficult to institutionalise the arrangements negotiated at government level. The polarised nature of Northern Ireland contributes to this difficulty, as does the relative autonomy of nationalist and unionist communities there. Moreover, although public opinion in the Republic is no longer actively committed to a united Ireland, no Irish government can ignore the strong sympathy that continues to exist for nationalists in Northern Ireland. In June 1996 only 10 percent of those surveyed stated that Northern Ireland should remain in the United Kingdom, 40 percent asserted that the Irish government was not reflecting nationalist opinion strongly enough, and overwhelming majorities believed that the British government and the Unionist parties were not contributing to a solution of the problem (*Irish Times*/MRBI Poll, June 1996).

Despite these obvious limits—and notwithstanding the difficulty, in general, of resolving conflicts over sovereignty and nationalism—a more positive reading of the situation is possible. As a result of diplomatic negotiation, considerable progress has been made on both sides over a ten-year period. Indeed, the situation in Northern Ireland suggests not only that liberal democracies do not go to war with each other but also that they are better placed than other types of regimes to devise the means to resolve even the most intransigent of conflicts (Doyle 1986). The biggest challenge for the Irish government in relation to Northern Ireland may well be yet to come.

Notes

The author would like to thank Jack Jones of the Market Research Bureau of Ireland for permission to cite the *Irish Times*/MRBI Polls.

References and Further Reading

Adams, Gerry, 1986. *The Politics of Irish Freedom*. Dingle: Brandon.

Akenson, Donald Harman, 1994. *Conor*. Montreal/Kingston: McGill-Queen's University Press.

Anderson, James, 1980. "Regions and religion in Ireland: A short critique of the 'Two Nations' theory," *Antipode* 12:1, pp. 44–53.

Barrington, Donal, 1957. "Uniting Ireland," *Studies* 46, pp. 379–402.

Barton, Brian, and Patrick J. Roche (eds.), 1994. *The Northern Question: Perspectives and Policies*. Aldershot: Avebury.

Davis, Earl E., and Richard Sinnott, 1979. *Attitudes in the Republic of Ireland Relevant to the Northern Ireland Problem*. Dublin: Economic and Social Research Institute.

Doyle, Michael W., 1986. "Liberalism and world politics," *American Political Science Review* 80:4, pp. 1151–1163.

FitzGerald, Garret, 1991. *All in a Life*. Dublin: Gill and Macmillan.

Follis, Brian, 1995. *A State Under Siege: The Establishment of Northern Ireland 1920–25*. Oxford: Clarendon.

Forum for Peace and Reconciliation, 1995. "Report of Proceedings—Volume 1, 28 October 1994." Dublin: Stationery Office.

Gallagher, Michael, 1990. "Do Ulster Unionists have a right to self-determination?" *Irish Political Studies* 5, pp. 11–30.

______, 1995. "How many nations are there in Ireland?" *Ethnic and Racial Studies* 18:4, pp. 715–739.

Girvin, Brian, 1986a. "National identity and conflict in Northern Ireland," pp. 105–134 in Brian Girvin and Roland Stürm (eds.), 1986. *Politics and Society in Contemporary Ireland*. Aldershot: Gower.

______, 1986b. "The Anglo-Irish Agreement 1985," pp. 150–165 in Brian Girvin and Roland Stürm (eds.), 1986. *Politics and Society in Contemporary Ireland*. Aldershot: Gower.

______, 1987. "The campaign," pp. 9–29 in Michael Laver, Peter Mair, and Richard Sinnott (eds.), *How Ireland Voted*. Dublin: Poolbeg.

______, 1993. "Social change and political culture in the Republic of Ireland," *Parliamentary Affairs* 46:3, pp. 380–398.

______, 1994. "Constitutional nationalism and Northern Ireland," pp. 5–53 in Brian Barton and Patrick J. Roche (eds.), *The Northern Question: Perspectives and Policies*. Aldershot: Avebury.

______, forthcoming. "The Republicanisation of Irish Society 1932–48," in *A New History of Ireland*, Vol. VII.

Girvin, Brian, and Roland Stürm (eds.), 1986. *Politics and Society in Contemporary Ireland*. Aldershot: Gower.

Handbook of the Ulster Question, 1923. Dublin: Stationery Office.

Harkness, David, 1969. *The Restless Dominion*. London: Macmillan.

Herz, Dietmar, 1986. "The Northern Ireland policy of the Irish Republic," pp. 135–149 in Brian Girvin and Roland Stürm (eds.), 1986. *Politics and Society in Contemporary Ireland*. Aldershot: Gower.

Heslinga, M. W., 1971. *The Irish Border as a Cultural Divide*. Assen: Van Gorcum.

Irish Law Reports, 1990. Dublin: Incorporated Council of Law Reporting for Ireland.

Irish Political Studies, 1985–1995. "Data Section."

Joyce, Joe, and Peter Murtagh, 1983. *The Boss: Charles J. Haughey in Government*. Dublin: Poolbeg.

Kant, Immanuel, 1795. "Perpetual peace: A philosophical sketch," pp. 93–130 in Hans Reiss (ed.), *Kant: Political Writings* (1991 ed.). Cambridge: Cambridge University Press.

Kennedy, Dennis, 1988. *The Widening Gulf*. Belfast: Blackstaff Press.

Keogh, Dermot, 1994. *Twentieth-Century Ireland: Nation and State*. Dublin: Gill and Macmillan.

Laver, Michael, Peter Mair, and Richard Sinnott (eds.), 1987. *How Ireland Voted*. Dublin: Poolbeg.

Lee, J. J., 1989. *Ireland: 1912–1985*. Cambridge: Cambridge University Press.

Lemass, Seán, 1959. *One Nation*. Dublin: Fianna Fáil.

Mac Greil, Michael, 1977. *Prejudice and Tolerance in Ireland*. Dublin: College of Industrial Relations.

Mair, Peter, 1987a. *The Changing Irish Party System*. London: Francis Pinter.

______, 1987b. "Breaking the nationalist mould: The Irish Republic and the Anglo-Irish Agreement," pp. 81–110 in Paul Teague (ed.), *Beyond the Rhetoric*. London: Lawrence and Wishart.

Mansergh, Martin, 1986. *The Spirit of the Nation: The Speeches and Statements of Charles J. Haughey, 1957–1986*. Cork: Mercier.

O'Brien, Conor Cruise, 1974. *States of Ireland*. London: Panther.

______, 1994. *Ancestral Voices: Religion and Nationalism in Ireland*. Dublin: Poolbeg.

O'Halloran, Clare, 1987. *Partition and the Limits of Irish Nationalism*. Dublin: Gill and Macmillan.

O'Leary, Brendan, 1987. "The Anglo-Irish Agreement: Meanings, explanations, results and a defence," pp. 11–40 in Paul Teague (ed.), *Beyond the Rhetoric*. London: Lawrence and Wishart.

______, 1995a. "Introduction: Reflections on a cold peace," *Ethnic and Racial Studies* 18:4, pp. 695–714.

______, 1995b. "Afterword: What is framed in the Framework Documents?" *Ethnic and Racial Studies* 18:4, pp. 862–872.

O'Leary, Brendan, and John McGarry. 1993. *The Politics of Antagonism: Understanding Northern Ireland*. London: Athlone.

Phoenix, Eamon, 1994. *Northern Nationalism: Nationalist Politics, Partition and the Catholic Minority in Northern Ireland 1890–1940*. Belfast: Ulster Historical Foundation.

Reiss, Hans, 1991. *Kant: Political Writings*. Cambridge: Cambridge University Press.

Report of the Committee on the Constitution, 1967. Dublin: Stationery Office.

Rose, Richard, 1971. *Governing Without Consensus*. London: Faber and Faber.

Sinnott, Richard, 1986. "The North: Party images and party approaches in the Republic," *Irish Political Studies* 1, pp. 15–32.

Whyte, John, 1990. *Interpreting Northern Ireland*. Oxford: Clarendon.

11

Anglo-Irish Relations and Constitutional Policy

PAUL ARTHUR

One of the most remarkable features of the Northern Ireland conflict since 1968 is the manner in which it has been redefined and its parameters extended. In the Downing Street Declaration of 19 August 1969, the British and Northern Ireland prime ministers declared that the problem was "entirely a matter of domestic jurisdiction. The United Kingdom Government will take full responsibility for asserting this principle in all international relationships." Implicitly, Labour ministers believed that the conflict had certain advantages in terms of domestic politics. One cabinet minister wrote in August 1969: "It has deflected attention from our own deficiencies and the mess of the pound. We have now got into something which we can hardly mismanage" (Crossman 1978: 620). The academic literature of this period reflected the same internal logic even if some attempt was made to put the problem in comparative perspective (Rose 1971: 447–473). Although the British government in the early 1970s was not averse to drawing examples from other countries such as the Netherlands, Belgium, and Switzerland (HMSO 1975: 43–46), the explicit assumption throughout the decade was that an internal settlement was the only realistic option.

Constitutional policy changed direction in the 1980s. Following a series of prime ministerial summits beginning in May 1980, the British and Irish governments signed the Anglo-Irish Agreement (AIA) on 15 November 1985. The Agreement was registered at the United Nations and warmly endorsed by the British and Irish publics, the United States, and the major states of Western Europe. It constituted a new recognition of the political reality that the Northern Ireland problem is inextricably linked to wider Anglo-Irish relations. Basically both governments were returning to the constitutional drawing board by accepting that the Government of Ireland Act of 1920 and the Anglo-Irish Treaty had merely quarantined an intense interstate conflict by attempting to contain it within the boundaries of Northern Ireland. Partition had been a fashionable enough mechanism for solving boundary problems created in the aftermath of World War I (Wright 1987: 262–289). But its aim of resolving conflict through the creation of more homogeneous states was not achieved in the Irish context—a failure most evident in the campaign of political violence since 1969. Thus, following a series of failed internal initiatives since the imposition of direct rule in 1972 (see Chapter 6), the British government reexamined the wider parameters of the problem.

This approach was reflected in the Anglo-Irish Agreement of 1985 and, more recently, in the *Joint Declaration for Peace* signed by John Major and Albert Reynolds in Downing Street in December 1993 and the Framework Documents of February 1995. The 1993 Declaration and the 1995 Framework Documents are a logical continuation of the Anglo-Irish Agreement of 1985. One of the important aspects of the AIA was that it eschewed purely internal frameworks and prioritized the Anglo-Irish process as the facilitator of future progress in constitutional policy. Thus the 1993 *Joint Declaration for Peace* (sometimes known as the *Downing Street Declaration*) reflected a vastly different political context than had existed when its namesake was written in August 1969. Northern Ireland no longer had its own government or prime minister, and the British and Irish governments had been working together for several years to find a common solution to the problem. Hence the aim of the 1993 Declaration was "to foster agreement and reconciliation, leading to a new political framework founded on consent and encompassing arrangements within Northern Ireland, for the whole island and between these islands" (*Joint Declaration for Peace,* 1993: paragraph 2). What was evident in each of the initiatives since 1985 was a shift in emphasis from the purely endogenous sources of conflict to include exogenous factors. In broadening the parameters of the conflict the governments thereby further internationalised it.

This chapter will explain the rationale for the new approach. It will allude to the failure of the endogenous initiatives and emphasise the ensuing alterations to the international system (Kratochwil 1986) and their impact on Anglo-Irish relations. It will be more concerned with the view from Dublin, London, Washington, and Brussels than (to quote Winston Churchill) "the dreary steeples of Fermanagh and Tyrone." This account will rely more on the literature on globalisation

(Parry 1993) and on cosmopolitan democracy (Held 1992) than on the (Woodrow) Wilsonian notion of the nation-state fashioned in the aftermath of World War I.

The International System and Anglo-Irish Relations

In 1969 the Republic of Ireland was a minor player on the margins of international politics. That role remained substantially the same over the next two decades, although its relationship with the United Kingdom changed dramatically. A range of factors help explain this changing relationship. First, the Republic's economy has grown rapidly and is now considered one of the "tiger economies" of the European Union (EU). The proportion of Ireland's exports going to Britain fell rapidly, from 75 percent in 1960 to 35 percent in 1988 to 26 percent by 1996. Correspondingly, the EU increased in importance: "From the 1970s the EU emerged as a critical arena of political and economic decision-making" (Ruane and Todd 1996: 236; FitzGerald, Gillespie, and Fanning 1996). It is the purpose of this chapter to explain the reasons not for this growth but, rather, for the psychological impact of such economic success on a small off-shore economy and, in particular, the consequences for its relationship with its more powerful neighbour to the east. British-Irish relations, noted historically for their asymmetry and Ireland's obsessive concern with partition, are an example of Robert Keohane and Joseph Nye's concept of "complex interdependence" (cited in Keatinge 1982: 308). In terms of devices for managing the international system, Ireland had always been considered to fall within Britain's "sphere of responsibility" (Kratochwil 1986: 48). That began to change after 1973, when both entered the European Economic Community as coordinate partners. In the following two decades Ireland's standing in the EU benefited from a more *communitaire* attitude than its larger neighbour (Department of Foreign Affairs 1996: 59; Tugendhat 1986). Ireland's "dependency syndrome" (Lee 1989: 627–628) diminished.

A second possible explanation for attitudinal change lies in the more dynamic influence of the Irish diaspora, particularly that in the United States. Successive generations of Irish nationalists suffered from the delusion that Irish-America had a huge influence on whomsoever happened to be president, and it was simply a matter of (to paraphrase Conor Cruise O'Brien) "the Micks pushing the Yanks to push the Brits to push the Prods into a united Ireland." This was a myth that clearly had little practical consequence from the 1920s onward. We shall see that a policy change occurs after Mrs. Thatcher became prime minister in 1979, a change that reflected a more constructive Irish-American approach and an acknowledgement that the Anglo-American "special relationship" had become less special in the intervening years (Arthur 1991).

A third source of attitudinal change was the evolving nature of political debate within Northern Ireland. Four initiatives based on an internal settlement failed between 1972 and 1986 (see Chapter 6). The Conservative government of 1970–1974 veered between coercion and conciliation, and culminated in the courageous attempt to move beyond the Westminster model with the power-sharing experiment of 1974. Its collapse after less than five months—ostensibly because the government recognised that there was an institutionalised Irish dimension to the problem—convinced Whitehall that normal standards of political behaviour did not pertain in the province. The failure of the Constitutional Convention eighteen months later, of the Atkins' initiative in 1980–1981, and of James Prior's experiment in rolling devolution underlined the zero-sum nature of local politics.

A fourth factor encouraging British governments to reevaluate their approach to Northern Ireland was the intensity of political violence. The rapid mobilisation of republican and loyalist paramilitaries, operating with considerable communal support, illustrated that Northern Ireland had a political culture driven by intimidation and a population ambiguous about the use of violence for political ends (Wright 1987: 112–163). The demography of violence suggested that there was a "control" mechanism (Darby 1986) and that it was predicated on the concept of a "Long War." In any case, its frequency would have persuaded government that the norms of liberal democracy were not applicable to the Northern Ireland problem. Equally, the longer the violence continued, the greater its capacity for inducing fatalism in the wider community. Governments needed to be prepared to take risks to break the cycle of violence. One approach was to look beyond standard models of governance and seek solutions from the international system.

Developments within Europe and the metamorphosis of the EEC into the EU were illustrations of changes in the nature of intergovernmental cooperation. These were also examples of the "variety of contradictory tendencies" found in the international scene (Kratochwil 1986). One tension is that although political order is premised on territorial sovereignty, increasingly interdependent economic and information markets are revising these traditional conceptions of territorial boundaries. For example, William Wallace (1986: 368) bemoans the fact that the United Kingdom's "preoccupation with sovereignty—in particular, with the nature of the formal European commitment—has distracted attention from the progressive informal encroachment of international linkages on British autonomy."

By contrast, the Irish Department of Foreign Affairs (DFA) had been more prescient in drawing the distinction between independence and sovereignty. A White Paper, *The Accession of Ireland to the European Communities* (1972), accepted that Ireland enjoyed very little economic sovereignty and that the decisive consideration had to be the national interest. Hence Irish foreign policy was guided by a sense of interdependence and by a recognition that sovereignty needed to be pooled (Lee 1989: 463–464). The DFA also accepted that a legal revolution was occurring within Europe and that this had the capacity to change the rules of the political game (Weiler 1990: 18–22).

Constitutional policy in relation to Northern Ireland had to pay obeisance to both the endogenous and the exogenous sources of conflict. Policymakers knew as early as 1972 that a solution could not be fashioned from a purely internal approach. Moreover, they recognised that a political culture existed in Northern Ireland that was alien to British political practice. There was not to be a British solution to a British problem. One reason was that they did not have complete control of exogenous factors such as developments within the EU and the political influence of the Irish diaspora. In addition, as an independent state the Republic of Ireland was no longer within Britain's sphere of responsibility. All of these developments pointed toward an Anglo-Irish process and general internationalisation of the Northern Ireland conflict.

Anglo-Irish Relations in the Thatcher Era

When Mrs. Thatcher entered Downing Street in May 1979 there was little in her record to suggest that she would play a pro-active role in relation to Northern Ireland. The 1979 Conservative manifesto had paid scant attention to the problem, save to stress the traditional policy of defeating terrorism and of maintaining the Union. A cryptic reference to future government stated that "in the absence of devolved government, we will seek to establish one or more elected regional councils with a wide range of powers over local services" (Conservative Party manifesto 1979). This pro-integrationist stance was in line with the thoughts of the Conservative opposition spokesman on Northern Ireland, Airey Neave, who had been assassinated by the Irish National Liberation Army (INLA) on 30 March 1979. Nor was there any reason to anticipate major opposition from Labour. The appointment of the new Secretary of State, Humphrey Atkins, a man without previous cabinet experience and little knowledge of Northern Ireland, seemed to confirm that a period of consolidation was under way.

Within a matter of months the prime minister did a U-turn. A consultative document, *The Government of Northern Ireland: A Working Paper for a Conference* (Cmnd. 7763), produced in November, sought no more than the "highest level of agreement . . . which will best meet the immediate needs of Northern Ireland." Only the Alliance Party endorsed the conference initially; in the end the UUP boycotted it on the grounds that it was a dereliction of the integrationist thrust of the manifesto. Since the UUP was the largest party, the conference became pretty meaningless and ground to a halt within four months. In any case, unionists may have been worried about further allusions to an "Irish dimension." In reality, a practical Irish dimension had been recognised as early as October 1972 in another government discussion paper, *The Future of Northern Ireland: A Paper for Discussion*. It contained three elements. First, Northern Ireland's constitutional status was guaranteed; secondly, functional cooperation was stressed—in keeping with the two states' entry into the EEC; and thirdly, greater emphasis was placed on anti-terrorism cooperation. Later, with the collapse of the Sunningdale experiment and the poor Dublin/London relations that ensued, the Irish dimension did not appear to be a central item on the government's agenda. Thus, some were surprised and suspicious when it reentered the equation, especially with Mrs. Thatcher in office.

The most graphic illustration of these fears was presented by Enoch Powell (1983: 19–20) when he examined the principles that, he asserted, guided Dublin, London, and Washington in driving toward a solution based on Irish unity. What was interesting about the Powell analysis was that he placed it in a geopolitical context. He appeared to be acknowledging that the international community was prepared to play its role in internationalising the means toward a solution to the conflict. In that respect, besides the British and Irish governments, there are two key players—the EU and the United States. During, and since, the Thatcher era, the visibility of the EU as a political actor was not as apparent as that of the United States. An important influence of the EU is that it provides a context for raising issues concerning transnational identities and the pooling of authority in different functional areas. Similar concerns, in relation to a postnational Europe and its impact on the Anglo-Irish conflict, have been enunciated by the SDLP leader (Hume 1996: 109–147).

The United States has played a more pro-active and incremental role—as we shall see when we examine the part played by the Clinton administration. The first overt signs of an active role date back to President Carter in August 1977. Following discussions with the British and Irish governments, he issued a statement in which he condemned violence, expressed support for a peaceful solution in which the Irish government would be involved, and promised U.S. investment assistance in the event of a settlement (Holland 1987: 127–128). Four points can be made about the Carter statement. The first is that it treated the Northern Ireland conflict as a legitimate concern of U.S. foreign policy—the phrase used by the American ambassador to Ireland was that the United States was "neutral but not indifferent" (*Irish Times,* 9 September 1977). The second is that the sentiments expressed were not far removed from those written into the preamble of the Anglo-Irish Agreement of November 1985. The third is that it skated over the "internal jurisdiction" issue by referring to three entities: Northern Ireland, Great Britain, and Ireland. The fourth is that the president specifically raised human rights and discrimination matters (which were to be exploited by Irish-American lobbyists in the coming years).

In retrospect, it can be argued that the statement established an American policy of intervention at three levels: mediation; the protection of human rights; and, at a geopolitical level, part of the process of controlling the "network of international terrorism." Others read American "intervention" as "interference." For example, during the 1979 general election, Speaker of the U.S. House of Representatives, Tip O'Neill, condemned successive British governments for treating Northern Ireland like a political football and demanded an early and major initiative to get political negotiations under way. His message was resented; yet in Mrs. Thatcher's first major interview with the foreign press she told the *New York Times* (12 November 1979) that she was prepared to take such a bold initiative. The result was the Atkins' Conference and the start of an Anglo-Irish process, with two prime ministerial summits in May and December 1980. The December summit in Dublin saw the most powerful British cabinet presence in Ireland since partition. These meetings set off alarm bells in unionist circles. Reference has already been made to Enoch Powell's analysis, which suggested that there was a policy to abolish Northern Ireland and incorporate the unified island within NATO. The beneficiary would be the United States, since, Powell asserted, it would block "the gravest of all the gaps in the American strategy for Europe." His suspicions may have been fueled by the rapidity with which British policy had changed after Mrs. Thatcher came to power. As recently as 5 May 1978 the two governments had issued a statement that said: "The British and Irish Governments have a different approach in the search for a long-term solution for peace and stability in Northern Ireland." Yet within two years they had embarked on an Anglo-Irish process that led to the Agreement of November 1985 and culminated, via the *Joint Declaration* (December 1993), in the Framework Documents (February 1995).

In May 1980 the prime minister and Taoiseach had reached agreement on "new and close political cooperation." That was followed a few days later by the first meeting of the RUC chief constable and Garda commissioner to discuss cross-border security arrangements. In December Thatcher and Haughey met again and agreed to inaugurate a series of Anglo-Irish studies on matters of common concern. In a significant phrase, both contemplated an examination of "the totality of relationships within these islands."[1] The Joint Studies Report of November 1981 recommended, among other things, the creation of an Anglo-Irish Intergovernmental Council to review policy toward Northern Ireland. It held thirty meetings between 2 November 1983 and 26 March 1985 and was the forum within which the Anglo-Irish Agreement was established in November 1985.

This is not to suggest that Dublin and London worked in perfect harmony. Relations were strained during the hunger strikes, and there was profound disagreement concerning the conduct of the Falklands War. In addition, the Irish government objected to Secretary of State James Prior's plan for "rolling devolution" (see Chapter 6), believing it to be unworkable. That much had been anticipated in the report of a joint steering group of British and Irish officials. It had recommended action to reduce misunderstanding on a variety of misconceptions relating both to public attitudes and to government policies. Specifically, it sought "institutional arrangements . . . deliberately framed to reduce suspicion and distrust, and measures to make more effective the prosecution of offenders who seek to evade justice by crossing from one side of the border to the other" (HMSO 1981: 36). That odd combination of requirements—institutional arrangements (however imprecisely described) *and* security cooperation—represented the separate and often contradictory priorities of the governments. Nonetheless, it would be true to say that megaphone diplomacy was replaced by reasoned discussion. Despite the deterioration in relations over the Falklands, for example, an Anglo-Irish summit was held in November 1983 with the purpose of rebuilding a better relationship. Another summit followed a year later, and it was to be the precursor for the 1985 Agreement.

Toward a Nationalist Consensus

Successive Irish governments and the SDLP leader, John Hume, had been wooing Irish-America since the early 1970s. Hume's efforts in that direction increased substantially after the failure of power sharing and the Constitutional Convention in the mid-1970s. He perceived his role to be twofold: discouraging Americans from supporting the IRA's "armed struggle" and encouraging the U.S. political system to be involved in seeking a solution to the conflict (White 1984: 183–196). The fruits of those efforts were evident after 1992 when Bill Clinton became president.

Nearer home, Irish constitutional nationalists set themselves the task of redefining Irish nationalism in the light of contemporary events and attitudes through the Forum for a New Ireland (see Chapter 10). It was a body drawn from the SDLP in the North and from Fianna Fáil, Fine Gael, and Labour in the South. In that respect it could claim to speak for the vast majority of the Irish people. Its first public meeting was held on 30 May 1983 and its report was published on 2 May 1984. Its preferred option was Irish unity, although it also suggested models of federalism/confederalism and of joint (British/Irish) authority over Northern Ireland. Any solution, the report concluded, could be achieved "only in agreement"; moreover it was prepared "to discuss other views which may contribute to political development" (New Ireland Forum Report: paragraph 5.10).

But the Forum was about more than its final report. Essentially, it moved the debate from the aspirational to the operational. It achieved several short-term objectives and was a brilliant piece of public relations in the context of "modernising" Irish nationalism through its use of public hearings with prominent individuals and groups (many of them indifferent to the claims of Irish nationalism) and its publication of enquiring and critical documents. It commanded international attention and persuaded others of the seriousness and tolerance of the nationalist project. It also enabled the SDLP to maintain a high positive profile at a time when it was boycotting the Northern Ireland Assembly (of 1982–1986). In turn, it made much of the Assembly business redundant and protected the SDLP's flank from the electoral mobilisation of Sinn Féin in the 1980s. There is evidence that Mrs. Thatcher recognised the importance of the developing Anglo-Irish process. In her address to a joint session of the U.S. Congress on 20 February 1984, she devoted a section to the Irish question. The speech can be read as a recognition of the depth of American interest: "Garret FitzGerald and I will continue to consult together in the quest for stability and peace in Northern Ireland. We hope we will have your continued support for our joint efforts to find a way forward."

Sinn Féin was decidedly not part of the Forum exercise. The Forum parties denied it a role and attempted to isolate it from the nationalist consensus. They disapproved fundamentally of its method of "the armalite and the ballot box." On the other hand, republicans believed that they represented the marginalised in Ireland and that their violence was a form of political communication in which the IRA fulfilled the role of purveyors of violence and Sinn Féin that of purveyors of political meaning. The policy had limited success in that republicans demonstrated that they could not be ignored nor defeated, but they recognised that they would have to abandon the armed struggle if they wanted to become part of the nationalist consensus. That self-understanding did not emerge until they acknowledged the enormity of the task they faced in the aftermath of the signing of the Anglo-Irish Agreement.

The Anglo-Irish Agreement: Catalyst for Negotiations?

The Agreement was a novel approach to a complex and intractable problem, an attempt made by the two authorities who claimed jurisdiction over the territory of Northern Ireland to settle the matter amicably. It was as if Britain and Ireland with the blessing of the international community had established themselves as a prestigious third party to oversee (and bring a sense of urgency to) the Northern Ireland problem. Morton Deutsch (1973) lists seven functions that a third party must perform in helping conflicting parties come to a constructive resolution of their conflict. One concerns the need to alter the asymmetries in motivation, power, or legitimacy between the parties.

The Agreement altered those asymmetries. The British ambassador in Dublin recognised that the AIA had profoundly alienated the unionist majority and said that there could be "no return to the dictatorship of the majority." He went on to make the telling point that the AIA "reflected a fundamental change in the politics of the North. I have no hesitation in saying that it was one of those rare diplomatic instruments which changes the game thereafter" (*Irish Times,* 22 June 1988). Events since 1985 bear out this prognostication. The majority's sense of powerlessness has been demonstrated in its failure to remove the threat implicit in the Agreement. Further, the IRA—in a 1985 Christmas message to its supporters—acknowledged that the security implications of the Agreement represented a powerful challenge to their armed struggle. At a stroke, then, the Agreement had altered the political geometry. It had highlighted the powerlessness of unionism and presented a major security threat to republicanism.

However, it is likely that the AIA was formulated with longer time horizons in mind, in an attempt both to alter the structure of incentives faced by the parties and to induce more general attitudinal changes in helpful directions. One of the shrewdest analyses written within weeks of the signing (and bearing evidence of considerable insider knowledge) was that of the former U.S. ambassador to Ireland, William Shannon. He cautioned that "the two governments have set in motion a process of change. The way ahead for this kind of intergovernmental co-operation is uncharted. It may be the end of the century before it finally becomes clear how far Northern Ireland has drifted from its old habits of conflict" (Shannon 1986: 870). More than a decade later the prescience of that remark has not been fully tested. What is clear is that it is inconceivable that there would have been the 1993 Declaration or the 1995 Framework Documents had there not been the Anglo-Irish Agreement, which established the context for the three-stranded approach.[2]

By formalising the efforts of the British and Irish governments to secure reconciliation in Northern Ireland, the Agreement provided unequivocal evidence that the problem was a joint one. It can also be seen as the second tier of mobilisation. Opponents of the New Ireland Forum—the first tier—made the mistake of assuming that it was no more than a public relations exercise in starry-eyed nationalism. With hindsight we can see it as an agenda rather than a blueprint for constitutional nationalists, and as a challenge to British policy makers. The response came in the signing of the Agreement whereby the two governments entered the debate as a prestigious third party with the support of much of the international community. The debate since 1986, and particularly after 1993, illustrates the degree to which the Anglo-Irish process has moved interpretations of the Northern Ireland conflict beyond the purely endogenous.

Attempts were made to ensure that both communities remained on board. Unionists were to be reassured by the affirmation in Article 1(a) of the AIA that "any change in the status of Northern Ireland would only come about with the consent of a majority of the people of Northern Ireland." However, that consent principle appeared to be undermined when they read that Dublin was to be given a consultative role as of right in regard to Northern Ireland policy within the framework of the Intergovernmental Council (IGC). This consultative mechanism was established by the creation of an intergovernmental conference to be serviced by senior officials from Dublin and London. Although certain articles were designed to act as a catalyst toward achieving power-sharing devolution by the local parties in place of an enhanced role for the IGC, unionists responded with bitter and sustained opposition. James Molyneaux, the UUP leader, on the day after the Agreement was signed, declared: "We are going to be delivered, bound and trussed like a turkey ready for the oven, from one nation to another" (Northern Ireland Assembly Report, vol. 18, p. 103). A massive demonstration on 23 November 1985 brought more than 10 percent of the entire Protestant population into Belfast city centre. The following day, a *Sunday Times* opinion poll found 49 percent of Protestants opposing the Agreement and only 14 percent in favour. Extraparliamentary reaction, including increased levels of loyalist paramilitary violence, failed to create any clear strategy to destroy or amend the Agreement. And when the Conservatives were reelected at the 1987 General Election with a clear victory, unionists were left with no specific policy save opposition to the Agreement.

Moreover, they were isolated, victims of the new asymmetry. The Agreement had been widely welcomed not only in Britain and Ireland but throughout the world. It had been ratified in the Commons by a majority of 426. The Dáil vote was much closer—88 to 75—but Irish public opinion was firmly in support. The significance of the international dimension was recognised in Article 10(a). In a bid to regenerate a depressed local economy the International Fund for Ireland was created to promote economic and social development in Northern Ireland and the six border counties in the Republic. The monies for the Fund came largely from the United States, but Canada, New Zealand, and the EU were also net contributors. A possible escape route for unionists lay in Article 11 of the Agreement, which promised a review of the workings of the intergovernmental conference after three years. However, when the review was reported in May 1989, it brought little comfort for unionists. Instead it underlined the durability of the Agreement by highlighting increased functional cooperation, although it promised to consider "changes in the scope and nature of the working of the Conference" (*Official Review of the Agreement* 1989: paragraph 29) so long as such changes did not interfere with the spirit of the Agreement.

Unionists made no attempt to take advantage of this offer. They did not realise fully that their resistance to change had been surmounted for the first time in this century. They did not appreciate that the Agreement had been built to withstand whatever loyalists threw at it. They did not read its two simple and profound messages: first, that the people of Northern Ireland represented a tiny percentage of the United Kingdom electorate; and secondly, that a "solution" was to be found in the larger play of British-Irish interests. In the meantime, there could be no proper debate about the future of the province until they came to terms with the new realities and new asymmetries. That process did not even begin until Peter Brooke became Secretary of State in 1989. In a series of speeches made early in his tenure, he set out to reassure dissidents of the Agreement on both sides. In retrospect, his impact on republicanism was very important. It is not so easy to detect movement on the unionist side, however. After only a hundred days in office, Brooke stated that an abandonment of violence by the IRA could lead to "imaginative steps" by the government. In a further speech made in his constituency on 9 November, he claimed that the British had no economic or strategic interest in the union, that it would accept unification by consent, and that there was a place for nonviolent republicanism. To counteract any unionist fears he announced in Belfast on 6 December that he "had no secret plan, no hidden agenda" (Arthur 1992: 111). In an address to the Bangor Chamber of Commerce a month later, he advised that he "would not wish to raise hopes unduly" but wanted to release unionism from its "internal exile" (Arthur 1992: 111). We shall see that it was a slow release, but at least a process had begun.

To induce unionists into the process, Mr. Brooke—with the acquiescence of the SDLP and the Irish government—made three concessions. First, he was prepared to consider an alternative to the Agreement; secondly, he agreed to a postponement of the intergovernmental conference to allow talks to get under way; and thirdly, he suggested that the secretariat officials could be employed elsewhere during this period. The Bangor speech also recognised that the parameters of the problem were contained within the aforementioned three-stranded relationship and led directly to the problem of the sequence in which these strands should be addressed (or whether they could be examined concurrently). All of these procedural difficulties slowed up the process, as the tortuous progress of the Brooke and Mayhew talks demonstrated.

Bringing Republicans into the Democratic Process

While this painfully slow process was being parsed, analysed, and dissected by pundits, a more private parallel process was under way involving republicans and emissaries for the government. It had its genesis in a public dialogue between the SDLP and Sinn Féin conducted between March and September 1988. That had been influenced in turn by an intense debate within republicanism that was under way in the aftermath of the Anglo-Irish Agreement. Ever since the collapse of the hunger strikes in 1981 and the electoral surge of Sinn Féin in the first half of the 1980s, Sinn Féin's strategists had begun to plan for an end to the armed struggle. They recognised that their people were war-weary and that, whereas they had the capacity to continue with the "Long War," they had no guarantee of victory. They knew, too, that they had been guilty of many "mistakes" that had succeeded in alienating their own supporters. The most prominent of these was the bomb in Enniskillen on Remembrance Sunday 1987, when they killed eleven innocent civilians, and that in Warrington in March 1993, which resulted in the death of two young boys. Finally, they recognised that the Agreement may have changed the nature of the political game forever. Indeed, the prominent republican Martin McGuinness stated publicly after Peter Brooke's first major speech that he was the first Secretary of State with some understanding of Irish history.

In the aftermath of the Enniskillen bomb, John Hume decided that it was a propitious psychological moment to challenge the IRA's campaign of armed struggle. He wrote to Gerry Adams on 17 March 1988 and pointed out that the armed struggle was doing more damage to those it alleged it was protecting; that it was too simplistic to state that the cause of all the violence is the British presence in Ireland; that it is the people, rather than the territory of Ireland, that have to be united; and that the IRA's methods and strategy had actually become more sacred than their cause. A series of meetings between the SDLP and Sinn Féin followed. They ended in September when it was clear that the gap between the parties was too wide, although each side promised to reconvene if the opportunity arose.

The process contained several interesting features. For one thing, it was the first time that Sinn Féin policies had been scrutinised so closely by those who aspired to the same end of Irish unity. The SDLP set the dialogue in a postnationalist framework and reminded Sinn Féin that Wolfe Tone and Patrick Pearse had called off the armed struggle rather than commit their people to further bloodshed. Secondly, the dialogue shifted Sinn Féin away from moral certitude. Over the next few years it opened its doors to those who sought to demonstrate the errors of the armed struggle. Thirdly, the dialogue rehearsed many of the issues that later appeared in the *Joint Declaration* of 1993: A putative "Forum for Peace and Reconciliation" was suggested by the SDLP and became part of the post-Declaration political furniture that enabled Sinn Féin to move from the margins and embrace the concept of inclusivity; the SDLP's blunt assertion that Britain no longer had any selfish strategic or economic interests in remaining in Ireland was also included in the Declaration; and, finally, the debate about self-determination was removed from its theological plinth and placed in the harsh political world of the late twentieth century.

The culmination of this process was the publication in February 1992 of a Sinn Féin discussion paper, *Towards A Lasting Peace in Ireland*, which recognised that unionist fears would have to be addressed. It also accepted that British withdrawal would come about over time through the cooperation of both governments in consultation with all the parties in Northern Ireland. Finally, it raised its eyes above the parapet by taking account of the international dimension and the political implications of the EU. This publication was a considerable political and psychological step for Sinn Féin, as great as its decision at the 1986 Ard-Fheis to enter Dáil Éireann if it won any parliamentary seats. In effect, the paper recognised the legitimacy of the Irish government for the first time since partition, as well as the rights of northern Protestants. A year later, in 1993, contact with the SDLP was renewed in a dialogue between John Hume and Gerry Adams. They issued a statement couched in the language of inclusion that recognised that any new agreement would be possible and durable only if it could earn and enjoy the allegiance of the different traditions of the island by accommodating diversity and providing for national reconciliation. These talks, however, were suspended on 25 September when both leaders presented the Irish government with a paper, the broad principles of which "[would] be for wider consideration between the two governments."

While this process was under way, a parallel dialogue was being held in secret. A line of communication between republicans and the British government had opened in mid-1990 and continued until 1993. It might be said that the *Joint Declaration for Peace* was the culmination of this secret dialogue. Less than three weeks after its signing, Sinn Féin published *Setting the Record Straight*, its account of the secret meetings. It is a fascinating document that illustrates the extent of mistrust between Sinn Féin and the government, as well as the latter's efforts to establish some trust. For example, it makes clear the fact that Sinn Féin was being kept abreast of what was going on during the Brooke and Mayhew talks. The lengths to which the government was prepared to go are described in a Sinn Féin report of a meeting with the government's representative on 23 March 1993:

> Any settlement not involving all of the people north and south won't work. A North/South settlement that won't frighten unionists. The final solution is union. It is going to happen anyway. The historical train—Europe—determines that. We are committed to Europe. Unionists will have to change. This island will be one (Sinn Féin 1993).

Despite the fact that the prime minister had told the House of Commons on 20 November 1993 that the thought of talking to Gerry Adams "would turn my stomach," we now know that these talks were helping to create the conditions that allowed John Major and Albert Reynolds to sign the *Joint Declaration* on 15 December 1993. Although the Declaration was insufficient as far as Sinn Féin was concerned, it allowed Sinn

Féin to find a place in the democratic process through paragraph 11 of the Declaration, where the Irish government signaled its intention to establish the Forum for Peace and Reconciliation "to make recommendations on ways in which agreement and trust between both traditions in Ireland can be promoted and established" (*Joint Declaration for Peace,* 1993). Although the Forum did not meet until late October 1994 (because the priority of the two governments during the first half of 1994 was to secure an IRA ceasefire), the Irish government nevertheless did enough to keep Sinn Féin involved in the process. The Irish government removed the broadcasting ban on Sinn Féin on 19 January 1994; Mr. Major followed suit on 16 September. The Dublin government also acted as a conduit between Sinn Féin and London as the former sought further clarification on the precise meaning of the *Joint Declaration.* Sir Patrick Mayhew's initial reaction was to argue that the Declaration was a free-standing document that needed no further explanation. Eventually he succumbed, and in April 1994 the government answered twenty specific questions put to it by Sinn Féin. That seemed to be enough for the republicans. The IRA announced its cessation of violence on 31 August 1994, but it refused to use the word *permanent;* nor would it accept the *Joint Declaration.*[3] Nevertheless, Mr. Major accepted as "a working assumption" that, three months after the cessation, the IRA had renounced violence for good, and his officials began a series of bilateral talks with Sinn Féin to be followed later, it was assumed, by meetings with ministers.

Collapse of the "First" Ceasefire

When the IRA planted a bomb in Canary Wharf in London on 9 February 1996, the formal peace process had come to an end, at least for the time being. By the early months of 1997 the fringe loyalist parties were still engaged in multiparty talks at Stormont, but their ceasefire was also beginning to unravel. It is the purpose of this chapter not to follow the minutiae of these events but simply to explain their significance for Anglo-Irish policy. After all, it was the Anglo-Irish process that had helped deliver peace: The questions that arose after Canary Wharf concerned the degree to which the governments had contributed to the collapse, and also whether they could resurrect the peace process.

One should not underestimate the impact of the EU and the United States in underpinning the original process. The former began to take action in the autumn of 1994 when the EU Commission created a special Task Force to look into further ways in which it could give practical assistance to Northern Ireland and the border counties to assist the peace process. It produced the "Delors package" (formally, the Peace and Reconciliation Programme), which would run for five years with a budget of 300 million ECUs for the first three years and with the financing for the final two years to be subject to review. Significantly, that support was not withdrawn after Canary Wharf. Similarly, the Clinton administration had been crucial in persuading republicans and loyalists to embrace the democratic process. When the president granted Gerry Adams a visa to visit the United States in January 1995, he was opposed by the British government and his own State and Justice Departments. Two further visits by Adams in 1995 and an agreement that Sinn Féin could raise funds in the United States made it more palatable to sell the process to republican activists. Similar treatment for loyalists had the desired effect. As we shall see, the United States continued to play a key role in an effort to restore the peace process.

The return to violence was a classic illustration of the tension between the endogenous and exogenous aspects of the conflict. The latter helped to create the conditions that laid emphasis on the notion of inclusivity and process, bringing the supporters of paramilitarism into democratic dialogue. But there were those who believed that the pace of change was getting out of control and that former gunmen should be forced to serve a longer political apprenticeship. They were keen to slow down the rate of change. Their wishes appeared to be granted when in March 1995 Sir Patrick Mayhew produced a further clarification of what was meant by a renunciation of violence. Among the twenty questions that Sinn Féin had posed to the government in May 1994 was question 18(a), which asked specifically: "The British Government has called on Sinn Féin to renounce violence. What does this mean?" The answer it received on that occasion was a fudge of paragraph 10 of the *Joint Declaration*, whereas in March 1995 the answer was much more specific. It was dubbed the "Washington 3" speech and referred to three elements on decommissioning: the acceptance of the principle of disarmament, the modalities by which it could be achieved, and the necessity to make some gesture on decommissioning as an act of good faith *prior* to all party talks. Both sets of paramilitaries balked at the inclusion of this third point, which they construed as an extra precondition and an admission of surrender. Republicans in particular believed that the absence of their campaign of violence and their democratic mandate entitled them to immediate entry into all-party talks. Washington 3 was to be the major hurdle blocking the peace process.

Its timing was interesting. It was launched within a month of the publication of the Framework Documents. The emphasis was firmly on the plural inasmuch as both governments were concerned with the totality of relationships and with arrangements for devolved structures in Northern Ireland. The text itself was complex and wordy and deliberately ambiguous because it had to offer something to everyone. In fact, the mainstream unionist parties appeared to be unhappy with it in varying degrees; and there is at least the suspicion that they used their parliamentary weight at Westminster to obtain concessions at a time when the government fretted about its dwindling majority. There were those who believed that the concessions were contained in the Washington 3 statement.

One potential escape route from this stalled process lay in the creation of an international decommissioning panel to establish the credentials of such a process. Following a period of procrastination, the governments released a "twin-tracks communiqué"—concerned with decommissioning and all-party talks—on 28 November 1995. Again, timing was important: The communiqué coincided with President Clinton's visit to Britain and Ireland. It injected a new dynamism into the process and gave the panel a fairly wide remit. It also set a tight schedule whereby the panel would report to the governments by mid-January 1996; the governments were to meet a month later "to review progress on preparatory talks for all-party negotiations [which] they have firm view to achieving . . . by the end of February 1996." The panel was chaired by former U.S. Senate Majority Leader George Mitchell (a friend of the president), and it included Canadian General Jean de Chastelain and a former Finnish prime minister, Harri Holkeri. Although they delivered their report on 22 January 1996, it was not enough to save the peace process.

The Mitchell team had produced an impressive report in record time, but the British government was not altogether happy with its findings because it made the stark point that "success in the peace process cannot be achieved solely by reference to the decommissioning of arms" (paragraph 51). Instead it uncoupled the issue of decommissioning and political talks through the enunciation of six principles of democratic participation and nonviolence (paragraph 20), as well as through the suggestion that some decommissioning could take place *during* (rather than prior to) all-party negotiations as part of a confidence-building process. The government responded before any party had time to digest its contents by calling an election for a Northern Ireland Peace Forum. Sinn Féin and the SDLP were unhappy with both the election and the Forum, believing the proposed election to be a diversion from inclusive negotiation. But the election was very much the desire of Mr. Major's allies in the UUP. They had included a similar proposal in a party position paper of February 1996, *The Democratic Imperative: Proposals for an Elected Body for Northern Ireland*. At a summit on 28 February, both governments committed themselves to convening all-party negotiations on 10 June through "an elective process [which] would offer a viable direct and speedy route to all-party negotiations." The elections were duly held on 30 May, but the only party to emerge with any real satisfaction was Sinn Féin, which took 15.5 percent of the poll—its highest ever recorded. That was not enough to get it into the negotiations since the IRA campaign was still operative. In any case, the multiparty negotiations moved at a snail's pace and were seriously damaged by the events of the marching season during the summer of 1996.

One incident in particular illustrated that the Northern Ireland problem was not simply about decommissioning but also highlighted the nature of an intimidatory and demotic culture. A year before the event in question, in July 1995, an Orange march took place in Portadown, where local Catholics objected to the march passing their houses. They determined that the same would not happen in 1996, a decision that was upheld initially by the RUC Chief Constable. When Orangemen mustered in very large numbers for four successive nights, he reversed the decision and allowed the march to proceed along its chosen route. The result was catastrophic. Serious and sustained rioting broke out in many centres throughout the province. A huge amount of material damage was caused and an innocent Catholic was murdered, allegedly on the orders of a well-known loyalist leader. Relations between the British and Irish governments came under huge strain. Allegations of widespread police brutality led to complaints from the independent Standing Advisory Committee on Human Rights "about the failure to maintain the supremacy of the rule of law and about the serious violations of human rights resulting therefrom." It considered that the events had led to "what is perhaps the widest gulf in understanding between the two communities for 20 years" (*Irish Times,* 9 August 1996). In short, the march led to the temporary collapse of political authority in Northern Ireland.

Developments during 1997 led to a renewal of cautious optimism after the despair of the summer of 1996 and facilitated a second opportunity to build a "peace process." The most important event was the election on 1 May of a new British Labour Party government with a large majority. Prime Minister Tony Blair quickly signaled that Northern Ireland would be a top priority for his government. He visited Northern Ireland within weeks of his election victory and, in a major speech designed to restart the stalled peace process, made it very clear that close cooperation between the British and Irish governments would continue. With the considerable authority afforded by his huge election victory, Blair offered the republican movement a stark choice:

> The IRA and Sinn Féin face a choice between negotiations and violence. Violence is the failed path of the past. I urge them to choose negotiations,

> once and for all. . . . I am ready to make one further effort to proceed with the inclusive talks process. My message to Sinn Féin is clear. The settlement train is leaving. I want you on that train. But it is leaving anyway, and I will not allow it to wait for you. You cannot hold the process to ransom any longer. So end the violence. Now. (speech by Prime Minister Blair, Belfast, 16 May 1997)

Adding that his government "would respond quickly to genuine moves to achieve peace," Blair signaled the seriousness of his intent by publicly announcing that he would allow government officials to meet Sinn Féin to "explain our position and to assess whether the republican movement genuinely is ready to give up violence and commit itself to politics alone" (speech by Blair, 16 May 1997). Thus the republican movement was presented with an ultimatum: Disavow violence and enter negotiations, or continue violence and face isolation and repression.

Related events, such as the election of a new Fianna Fáil–led coalition government in Dublin and, especially, Sinn Féin's impressive electoral performance at the 1997 Westminster and District Council elections, contributed to the renewal of the IRA's ceasefire in July 1997. The government made it clear that there would be no lengthy "decontamination" period this time, and within six weeks of the ceasefire Sinn Féin was invited to the new round of negotiations that started on 15 September 1997. The "peace process" had been given a second chance.

Conclusion

The main argument of this chapter is that constitutional policy has changed and that Anglo-Irish relations have been modified accordingly. In earlier years it was clear that Northern Ireland policy was solely a matter for the United Kingdom government. The concept of the "Irish dimension" was introduced in the 1970s, but it was more aspirational than operational. As of the 1980s a pattern was established whereby the British and Irish governments held summits on a regular basis. The result was closer cooperation and a breakdown in historic misconceptions, culminating in the signing of the Anglo-Irish Agreement in November 1985. The Agreement gave the Irish government a formal role in relation to Northern Ireland policy that fell short of joint authority. This is not to suggest that Anglo-Irish relations were always sweetness and light and without tensions. Nevertheless, the continuation of an Anglo-Irish process over a decade and a half underlined the degree to which unionism was being marginalised in British politics. The publication of the *Joint Declaration* in December 1993 and of the Framework Documents in February 1995 was further evidence that both governments assert the centrality of an Anglo-Irish approach to the Northern Ireland conflict.

Given the sophistication and longevity of the campaign of violence, it was hardly surprising that the British government turned its back on seeking a purely internal solution to the problem. But closer cooperation might have resulted in any case. The United Kingdom and Ireland are coordinate members of the EU. The (Woodrow) Wilsonian model of the nation-state no longer has the same validity as we approach the millennium (Hobsbawm 1990). Globalisation has encouraged the growth of functional regimes. In addition, the Anglo-American "special relationship" may not be quite so special any longer (Arthur 1991). All of these factors have had an impact on Anglo-Irish relations and assisted in internationalising the conflict, thus enabling the United States and the EU to play a more active role as prestigious third parties.

Internationalisation has helped, too, in allowing the local parties to the conflict to find more space and to examine the problems afresh. One need only look at Sinn Féin's policy document, *Towards a New Ireland* (1992), to see the impact of these wider horizons. It recognised that traditional sovereignties are eroding, jurisdictions are in flux, and boundaries are altering. It alluded to the demand for political democracy in Eastern Europe, to the reunification of Germany, to economic restructuring under EU integration, and to an Irish republicanism that "has its roots in the crucible of Europe during the great French revolution." And it saw the political and economic transformation of Europe as providing "a golden opportunity for Ireland to finally resolve its British problem." The fact that such views are not dissimilar to those of the SDLP leader (Hume 1996: 134–147) suggests a shift from an ethnocentric to a polycentric nationalism "which respects the other and sees each nation as enriching a common civilisation" (Tamir 1995: 430). In other words, Anglo-Irish policy has helped to reshape the question. By itself, this outcome does not provide a solution. That can emerge only when we confront the ghosts of history: "But if the focus remains on the past, the past will become the future, and that is something no one can desire" (Report of the International Body [The Mitchell Commission] 1996: paragraph 16).

References and Further Reading

Arthur, Paul, 1991. "Diasporan intervention in international affairs." *Diaspora* 1:2, pp. 143–162.

Arthur, Paul, 1992. "The Brooke Initiative," *Irish Political Studies* 7, pp. 111–115.

Arthur, Paul, 1996. "Time, territory, tradition and the Anglo-Irish 'Peace' Process," *Government and Opposition* 31:4, pp. 426–440.

Crossman, Richard, 1978. *The Diaries of a Cabinet Minister: 3*. London: Jonathan Cape.

Darby, John, 1986. *Intimidation and the Control of Conflict in Northern Ireland*. Dublin: Gill and Macmillan.

Department of Foreign Affairs 1996. *Challenges and Opportunities Abroad: White Paper on Foreign Policy*. Dublin: Stationery Office.

Deutsch, Morton, 1973. *The Resolution of Conflict: Constructive and Destructive Processes*. New Haven: Yale University Press.

FitzGerald, Garret, Paul Gillespie, and Ronan Fanning, 1996. "Britain's European Question: The Issues for Ireland," pp. 5–71 in Paul Gillespie (ed.), *Britain's European Question: The Issues for Ireland*. Dublin: Institute of European Affairs.

Haagerup, Neils, 1984. *A Report on Northern Ireland*. Strasbourg: European Parliament.

Held, David (ed.), 1992. "Prospects for democracy," *Political Studies*, Special Issue No. 40. Oxford: Blackwell.

Holland, Jack, 1987. *The American Connection: U.S. Guns, Money and Influence in Northern Ireland*. New York: Viking.

HMSO, 1975. *The Government of Northern Ireland: A Society Divided*. Belfast.

HMSO, 1981. *Anglo-Irish Joint Studies: "Joint Report and Studies"* (Cmnd. 8414). London.

Hobsbawm, Eric, 1990. *Nations and Nationalism Since 1780*. Cambridge: Cambridge University Press.

Hume, John, 1996. *Personal Views: Politics, Peace and Reconciliation in Ireland*. Dublin: Town House.

Keatinge, Patrick, 1982. "An odd couple? Obstacles and opportunities in inter-state political co-operation between the Republic of Ireland and the United Kingdom," pp. 305–353 in Desmond Rea (ed.), *Political Co-operation in Divided Societies*. Dublin: Gill and Macmillan.

Kratochwil, Emil, 1986. "Of Systems, boundaries and territoriality: An enquiry into the formation of the state system," *World Politics* 39:1.

Lee, Joseph, 1989. *Ireland 1912–1985: Politics and Society*. Cambridge: Cambridge University Press.

O'Leary, Brendan, and John McGarry, 1993. *The Politics of Antagonism: Understanding Northern Ireland*. London: Athlone Press. (2nd edition published in 1996.)

Parry, Geraint (ed.), 1993. "Globalization: The interweaving of foreign and domestic policy-making," *Government and Opposition* 28:2, pp. 143–288.

Powell, Enoch, 1983. "Dev and devolution," *The Spectator* 8, pp. 19–20. January.

Rea, Desmond (ed.), 1982. *Political Co-operation in Divided Societies*. Dublin: Gill and Macmillan.

Rose, Richard, 1971. *Governing Without Consensus: An Irish Perspective*. London: Faber and Faber.

Ruane, Joseph, and Jennifer Todd, 1996. *The Dynamics of Conflict in Northern Ireland: Power, Conflict and Emancipation*. Cambridge: Cambridge University Press.

Shannon, William, 1986. "The Anglo-Irish Agreement," *Foreign Affairs* 64:4, pp. 835–850.

Sinn Féin, 1992. *Towards a Lasting Peace in Ireland*. Dublin.

Sinn Féin, 1993. *Setting the Record Straight*. Dublin.

Tamir, Y., 1995. "The enigma of nationalism," *World Politics* 47.

Tugendhat, Christopher, 1986. *Making Sense of Europe*. Harmondsworth: Viking.

Wallace, William, 1986. "What price independence? Sovereignty and interdependence in British Politics," *International Affairs* 62:3, pp. 367–389.

Weiler, Joseph, 1990. "The European Community in change: Exit, voice and loyalty," *Irish Studies in International Affairs* 3:2, pp. 15–25.

White, Barry, 1984. *John Hume: Statesman of the Troubles*. Belfast: Blackstaff Press.

Wright, Frank, 1987. *Northern Ireland: A Comparative Analysis*. Dublin: Gill and Macmillan.

12

"Futures"

PAUL MITCHELL

Despite[1] numerous government initiatives, the current phase of the Northern Ireland conflict has stretched to almost thirty years. The failure of all attempts to end the conflict adequately explains why it is said to have an intractable nature and cautions against any assumption that there exists a formula—no matter how just and balanced—that will readily be embraced by the principal communities and protagonists in Northern Ireland. Given the protracted and enduring nature of the conflict, it is axiomatic that no one has proposed a settlement that has received universal acclaim. And no one will. The "solution" in terms of a near-perfect model for reconciling differences is not waiting to be invented.

Indeed, it is probably better to speak of "settlements" than "solutions," while retaining the prospect that the former, if fair and balanced, eventually will evolve into the latter. Previous chapters have analysed the evolution of initiatives such as the Anglo-Irish Agreement, the *Joint Declaration for Peace* and the Framework Documents. Here we step back from the detail of the multiple documents, processes, and communiqués and examine the merits and faults of a small set of thinkable futures. All prescriptions have costs and benefits, risks and certainties. But clearly some costs are worse and some benefits are better than others, and it is with this in mind that I evaluate the broad types of settlement discussed herein.

Assumptions and Diagnoses

Prescriptions flow from explanation, which in turn results from a mixture of value judgements and (one hopes) reasoned and reasonable reflection on the available evidence. Academic commentary on particular ethnic conflicts is notoriously partisan, and book reviews often reveal more about the reviewer than the book. Since this is regularly the case with the Northern Ireland conflict, it is worth being explicit about the assumptions that inform this chapter. Two propositions are fundamental and interrelated.

First, at the conflict's core is what Walker Connor has labeled an "ethno-national" antagonism (1994): a clash of national identities with Northern Ireland representing the territorial line of retreat of British and Irish state and nation building failures (O'Leary and McGarry 1993: 107–108). Irish Catholics throughout the island were never integrated into the British state as equals, and Northern Protestants were never attracted in large numbers by the idea of a united Ireland. A standoff of national allegiances ensued. Any analysis that elides this conflict of national identities is missing the point.[2] Thus the conflict is not primarily religious, cultural, or class based; it is not imperial, colonial, or even settler-native—although elements of all these have been contributory either in the past or the present. The rival communities in Northern Ireland are of course often referred to by the convenient labels "Catholic" and "Protestant." But to conclude that the antagonism is religious is to confuse the ethnic boundary marker for the essence of the conflict. It is unlikely that ecumenism or widespread secularisation would lead to the withering of rival national identities.[3]

Once mobilised, national conflicts cannot be wished away or engineered out of existence by greater economic equality, pluralisation, or acculturation, although each of the above may be helpful in its own right. An important feature of ethnic and national identities—one that contributes to their intense and enduring nature—is their ability to be premised on any evidence of (alleged) common ancestry and experience. "The point is simple, but often refused: as long as groups have any way of telling each other apart—names or clothes can be substituted for religion or language—ethno-national divisions can be maintained" (McGarry and O'Leary 1995a: 357). The relevant conclusion is that only those approaches that tackle the core of the problem—national identities in conflict—have any prospect of enduring success.

The second proposition is that the status quo is unacceptable and an important part of the problem. Northern Ireland has never been a functioning liberal democracy, has never been widely regarded as legitimate, and has cost almost 3,300 lives since 1969. Nationalists objected to the manner (and fact) of the partition that created Northern Ireland, and neither unionist governments nor the British government since 1972 have been able and/or willing to reform Northern Ireland so as to warrant any expectation that most Catholics will identify with the British state. Thus, "the claim that Northern Ireland is and should be (exclusively) British is part of the problem" (O'Leary, Lyne, Marshall, and Rowthorn 1993: 89). A sometimes overlooked aspect of the current constitutional position is that the British government and people no longer assert exclusive sovereignty over Northern Ireland. On the contrary, it is the official policy of the British government (stated in the *Joint Declaration for Peace* and repeated in *A New Framework for Agreement*) that it would "introduce the necessary legislation" to facilitate a united Ireland if a majority of the people of Northern Ireland were to express their consent. Thus the formal constitutional status quo is that Northern Ireland is currently exclusively British but could be exclusively Irish as soon as a simple majority so desires. This position not only disregards important realities of the conflict but exacerbates unnecessary fears and raises expectations that cannot be realised. The escape route from this zero-sum trap is to reject majoritarian thinking, a principle of exclusion that is ill-advised and dangerous in ethno-national conflicts.

The following sections outline and evaluate four broad families of prescriptions: integration projects, whether motivated by unionist, nationalist, or liberal concerns; separation schemes; independence; and proposals for sharing sovereignty and authority. A final section examines feasibility and current options.

Integration Projects

Of all the broad categories of prescription, integration projects are the most diverse both in motivation and effect. Essentially there are partisan and nonpartisan proposals that urge national or civic integration respectively. Partisan projects are explicitly or implicitly unionist or nationalist and advocate resolving the conflict by definitively integrating Northern Ireland with the British or Irish states respectively. Nonnational civic integrationists usually recognise the zero-sum nature of the constitutional divide and recommend bypassing or "transcending" it by concentrating on "civil society," "bottom-up" or "emancipatory" strategies, policies designed to promote equality and contact between the divided communities through reform of public policies, and sometimes a "deconstruction" of the roots of antagonism.

Partisan Integration

National integrationists argue that Northern Ireland's equivocal constitutional status should be ended by rendering it either exclusively

British or Irish. Unionist integrationists want the British government to end Northern Ireland's current conditional membership in the union (based on a local majority being opposed to a united Ireland) and fully integrate it into the British state on a permanent basis.[4] The argument is that Northern Ireland's uncertain status simultaneously exacerbates unionist anxieties and encourages Irish nationalists and republicans to believe that their ultimate goals are achievable. It is claimed that administrative integration into the United Kingdom would reassure unionists, thus allowing an equitable reform of the Northern Ireland state and possibly even power sharing with Catholics. In other words, if only Northern Catholics would forsake their Irish nationalism in favour of the British state, they could be included as full and equal citizens. Such accounts stress the economic benefits and high quality of citizenship that could be afforded Northern Catholics under "positive direct rule" if they would relinquish Irish nationalism or republicanism. The most compelling way to see the error of these excessively materialist accounts is to consider the counterfactual: Would unionists drop their objections to a united Ireland if it could be demonstrated that they would be fully integrated into an increasingly wealthy and pluralist Southern state?

There are also those who advocate electoral integration, arguing that the sectarian choices on offer in Northern Ireland could be bypassed or even transformed if only the main British political parties would contest elections in Northern Ireland (Roberts 1987; Aughey 1989; Wilson 1989). Although it is tempting to believe that nonethnic parties or new leaders might make the difference, these writers overestimate the importance of political parties once an ethno-national conflict has developed. The comparative evidence is clear: Once ethnic sentiments are mobilised beyond a certain point, multiethnic parties are typically unstable and will usually be replaced by rival parties projecting an exclusive ethnic appeal. In Belgium the main political parties—Liberal, Social Democrat, and Christian Democrat—organised across the linguistic divide and throughout the state. However, the increased salience of ethnic conflict since the 1960s resulted in these parties' bifurcation into linguistically exclusive parties. Thus, for example, the Belgian Socialist Party was replaced by separate Flemish and Walloon Socialist parties. Indeed, since the fragmentation of the socialists, this process has been replicated in the other ideological families, so that the party system has doubled in size.[5]

There are three impressive objections to electoral integration. First, as suggested above, it simply will not work. As Donald Horowitz puts it: "In an ethnic party system, the choice for a Left party is to adapt and become essentially an ethnic party or to wither and die" (1985:

338). In Northern Ireland efforts to forge class alliances by means of an ambivalent posture on the constitutional question have always resulted in the marginalisation of those who persevere. The prognosis is the same for conservative parties: Whatever their original intentions, multiethnic parties become marginalised or partisan or both. The fate of the Northern Ireland Conservatives is a case in point. Secondly, the local "sectarian" parties are democratic and attract about 90 percent of votes cast at each election. Thirdly, electoral integration projects are not neutral. After all, it is *British* electoral integration that these authors advocate (O'Leary et al. 1993: 123; O'Leary and McGarry 1993).[6] John Whyte's judgement bears repeating: "Electoral integration is a dead end, and the attempt to explore it only postpones the search for a settlement" (Whyte 1990: 221).

The Irish nationalist integration project is premised on the same logic and was clearly expressed by Gerry Adams in his 1995 address to Sinn Féin's *Ard-Fheis:* "Unionists are an Irish national minority with minority rights." In this formulation, unionists only have rights as future Irish citizens.[7] Since the partition of Ireland was illegitimate, only the Irish people as a whole have a right to self-determination; therefore, unionists have no justification for opting out of their birthright. The republican position has essentially been that Northern unionists suffer from a debilitating false consciousness, and that once the British state withdraws unionists will face reality and reconcile themselves to their Irish identity. Republicans have regularly underestimated or simply dismissed the willingness of unionists to oppose and fight against Irish territorial unification.

Both national integration projects—unionist and Irish nationalist—are patronising and flawed. They are patronising because they do not accept that the other side's beliefs are sincerely held, judging that once the preferred constitutional arrangements fall into place the unionist or nationalist community, faced with its minority status, will "wise up" (per the local vernacular) and operate the new constitution to their maximum advantage.[8] The logic is flawed, however: If the primary conflict is a clash of national identities, then there is no basis for assuming that either side would be prepared to trade away its identity for any socially and economically favourable integration into a rival nation-state. Ethnic groups once nationally mobilised on their own homeland do not typically decide which nation to join based on an instrumental calculation of material gain.

The appropriate conclusion, as Brendan O'Leary and John McGarry have argued, is that integration projects are more of a symptom of conflict than a solvent:

> [T]oo many parties to the conflict are presently integrationists, but on their own terms. Unionists wish to integrate Northern Ireland into the UK, administratively, electorally, or culturally. In so doing they ignore or diminish the importance of their minority's Irish national identity. Irish nationalists, north and south, have and do seek the integration of Northern Ireland into an all-Ireland state. In so doing they ignore or diminish the importance of the British and religious identity of "their minority," Ulster unionists. Each community has an "integration project"; each is majoritarian, at the expense of its own minority. (O'Leary and McGarry 1993: 307; see also O'Leary et al. 1993: 121)

These national integration projects are an assault on their rivals' national identity; they are exclusionary, unbalanced, and unfair and, as such, have no prospect of helping to resolve the conflict.

Civic Integration and "Bottom-Up" Strategies

A wide variety of other approaches recognise that national identities are sincerely held, that they tend to encourage zero-sum politics, and that a constitutional settlement is unlikely to be forthcoming. For example, Richard English argues that there is no solution that can be implemented, that negotiations are dangerous,[9] and that only "demographic, economic and wider political changes" have any prospect of ending the conflict "within a generation" (1997: 25). He essentially contends that because the constitutional issue is "too hot to handle" it should be left well alone and Anglo-Irish efforts should instead concentrate on reforming Northern Ireland. Similar to the unionist integrationist position, English's further assertion is that "serious nationalist grievances (regarding employment, marches, policing) are more likely to be addressed once unrealistic nationalist hopes have been removed and unnecessary unionist fears have been assuaged" (1997: 25). However, English is not naive enough to believe that such reforms will end the conflict: "[M]ost nationalists in Northern Ireland are unlikely to endorse Northern Ireland in whatever shape it emerges" (1997: 25). His willingness to accept a reformed status quo is of course an implicitly unionist position.

A surprising number of commentators, although they recognise the national nature of the conflict, continue to emphasise materialist agendas as though the conflict were mainly about civil rights. Indeed, Paul Bew and Henry Patterson recommend avoiding the constitutional question altogether: The "centre of the tasks" of any British government, they argue, "must be the attempt to deal with the necessary reformist agenda in a way that clearly separates it from conflicting aspirations on the constitutional future of Northern Ireland....

[W]hile leaving 'ultimate' constitutional aspirations untouched, it would provide for a more expansive and positive form of citizenship within Northern Ireland" (Bew and Patterson 1990: 217). Reform of the state in the direction of socioeconomic equality, parity of esteem, and legal and policing reforms would of course be helpful and an important part of any progressive framework. However, sidestepping what is implicitly recognised as the heart of the conflict—namely, constitutional aspirations—is a recipe for its continuation.[10] Walker Connor has repeatedly warned that the materialist foundations of ethnic conflict are greatly exaggerated (Connor 1994).[11] Only those approaches that directly address the core problem of national identities have any prospect of success.

A range of explicitly nonpartisan proposals recognise the centrality of national identity in the ongoing stalemate and recommend that some progress may be made by taking actions to depolarise the segmented communities (Wilford 1992) or by "deconstruct[ing] the root causes of conflict" (Todd 1995a: 171).[12] Neither of these complementary approaches is intended as an alternative to the search for a political settlement; rather, each has been deemed an aid in arriving at the "preconditions for a settlement" (Todd 1995a: 171). Wilford focuses on public policy initiatives such as fair employment, integrated education, and community relations schemes, which he sees as possible means of advancing desegregation and pluralism through intercommunal contact (Wilford 1992: 38). And although he does not suggest that such policies are panaceas for Northern Ireland's ills,[13] he interprets these bottom-up approaches as a necessary corrective to the top-down character of classic consociational prescriptions. The latter are indeed elite-led, but Wilford tends to overstate the immutability of community relations under consociational political settlements.[14] Although some consociational architecture—as in pre–civil war Lebanon—did suffer from fixity, power-sharing institutions can be designed along more flexible lines. Institutionalised power sharing and proportionality do not require frozen community relations, only a fair and inclusive relationship to political authority.

Judging that none of the available constitutional settlements can currently attract sufficient consent, Todd (1995a, 1995b) and Ruane and Todd (1996) recommend an "emancipatory process" whose "primary aim is to deconstruct the root causes of conflict so that participants are freed to reconstruct alternative relationships among themselves" (Todd 1995a: 171). Even though this approach represents a genuine attempt to avoid the pitfalls of imposed settlements through a participatory process, it is ultimately rather too thin on specifics. Apart from encouraging general social processes that may already be under way, it specifies few concrete mechanisms of change. The logic is as follows: "No existing proposal can attain sufficiently wide agreement. That is why the process of dismantling and deconstructing the conditions of conflict is essential. Emancipation involves a commitment to real change in social structures" (Todd 1995a: 174). The problem is that, although such social change would be intrinsically helpful, it may not do much about ethnic conflict: Such identities are not easily "reconstructed" along more amenable lines. The approach as a whole probably underestimates the extent to which political divisions in protracted ethno-national conflict are relatively independent of changes in the social structure. This is not to say that there is no connection—that ethnic conflicts are impervious to social change. Rather, the aim is to recognise the resilience of ethnic antagonisms in the face of changes in economic, social, and cultural conditions. The ascriptive nature of ethnic identities means that ethnic conflicts tend to be intense, enduring, and stubbornly resistant to purely material or social change. Political change is required.

Bottom-up approaches are premised on a liberal article of faith—namely, that contact promotes toleration and understanding.[15] On this point, however, the evidence is at best mixed and indecisive. Although it is a plausible tenet in liberal democracies (though even here it can be challenged), it is less convincing in ethno-national conflicts where grievances are intensely held and violence is a real possibility. A number of specialists on ethnic conflict have noted that contact is as necessary for violence as it is for friendship (e.g., Connor 1994; Horowitz 1985). As McGarry and O'Leary put it: "[I]n deeply divided territories, increased exposure to the 'other' may make group members more aware of what their group has in common and what separates them from others. Exposure may cement group solidarity rather than diffuse it" (1995b: 855). This debate highlights a philosophical difference of opinion as to the most prudential path for public policy in protracted ethnic conflicts. One school believes that ethnic differences in polarised conflicts are likely to be enduring realities and, hence, that the best course of action in the short term is to treat them as realities that should not be wished away but, rather, accommodated and respected. In consociational language the ethnic communities become building blocks in a balanced settlement. The bottom-up or civil society school believes that the consociational approach "conveys a rather bleak view of humanity" (Wilford 1992: 31). In contrast, advocates of civil society approaches tend to treat ethnic identities as more fluid and recommend strategies of pluralisation, deconstruction, and the transcending of traditional identities (Todd 1995; Ruane and Todd 1996). But the problem with the latter is that transcending identities is a decidedly long-term endeavour and that, in the meantime, attempts at anything other than entirely voluntary integration are dangerous, creating new opportunities for conflict. The reality is that most people in mobilised conflicts do not want to be integrated. For example, "many northern nationalists insist that they want equality and autonomy rather than equality and integration" (McGarry and O'Leary 1995b: 856).

In sum, any reconciling effects due to increased voluntary contact between communities, deconstruction, or emancipation would be helpful in conditions of debilitating polarisation. However, there are at least two reasons to doubt the political significance of desegmentation strategies in such intractable conflicts. First, there is little evidence to suggest that much reconciling is taking place beyond certain cosmopolitan enclaves. Most ethnic partisans do not want to be emancipated any more than they want to be integrated. The limited progress that is sometimes made in terms of inter-ethnic understanding is frequently eclipsed by the latest polarising event that quickly reasserts intra-ethnic solidarities. Secondly, even if bottom-up (or civil society) approaches could make progress that had political implications for the conflict, the likelihood is that it would be a case of too little, too late, and too slow.

Separation

For most, separation—by means of a repartition of Northern Ireland—is not a tenable future. Nevertheless, it is worth some examination because it is the logical alternative to and possibly the consequence of the failure of all other initiatives. Also to some extent it is already happening—informally—in terms of the increasing spatial segregation of the communities in Northern Ireland.

At least in the abstract, the partition of divided territories into new states can be just because it is consistent with the mutual self-determination of peoples. In the Irish case a repartition would involve creating a smaller British Northern Ireland in the northeast and a larger Republic of Ireland that would absorb as much of the nationalist population as is feasible. The latter qualification highlights the difficulty. The main selling point of partition as a means of eliminating conflict is the assumption that the probable outcome will be more homogeneous states (as well as the ancillary assumption that more homogeneous states will lead to lower levels of conflict). Unfortunately, these assumptions are rarely met in practice because a successful partition must fulfil two conditions. First, the seceding region must not contain people who do not want to leave (the southern and western regions joining the Republic of Ireland must contain no or few unionists). Secondly, the seceding region must contain all or almost all of those who want to leave (nationalists who want to leave must not be left behind in the rump Northern Ireland state). Of course, the unionist and nationalist communities in Northern Ireland are too geographically interspersed to fulfil either of these conditions. Any proposed repartition line would leave large numbers of people on the "wrong side" of the new border.

Liam Kennedy's careful account of repartition scenarios makes it clear that the new border would be unwieldy (much like the current situation in Bosnia) and most likely would involve enclaves detached from the "national" territory (Kennedy 1986, 1991). As an obvious example, consider that about 100,000 Catholics live in West Belfast, which therefore becomes an Irish enclave within British Ulster in three of Kennedy's four scenarios.[16] Belfast is not the only problem: There are Protestant-majority areas even in parts of mostly nationalist Fermanagh and Tyrone. Moreover, even Kennedy's best scenario—namely, Option 1 (and I say *best* in the sense of minimising minorities)—entails detached enclaves in Belfast and Fermanagh and still leaves large numbers of people in the "wrong" state. For example, at the time of Kennedy's calculations, the minority in Northern Ireland (i.e., the cultural Catholic population, with no Protestants "displaced") was 39.1 percent. As a result of Option 1, then, the size of the Catholic minority in the truncated British Ulster would be reduced from 39.1 percent to 20.2 percent (in other words, about half of Northern Ireland's Catholics would join the Republic of Ireland and half would be left behind in British Ulster). However, a further result of the repartition is that about 75,000 Protestants (about 8 percent of Northern Ireland Protestants) would find themselves displaced on the wrong side of the border, compared with none in the status quo.

Thus the result is certainly more balanced in that displacement is shared, but the repartition is not obviously better than the existing position. Indeed, there are reasons to believe that a repartition could be a good deal worse than the status quo. One reason is obvious: Since no "perfect" partition is feasible, any attempt would leave smaller and more vulnerable minorities on either side of the new border. Another is that a partition, or even the prospect thereof, may induce demonstration effects and preemptive behaviour. A demonstration effect arises when a secession encourages others to "have a go" at achieving their own secession; a Northern Irish version of this would be "salami-partitions—as border-area after border-area developed nationalist-majorities" (O'Leary et al. 1993: 103). Preemptive action occurs when the prospect of a partition encourages groups to "cleanse" the area of the ethno-national rival as has happened most clearly in the former Yugoslavia.

In sum, repartition, though potentially just and balanced, is a decidedly poor option for Northern Ireland and has negligible support.[17] It should be contemplated only if it is judged to be the least objectionable of a bad set of alternatives. Indeed, Horowitz concludes that, as a general solution to ethnic conflict, "it ought not to be the policy of choice but of desperation" (1985: 592). In Northern Ireland the only scenario desperate enough to make repartition attractive would be an all-out ethnic war.

Independence

An independent Northern Ireland is possibly the only major "option" that is even less likely than a repartition, despite being considerably more popular. According to a September 1996 *Irish Times*/MRBI Poll, "Northern Ireland as an independent state" was the first preference of 4 percent of respondents. It was also the second preference of 15 percent; however, this apparent popularity masks a partisan divide. Only 1 percent of Catholics chose independence as their second preference, compared to 24 percent of non-Catholics (*Irish Political Studies* 1997: 182–183). Superficially, independence seems fair because it rules out each side's first preference: integration into either the British or Irish states. Advocates of independence (e.g., the UDA's New Ulster Political Research Group 1979; Murphy 1984; de Paor 1990; Moore and Crimmins 1991) essentially argue that internal accommodation will be feasible once London and Dublin are removed from the conflict. However, this reasoning overestimates the exogenous roots of conflict and seriously underestimates the internal basis of antagonism. Even if an independent Northern Ireland were financially viable, which is doubtful, it would not be stable. Comparative experience suggests that the direct consequence of divided lands achieving independence is more likely to be ethnic war than reconciliation. Given that the communities in Northern Ireland have shown little willingness to share power and authority at the bidding of successive British and Irish governments, there is little reason to believe that they would do so on their own. With independence, the minority would fear majority tyranny, unionists would lose their British links, and republican paramilitaries would most likely be encouraged, believing that with British troops gone their goals would be realisable.

In short, "if there were enough trust between the communities in Northern Ireland, independence would probably be viable—but it would probably not be necessary" (Whyte 1990: 223). At best, independence is the product of wishful assumptions; at worst, of partisan calculations. It is much less likely to lead to accommodation than to a melt-down into an ethno-national war, which in turn would necessitate a messy repartition of territory.

Sharing Sovereignty and Authority

The logic of this prescription is quite simple. Since the core of the problem is a clash of identities in which traditional partisans assert that Northern Ireland has to be exclusively British or exclusively Irish, then the only way out of this sovereignty trap is for Northern Ireland to become simultaneously British and Irish. Claiming that Northern Ireland has to be British *or* Irish frames the conflict in all-or-nothing terms, whereas scenarios for separation are not feasible given the distribution of the population. Thus the most desirable response is to share authority and sovereignty, a normatively enlightened approach that prioritises recognition and institutional expression of each community's identity. Since the conflict is partly the joint product of British and Irish failures, it is only right that they should jointly be responsible for taking steps to end it. Each government and people should recognise that British and Irish claims to Northern Ireland are equally valid.

Though not a new idea, the most imaginative and detailed shared authority proposal has been outlined by O'Leary and McGarry (1993; O'Leary et al. 1993).[18] The aim of their proposal is to directly address both the internal and external dimensions of the conflict and to reconcile them in a manner that is fair, balanced, and stable. Essentially they propose a set of consociational arrangements (power sharing, proportionality, and community autonomy) within the framework of joint British and Irish sovereignty. The model as a whole incorporates an elaborate system of checks and balances as well as a division and fusion of executive and legislative powers that interlock. The key features of the shared authority proposal are as follows:[19]

- *Constitution of Northern Ireland*: Britain and the Republic of Ireland become co-sovereigns of the region, and citizens of Northern Ireland are free to choose British or Irish or dual citizenship. There would be two heads of state—the British monarch and the Irish president—and all national insignia and cultures would be equally respected. Amendments would be made to British public law and Articles 2 and 3 of the Irish constitution as part of the process of entrenching joint sovereignty.

- *Shared Authority Council of Northern Ireland* (SACNI): This chief executive body would consist of five members, three elected in Northern Ireland by single transferable vote and two appointed, one each by the Prime Minister and Taoiseach from their cabinets.[20] The SACNI would appoint ministers to run government departments and be ultimately responsible for defence and security.
- *Assembly of the Peoples of Northern Ireland*: This assembly would be equipped with an extensive committee structure to scrutinise ministerial departments. Apart from certain legislative powers (see O'Leary et al. 1993 for details), it would elect a Speaker and a Deputy Speaker. And each of these (most likely one unionist and one nationalist) would have equal powers in determining whether any bills threaten national or religious rights or freedoms. If either official so finds, he or she can ask for a ruling by the Supreme Court, which, like all other institutions, would be proportionally composed.

An important aspect of O'Leary and McGarry's prescription is that it is designed to be semi-permanent or, as they prefer to say, "durable." A key problem with previous joint authority proposals is that they were envisaged as transitional arrangements—as halfway houses to a united Ireland. This was the case, for example, with the SDLP's 1972 policy document *Towards a New Ireland*, which called for joint sovereignty as "an interim system of government," during which time the British government should "positively encourage" a united Ireland by consent (SDLP 1972: 4–7). The response of unionists was summed up in *Peace, Order and Good Government*, the Ulster Unionist Party's manifesto for the 1973 Assembly elections: "We totally reject any attempts by the Dublin Government to interfere in the internal affairs of Northern Ireland, nor will we allow any Council of Ireland to become a stage on the road to Irish Unity" (Unionist Party 1973: 11).[21]

Hence most proposals for sharing sovereignty are vulnerable to the reasonable unionist objection that they are really nationalist schemes to achieve a united Ireland by stealth. O'Leary and McGarry's proposals have no such motivation; they are explicitly designed to prevent shared authority from becoming a mechanism for imposing a united Ireland (or anything else) without widespread consent. First, the new *Constitution of Northern Ireland* would be entrenched in British public law and in the *Constitution of Ireland*. Secondly, the new Northern Ireland constitution could be changed only with the consent of three-quarters of those voting in a referendum in Northern Ireland.[22]

The constitution is deliberately designed to be inflexible on issues of sovereignty in order to prevent the current or future majority from imposing its will on the current or future minority. With such a decision rule in place, neither community could be coerced into an exclusively Irish or exclusively British state. Given that each side's sovereignty claims are mutually incompatible, the shared sovereignty idea splits the difference: "Each community would obtain the protection of its nation-state at the expense of having to share the territory, sovereignty and political power with the other community and its nation-state" (McGarry and O'Leary 1995a: 370).

It is now the conventional wisdom of both governments that any proposed settlement has to be "boycott-proof" to the extent possible. Since most desirable approaches require the participation of the local parties, each side has the ability to undermine the new processes by boycotting or destabilising them. Ultimately, since a party cannot be forced to participate constructively, any proposed settlement must specify a default mechanism should the new institutions malfunction due to boycotts or wrecking manoeuvres. If this were to happen during shared authority, the default would effectively be joint direct rule of Northern Ireland by the British and Irish governments.

The advantages for nationalists are obvious. Shared sovereignty and authority would be a significant improvement on the status quo. Their national identity would be institutionally expressed and elevated to an equal position with that of unionists. And their interests would be protected by the increased role of the government of the Republic of Ireland.

The advantages for unionists are less obvious, yet clearly important given the hostile unionist reaction to the Anglo-Irish Agreement. It is worth examining unionist incentives in a little more detail since these are usually the weak link in the reasoning of most plans for change. Specifically, O'Leary and his colleagues acknowledge that unionists are not "sympathetic to any alteration in indivisible British sovereignty over Northern Ireland" (1993: 56). They make two further points in this connection. First, they assert that the unionist position is not reasonable and that it is based on "an illiberal theory of self-determination" (1993: 56). Essentially many unionists argue that they alone have a right to self-determination because they are a local majority. However, "what is sauce for the goose should also be sauce for the gander. If unionists maintain that the majority within the United Kingdom should not be able to over-rule the preferences of the majority within Northern Ireland then they must also concede that the majority within Northern Ireland has no right to over-rule the preferences of the minority within Northern Ireland" (O'Leary et al. 1993:

57).[23] The logic here is well founded: Majoritarian thinking is an intrinsic part of the problem, and claims to self-determination must be reciprocal to be just.

Secondly, O'Leary and his colleagues assert that the constitutional position of unionists is more secure with shared sovereignty in the sense that a united Ireland would be improbable. The logic here is that the present constitutional position allows Northern Ireland to become part of the Republic of Ireland as soon as a simple majority for this outcome emerges in Northern Ireland. Given demographic changes and increased nationalist voting, unionists conceivably may find themselves the minority community sometime during the next few decades. The proposal is that shared authority should continue even if unionists are no longer the majority community. Instead of the current situation in which a nationalist simple majority can trigger a change in Northern Ireland's constitutional status, under shared authority it would require a three-quarters majority to do so. Therefore, "under our model unionists will undoubtedly be better protected against their worst-case outcome than they are at present. . . . The proof of this argument is that many nationalists will find this feature of our model its most objectionable element" (O'Leary et al. 1993: 61).

There are, however, some counterarguments suggesting that unionists are unlikely to consent to shared sovereignty. First, whereas the constitutional entrenchment suggested by O'Leary and his colleagues protects unionists against their "worst-case outcome" (a united Ireland), it embraces shared authority, an outcome that they also do not like very much. Indeed, according to the September 1996 *Irish Times*/MRBI Poll cited throughout this chapter, the joint authority option was the first preference of only 3 percent of non-Catholics (among seven choices, only a united Ireland was more unpopular).[24] Although it can credibly be argued that neither side really loses anything much by pooling sovereignty and authority, the reality is that in mobilised conflicts where only one side's (unionist) identity is entrenched, sharing will usually be perceived as losing. Secondly, the incentive to negotiate a compromise now is partly based on a fear of being in a weakened bargaining position in the future when unionists *might* be a minority. Even if this were the case (which is doubtful given that a substantial minority of Catholics favour "unionist" options),[25] unionists no doubt calculate that they cannot be coerced into a united Ireland in the near future any more than they could have been in 1920, when they were also a "minority" on the island. Thirdly, even if (as seems likely) unionists are concerned about their constitutional position weakening in the future, the shared authority model makes implicit assumptions that unionists' (or for that matter any politician's) time horizons are long enough to encourage a prudential judgement. But to be confident of such assumptions, we would need to know how unionists discount future costs and benefits. Is it really the case that unionists would rather accept an immediate and tangible cost now—the weakening of their constitutional position that "sharing" is perceived to involve—in order to avoid a possible greater cost in the future? This seems unlikely.

Nevertheless, the concept of sharing authority and sovereignty has much to recommend it. It directly addresses the core of the problem and "splits the difference" by guaranteeing the institutional expression of both British and Irish identities unless or until the people of Northern Ireland decide otherwise by widespread consent (using a high threshold of two-thirds or three-quarters popular approval). It is an imaginative response to an unusual conflict that has the merit of challenging traditional assumptions concerning the "indivisibility of sovereignty" and the sanctity of majorities. The problem is that it does not have the consent of the unionist community at present and therefore could only be imposed. The two governments currently appear unwilling to take the course of imposing shared authority.

In the second edition of their book, O'Leary and McGarry recognise that shared authority, though desirable, is not feasible at present: It "has the merit of justice, if not consensus, but lacks the agents to execute it" (1996: 368). Instead, they propose a functional equivalent styled as a "double protection" system that would guarantee the same rights to unionists, should they ever become part of a united Ireland, as would be enjoyed by nationalists in a reconstructed Northern Ireland.[26] The reason that O'Leary and McGarry believe this approach to be more feasible is that it does not involve any change in Northern Ireland's current constitutional status, which would remain exclusively British, at least until a majority decides otherwise (this, after all, is the constitutional position of both governments). In addition to the constitutional status quo, the double protection package contains both internal and external dimensions. The internal settlement involves an assembly and executive that are elected proportionally and includes power sharing. But for the model to have any prospect of success, its internal features must be supplemented by "external" Irish dimensions. McGarry and O'Leary suggest a variety of these, ranging from the Intergovernmental Conference (established by the Anglo-Irish Agreement) acting as the safeguard of the settlement (with the right to veto any policy that threatens fundamental rights) to numerous cross-border bodies with functional powers in specific areas. Whatever the format of the Irish dimensions, "pure internalisation" must be avoided: "It is crucial for the nationalist minority that there be some institutional link between Northern Ireland and the Republic" (McGarry and O'Leary 1995a: 379). Clearly, any settlement without significant Irish dimensions has no prospect of success.

Essentially the idea is that authority would be shared, but not sovereignty.[27] The Anglo-Irish intergovernmental conference would guarantee the overall settlement, and a "swing constitution" would provide double protection: Unionists and nationalists would have the same rights irrespective of whether Northern Ireland remains within the United Kingdom or later becomes part of the Republic of Ireland (McGarry and O'Leary 1995a: 398). However, although the foregoing is a creative response to the difficulties of achieving unionist consent for shared sovereignty and authority, it is hard to envision that unionists would be much more enthusiastic about this formulation. In addition, since it (reluctantly) embraces majoritarianism with regard to sovereignty, it is considerably less just than the earlier proposal—a fact that the authors acknowledge (O'Leary and McGarry 1996: 368).

Conclusion

There are logical and normative problems with all of the thinkable futures for Northern Ireland. The prescriptions most widely advocated by the protagonists are variations of national integration projects. In the poll cited throughout this chapter, 82 percent of non-Catholic respondents chose exclusively British options, whereas 39 percent of Catholics chose a united Ireland (*Irish Political Studies* 1997: 182). Although as aspirations these desires are legitimate, no exclusively British or Irish settlement would be fair or stable and, therefore, will not be permitted by the sovereign governments. A united Ireland will not be imposed, unionist majority rule in Northern Ireland will not be allowed, and neither will direct rule without Irish dimensions, the position before the Anglo-Irish Agreement. Nevertheless, these partisan and incompatible desires are enduring realities.

From the perspective of many nonpartisan observers, some variation on shared sovereignty and authority would be an acceptable settlement—far from perfect, but a good deal fairer than partisan integration and less dangerous than repartition or independence. Of course, fairness and balance are a matter of perspective. Shared authority looks balanced in the abstract or as a set of institutions for a new multiethnic state in a virgin territory—if that were possible. But in reality there is always a status quo position (irrespective of competing views as to its legitimacy), and prescriptions will understandably be judged by participants in terms of the costs and benefits of departing from where they are, as well as where they wish to be. And the problem with any proposal that might reasonably be judged to be something that most nationalists could accept is that it involves a process of change in which most of the costs are borne by unionists. A recent survey of flexibility and intransigence concludes: "Protestants and unionists are resistant to multiple forms of constitutional change because it is they who have to do the changing; Catholics and nationalists are more amenable to change because for them most feasible changes would mark a net incremental improvement on the status quo" (Evans and O'Leary 1997: 45)

Where does this leave us? A new talks process began in September 1997, including Sinn Féin for the first time. The DUP and the U.K. Unionist Party boycotted the talks because of Sinn Féin's inclusion, whereas the UUP was authorised by its governing body to take part in negotiations, though its leaders refused to engage directly with representatives of Sinn Féin. Although there was a responsibility to exhaust diplomatic and negotiating efforts in the hope that the process would alchemize reciprocal concessions, nothing in the last thirty years of interparty talks suggested that a breakthrough was either likely or imminent. Most feared that negotiations would resemble previous efforts: interminable procedural wrangles, with each party seeking to blame the others for the collapse of talks. Comparative experience of such conflicts warned against facile optimism: "[S]uch conflicts are seldom resolved or finally settled" (Esman 1994: 46). And after all, for many years the "peace process" had been mostly process and little peace.

However, the future is often better than the past, even in the case of protracted ethnic conflicts. During 1997, new administrations came to power in both capitals: a British government with a large majority and an Irish government led by Fianna Fáil. These developments improved the prospects for progress when difficult choices had to be faced. In addition, the structure of incentives facing some of the key regional parties had altered such that the costs of failure increased. For unionists, local political responsibility could be restored only through an agreement to share power, identity, and (potentially) sovereignty with the nationalist community. In the meantime, the regional political vacuum had failed to freeze the status quo and instead accelerated and institutionalised cooperative binational endeavours by the British and Irish governments. Another negotiating failure could be projected to reinforce these trends whilst leaving the UUP in "internal exile" and, in any case, would not prevent the imposition of further Irish dimensions by the two governments. For most republicans, and certainly for the Sinn Féin leadership, the costs of failure were also high. Failure is especially costly when practical alternatives are absent. Having already concluded that a renewed military offensive was unwinnable—leading at best to a renewed polarised stalemate—and with strong signals within both communities that no return to the situation of the 1970s or even the 1980s would be tolerated, the Sinn Féin leadership had invested heavily in a political agreement.

Nevertheless, when a political agreement was reached by eight of the parties on 10 April 1998, most observers, if they are honest, were as astonished as their contemporaries had been when the Berlin wall was breached and Mandela was released from prison. The historic agreement, subsequent referenda, elections, and prospects for the future are extensively analysed in the epilogue to this book.

Fintan O'Toole has remarked: "[T]he search for peace has turned a place nobody quite wanted into a place that nobody claims. Northern Ireland has become a new kind of political space. Its people are in an extraordinary position—free to be anything they can agree to become. They have escaped from nations" (*New Yorker,* 27 April 1998, p. 56). For all the aptness of Milton Esman's sage words concerning the difficulties of definitively ending ethnic conflicts, the next few years offer the best opportunity in decades to construct a brighter future—and to render Esman's warning a self-denying prophecy.

Notes

Thanks to Richard English, Gitta Frank, Richard Jay, Brendan O'Leary, Jennifer Todd, and Rick Wilford for commenting on drafts of this chapter. Thanks also to the students taking the M.A. in Irish Politics at QUB during 1997 who were subjected to a version of the chapter. The usual disclaimers apply.

References and Further Reading

Aughey, Arthur, 1989. *Under Siege: Ulster Unionism and the Anglo-Irish Agreement.* London: Hurst and Company.

Bew, Paul, and Henry Patterson, 1990. "Scenarios for progress in Northern Ireland," pp. 206–218 in John McGarry and Brendan O'Leary (eds.), *The Future of Northern Ireland.* Oxford: Clarendon Press.

Bew, Paul, Henry Patterson, and Paul Teague, 1997. *Between War and Peace: The Political Future of Northern Ireland.* London: Lawrence and Wishart.

Connor, Walker, 1994. *Ethnonationalism: The Quest for Understanding.* Princeton: Princeton University Press.

de Paor, Liam 1990. *Unfinished Business: Ireland Today and Tomorrow.* London: Hutchinson.

Deutsch, Karl, 1969. *Nationalism and Its Alternatives.* New York: Knopf.

English, Richard, 1997. "Challenging peace," *Fortnight* No. 362, pp. 24–25.

Esman, Milton, 1994. *Ethnic Politics*. Ithaca, N.Y.: Cornell University Press.

Evans, Geoffrey, and Brendan O'Leary, 1997. "Frameworked futures: Intransigence and flexibility in the Northern Ireland elections of May 30 1996," *Irish Political Studies* 12, pp. 23–47.

Horowitz, Donald, 1985. *Ethnic Groups in Conflict*. Berkeley/Los Angeles: University of California Press.

Irish Political Studies, vol. 12, 1997. "Data Section," pp. 148–210.

Kennedy, Liam, 1986. *Two Ulsters: A Case for Repartition*. Belfast.

Kennedy, Liam, 1991. "Repartition," pp. 137–161 in John McGarry and Brendan O'Leary (eds.), *The Future of Northern Ireland*. Oxford: Clarendon Press.

Mitchell, Paul, 1995. "Party competition in an ethnic dual party system," *Ethnic and Racial Studies* 18:4, pp. 773–796.

McGarry, John, and Brendan O'Leary, 1995a. *Explaining Northern Ireland*. Oxford: Blackwell Publishers.

______, 1995b. "Five fallacies: Northern Ireland and the liabilities of liberalism," *Ethnic and Racial Studies* 18:4, pp. 837–861.

Moore, Margaret, and James Crimmins, 1991. "The case for negotiated independence," pp. 242–267 in John McGarry and Brendan O'Leary (eds.), *The Future of Northern Ireland*. Oxford: Clarendon Press.

Murphy, Dervla, 1984. *Changing the Problem: Post-Forum Reflections*. Gigginstown: Lilliput Press.

New Ulster Political Research Group, 1979. *Beyond the Religious Divide*. Belfast.

O'Leary, Brendan, and John McGarry, 1993. *The Politics of Antagonism: Understanding Northern Ireland*. London: Athlone Press.

______, 1996. *The Politics of Antagonism: Understanding Northern Ireland*, 2nd ed. London: Athlone Press.

O'Leary, Brendan, Tom Lyne, Jim Marshall, and Bob Rowthorn, 1993. *Northern Ireland: Sharing Authority*. London: Institute for Public Policy Research.

Roberts, Hugh, 1987. "'Sound stupidity': The British party system and the Northern Ireland question," *Government and Opposition* 22:3, pp. 315–335.

Ruane, Joseph, and Jennifer Todd, 1996. *The Dynamics of Conflict in Northern Ireland*. Cambridge: Cambridge University Press.

SDLP, 1972. *Towards a New Ireland*. Belfast.

Todd, Jennifer, 1995a. "Beyond the community conflict: Historic compromise or emancipatory process?" *Irish Political Studies* 10, pp. 161–178.

______, 1995b. "Equality, plurality and democracy: Justifications of proposed constitutional settlements of the Northern Ireland conflict," *Ethnic and Racial Studies* 18:4, pp. 818–836.

Unionist Party, 1973. *Peace, Order and Good Government*. Belfast.

Whyte, John, 1990. *Interpreting Northern Ireland*. Oxford: Oxford University Press.

Wilford, Rick, 1992. "Inverting consociationalism? Policy, pluralism and the post-modern," pp. 29–46 in Brigid Hadfield (ed.), *Northern Ireland: Politics and the Constitution*. Buckingham: Open University Press.

Wilson, Tom, 1989. *Ulster: Conflict and Consent*. Oxford.

13

Epilogue

RICK WILFORD

At the referendum on 22 May 1998, on a turnout of 81 percent, the Northern Ireland electorate endorsed the Agreement arrived at on Good Friday, 10 April 1998, by eight[1] of the province's ten political parties elected to the Forum in 1996. The scale of the endorsement—71 percent for and 29 percent against—appeared definitive; yet no sooner had it been declared (on the afternoon of 23 May) than the unionist politicians who opposed the Agreement claimed that a majority of the unionist electorate had voted against it. Such claims, and counterclaims by the proponents of the Agreement, were settled by an exit poll that reported that majorities of *both* communities had voted "Yes" (*Sunday Times,* 24 May 1998). Although only a narrow majority of the unionist electorate supported the Agreement, thereafter none could deny the breadth of popular support for a set of proposals that offered the opportunity and the challenge for Northern Ireland to embark on a political trajectory free from political violence. Having passed the referendum hurdle, the parties readied themselves for the 25 June election that would determine the identity of those charged to set up and implement the institutions defined by the Agreement. In the sections that follow, the main terms of that Agreement are outlined and the results of both the referendum campaign and the ensuing election held on 25 June 1998 are discussed.

The Good Friday Agreement

After almost two years of negotiation, the talks process begun after the Forum election of 1996 reached its climax with the announcement that the parties to the talks had agreed upon a set of proposals for the future governance of Northern Ireland. The structures envisaged by the Agreement were expressed in terms of the three strands originally defined by the former Secretary of State, Peter Brooke, in 1990. Strand 1 was concerned with institutional arrangements within Northern Ireland; Strand 2, with cross-border relationships between Belfast and Dublin; and Strand 3, with east-west relations—that is, between the island of Ireland, north and south, and Great Britain.

The three strands are integrally interrelated: They have to stand together, else the Agreement will fail. Accordingly, unionists accepted a provision for cross-border bodies (Strand 2); nationalists and republicans endorsed the creation of a new Assembly within Northern Ireland (Strand 1); and all the participants consented to the establishment of a novel British-Irish Council encompassing the U.K. and the Republic of Ireland (Strand 3). The unionists' "price" for the Agreement was the abandonment by the Irish Republic of its formal territorial claim to the six counties that constitute Northern Ireland, and the *quid pro quo* for nationalists and republicans was the repeal of the 1920 Government of Ireland Act. In place of these conflicting pieces of constitutional legislation, the parties to the talks and both the British and Irish governments accepted that Northern Ireland's constitutional status would henceforth be determined by the exercise of popular sovereignty by its electorate through a referendum. Thus, "consent" became the new constitutional imperative, a political reality to be embodied for the first time in the constitution of the Irish Republic.

The language of the Agreement placed a premium on consent, pluralism, consensus, and accommodation. Its signatories committed themselves to "partnership, equality and mutual respect" and reaffirmed their "total and absolute commitment to exclusively democratic and peaceful means of resolving differences on political issues." Acknowledging the "substantial differences between our continuing, and equally legitimate, political aspirations," the parties pledged their willingness to "work to ensure the success of each and every one of the arrangements established under this agreement" and accepted the fact that those arrangements were "interlocking and interdependent"—especially with respect to the Assembly and the North-South Ministerial Council, which were "so closely inter-related that the success of each depends on that of the other." In effect, the political parties not only had to accept the legitimacy of each strand but also had to make good-faith efforts to ensure that they worked.

Strand 1: Democratic Institutions in Northern Ireland

The durability of consociational thinking (see Chapter 6) is evident in relation to the 108-member Assembly. The intention was to provide for an inclusive legislative and executive institution, elected by PR-STV, that was subject to a variety of safeguards designed to "protect the rights and interests of all sides of the community." Application of the principle of proportionality was not confined to the electoral system but, rather, was extended to the allocation of seats around the cabinet ("Executive Committee") table, the composition of Assembly Committees, and the allocation of Committee Chairs: Relative party strengths in the Assembly (i.e., seats won at the election) governed the distribution of these posts.

The method of decisionmaking is further proof of the legacy of consociationalism. The Agreement requires items that are designated as "key decisions" by the Agreement—including the election of the Chair of the Assembly (akin to the Speaker in the House of Commons) and his or her deputy, the election of the First and Deputy First Ministers, the standing orders of the Assembly, and budget allocations to the Northern Ireland departments—to be taken on a cross-community basis. Two alternative voting procedures are applied to such key decisions as the means of realising the principle of bi-communalism: They are to be taken *either* on the basis of "parallel consent," whereby a majority of those present and voting, including a majority of the unionist and nationalist designations, concur with the decision, *or*, failing that more robust test of cross-community support, by means of a "weighted majority,"—that is, 60 percent of members present and voting, including at least 40 percent of both unionist and nationalist members. Although a number of key decisions are predetermined (see above), a provision in the Agreement also enables thirty members of the Assembly to bring forward a "petition of concern" to designate an issue as a key decision, thereby triggering the cross-community voting procedure.

To enable either test of bi-communal support to be applied, those elected to the Assembly are required to register a designation of identity as "nationalist," "unionist," or "other." Although this requirement may be criticised for freezing Assembly members into their respective communal blocs, it does provide a safeguard against majoritarianism on "key decisions": All other decisions will be subject to normal voting procedures; that is, a simple majority will prevail. An additional safeguard is provided by the incorporation of the European Convention on Human Rights (ECHR) into Northern Ireland, possibly supplemented by a Bill of Rights (which all parties support) overseen by a newly proposed Human Rights Commission. The Assembly and all public bodies will be subject to this new regime of rights, and all key decisions and legislation emanating from the Assembly will be "proofed" to ensure full compliance with the ECHR and any Bill of Rights for Northern Ireland. The final safeguard is provided by the creation of a multipurpose Equality Commission, which will monitor the statutory obligation to promote equality of opportunity and parity of esteem between the two main communities and to investigate individual complaints against public bodies.

Cushioned by this wide array of safeguards, the Assembly initially will have devolved to it full legislative and executive authority for those "transferable" matters administered by the six Northern Ireland Government Departments—namely, Agriculture, Economic Development, Education, Environment, Finance and Personnel, and Health and Social Services. Authority for "reserved" and "excepted" matters will remain at Westminster. Assembly members will elect the Chair and Deputy Chair on a cross-community basis, and a system of Assembly Committees paralleling the devolved departments will be constituted along proportional lines. The Chairs and Deputy Chairs of these committees will be allocated using the d'Hondt system,[2] and the membership will be chosen in "broad proportion" to party strengths in the Assembly. Thus, the committees will have a consociational character and are charged to scrutinise their associated departments, to assist in related policy developments, and to initiate legislation. As such, the committees will be powerful, multifunctional agencies through which consensual working arrangements may be instituted and developed.

Executive authority will reside with the First and Deputy First Ministers, elected by the Assembly on a cross-community basis, and up to ten Ministers. The ministerial posts will be allocated to parties by way of the d'Hondt system according to the number of seats held by each party in the Assembly. The Ministers will constitute the Executive Committee (cabinet), which will be convened, and presided over, by the First and Deputy First Ministers. Thus, unlike the British cabinet, the Executive Committee will be multiparty (indeed, coalitional) in its composition and will require an accommodatory and coalescent style in order to operate successfully. Collective responsibility may, however, prove difficult to accomplish. Although Ministers will enjoy full executive authority in their respective areas of responsibility, their actions must be agreed upon by the Executive Committee and must secure the endorsement of the Assembly as a whole: In cases where any Minister or the Executive Committee proposes to introduce a key decision, it will be subject to the cross-community voting procedures within the Assembly. In order to sit on the Executive, potential Ministers must sign a Pledge of Office that, among other things, requires each of them to commit themselves to nonviolence and exclusively democratic and peaceful means and to discharge *all* the duties of the office. Thus, for instance, none could refuse to participate in the creation and implementation of cross-border bodies (see below). In short, taking up a ministerial post obliges the members of the Executive to make every good-faith effort to fulfil *all* aspects of the Agreement.

The fact that the roles of the First and Deputy First Ministers will be performed by a unionist and a nationalist politician, respectively, epitomises the power-sharing or consociational character of the new institutions. The incumbents will convene and preside over the Executive Committee, which is charged to agree upon and prioritise executive and legislative proposals, to agree upon a common position on its programme, and to propose an annual budget. In particular, the First and Deputy First Ministers, who are jointly elected and effectively co-equal in their political authority, will have primary responsibility for dealing with Northern Ireland's external relationships, notably in relation to the Republic of Ireland, as set out in Strand 2 of the Agreement.

The Executive is not the only fount of legislation. Whereas Ministers can propose legislation, the Assembly is the prime source of authority in respect of all devolved responsibilities; its members, acting either as individuals or as members of the Assembly's committees, can also initiate legislation in devolved areas. Any such legislation must, however, comply with the ECHR and any Northern Ireland Bill of Rights that may supplement it. Where parity is normally maintained—in respect of social security payments, for instance—provision is made for the Assembly to opt in to U.K.-wide legislation. Thus, in certain important policy areas the legislative yardstick for Northern Ireland will reside at Westminster.

Indeed, consistent with previous attempts to create devolved structures within Northern Ireland, the U.K. parliament and its executive, embodied in the role of Secretary of State, will continue to exert a strategic role in relation to both reserved and excepted matters (see Chapter 6). Thus, the Northern Ireland Office will retain responsibility for these matters, although the Agreement does allow the Secretary of State—whose cabinet status is undiminished by the new arrangements—to consult regularly with the Assembly and the Ministers on reserved matters and to exercise permissive authority for it to legislate in these areas, subject to parliamentary control at Westminster. Given the scrutinising role of the Assembly in relation to transferred matters, the remits of the Westminster-based Northern Ireland Grand and Select Committees will be restricted to excepted and reserved matters. Hence the parliamentary dimension of Northern Ireland will be redefined, if not weakened.

In its essential design, the provisions for Strand 1 are highly reminiscent of the arrangements put in place for the 1973–1974 experiment in power sharing, to the extent that at least one cynic has described the 1998 Agreement as "Sunningdale for slow learners"! Indeed, the integral "Irish dimension" (see the discussion of Strand 2 below) renders the comparison even more persuasive. However, the dramatically altered political climate created by the ceasefires, as well as the breadth of support accorded to the Agreement via the referendums held simultaneously in Northern Ireland and the Irish Republic on 22 May, lent a compelling popular legitimacy to the proposals that was denied to both the 1974 and 1982 Assemblies. The demands for a stable peace that emanated from virtually all quarters of the province found some due (and additional) reward in a novel aspect of the Strand 1 proposals—namely, the provision for a consultative Civic Forum that had been proposed during the talks process by the Northern Ireland Women's Coalition. The purpose of the Forum is to provide a mechanism through which representatives of the voluntary, business, and trade union sectors, together with other sectional interests agreed upon by the First and Deputy First Ministers, can be consulted on social, economic, and cultural issues. Although the Forum will enjoy only advisory status, it nevertheless provides for what may be loosely termed "societal corporatism" as an adjunct to the formal representative institutions.

Such are the institutional provisions for the internal governance of Northern Ireland. Note, however, that for an initial period the Assembly will have only a "shadow" existence; in other words, the Assembly's legislative and executive powers will not become operative until six months after its election. Nevertheless, the "shadow" ministerial team, once elected (in the case of the First and Deputy First Ministers) and appointed (as is true of their Executive Committee colleagues) will begin a programme of work related to Strand 2 of the Agreement during their initial period of office.

Strand 2: The North/South Ministerial Council

Provision for the "Irish dimension" (see Chapter 6) has defined the variable geometry of earlier devolution proposals: During 1998 it became a necessary part of the design. In the form of the proposed Council of Ireland, this dimension was the operative cause of the failure of the 1973–1974 scheme; yet some twenty-five years later, representatives of those unionist and loyalist groups who had been instrumental in toppling the power-sharing Executive were party to the creation of new, accountable arrangements that institutionalised a role for Dublin in the internal governance of Northern Ireland.

The context for such a sea-change in the attitude of many loyalists was a commitment to politics, itself prompted by the initial ceasefire by the republican movement. Indeed, so strong was that commitment that it survived the breach of the ceasefire in February 1996 and remained essentially intact up to and beyond the PIRA's renewal of its "complete cessation of military operations" starting at midnight on 20 July 1997. Unionist and loyalist antipathy toward the Anglo-Irish Agreement of 1985 had not diminished: If anything, the prospect of democratising the role of Dublin in the internal affairs of Northern Ireland was a compelling one, provided that the territorial claim over the "six counties" contained in the Irish Constitution was abandoned. Sinn Féin and other republicans opposed such constitutional reform and, moreover, favoured free-standing cross-border bodies wholly detached from any potential representative assembly within Northern Ireland. However, the Irish government did undertake to drop the irredentism of Articles 2 and 3 of the 1937 constitution (subject to referendum), and it agreed that the new north-south institutions would be inextricably linked to the new Assembly, thereby locking its prospective members into all-Ireland functional bodies.

The 1998 Agreement proposed the establishment of a North/South Ministerial Council to bring together those with executive responsibilities on both sides of the border "to develop consultation, co-operation and action within the island of Ireland . . . on matters of mutual interest within the competence of the Administrations, North and South." Thus, participation in the Council, which will be serviced by a joint Secretariat staffed by Northern Irish and Irish civil servants, is an essential responsibility of the new Executive Committee. Such participation will occur at the highest level, inasmuch as committee members will meet with their counterparts in the Republic (namely, the Taoiseach and relevant Ministers) and in a variety of formats. These include twice-yearly plenary meetings; regular and frequent sectoral meetings between relevant Ministers; and other formats as appropriate to consider cross-sectoral issues (including external relationships with the European Union) and to resolve any disagreements that may arise.

The agendas for these meetings, whatever their format, will be subject to prior agreement, and each side can propose any matter for consideration or action. Any and all Council decisions must be agreed upon by both sides—effectively providing for a mutual veto, another characteristic feature of the classic consociational model—and are subject to the prevailing rules for democratic authority and accountability in force in the Assembly and the Irish parliament (Oireachtas). In circumstances where decisions are taken at Council level that exceed the limits of authority of those Ministers attending, such decisions must secure the approval of both the Assembly (by a simple majority, a weighted majority, or parallel consent, as appropriate) and the Oireachtas. Hence the autonomy of the Council will be strictly bounded by the requirements of unanimity within and between the Executive Committee and the Irish cabinet, and by the authority of both the Assembly and the Irish parliament, and it will be limited to those matters devolved to Northern Ireland.

Following the election to the Assembly, and the joint election by its members of the First and Deputy First Ministers, the Council will meet in transitional form—that is, before legislative and executive powers are transferred to Northern Ireland—to establish their operating procedures and, most significantly, to review the potential for cross-border cooperation "where implementation will be of mutual benefit" in twelve subject areas indicated by the Agreement.[3] Within the first four months of its existence (no later than 31 October 1998), the transitional or "shadow" Council is charged to agree upon at least six matters for cooperation and implementation through existing bodies in each jurisdiction and upon a further six through the creation of new implementation bodies on a cross-border or all-island level. These bodies are expected to come into operation as powers are transferred to the Executive Committee and the Assembly (approximately six months after the election); legislative authority for these bodies will rest with the Assembly. No requirement exists for such cross-border cooperation to develop beyond the initial dozen subject areas: Any expansion would be subject to agreement within the Council and would require the endorsement of both the Assembly and the Oireachtas. Neither the Council nor the Assembly can stand alone: As the Agreement stipulates, "[They] are mutually interdependent. . . . [O]ne cannot successfully function without the other." Cross-border cooperation and action are thereby an integral aspect of the new political arrangements. The Agreement also provides for consideration to be given to the creation of two other north-south institutions: first, a joint parliamentary forum in which equal numbers of representatives from the Assembly and the Irish parliament may discuss matters of mutual interest and concern; and, secondly, a jointly appointed consultative civic forum to provide advice to politicians in both jurisdictions on social, economic, and cultural and miscellaneous matters.

The creation of the mandatory cross-border institutions will establish a rich network of executive mechanisms through which reciprocal cooperation, action, and influence will be realised. At the Council level, authority will be a two-way street and will be accountable to politicians on both sides of the border, rather than sheltered from their democratic scrutiny as was the case with the bilateral mechanisms put in place by the Anglo-Irish Agreement of 1985.

Strand 3: The British-Irish Council and the British-Irish Intergovernmental Conference

Strand 2 does provide for an external dimension by enabling the Council to consider the European Union (EU) aspects of relevant north-south matters and commits both the British and Irish governments to take into account and represent the Council's views of the European Union's policies and programmes at relevant EU meetings. This rather extrovert aspect of the Agreement is compounded by Strand 3, which creates something resembling a confederal arrangement embracing the whole of the U.K. and the Republic of Ireland in the form of a British-Irish Council (BIC).

This Council, established under a new British-Irish Agreement (which "subsumes" the Anglo-Irish Agreement of 1985), is intended to "promote the harmonious and mutually beneficial development of the totality of relationships among the peoples of these islands." It will include representatives of the British and Irish governments, the devolved institutions in Northern Ireland, Scotland, and Wales, representatives from the Isle of Man and the Channel Islands, and, prospectively, members of any future tiers of regional government in England. This expansive institution, which will meet twice a year at a "summit" level, in sectoral formats and in other formats to consider cross-sectoral matters, is not intended to be merely a talking-shop. Its participants will exchange information, and discuss and consult on matters of mutual interest within their respective spheres of competence; but they may also agree upon common policies and actions on either a multilateral or bilateral basis in policy areas such as transport, agriculture, the environment, education, health, cultural matters, and approaches to EU issues. Any agreed policies and actions are to be voluntary and subject to the unanimity rule: Representatives may opt in or out of such policies. Any joint action that is agreed upon between two members of the BIC will not require the prior approval of the others and will operate independently of it. To help lend a sense of identity and unity to the BIC, the elected institutions from which its members are drawn will be encouraged to establish and develop interparliamentary links, using the existing British-Irish interparliamentary body as its model.

The 1998 Agreement exerts a profound effect upon the Anglo-Irish Agreement of 1985, requiring the establishment of a new British-Irish Agreement to deal with the "totality of relationships" between the two governments. This entails the creation of a standing British-Irish Intergovernmental Conference whose purpose is to promote "bilateral co-operation on matters of mutual interest within the competence of both Governments." Given the nature of the powers devolved to Northern Ireland, such cooperation will be limited to nondevolved matters including security, rights issues, criminal justice, prisons, and policing.

The 1998 Agreement does not entail a derogation from the sovereignty of either government and so does not introduce a regime of joint authority in relation to Northern Ireland. The Agreement does, however, recognise the Irish government's "special interest in Northern Ireland" and enables it to put forward views and proposals within the spheres of competence allotted to the British-Irish Intergovernmental Conference. Any decisions must be by agreement, and the participants—who at the summit level will include both prime ministers and, more routinely, the appropriate ministerial teams—are mandated to "make determined efforts to resolve disagreements between them." In particular, both governments will seek to facilitate cooperation in security matters, and, unless and until responsibility for reserved matters is devolved to a Northern Ireland administration, they are committed to "intensify co-operation on the all-island or cross-border aspects of these matters." Thus, all other things being equal, increased functional cooperation will exist between, for example, the Royal Ulster Constabulary (RUC) and the Gardai through extant agencies and channels rather than through newly created cross-border implementation bodies.

An important difference between the Intergovernmental Conference established by the 1985 Anglo-Irish Agreement and this more recent one is that the latter will be accessible to "relevant" executive members of the new administration in Northern Ireland (most probably the First and Deputy First Ministers) to discuss nondevolved matters, thereby defending it against the charges of secrecy and mystification so commonly and legitimately levelled by the unionist community at its predecessor. This access will also extend to the planned triennial review of the workings of the new British-Irish Agreement, rendering the relevant Anglo-Irish relationship effectively accountable to the Executive Committee in the north and, thereby, to the Northern Ireland Assembly. The Intergovernmental Conference will also contribute to any future review of the workings of the wider Agreement, even though it is not empowered to "override" the democratic arrangements established under the terms of that Agreement. These arrangements thereby confer a considerable degree of autonomy to the Assembly members; however, unlike the nascent Scottish parliament, the new Northern Ireland Assembly will not enjoy any tax-varying powers: The purse strings will be firmly held by the U.K. Treasury. The latter will determine a block grant for devolved matters that, subject to its special cross-community voting procedures, the Assembly will then allocate to the relevant departments.

Together, the three strands or pillars interlock to provide the complex architecture of the 1998 Agreement. They rest upon the foundation of popular consent for any future change in the constitutional status of Northern Ireland and upon an aggregate of rights, safeguards, and a statutory obligation (monitored by a new Human Rights Commission) to promote equality of opportunity in relation to religion, political opinion, gender, race, disability, age, marital status, dependants, and sexual orientation. The new Human Rights Commission will advise the U.K. government on those rights supplementary to the ECHR that are required to constitute a Bill of Rights for Northern Ireland and that will reflect the principles of mutual respect for the identity and ethos of both communities and parity of esteem. Equally, the Irish government is committed to introduce an equivalent level of protection of human rights within its own jurisdiction and to establish its own Human Rights Commission with a mandate and remit equivalent to that within Northern Ireland. Furthermore, the Agreement envisages a joint committee of both commissions to act as a forum for the consideration of human rights issues throughout the island of Ireland and to consider drafting a charter of agreed measures, to be endorsed by all democratic parties, "for the protection of the fundamental rights of everyone living in the island of Ireland."

Economic, Social, and Cultural Issues

An additional underpinning to the Agreement is provided by the U.K. government's commitment to make "rapid progress" with both a regional and an economic development strategy, as well as to formulate measures on employment equality that are consistent with its broader purpose of pursuing the goal of social inclusion. More specifically, it has undertaken to strengthen existing anti-discrimination legislation in Northern Ireland and to take a number of other measures aimed at combating unemployment and progressively eliminating the differential unemployment rates between the two communities.

On the cultural front, all the participants have acknowledged respect for the linguistic diversity and cultural wealth of the island of Ireland, and the British government has signified its readiness, "where appropriate and where people so desire it," to promote the Irish language by, among other things, placing a statutory duty on the Department of Education "to encourage and facilitate Irish medium education." A related measure is the commitment by the British government to consider signing the Council of Europe Charter for Regional Minority Languages and by the Irish government to proceed with ratification of the Council of Europe's Framework Convention on National Minorities (already ratified by the U.K.). The potency of symbols and emblems is acknowledged within the Agreement, and its signatories are mandated to ensure that they will be used in a manner that promotes mutual respect rather than division.

The Agreement also acknowledges the suffering inflicted on the victims of the troubles and recognises the need for well-resourced services to meet their needs. In addition, it commends the efforts of both statutory and voluntary organisations engaged in the work of developing reconciliation and mutual understanding within and between communities—work that has "a vital role in consolidating peace and political agreement." Thus, the signatories are pledged to look sympathetically at increased funding for the work of reconciliation and, in particular, to consider initiatives designed to encourage both integrated education and mixed housing as contributory means to that end.

Security, Decommissioning, Policing, Justice, and Prisoners

During the ensuing referendum and election campaigns, the fabric of the Agreement represented by its three strands proved somewhat less controversial and emotive than the issues of decommissioning by the paramilitaries, reform of the RUC, and the accelerated release of prisoners convicted of scheduled offences. The decommissioning of arms had cast a long shadow over the talks process and continued to do so. The relevant section in the Agreement reiterated the commitment of the talks participants to "the total disarmament of all paramilitary organisations" and to the use of their influence to achieve that aim within two years of the pending referendums in both parts of the island of Ireland. The process of decommissioning, scheduled to begin at the end of June 1998, is to be monitored and verified by the Independent International Commission on Decommissioning (the Mitchell Commission) set up in November 1995. A similar time frame was stipulated for the planned early release of paramilitary prisoners. By the end of June 1998, legislation was enacted in both the Westminster and Dublin parliaments, providing for the accelerated release scheme of all "qualifying" prisoners—namely, those affiliated with organisations that had established and maintained an "unequivocal ceasefire." (Those associated with organisations failing to declare such a ceasefire do not qualify for early release.) The intention was to free, on license, all qualifying prisoners by June 2000. Reading between the lines, one finds it difficult to avoid the conclusion that the timetables specified for both decommissioning and the release scheme were merely coincidental.

On the security front, the British government and the signatories to the Agreement expressed their desire to see a normalisation of security arrangements and practices in Northern Ireland. In pursuit of this objective, the British government undertook to reduce troop levels and to remove both the security installations and the emergency powers consistent with the assessment of the level of threat obtaining in the province. Similarly, the Irish government undertook to reform and dispense with elements of its emergency legislation as circumstances permitted. Such readiness on the part of both administrations was indicative of the shared ambition to see Northern Ireland become, in the words of the Agreement, "a normal peaceful society."

The remaining aspects of this part of the Agreement related to policing and the criminal justice system, each of which has an eruptive potential. The participants to the talks shared the belief that the Agreement created the opportunity for a new beginning in policing, with a new police service that would attract support and consent from all sections of the community, would be representative in its composition, and would routinely be unarmed. The key principles of this police service would be its professionalism, effectiveness, efficiency, fairness, impartiality, freedom from partisan control, and accountability both under the law and to the wider community. To realise these principles the signatories to the Agreement endorsed the establishment of an Independent Commission on Policing that would consult widely and bring forward a report by the summer of 1999. Shortly after the publication of the Agreement, the British government appointed Chris Patten (a former Conservative MP, junior minister in the Northern Ireland Office, and Britain's last governor of Hong Kong) to chair the commission.

In a move paralleling the creation of the Policing Commission, the British government announced a comprehensive review of the criminal justice system in Northern Ireland, covering such issues as appointments to the judiciary, the supervision of an independent prosecution service, law reform, cooperation between the criminal justice agencies on both parts of the island of Ireland, and the possibility of establishing a Department of Justice under the aegis of the new Assembly. This last measure signaled the intent of the government to devolve reserved matters to Northern Ireland, all other things being equal. The review team, led by Jim Daniell (director of Criminal Justice at the Northern Ireland Office) and including a number of independent assessors, is charged to produce its report by the autumn of 1999.

The Referendum

As noted, certain key aspects of the Agreement—decommissioning and the reviews of both policing and the criminal justice scheme—were not wholly resolved by the participants to the talks but, rather, hinged on future developments within the wider body politic. Though a remarkable achievement, the forging of the Agreement was not without its immediate casualties. Besides those unionists (the DUP and the U.K. Unionists) who had walked out of the talks when Sinn Féin was permitted to participate following the restoration of the PIRA's ceasefire, there were members of the Ulster Unionist Party's negotiating team who took particular exception to certain aspects of the document, especially the prisoner release scheme, the proposed reform of the RUC, and the looming prospect that Sinn Féin would become members of the Executive Committee before any paramilitary weapons were decommissioned.

Many participants were affected by the strains of coming to an agreement before the deadline stipulated by the talks chairman, George Mitchell, and endorsed by both prime ministers. Mitchell's insistence that the parties would have to justify any failure to agree, and his production of a confidential paper early in the final week of the talks delineating the outstanding areas of disagreement, concentrated minds wonderfully. Yet the initial deadline—midnight, 9 April—passed without agreement and intensive efforts were made throughout the night to bridge the remaining differences among the participants. These efforts were by no means confined to the parties at the talks; indeed, they also involved Tony Blair, the British Premier (who took up temporary residence in Northern Ireland in the final few days of the talks); his Irish counterpart, Bertie Ahern (who ferried between Belfast and Dublin over the same period to attend the funeral of his mother who died suddenly at the height of the negotiations); and, via George Mitchell, U.S. President Bill Clinton. Each of these leaders sought and eventually succeeded in helping to maintain the momentum of the talks.

Nevertheless, until late in the afternoon of 10 April, it was uncertain that there would be an Agreement. At the eleventh hour, following a meeting of the Ulster Unionist Party (UUP) delegation (which, by a majority, decided to accept the Agreement in its entirety), a number of UUP members walked out of the talks, including the youngest of its MPs, Jeffrey Donaldson—thereby reinforcing the prospect that the referendum campaign would be an acrimonious one within the wider unionist family. And so it proved.

The unionist politicians opposed to the Agreement—the Democratic Unionist Party (DUP), the U.K. Unionists, and five of the UUP's MPs (half its parliamentary representation)—forged a strategic coalition under the improvised label of United Unionists. Donaldson did not join forces with the disaffected unionists but, instead, chose to make known his opposition alone. The pro-Agreement parties did not—indeed, given their ideological diversity, could not—unite to mobilise the "Yes" vote but, rather, campaigned under their respective party umbrellas. There was, however, an official "Yes" campaign funded by the British government, but it was a rather lacklustre affair.

The opponents to the Agreement focused upon the perceived threat to the Union of Northern Ireland and Great Britain posed by the repeal of the 1920 Government of Ireland Act, in the process discounting both the proposed changes to Articles 2 and 3 of the Irish Constitution (which replaced the territorial claim with an aspiration to unify the island) and the primacy attached to popular consent for any change in the constitutional status of the province. But among unionists it was the prisoner release scheme, the issue of decommissioning, and the likelihood of police reform that stirred the greatest passions during the period leading up to the referendum. Within the republican community dissent also emerged, focusing upon what was perceived to be capitulation by Sinn Féin on a number of core principles—namely, acceptance of the proposed changes to the Irish constitution, retreat from its earlier insistence upon free-standing cross-border bodies immune from a unionist veto, endorsement of a new—and effectively partitionist—Northern Ireland Assembly, and the implied linkage between decommissioning and the prisoner release scheme.

Following two specially convened plenary conferences held in Dublin, the rank and file of Sinn Féin delegates voted overwhelmingly to accept the terms of the Agreement, thereby marginalising republican opposition on both sides of the border. Within the UUP, dissent was extensive and potentially much more damaging. Six of its ten MPs were anti-Agreement, five of them openly and vocally so—as was Lord Molyneux, David Trimble's immediate predecessor as party leader. However, Trimble carried a vote of his party executive on 11 April by 55 votes to 23 and, a week later, secured a similar margin of victory at the party's ruling Council. Following a heated debate, 72 percent of its 800 or so members supported the Agreement.

Aside from a small fraction of dissident republicans, opposition to the Agreement in the Republic of Ireland was minimal and centred upon the proposed changes to the 1937 constitution. The simultaneous referendums in both jurisdictions were provided for by the Agreement, and, in the case of the Republic, the only issue of contention was whether or not there should be two questions on the ballot paper: one pertaining to the Agreement and another related to the proposed changes to the constitution. Ultimately, both issues were conflated into one question: "Do you approve of the proposal to amend the Constitution contained in the undermentioned Bill?"[4] With all the parties in the Republic in the pro-Agreement camp, the result was something of a foregone conclusion, the only concern being the scale of the turnout. In fact, the turnout—at 56.3 percent—was rather disappointing. However, the scale of the pro-Agreement vote was emphatic,[5] with 1,442,583 (94.4 percent) in favor and just 85,748 (5.6 percent) against.

In Northern Ireland the referendum question was no less convoluted: "Do you support the agreement reached in the multi-party talks on Northern Ireland and set out in Command Paper 3883 [the Good Friday Agreement]?" The intense emotions stirred by the campaign were reflected by the exceptionally high turnout of 81.1 percent. Although no one anticipated a defeat for the pro-Agreement parties, interest centred on the balance of support within the unionist electorate. The outcome was 676,966 votes (71.12 percent) for the Agreement and 274,879 (28.88 percent) against. Two exit polls (*Sunday Times,* 24 May 1998; Radio Telefís Eíreann, 23 May 1998), which appeared shortly after the polling stations closed, showed that a narrow majority of the unionist community had supported the Agreement and that in seventeen of the province's eighteen Westminster constituencies there was a pro-Agreement majority, the one exception being Dr. Ian Paisley's redoubt of North Antrim. On the island as a whole, the result indicated that 85 percent of those who had voted were in the "Yes" camp.

The Assembly Election

Had there been a victory for its opponents in either jurisdiction, the Agreement could not have been implemented. Moreover, had a majority of the unionist voters in Northern Ireland voted against the Agreement, then in political terms it would have been a dead letter. In actuality, however, the level of support was such that the next stage of the unfolding drama, the elections to the Assembly, could proceed.

As during the referendum campaign, attention centred upon the contest among the unionist parties, although the struggle between the Social Democratic and Labour Party (SDLP) and Sinn Féin for popular ascendancy within the nationalist electorate was also rejoined—the leader of the SDLP, John Hume, having rejected the overtures made by the Sinn Féin president, Gerry Adams, for an electoral pact shortly after the referendum result was declared. Given the support for the Agreement, there was never any real doubt that a pro-Agreement majority would prevail in the new Assembly. However, if the anti-Agreement parties won 30 seats, they could petition for a range of issues to be designated as "key decisions," thereby triggering the required cross-community voting procedures and slowing down business in the Assembly. And if they secured an additional 5 or 6 seats, they would claim a majority of the unionist representation and be in a position to wreck the institution, thereby undermining the Agreement. Much was at stake, especially for the UUP and its leadership.

Given the division within the UUP, candidate selection became a major issue. The rules of the party require that a sitting MP needs special dispensation from the party executive to run for another public office. This dispensation was given to Trimble and his deputy, John Taylor; but it was withheld from the recalcitrant opponent of the Agreement, Jeffrey Donaldson, the only other UUP MP to seek nomination. The decision to exclude Donaldson as an official UUP candidate soured relations within the party to an even greater degree.

The election, held on 25 June, was based on the province's eighteen Westminster constituencies, each returning six members via PR-STV. When nominations closed, there were 296 candidates vying for the 108 seats. On the pro-Agreement side they included 38 for the SDLP, 37 for Sinn Féin, 22 for the Alliance Party, 12 for the Progressive Unionists, and 8 for the Northern Ireland Women's Coalition. The UUP's constituency associations nominated 48 official candidates, 6 of whom had voted against the Agreement at the referendum. In addition, a number of UUP members ran as independent candidates opposed to the Agreement; one of these—a member of the party's executive—ran against David Trimble in the latter's Westminster constituency of Upper Bann, thereby signaling the extent of disaffection within the ranks. The dissident Ulster Unionists fought alongside the DUP's 34 and the U.K. Unionist Party's 13 candidates in opposing the terms of the Agreement and had the potential to become a disruptive, even destructive, opposition bloc in the Assembly. In the end, this threat was not quite realised. After two days of vote counting, the final picture emerged on Saturday, 27 June (see Table 13.1).

For the first time in Northern Ireland's history a nationalist party, the SDLP, emerged with the largest vote share, as measured by the proportion of first preference votes it polled: It secured 22 percent of first preference votes and 24 seats (22.2 percent of the total) in the Assembly. By contrast, the UUP's share of first preference votes was, at

TABLE 13.1 NI Assembly Election: 25 June 1998

Party	V (% of First Preferences)	% Change Since 1996	Seats (N)	Seats (%)	Seat 'bonus' (S-V)
SDLP	22.0	+0.6	24	22.2	0.2
UUP	21.3	−2.9	28	25.9	4.6
DUP	18.1	−0.7	20	18.5	0.4
Sinn Féin	17.6	+2.2	18	16.7	−0.9
Alliance	6.5	0.0	6	5.6	−0.9
UK Unionists	4.5	+0.8	5	4.6	0.1
Progressive Unionists	2.5	−0.9	2	1.9	−0.6
Women's Coalition	1.6	+0.6	2	1.9	0.3
Independent Unionists	1.3	+1.3	3	2.8	1.5
Others	4.5	+0.3	0	0	−4.5
Total			108	100	
Turnout 69.9%					
Disproportionality (LSq index)					3.4

21.3 percent, its lowest ever recorded; yet the party continued to benefit from the sizeable "seat bonus" that has traditionally accrued to it at all Northern Ireland elections.[6] Specifically, the electoral system yielded the UUP 26 percent of seats in the Assembly based on only 21 percent of the votes, thus confirming the party's fluctuating fortunes in the recent past (Wilford 1998). The fragmentation of the unionist vote continued. The slight increase in the U.K. Unionists' support since the 1996 Forum election and the performance of the Independent Unionists opposed to the Agreement did not compensate for the larger fall in the votes of the two major unionist parties, such that the unionist bloc as a whole significantly declined. Equally, if not more, important was the apparent abstentionism of its electors: Rather than bring themselves to vote for anti-Agreement candidates, they chose to stay away from the polls. In that respect, the anti-Agreement parties maintained the mobilisation of their voters, whereas the pro-Agreement unionist parties did so rather less successfully.

Though a disappointing result for the UUP, an overall 73 percent of the electorate had given its first preference votes to pro-Agreement candidates, yielding a total of 80 seats and just 28 seats for the anti-Agreement parties (the DUP, the U.K. Unionists, and the three

Independent Unionists). More significant was the fact that the latter did not achieve the "magic" figure of 30 seats, which would have enabled them to use the device of a "petition of concern" to impede the business of the Assembly on its "key decisions." In addition, the balance of seat shares meant that the more robust test of cross-community voting in the Assembly (i.e., the "parallel consent" procedure) would prevail, provided that the two successful UUP candidates who had voted against the Agreement at the referendum remained loyal to the party leadership.

The situation within the "unionist family" is delicately poised, and a realignment of its constituent parties along a pro- and anti-Agreement axis is not unforeseeable. Within the nationalist electorate, Sinn Féin's increased vote share—its highest yet—maintains the electoral pressure on the SDLP. Only two of the four smaller parties involved in forging the Agreement—the Progressive Unionists and the Women's Coalition—secured representation in the Assembly, leaving the Ulster Democratic Party (UDP) and Labour to lick their electoral wounds. The failure of the UDP is perhaps ominous: Its close relationship with the largest of the loyalist paramilitary organisations, the Ulster Defence Association, may give those more disposed to violence reason to question a reliance on politics.

The newly elected Assembly met for the first time on 1 July 1998, when its major business was the election of the First and Deputy First Ministers. The only nominees for the joint ticket were David Trimble, the UUP leader, and Seamus Mallon, the deputy leader of the SDLP. They were duly elected on the basis of parallel consent. However, the first session of the Assembly closed with a time-limited debate on the controversial decision by the Parades Commission to prevent the Orange Order from marching along Garvaghy Road (Drumcree), which borders a nationalist housing estate. Following the debate, the Assembly adjourned for approximately three months. As protests by the Order and widespread loyalist disorder spread throughout Northern Ireland, the apparent "new" politics—signified both by the referendum result and by the electoral success of the pro-Agreement parties—threatened to be engulfed by the atavism of ethnic conflict, thereby placing the new Assembly in a condition of considerable jeopardy.

References and Further Reading

Gallagher, Michael, 1996. "Ireland: The referendum as a conservative device?" in Michael Gallagher and Pier Vincenzo Uleri (eds.), *The Referendum Experience in Europe*. London: Macmillan.

Wilford, Rick, 1998. "The 1997 Westminster Election in Northern Ireland," *Irish Political Studies* 13, 145–152.

Notes

Chapter One

1. The July 1995 Siege of Drumcree was another episode in the ongoing controversy concerning marches through the residential areas of the rival community. On this occasion, unionist determination to force an Orange Order march through a Catholic area of Portadown led to rioting between the marchers and the Royal Ulster Constabulary (RUC) (see Cochrane, 1997: 337–390).

2. It was during this year that nonsectarian rioting broke out in Belfast in protest over the low level of unemployment benefit as compared to payments in the rest of the United Kingdom.

Chapter Three

1. In focusing on religious background and social class, we have not intended to downplay inequalities that arise from other sources, most notably gender. More pervasive in determining patterns of physical segregation, however, are class and religious differences—of necessity, since gender inequalities exist within households whereas religious and class differences distinguish between families and households.

2. These questions extend beyond the usual uncertainty surrounding any attempts at population forecasting—including information regarding the future level of emigration or changes that might occur in fertility rates.

3. Of course, the match between wards and local communities is by no means exact, and the match between the religious composition of a ward and the degree of integration between Catholics and Protestants is even less so. A ward may be heterogeneous in its religious composition even while displaying considerable internal religious segregation.

4. Note that these figures reflect the responses of those who reported some religious affiliation in the census; we have made no adjustment for the "Nones" or nonresponses.

5. Although it is generally accepted that discrimination existed, the magnitude of this discrimination is still a contentious issue (Hewitt, 1981, 1983, 1985; O'Hearn 1983, 1985, 1987: see also Whyte 1983).

6. Strictly speaking, however, we would require, at a minimum, details about individual social mobility (which we lack) to determine whether or not

those upwardly mobile Catholics who were moving into the middle class became less nationalistic in their preferences upon arriving there.

Chapter Four

1. The actual parliament building at Stormont was opened as late as 1932. The first meeting of the parliament of Northern Ireland was held at Belfast City Hall and then moved to the Presbyterian College beside Queen's University. Nevertheless, following general convention, the term *Stormont* will be used to refer to the entire period up to 1972 (O'Leary, Elliott, and Wilford 1988: 29).

2. PR-STV for regional elections was abolished *via* the Methods of Voting and Redistribution of Seats (Northern Ireland) Act of 1929.

3. Even as late as 1967, the retention of ratepayer suffrage meant that 220,000 adults who were eligible to vote in Westminster elections were disenfranchised in local government elections in Northern Ireland (Elliott 1992: 79). The ratepayer franchise was abolished in Great Britain in 1945.

4. This electoral malpractice derives its name from Governor Elbridge Gerry of Massachusetts, who in 1812 managed to "concoct an outrageously elongated and twisted district that looked like a salamander and was called Gerry's Mander by his opponents" (Taagepera and Shugart 1989: 15–16; Riker 1986: 66–77).

5. In cases where the entire country serves as one large constituency, as in the Netherlands and Israel, gerrymandering is logically impossible.

6. The gerrymander was so well known that all three seats were not normally contested. The year 1949 was the first in which all three seats were contested.

7. The partisan distribution of the constituency of Fermanagh/Tyrone in 1921 and 1925 was four nationalists and four unionists. Craig's aim was to maintain this distribution: "The duty that fell to me was to see how, when these two counties that were combined, Fermanagh and Tyrone, were separated again, they could give fair representation of four members to this side of the House and four members to that side" (NI House of Commons Debates, Vol. 10, Col. 1450, 26 March 1929, quoted in Osborne 1979: 45). Of course, his use of the word *fair* was a misnomer. First, on the basis of population quotas, Fermanagh was not entitled to a third seat (Antrim and Londonderry had prior claims) (Osborne 1979). Secondly, if Fermanagh was to have three seats, it should have returned two nationalists and one unionist. The inverse result was achieved by means of the gerrymander outlined above.

8. The unionist share of the vote has probably been affected by differential turnout. Four constituencies in strong unionist areas (South Antrim, East Antrim, North Down, and Strangford) had turnouts below 60 percent, whereas some other seats in which nationalists did well had very high turnouts, reflecting the competitive nature of those contests. Nevertheless, differential turnout is itself an important competitive dynamic in ethnic party systems (see Chapter 5).

9. For a comprehensive and very accessible guide to PR-STV, see Sinnott 1993. For a good introduction to electoral systems generally, see Gallagher, Laver, and Mair (1995: ch. 11). This section draws on both of these sources.

10. The one exception was the election of the 1996 Forum, which was a unique variation on the principle of list system PR.

11. It is thus important to realise that STV in single-member constituencies (e.g., the method used for by-elections during the 1982–1986 Northern Ireland Assembly, as well as for electing the president of Ireland) is not a form of proportional representation. STV in single-seat constituencies is equivalent to the alternative vote (AV), a majority system. Hence the designation PR-STV is used in this chapter.

12. In some nonpreferential list systems (e.g., in Germany) the party organisation alone decides on the rank order of its candidates on the party list. Party voters thus have no opportunity to chose among a party's candidates. A wide range of other European countries have preferential list systems, which to varying degrees allow the voter to express a preference among party candidates (Gallagher, Laver, and Mair 1995: 285–286).

13. Nevertheless, there is no getting around the fact that PR-STV is a relatively complex electoral system. As Michael Gallagher comments: "The complexity involved might well be a price worth paying for the greater power it gives to the voters to express their preferences, and indeed a sophisticated electorate can relish watching the vote transfers reveal their information over the course of a count, but the initial impression STV makes on the uninitiated is one of convolution and complexity" (Gallagher 1996/1997: 5).

14. Once the number of surplus votes going to each candidate is calculated, the mechanical matter arises as to which actual ballot papers should be physically transferred. For elections to the Dáil the rule is that the papers to be transferred are taken from the last papers to be filed in the sub-parcel. If these papers do not constitute a random sample, some distortion could be introduced since these transferred papers may make a difference to subsequent counts if their later preferences are examined (see Sinnott 1993, 1995; Gallagher and Unwin 1986).

15. Notice, then, that it is possible to be elected without reaching the quota. In fact, a quota is not the same thing as a threshold. A quota is a sufficient but not necessary condition of being elected, whereas a threshold is a necessary condition (Sinnott 1993: 70).

16. Other more theoretical criticisms of STV have been made. The most common is that it is not a monotonic system. An electoral system that is nonmonotonic can produce paradoxical results whereby, in certain circumstances, a candidate could be disadvantaged by receiving a higher vote. Although this outcome sometimes occurs (Gallagher 1993: 78; Gallagher 1996/1997), it appears to be very rare and is therefore of limited practical significance. Indeed, Northern Ireland's chief electoral officer found no evidence of nonmonotonicity during the last twenty-two years of elections in the region (Bradley 1995; Farrell 1997).

17. A related criticism is that STV places candidates of the same party in competition with each other because they are vulnerable to losing their seats to

a party colleague. An argument often heard in the Republic of Ireland is that TDs respond to this fear by engaging in vast amounts of constituency work at the expense of national-level decisionmaking in the Dáil (see Gallagher and Komito 1993). Although there is considerable doubt that STV is primarily responsible for the localism in Irish politics, this possible criticism of STV is less relevant in Northern Ireland simply because it has lacked a regional parliament for most of the last thirty years. Indeed, since none of the Assemblies, Conventions, or Forums to date have ever survived more than one election, all members lost their seats through the abolition of these bodies.

18. STV also allows electors to vote for a very popular candidate without wasting their vote even though their additional vote for the candidate is superfluous (Taagepera and Shugart 1989: 26).

19. Several radio and television political correspondents added to the confusion by describing second-stage seat allocation as the "second count" as though the election involved STV.

20. Overall disproportionality was 3.9 (LSq index). But if the constituency elections alone had been considered (i.e., before the seats allocated by regional list were added), disproportionality would have risen sharply to 7.5.

21. The small number of Westminster seats (17–18) places some practical limitations on the extent of fragmentation.

22. Note, however, that the data on Northern Ireland represent the period 1981–1997 whereas Lijphart's data on the countries mentioned are based on the period 1945–1990.

Chapter Five

1. In addition, note that the parties of the centre-right are much stronger and those of the left are correspondingly weaker in Ireland than is typically the case in the rest of Europe (Mair 1993).

2. Sinn Féin won 6 seats in the first election to the Northern Ireland parliament in 1921, but this is quite a different party from Provisional Sinn Féin, which has been contesting elections since 1982.

3. For example, during 1921–1969 alone (i.e., the period before the fragmentation of the 1970s), parties with forty different labels contested elections; and, of these, twenty-two were successful in terms of winning a seat (Elliott 1992: 92).

4. Hegemonic control is "coercive and co-optive rule which successfully manages to make unworkable an ethnic or nationalist challenge to the state order" (O'Leary and McGarry 1993: 109; see also Lustick 1979).

5. The NILP peaked at 26 percent of the votes cast in 1962, but even this represented only 8.5 percent of the total electorate. Nationalist and republican abstentionism and the extremely large number of uncontested seats during the period tend to inflate perceptions of the NILP's popularity (McGarry and O'Leary 1995: 154–157).

6. The prediction is the same for right-wing parties such as the Northern Ireland Conservatives in the 1990s.

7. Indeed, the multitude of party labels in the last thirty years tends to exaggerate perceptions of the extent of fractionalisation in the Northern Ireland party system. Throughout the period 1973–1997 the "effective number of parties" has ranged between slightly more than four and slightly fewer than six (see the last column of Table 5.1). For example, although twenty-three "parties" contested the 1996 Forum elections, the effective number of parties was slightly less than six ($N = 5.84$).

8. Hume had earlier been offered the Nationalist Party nomination for Eddie McAteer's Foyle division, but he refused and subsequently won the seat as an independent (McAllister 1977: 23).

9. The bi-confessional but "constitutionally unionist" Alliance Party also became an established feature of the modern party system, although its support has been fairly modest, averaging 7.2 percent since the early 1970s.

10. The words *segment* and *bloc* are used interchangeably in this chapter, referring to the main political communities in Northern Ireland, unionist and nationalist. This is not to say that no other identities exist, or that there is no differentiation within communities. Rather, what is being asserted is that, in electoral terms, the constitutional conflict is primary and that most people want to be constitutionally linked to or at least protected by its preferred nation-state.

11. I say "*probable* tactical voting" because, although there is circumstantial evidence of such an effect, its existence cannot be known for sure without an election study that directly tracks past and current voting behaviour at a disaggregated individual level.

12. This point is borne out by the author's observation of the SDLP's 1995 conference debate on electoral strategy at Newcastle, Co. Down.

13. Sinn Féin also replaced the DUP as Northern Ireland's third largest party at both elections in 1997.

14. A bitter irony for SDLP workers in West Belfast was that Sinn Féin used pictures of John Hume together with Gerry Adams as part of the latter's successful bid to reclaim the Westminster seat in 1997.

15. The relative fortunes of the two main unionist parties is somewhat complicated by the success of a range of other smaller unionist parties that collectively took 9.3 percent of the vote.

Chapter Eight

1. "Community policing" generally refers to efforts to cultivate ties to local communities in order to facilitate local problem solving and crime control.

Chapter Nine

1. The study of women's political participation cited in this chapter was funded by the Economic and Social Research Council (under the title "The Political Participation, Interests and Attitudes of Women in Northern Ireland"

[grant number R000232726]) and conducted by the author, R. L. Miller, F. Donoghue, and, in part, Y. Bell between 1991 and 1993. The concurrent study of women councillors cited in the text was funded by the Nuffield Foundation and was carried out by the same research team.

2. For further details on the singular electoral system devised for the Forum election, see Chapter 4 of the present volume.

3. The phrase *armed patriarchy* is attributed by Monica McWilliams (1995: 34) to the late Cathy Harkin.

4. The 9 women who sat at Stormont, 6 of whom were Unionists, were returned on twenty-nine separate occasions. Dame Dehra Parker (Unionist) was the only woman to serve as a minister in the Stormont regime and was herself elected nine times.

5. These data were supplied by the Central Secretariat, Stormont, in February 1995.

6. Brook Centres offer nondirective advice and counseling on reproductive matters and are geared especially to the needs of young people.

7. Election literature produced by the NIWC stated that "its strength on the constitutional issue [lay] in not taking a fixed position but in working with the fixed positions and other positions to achieve political accommodation. The Women's Coalition is dedicated to drawing on all the different views, ideas and options to achieve a workable solution" (NIWC Candidate Briefing Document, Belfast, 1996).

8. See, for example, the Women's Research and Development Agency report entitled *Women and Citizenship: Power, Participation and Choice* (Belfast: EOCNI, 1995).

Chapter Ten

1. My colleague James Kellas has pointed out that Gibraltar is a point of contention between Spain and the United Kingdom. However, as Gibraltar is a Crown colony, not an integral part of the British state, the situation in respect of Gibraltar is more analogous to the Falklands Islands than to Northern Ireland.

2. A distinction should be made between the policy adopted by the SDLP and Fianna Fáil in this respect and the unease among a minority of both parties concerning the realism of such a policy.

3. The results of this and other polls by the Market Research Bureau of Ireland (MRBI) appeared in the *Irish Times*.

4. In the 1991 poll the question read as follows: "Articles 2 & 3 of the Constitution state the Republic's claim to jurisdiction over the island of Ireland. Are you in favour or not in favour of the claim contained in these articles?" A year later, in the September 1992 poll, the wording was quite different: "Articles 2 & 3 of the Constitution which claim jurisdiction over all of Ireland are being discussed by the Irish and British Governments and the Northern Parties. Do you think the *claim* in Articles 2 & 3 should be retained, or should the claim be changed to an *aspiration*?" (The emphasis in the latter has been added.)

Chapter Eleven

1. The phrase has been attributed to Brian Lenihan, who at the time was the Irish minister for foreign affairs (O'Leary and McGarry 1993: 219).

2. The three-stranded approach continues to structure negotiations. Strand One (or "North-North") relates to negotiations between the local parties concerning the internal government of Northern Ireland. Strand Two (or "North-South") negotiations pertain to the relationship between Northern Ireland and the Republic of Ireland. And Strand Three (or "East-West") talks concern the relationship between Britain and Ireland.

3. In return, the loyalist paramilitaries announced a cessation of violence on 13 October 1994.

Chapter Twelve

1. It is worth resisting the temptation to begin the sentence "Because of. . . . "

2. This is not to suggest that all Protestants are unionists, that all Catholics are Irish nationalists, that no other identities exist, or that there is no differentiation within communities. Rather, the point is that the national conflict is primary and that most people in each community want to be constitutionally linked to or at least protected by its preferred nation-state.

3. An old European definition of a nation—originally intended as a joke—is more intuitive than many more convoluted academic definitions: "A nation is a group of people united by a common error about their ancestry and a common dislike of their neighbours" (Deutsch 1969: 3; Connor 1994: 114).

4. In a September 1996 *Irish Times*/MRBI Poll, three exclusively British options were the first preferences of 54 percent of all respondents (17 percent of Catholics versus 82 percent of non-Catholics chose these options). The three options and the respective levels of support among Catholics and non-Catholics were as follows: "A return to majority rule and a Parliament at Stormont" (2 percent versus 20 percent); "A local Parliament for NI within the UK with power-sharing between the local parties" (12 percent versus 29 percent); and "NI becoming more fully part of the UK" (3 percent versus 33 percent) (*Irish Political Studies* 1997: 182–183).

5. Donald Horowitz (1985) provides numerous examples of similar processes in non-European contexts.

6. There are many, mainly unionist, advocates of British electoral integrationism in Northern Ireland. But whereas the desire to circumvent the local sectarian parties is mostly sincere, the thinking is wishful. There is no prospect of the British parties posing a serious electoral challenge to the local parties even if all of the former contested elections. The fate of the Northern Ireland Conservatives is instructive: marginal and increasingly partisan. The local parties *are* democratic. It is better to deal with that reality than to invent a more agreeable future based on unwarranted assumptions.

7. The September 1996 *Irish Times*/MRBI Poll offered one purely Irish option—"NI as part of a united Ireland"—which was the first preference of 17

percent. Thirty-nine percent of Catholics chose this option, compared to only 1 percent of non-Catholics. A further 39 percent of Catholics chose two other British/Irish options (*Irish Political Studies* 1997: 182–183).

8. As John Whyte puts it: "[A] united Ireland and integration with Britain . . . are based on the assumption that one side or the other in Northern Ireland is not too serious about its national aspirations and can be induced to abandon them" (1990: 226).

9. English objects to the two governments' policy of attempting to draw representatives of the political extremes into constitutional politics—a policy, he asserts, that creates "greater division between non-violent parties in the middle ground" (1997: 24). However, having the extreme parties outside of the process is just as likely to create difficulties for the constitutional parties if the former (as is likely) engage in a politics of ethnic out-bidding that pulls the moderate parties apart (see Mitchell 1995). English also objects to the two governments' attempts to draw the paramilitaries into constitutional politics because they have killed people. But surely it is precisely because the political extremes do most of the killing that they need to be included in the process if there is to be any realistic chance of ending it. As Fergus Finlay, a consummate strategist and advisor to the former leader of the Irish Labour Party, once put it: Negotiations to resolve the conflict without Sinn Féin "aren't worth a penny candle."

10. In a more recent book Bew and Patterson (along with Paul Teague) seem to be more reconciled to cross-border North-South institutions as a *quid pro quo* for the maintenance of the union with Britain. The book is rather thin on prescription (especially since it is subtitled *The Political Future of Northern Ireland*) and in its last paragraph appears to place the primary burden of compromise on nationalists: "Ultimately, though, the odds are stacked against a settlement. A significant part of nationalist Northern Ireland now finds it hard in principle to accept any compromise unionists might be prepared to live with" (Bew, Patterson, and Teague 1997: 215).

11. For an extensive review and critique of materialist interpretations of the Northern Ireland conflict see McGarry and O'Leary 1995a, chapter 7. More generally, see Horowitz 1985 and Esman 1994.

12. Commenting on an earlier draft of this chapter, Jennifer Todd pointed out that in Ruane and Todd's (1996) interpretation, conflicting nationalisms—though important—are not "primary." Specifically, they interpret the conflict as an "overdetermined communal conflict."

13. Wilford cautions that "it would be mistaken to assume that policies which celebrate cultural pluralism will beget political pluralism as a matter of course" (1992: 45).

14. Todd (1995) and Ruane and Todd (1996) also argue that approaches that advocate a "dualist" constitutional settlement—thus "forcing the communities to accept an egalitarian compromise—tend to freeze community divisions" and to underestimate "differentiation within and between the communities" (Todd 1995: 170–171). Whereas the foregoing is a common objection to "ethnic conflict approaches," the reality is that the communities themselves tend to downplay internal diversity and to emphasise solidarity vis à vis their ethnic rivals when polarisation is high—as it often is in protracted conflicts. Diversity can flourish only when the perceived threat recedes.

15. In this connection, consider Wilford's argument: "Experimentation has shown that prolonged and intense contact, especially where it entails co-operation in problem-solving, can assist markedly in overcoming mutual distrust, incomprehension and suspicion, thereby significantly reducing stereotypical behaviour among all the parties" (1992: 38).

16. Of course, Kennedy's demographic assumptions are probably out of date by now.

17. In a July 1991 poll cited by O'Leary and McGarry, repartition was the first preference of only 1 percent of people in Northern Ireland (1993: 286). (Since repartition is not widely regarded as a feasible option, most polls do not include it.)

18. Note that some versions are labeled "joint" and others entail "shared" authority or sovereignty. Despite some small differences ("shared" implies the participation of Northern Irish politicians whereas "joint" suggests something closer to joint direct rule), the intuitive logic is similar: Majoritarian thinking must be ruled out and minorities systematically included.

19. For the full institutional architecture, see O'Leary et al. (1993). Ancillary aspects of the model—such as policing, the judicial system, and the financial implications of shared authority—can also be found in the above work, but they are omitted here in the interests of brevity.

20. In a personal communication with the author, O'Leary stated that he now prefers that the SACNI should have seven members, five elected in Northern Ireland and one each from the U.K. and Irish governments.

21. In the 1990s, unionists objected to the language of self-determination in the *Joint Declaration for Peace*, judging (correctly) that such language was a symbolic overture to nationalists. Ironically, the Unionist Party's 1973 manifesto demanded that "there must be acceptance by the Republic of the right of the people of Northern Ireland to self-determination" (Unionist Party 1973: 10).

22. Although a high threshold for constitutional change is indispensable, the exact figure is a matter of judgement. O'Leary and his colleagues (1993) suggest three-quarters; elsewhere, McGarry and O'Leary (1995a) mention two-thirds as high enough consent.

23. This is *not* a "convenient" partisan argument: The logic applies equally to nationalists. As O'Leary and his colleagues point out, "if they reject the right of a majority in Northern Ireland to impose its will on the minority they must logically accept that the nationalist majority in Ireland as a whole has no right to impose its will on the unionist minority in Ireland as a whole" (1993: 57).

24. It might reasonably be countered that the joint authority option in all opinion polls is probably interpreted as the traditional "transitional" kind (on the road to a united Ireland) rather than in terms of "durable" shared authority. The finding reported in the text may thus overestimate unionist antipathy.

25. In the September 1996 *Irish Times*/MRBI Poll referred to in the text (and in Notes 4 and 7), 17 percent of Catholics selected exclusively U.K. options.

26. Limited space precludes detailed discussion of this variant of their prescriptions. However, details of the "double protection" model can be found in McGarry and O'Leary 1995a: 372–382, 396–403.

27. McGarry and O'Leary assert that the double protection model is not joint authority because "these mechanisms do not positively involve either

the British or Irish states in governing Northern Ireland, but rather provide a check against a possible internal abuse of power within Northern Ireland itself" (1995a: 381). Although some such safeguard is indeed desirable, there is little doubt that providing the Anglo-Irish IGC with veto powers would be regarded by many unionists as "tantamount to joint authority."

Epilogue

1. The eight parties were the Ulster Unionist Party, the Social Democratic and Labour Party, Sinn Féin, the Progressive Unionist Party, the Ulster Democratic Party, the Alliance Party, Labour, and the Women's Coalition.

2. In this application of d'Hondt, the number of seats won by a political party are divided, initially, by 1 so that the party with the greatest number of seats wins the first place around the Executive Committee table. Then, the seat total for Party A—which secured the first place—has its total number of seats divided by 2, while the remaining parties have their totals again divided by 1. The party with the highest average (in this case, the next largest party) then wins second place on the committee. Each time a party wins a seat, its divisor increases by one. In the case of the 10-member Executive Committee, the application of d'Hondt produced 3 seats for both the UUP and the SDLP and 2 each for the DUP and Sinn Féin. The d'Hondt divisor favours larger parties in most circumstances, such that in this case the UUP and the SDLP together received 60 percent of places on the Executive Committee (3 each) based on just 48 percent of Assembly seats (and an even smaller proportion of first preference votes). An alternative allocation rule (the Sainte-Lague divisor) would have given 1 place to the Alliance Party at the expense of the SDLP.

3. The twelve possible areas for north/south cooperation indicated in the Agreement are agriculture (animal and plant health), education (teacher qualifications and exchanges), transport (strategic planning), environment (including water quality and pollution), inland waterways, social security/social welfare (including fraud control and entitlements of cross-border workers), tourism (promotion and marketing), relevant EU programmes, inland fisheries, aquaculture, health (accident and emergency services and other related cross-border issues), and urban and rural development.

4. The "Bill" referred to here was the Nineteenth Amendment of the Constitutional Bill, which provided for the constitutional changes arising from the Agreement.

5. Though disappointingly low, the turnout at the referendum did exceed the average (54.2 percent) for the first seventeen amendments to the Constitution held between 1959 and 1995. In this connection, see Gallagher (1996: 90).

6. See Table 4.4 for evidence of this pattern. Note also that the 1998 Assembly election was impressively proportional (given an LSq index of 3.4, excluding independents and "others") and similar to local government elections.

About the Editors and Contributors

Paul Arthur is professor of politics and course director for Peace and Conflict Studies at the University of Ulster, Jordanstown. The author of several books on Northern Ireland, he has been a senior visiting fellow at the United States Institute of Peace.

Richard Breen is professor of sociology at Queen's University of Belfast and is currently on leave in the Department of Political and Social Sciences at the European University Institute in Florence, Italy. He has published a large number of papers on social stratification and inequality and is at work on a book dealing with the relationship between social class and ethnic divisions in Northern Ireland.

Feargal Cochrane is a research officer at the Centre for the Study of Conflict, University of Ulster, Coleraine. A former research fellow at the Institute of Irish Studies, Queen's University, Belfast, he is the author of *Unionist Politics and the Politics of Unionism Since the Anglo-Irish Agreement* (1997) and of several articles on politics in Northern Ireland.

Paula Devine is a research officer at the Centre for Child Care Research, Queen's University, Belfast. She previously worked at the Centre for Social Research, also at Queen's, where she specialised in quantitative social research and secondary analysis. She is closely associated with the Northern Ireland Social Attitudes Survey series as both joint author and joint editor.

Gordon Gillespie is a research fellow in the Department of Politics at Queen's University, Belfast, and is currently working on a study of the politics of the voluntary sector in Northern Ireland. He has written extensively on aspects of politics and culture in Northern Ireland. Among his books are the co-authored *Northern Ireland: A Chronology of the Troubles 1968–1993* (1993) and *The Northern Ireland Peace Process 1993–1996: A Chronology* (1996).

Brian Girvin is senior lecturer in politics at the University of Glasgow. He has written extensively on Irish politics, nationalism, and political culture and is the author of several books including *The Right in the Twentieth Century: Conservatism and Democracy* (1994). He is currently completing a book entitled *Nationalism and Irish Political Culture: Political Change in Ireland 1937–1997*.

Alan Greer is senior lecturer in politics at the University of the West of England. He is the author of *Rural Politics in Northern Ireland* (1996) and of several articles on politics and public policy in Northern Ireland and Great Britain.

Adrian Guelke is professor of comparative politics at Queen's University, Belfast. He is the author of *The Age of Terrorism and the International Sys-*

tem (1995) and *Northern Ireland: The International Perspective* (1998). He also edits *The South African Journal of International Affairs*.

Paul Mitchell is lecturer in politics at Queen's University, Belfast. The author of a wide range of articles and chapters in the fields of political competition in parliamentary democracies and competition and conflict regulation in ethnically divided societies, he is currently co-editing the forthcoming *How Ireland Voted 1997*.

Ronald Weitzer is associate professor in the Department of Sociology at George Washington University, Washington, D.C. He has written extensively on policing issues in both Northern Ireland and South Africa and is currently writing a book on police-minority relations in the United States.

Rick Wilford is reader in politics at Queen's University, Belfast. His most recent books include the co-authored *Women and Political Participation in Northern Ireland* (1996) and the co-edited *Women, Ethnicity and Nationalism: The Politics of Transition* (1998). He is also joint contributing editor of the forthcoming *Contesting Politics: Women in Ireland, North and South*.

Index